Fodor's 98
The Bahamas

W9-BJN-797

The complete guide, thoroughly up-to-date

Packed with details that will make your trip

The must-see sights, off and on the beaten path

What to see, what to skip

Mix-and-match vacation itineraries

City strolls, countryside adventures

Smart lodging and dining options

Essential local do's and taboos

Transportation tips, distances and directions

Key contacts, savvy travel tips

When to go, what to pack

Clear, accurate, easy-to-use maps

Background essay

Fodor's Travel Publications, Inc.
New York • Toronto • London • Sydney • Auckland
www.fodors.com/

Fodor's The Bahamas

EDITOR: Stephen Wolf

Editorial Contributors: Robert Andrews, David Brown, Rachel Christmas Derrick, Ian Glass, Gordon Lomer, Allyson Major, Jessica Robertson, Heidi Sarna, Helayne Schiff, Mary Ellen Schultz, M. T. Schwartzman (Gold Guide editor), Dinah A. Spritzer

Editorial Production: Stacey Kulig

Maps: David Lindroth, *cartographer*; Steven K. Amsterdam, *map editor*

Design: Fabrizio La Rocca, *creative director*; Guido Caroti, *associate art director*; Jolie Novak, *photo editor*

Production/Manufacturing: Mike Costa

Cover Photograph: Wayne Levin

Copyright

Special Sales

Fodor's Travel Publications are available at special discounts for bulk purchases for sales promotions or premiums. Special editions, including personalized covers, excerpts of existing guides, and corporate imprints, can be created in large quantities for special needs. For more information, contact your local bookseller or write to Special Markets, Fodor's Travel Publications, 201 East 50th Street, New York, NY 10022. Inquiries from Canada should be directed to your local Canadian bookseller or sent to Random House of Canada, Ltd., Marketing Department, 1265 Aerowood Drive, Mississauga, Ontario L4W 1B9. Inquiries from the United Kingdom should be sent to Fodor's Travel Publications, 20 Vauxhall Bridge Road, London SW1V 2SA, England.

PRINTED IN THE UNITED STATES OF AMERICA

10 9 8 7 6 5 4 3 2 1

CONTENTS

ON THE ROAD WITH FODOR'S

WE'RE ALWAYS THRILLED to get letters from readers, especially one like this:

It took us an hour to decide what book to buy and we now know we picked the best one. Your book was wonderful, easy to follow, very accurate, and good on pointing out eating places, informal as well as formal. When we saw other people using your book, we would look at each other and smile.

Our editors and writers are deeply committed to making every Fodor's guide "the best one"—not only accurate but always charming, brimming with sound recommendations and solid ideas, right on the mark in describing restaurants and hotels, and full of fascinating facts that make you view what you've traveled to see in a rich new light.

About Our Writers

Our success in achieving our goals—and in helping to make your trip the best of all possible vacations—is a credit to the hard work of our extraordinary writers.

New York–based freelance writer **Rachel Christmas Derrick** has been revisiting the Bahamas for more than fifteen years. Her articles about these Atlantic islands and other locales around the world have appeared in numerous newspapers and magazines, including the *New York Times*, the *Washington Post*, the *Boston Globe*, the *Los Angeles Times*, *Travel & Leisure*, *Newsweek*, *Essence*, and *Ms*.

Gordon Lomer, a Canadian freelance writer who wrote our special diving and boating coverage for Destination: The Bahamas chapter, is a certified diving instructor who spent 10 years in the Bahamas reporting on diving, fishing, and yachting events for the Bahamas News Bureau.

Jessica Robertson and **Allyson Major** updated the New Providence and Grand Bahama Island chapters. Born in England, bred in the Bahamas and schooled in Pennsylvania and Mexico, Jessica covers the nation for the Broadcasting Corporation of the Bahamas. She has visited almost all of the populated islands in the country (and some of those occupied only by hermit crabs and seagulls), but calls Nassau home. Allyson is a feature write for the Nassau Tribune, one of two dailies in the Bahamas. Her work takes her island hopping much of the time, but she, too, spends most of her days and nights in Nassau.

We'd also like to thank a number of people and organizations: Barbara Zirl and Lisa Dawson at Bozell Public Relations; Charity Armbrister and Maxine Williamson at the Bahamas Ministry of Tourism (New Providence Island); Carmeta Miller at the Grand Bahama Island Tourism Board; Deborah Simorne at Grand Bahama Beach Hotel; Chris Allison at UNEXSCO on Grand Bahama Island; and Keith Fox at Solomon's Wholesale Club in Freeport.

New This Year

Rachel Christmas Derrick has also added a host of new dining and lodging places—from the only hotel on luscious, undeveloped Stocking Island to local favorites for cracked conch—in the Out Islands to this edition.

And this year, Fodor's joins Rand McNally, the world's largest commercial mapmaker to bring you a detailed color map of the Bahamas. Just detach it along the perforation and drop it in your tote bag.

On the Web, check out Fodor's site (www.fodors.com/) for information on major destinations around the world and travel-savvy interactive features. The Web site also lists the 85-plus radio stations nationwide that carry the Fodor's Travel Show, a live call-in program that airs every weekend. Tune in to hear guests discuss their wonderful adventures—or call in to get answers for your most pressing travel questions.

How to Use This Book

Organization

Up front is the **Gold Guide,** an easy-to-use section divided alphabetically by topic.

Under each listing you'll find tips and information that will help you accomplish what you need to in the Bahamas. You'll also find addresses and telephone numbers of organizations and companies that offer destination-related services and detailed information and publications.

The first chapter in the guide, Destination: The Bahamas, helps get you in the mood for your trip. "In the Wake of Columbus" provides a short history of the island country, What's Where gets you oriented, New and Noteworthy cues you in on trends and happenings, Fodor's Choice showcases our top picks, and Festivals and Seasonal Events alerts you to special Bahamian events you'll want to seek out.

We have a new Pleasures and Pastimes chapter this year, which brings together a wealth of information—including mini-guides on casino gambling and on diving and sailing in Bahamian waters—as well features on the Junkanoo and Goombay celebrations and what local Bahamian culinary delights to look for.

Chapters on New Providence and Grand Bahama islands are divided into sections on exploring, dining, lodging, nightlife and the arts, outdoor activities and sports, and shopping, and the chapters end with sections called A to Z, which tell you how to get there and get around and provide important contacts and resources. The Out Islands and the Turks and Caicos Islands chapters cover these smaller islands (and groups of islands) individually in alphabetical order.

At the end of the book you'll find a Portrait of the Bahamas, in which inveterate traveler William G. Scheller follows the path of Columbus through the Bahamian islands.

Icons and Symbols

★   Our special recommendations
✕   Restaurant
☷   Lodging establishment
✕☷   Lodging establishment whose restaurant warrants a special trip
☺   Good for kids (rubber duckie)
☞   Sends you to another section of the guide for more information
✉   Address
☎   Telephone number
☉   Opening and closing times

✉   Admission prices (those we give apply to adults; substantially reduced fees are almost always available for children, students, and senior citizens)

Numbers in white and black circles that appear on the maps, in the margins, and within the tours correspond to one another.

Dining and Lodging

The restaurants and lodgings we list are the cream of the crop in each price range.

Hotel Facilities

We always list the facilities that are available—but we don't specify whether they cost extra: When pricing accommodations, always ask what's included. In addition, assume that all rooms have private baths unless otherwise noted.

Restaurant Reservations and Dress Codes

Reservations are always a good idea; we note only when they're essential or when they are not accepted. Book as far ahead as you can, and reconfirm when you get to town. Unless otherwise noted, the restaurants listed are open daily for lunch and dinner. We mention dress only when men are required to wear a jacket or a jacket and tie. Look for an overview of local habits in the Gold Guide.

Credit Cards

The following abbreviations are used: **AE,** American Express; **DC,** Diners Club; **MC,** MasterCard; and **V,** Visa.

Please Write to Us

You can use this book in the confidence that all prices and opening times are based on information supplied to us at press time; Fodor's cannot accept responsibility for any errors. Time inevitably brings changes, so always confirm information when it matters—especially if you're making a detour to visit a specific place. In addition, when making reservations be sure to mention if you have a disability or are traveling with children, if you prefer a private bath or a certain type of bed, or if you have specific dietary needs or other concerns.

Were the restaurants we recommended as described? Did our hotel picks exceed your expectations? Did you find a museum we recommended a waste of time? If you have complaints, we'll look into them and revise our entries when the facts warrant it. If you've discovered a special place that we haven't included, we'll pass the information along to our correspondents and have them check it out. So send us your feedback, positive *and* negative: email us at editors@fodors.com (specifying the name of the book on the subject line) or write the Bahamas editor at Fodor's, 201 East 50th Street, New York, NY 10022. Have a wonderful trip!

Karen Cure
Editorial Director

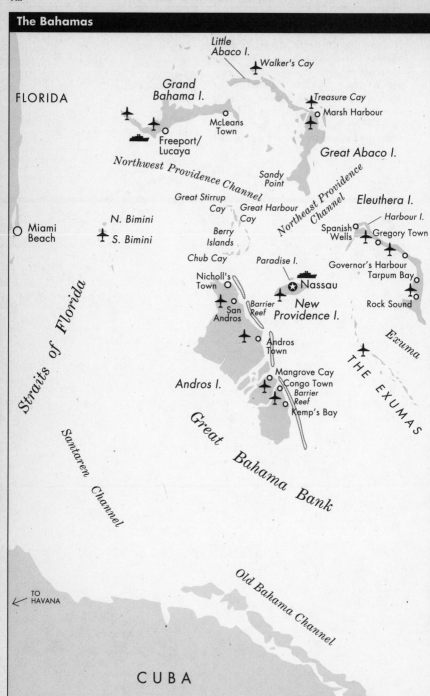

FLORIDA

Little Abaco I.

Walker's Cay

Grand Bahama I.

Treasure Cay

Marsh Harbour

McLeans Town

Freeport/Lucaya

Great Abaco I.

Northwest Providence Channel

Sandy Point

Great Stirrup Cay

Great Harbour Cay

Northeast Providence Channel

Eleuthera I.

Harbour I.

Spanish Wells

Gregory Town

Miami Beach

N. Bimini

S. Bimini

Berry Islands

Governor's Harbour

Tarpum Bay

Chub Cay

Paradise I.

Nassau

Nicholl's Town

Barrier Reef

San Andros

New Providence I.

Rock Sound

Straits of Florida

Andros Town

Exuma

Andros I.

Mangrove Cay

Congo Town

Barrier Reef

Kemp's Bay

THE EXUMAS

Great Bahama Bank

Santaren Channel

Old Bahama Channel

TO HAVANA

CUBA

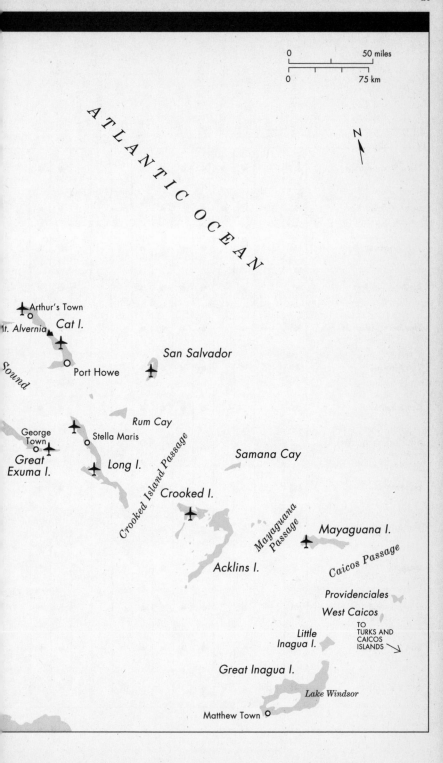

Island Finder

	Cost of Island	Number of rooms	Nonstop flights (from the U.S.)	Cruise ship port	U.S. dollars accepted	Historic sites	Natural beauty	Lush	Arid	Mountainous	Rain forest	Beautiful beaches	Good roads	
New Providence	$$$	7460	●	●	●	●	●					●	●	
Grand Bahama	$$	3039		●	●		●					●	●	
The Abacos	$$$	513	●		●	●	●	●				●	●	
Andros	$$	149	●		●	●	●	●				●	●	
The Berry Islands	$$$	44	●		●	●	●	●				●	●	
The Biminis	$$	118	●		●	●	●	●				●	●	
Cat Island	$$	66			●	●	●	●				●	●	
Crooked & Acklins Islands	$$	12			●	●	●					●		
Eleuthera	$$$	520	●		●	●	●	●				●	●	
The Exumas	$$	157	●		●	●	●	●				●	●	
Inagua	$	25			●		●							
Long Island	$$$	59	●		●	●	●	●				●	●	
San Salvador	$$$	302	●		●	●	●	●				●	●	
Turks & Caicos	$$$	1,205		●	●				●			●		

Public transportation	Fine dining	Local cuisine	Shopping	Music	Casinos	Nightlife	Diving and Snorkeling	Sailing	Golfing	Hiking	Ecotourism	Villa rentals	All-inclusives	Luxury resorts	Secluded getaway	Good for families	Romantic hideaway
•	•	•	•	•	•	•	•	•	•		•	•	•	•		•	
•	•	•		•	•	•	•	•	•		•			•		•	
		•	•	•	•		•	•	•		•	•	•	•	•	•	•
		•					•	•			•	•	•	•	•	•	•
	•	•					•	•	•		•	•	•	•	•	•	•
	•	•	•	•		•	•	•			•			•	•	•	•
		•					•	•		•	•	•			•	•	•
		•					•						•		•		
	•	•	•	•			•	•						•		•	•
	•	•		•		•	•	•			•	•	•	•	•	•	•
		•					•				•	•					
	•	•		•		•	•				•			•	•	•	•
	•	•					•	•			•		•	•	•		•
		•			•		•	•	•			•	•	•	•		•

SMART TRAVEL TIPS A TO Z

Basic Information on Traveling in the Bahamas,
Savvy Tips to Make Your Trip a Breeze, and
Companies and Organizations to Contact

A

AIR TRAVEL

Most flights to the Bahamas—to Nassau, Freeport, and the Out Islands alike—connect through Miami, Orlando, or Atlanta, depending on the airline. If you are flying to the Out Islands, consider whether you would rather make one connection through a Florida city, or two—through a Florida city and Nassau.

MAJOR AIRLINE OR LOW-COST CARRIER?

Most people choose a flight based on price. Yet there are other issues to consider. Major airlines offer the greatest number of departures; smaller airlines—including regional, low-cost and no-frill airlines—usually have a more limited number of flights daily. Major airlines have frequent-flyer partners, which allow you to credit mileage earned on one airline to your account with another. Low-cost airlines offer a definite price advantage and fewer restrictions, such as advance-purchase requirements. Safety-wise, low-cost carriers as a group have a good history, but **check the safety record before booking** any low-cost carrier; call the Federal Aviation Administration's Consumer Hotline (☞ Airline Complaints, *below*).

➤ MAJOR AIRLINES: **Delta** (☎ 800/221–1212) flies to Nassau and Freeport. **Continental** (800/525–0280) and **US Airways** (☎ 800/428–4322) fly to Nassau only. From Canada, **Air Canada** (☎ 800/676–7725) flies to Nassau and Freeport.

➤ SMALLER AIRLINES: **American Eagle** (☎ 800/433–7300) flies to Nassau, Freeport, Governor's Harbour, Marsh Harbour, and George Town; **Bahamasair** (☎ 800/222–4262) connects through Miami, Orlando, and Fort Lauderdale to Nassau, Freeport, Treasure Cay, George Town, Eleuthera (North Eleuthera and Governor's Harbour airports), and Stella Maris

on Long Island, and through Nassau to Marsh Harbour, Acklins, Crooked Island, Andros, Cat Island, Eleuthera (North Eleuthera, Governor's Harbour, and Rock Sound), Great Exuma, Inagua, Long Island, and San Salvador; **Comair** (☎ 800/354–9822) flies to Nassau and Freeport; **Carnival Airlines** (☎ 800/824–7386) and **Paradise Island Airlines** (☎ 800/786–7202) fly only to Nassau; and **Pan Am Air Bridge** (☎ 800/424–2557) flies to Paradise Island (New Providence) and to Bimini.

➤ FROM THE U.K.: **British Airways** (☎ 0345/222–111) flies twice weekly to Nassau from London Gatwick. There is an even wider choice of flights via Miami—on **British West Indian Airways** (☎ 0181/570–5552), **Caledonian** (✉ Golden Lion Travel, ☎ 01293/567–800), and **Virgin Atlantic** (☎ 01293/747–747)—with competitive prices. Contact **American Airlines** (☎ 0345/789–789) or **Bahamasair** (☎ 0171/437–8766 or 0171/437–3542) for flights to the islands from Miami.

➤ WITHIN THE BAHAMAS: **Bahamasair** (☎ 242/377–5505), the national airline, has interisland routes; its schedule to some of the islands is limited. To reach the remoter islands, charter a plane at Nassau International Airport: **Cleare Air** (☎ 242/377–0341), **Congo Air** (☎ 242/377–8329), **Pinders Charter Service** (☎ 242/377–7320), **Reliable Air Services** (☎ 242/377–7335), **Sandpiper Air** (☎ 242/377–5751), **Sky Unlimited** (☎ 242/377–8993), **Taino Air Service** (☎ 242/327–5336).

GET THE LOWEST FARE

The least expensive airfares to the Bahamas are priced for round-trip travel. Major airlines usually require that you **book far in advance** and **stay at least seven days** and no more than 30 to get the lowest fares. Ask about "ultrasaver" fares, which are the cheapest; they must be booked 90 days in advance and are nonrefundable. A little more expensive are "supersaver" fares, which require only a 30-day advance purchase. Remember that penalties for refunds or scheduling changes are stiffer for international tickets, usually about $150. International flights are also sensitive to the season: **Off-season fares are cheapest.** If your destination or home city has more than one gateway, **compare prices to and from different airports.** Also price flights scheduled for off-peak hours, which may be significantly less expensive.

To save money on flights from the United Kingdom and back, **look into an APEX or Super-PEX ticket.** Both should be booked in advance and have certain restrictions, though they can sometimes be purchased right at the airport.

DON'T STOP UNLESS YOU MUST

When you book, **look for nonstop flights,** and **remember that direct flights stop at least once.** International flights on a country's flag carrier are almost always nonstop; U.S. airlines often fly direct. Try to **avoid connecting flights,** which require a change of plane and can increase the chance of baggage delay or loss. Two airlines may jointly operate a connecting flight, so ask if your airline operates every segment—you may find that your preferred carrier flies you only part of the way.

USE AN AGENT

Travel agents, especially those who specialize in finding the lowest fares (☞ Discounts & Deals, *below*), can be especially helpful when booking a plane ticket. When you're quoted a price, **ask your agent if the price is likely to get any lower.** Good agents know the seasonal fluctuations of airfares and can usually anticipate a sale or fare war. However, waiting can be risky: The fare could go *up* as seats become scarce, and you may wait so long that your preferred flight sells out. A wait-and-see strategy works best if your plans are flexible, but if you must arrive and depart on certain dates, don't delay.

CHECK WITH CONSOLIDATORS

Consolidators buy tickets for scheduled flights at reduced rates from the airlines then sell them at prices that beat the best fare available directly from the airlines, usually without advance restrictions. Sometimes you can even get your money back if you need to return the ticket. Carefully read the fine print detailing penalties for changes and cancellations, and **confirm your consolidator reservation with the airline.**

➤ CONSOLIDATORS: **United States Air Consolidators Association** (✉ 925 L St., Suite 220, Sacramento, CA 95814, ☎ 916/441–4166, FAX 916/441–3520).

AVOID GETTING BUMPED

Airlines routinely overbook planes, knowing that not everyone with a ticket will show up, but sometimes everyone does. When that happens, airlines ask for volunteers to give up their seats. In return these volunteers usually get a certificate for a free flight and are rebooked on the next flight out. If there are not enough volunteers the airline must choose who will be denied boarding. The first to get bumped are passengers who checked in late and those flying on discounted tickets, **so get to the gate and check in as early as possible,** especially during peak periods.

Always **bring a photo ID to the airport.** You may be asked to show it before you are allowed to check in.

ENJOY THE FLIGHT

For better service, **fly smaller or regional carriers,** which often have higher passenger-satisfaction ratings. Sometimes you'll find leather seats, more legroom, and better food.

For more legroom, **request an emergency-aisle seat;** don't, however, sit in the row in front of the emergency aisle or in front of a bulkhead, where seats may not recline.

If you don't like airline food, **ask for special meals when booking.** These can be vegetarian, low cholesterol, or kosher, for example.

Some carriers have prohibited smoking throughout their systems; others allow smoking only on certain routes or even certain departures from that route, so **contact your carrier regarding its smoking policy.**

COMPLAIN IF NECESSARY

If your baggage goes astray or your flight goes awry, complain right away. Most carriers require that you file a claim immediately.

➤ AIRLINE COMPLAINTS: U.S. Department of Transportation **Aviation Consumer Protection Division** (✉ C-75, Washington, DC 20590, ☎ 202/366–2220). **Federal Aviation Administration (FAA) Consumer Hotline** (☎ 800/322–7873).

AIRPORTS & TRANSFERS

The major gateways to the Bahamas include **Nassau** (☎ 809/377–7281), on New Providence Island, and **Freeport** (☎ 809/352–6020), on Grand Bahama Island. There are also direct flights from Florida to Marsh Harbour and Treasure Cay in the Abacos.

B

BUSINESS HOURS

Banks are open Monday–Thursday 9:30–3 and Friday 9:30–5. Principal banks are Bank of the Bahamas, Bank of Nova Scotia, Barclays Bank, Canadian Imperial Bank of Commerce, Chase Manhattan Bank, Citibank, and Royal Bank of Canada.

Shops in the Bahamas are open Monday–Saturday 9–5. Bahamian stores are permitted to open on Sunday, but most choose to remain closed. **Best shopping times are in the morning**, when streets are less crowded. Remember that when you're shopping in Nassau, you'll be competing with the hordes of passengers that pour off cruise ships at Prince George Wharf daily.

C

CAMERAS, CAMCORDERS, & COMPUTERS

Always **keep your film, tape, or computer disks out of the sun.** Carry an extra supply of batteries, and **be prepared to turn on your camera, camcorder, or laptop** to prove to security personnel that the device is real. Always **ask for hand inspection of film,** which becomes clouded after successive exposure to airport X-ray machines, and **keep videotapes and computer disks away from metal detectors.**

➤ PHOTO HELP: Kodak Information Center (☎ 800/242–2424). *Kodak Guide to Shooting Great Travel Pictures,* available in bookstores or from Fodor's Travel Publications (☎ 800/533–6478; $16.50 plus $4 shipping).

CUSTOMS

Before departing, **register your foreign-made camera or laptop with U.S. Customs** (☞ Customs & Duties, *below*). If your equipment is U.S.-made, call the consulate of the country you'll be visiting to find out whether the device should be registered with local customs upon arrival.

CAR RENTAL

Rates in Nassau begin at $53 a day and $288 a week for an economy car with air-conditioning, manual transmission, and unlimited mileage.

➤ MAJOR AGENCIES: **Budget** (☎ 800/527–0700, 0800/181181 in the U.K.). **Dollar** (☎ 800/800–4000, 0990/565656 in the U.K., where it is known as Eurodollar). **Hertz** (☎ 800/654–3001, 800/263–0600 in Canada, 0345/555888 in the U.K.).

CUT COSTS

To get the best deal, **book through a travel agent who is willing to shop around.**

Also **ask your travel agent about a company's customer-service record.** How has it responded to late plane arrivals and vehicle mishaps? Are there often lines at the rental counter, and, if you're traveling during a holiday period, does a confirmed reservation guarantee you a car?

NEED INSURANCE?

When driving a rented car you are generally responsible for any damage to or loss of the vehicle. You also are liable for any property damage or personal injury that you may cause while driving. Before you rent, **see what coverage you already have** under the terms of your personal auto-insurance policy and credit cards.

BEWARE SURCHARGES

Note that some rental agencies charge extra if you return the car before the time specified on your contract. To avoid a hefty refueling fee, **fill the** tank just before you turn in the car, but be aware that gas stations near the rental outlet may overcharge.

MEET THE REQUIREMENTS

In the Bahamas your own driver's license is acceptable for up to three months. An International Driver's Permit is a good idea; it's available from the American or Canadian automobile association, or, in the United Kingdom, from the Automobile Association or Royal Automobile Club.

CASINO GAMBLING

For information on **casino gambling** in the Bahamas, ☞ Cashing In: A Casino Gambling Primer *in* Chapter 2, Pleasures and Pastimes.

CHILDREN & TRAVEL

CHILDREN IN THE BAHAMAS

Be sure to plan ahead and **involve your youngsters** as you outline your trip. When packing, include things to keep them busy en route. On sightseeing days try to schedule activities of special interest to your children. If you are renting a car don't forget to **arrange for a car seat** when you reserve. Most hotels in the Bahamas allow children under a certain age to stay in their parents' room at no extra charge, but others charge them as extra adults; be sure to **ask about the cutoff age for children's discounts.** Club Med, Breezes, Sandals and some small inns discourage or don't permit children; be sure to ask.

FLYING

As a general rule, infants under two not occupying a seat fly at greatly reduced fares and occasionally for free. If your children are two or older **ask about children's airfares.**

The adult baggage allowance typically applies to children paying half or more of the adult fare. When booking, **ask about carry-on allowances for those traveling with infants.** In general, for babies charged 10% of the adult fare you are allowed one carry-on bag and a collapsible stroller, which may have to be checked; you may be limited to less if the flight is full.

According to the FAA it's a good idea to use safety seats aloft for children weighing less than 40 pounds. Airlines, however, can set their own policies: U.S. carriers allow FAA-approved models but usually require that you buy a ticket, even if your child would otherwise ride free, since the seats must be strapped into regular seats. Airline rules vary regarding their use, so it's important to **check your airline's policy about using safety seats during takeoff and landing.** Safety seats cannot obstruct any of the other passengers in the row, so get an appropriate seat assignment as early as possible.

When making your reservation, **request children's meals or a free-standing bassinet** if you need them; the latter is available only to those seated at the bulkhead, where there's enough legroom. Remember, however, that bulkhead seats may not have their own overhead bins, and there's no storage space in front of you—a major inconvenience.

CONSUMER PROTECTION

Whenever possible, **pay with a major credit card** so that you can cancel payment if there's a problem, provided that you have documentation. This is a good practice whether you're buying travel arrangements before your trip or shopping at your destination.

If you're doing business with a particular company for the first time, **contact your local Better Business Bureau and the attorney general's offices** in your state and the company's home state. Have any complaints been filed?

Finally, if you're buying a package or tour, always **consider travel insurance** that includes default coverage (☞ Insurance, *below*).

➤ LOCAL BBBs: **Council of Better Business Bureaus** (✉ 4200 Wilson Blvd., Suite 800, Arlington, VA 22203, ☎ 703/276–0100, ℻ 703/525–8277).

CRUISING

Carnival Cruise Lines (✉ 3655 N.W. 87th Ave., Miami, FL 33178, ☎ 800/327–9501) offers three-day trips to Nassau and four-day trips to Nassau and Freeport. The *Fantasy,* which holds 2,044 passengers, leaves from Port Canaveral on Thursday and Sunday. The 2,040-passenger *Ecstasy* leaves from the Port of Miami on Friday and Monday.

SMART TRAVEL TIPS / THE GOLD GUIDE

Celebrity Cruises (✉ 5201 Blue Lagoon Dr., Miami, FL 33126, ☎ 800/437–3111) stops in Nassau with their 1,750-passenger cruise ship *Century,* which leaves every other Saturday from the Port of Miami on a seven-night eastern Caribbean cruise.

Discovery Cruises (✉ 1850 Eller Dr., Suite 402, Fort Lauderdale, FL 33316, ☎ 800/937–4477) has one-day trips to Freeport. The *Discovery I,* which holds 1,250 passengers, leaves from the Port of Fort Lauderdale every Sunday, Monday, and Wednesday, and from the Port of Everglades on Friday. The *Discovery Sun,* which holds 1,050 passengers, leaves from the Port of Miami on Tuesday, Thursday, and Saturday.

Dolphin & Majesty Cruise Line (✉ 901 South America Way, Miami, FL 33132, ☎ 800/222–1003 or 800/532–7788) offers three- and four-day cruises to Nassau aboard the *Ocean-Breeze,* with room for 776 passengers, and three-day trips to Nassau aboard the *Royal Majesty,* which can take 1,056 passengers. The 588-passenger *SeaBreeze* stops in Nassau on its seven-day eastern Caribbean cruise. All cruises depart from the Port of Miami.

Kloster/Norwegian Cruise Line (✉ 95 Merrick Way, Coral Gables, FL 33134, ☎ 800/327–7030) has three-day cruises to Nassau, departing every other Friday. The liner is the *Leeward,* which holds 950 passengers and operates out of Miami.

Premier Cruise Lines (✉ Box 573, 400 Challenger Rd., Cape Canaveral, FL 32920, ☎ 800/515–7890), the official cruise line of Walt Disney World, sends its Big Red Boats, the 1,550-passenger *Atlantic* and the 1,800-passenger *Oceanic,* on three- or four-day loops to Nassau and Freeport-Lucaya from Port Canaveral. The three-night cruises depart Thursday and Friday; the four-night cruises, Sunday and Monday.

Royal Caribbean Cruise Line (✉ 1050 Caribbean Way, Miami, FL 33132, ☎ 800/327–6700) offers three- and four-day cruises aboard the 1,600-passenger *Nordic Empress,* departing every Monday and Friday from Miami. Three-day cruises sail to Nassau and Coco Cay; four-day cruises sail to Nassau, Coco Cay, and Freeport.

SeaEscape Cruise Lines (✉ 140 S. Federal Hwy., Dania, FL 33004, ☎ 800/327–2005) offers one-day cruises to Freeport. The 1,170-passenger *SeaEscape* departs from Fort Lauderdale on Monday, Wednesday, Friday, and Sunday.

CUSTOMS & DUTIES

When shopping, **keep receipts** for all of your purchases. Upon reentering the country, **be ready to show customs officials what you've bought.** If you feel a duty is incorrect, appeal the assessment. If you object to the way your clearance was handled, get the inspector's badge number. In either case, first ask to see a supervisor, then write to the port director at the address listed on your receipt. Send a copy of the receipt and other appropriate documentation. If you still don't get satisfaction you can take your case to customs headquarters in Washington.

ENTERING THE BAHAMAS

Customs allows you to bring in 50 cigars or 200 cigarettes or 1 pound of tobacco and a quart of liquor and 1 quart of wine in addition to personal effects and all the money you wish. But **don't even think of smuggling** in marijuana or any kind of narcotic. Justice is swifter in the Bahamas than in the United States. Expect conviction and severe punishment within three days, which could certainly put a damper on your vacation.

You would be well advised to **leave pets at home,** unless you're considering a prolonged stay in the islands. An import permit is required from the **Ministry of Agriculture and Fisheries** (✉ Box N 3028, Nassau, ☎ 242/325–7413) for all animals brought into the Bahamas. You'll also need a veterinary health certificate issued by a licensed vet within 24 hours of embarkation. The permit is good for 90 days from the date of issue.

ENTERING THE U.S.

You may bring home $400 worth of foreign goods duty-free if you've been out of the country for at least 48 hours and haven't already used the $400 allowance or any part of it in the past 30 days.

Travelers 21 and older may bring back 1 liter of alcohol duty-free.

In addition, you are allowed 200 cigarettes and 100 non-Cuban cigars. Antiques, which the U.S. Customs Service defines as objects more than 100 years old, enter duty-free, as do original works of art done entirely by hand, including paintings, drawings, and pieces of sculpture.

You may also send packages home duty-free: up to $200 worth of goods for personal use, with a limit of one parcel per addressee per day (and no alcohol or tobacco products or perfume worth more than $5); label the package PERSONAL USE and attach a list of its contents and their retail value. Do not label the package UNSOLICITED GIFT, or your duty-free exemption will drop to $100. Mailed items do not affect your duty-free allowance on your return.

➤ INFORMATION: **U.S. Customs Service** (Inquiries, ✉ Box 7407, Washington, DC 20044, ☎ 202/927–6724; complaints, ✉ Commissioner's Office, 1301 Constitution Ave. NW, Washington, DC 20229; registration of equipment, ✉ Resource Management, 1301 Constitution Ave. NW, Washington, DC 20229, ☎ 202/927–0540).

ENTERING CANADA

If you've been out of Canada for at least seven days you may bring in C$500 worth of goods duty-free. If you've been away for fewer than seven days but more than 48 hours, the duty-free allowance drops to C$200; if your trip lasts 24–48 hours, the allowance is C$50. You may not pool allowances with family members. Goods claimed under the C$500 exemption may follow you by mail; those claimed under the lesser exemptions must accompany you.

Alcohol and tobacco products may be included in the seven-day and 48-hour exemptions but not in the 24-hour exemption. If you meet the age requirements of the province or territory through which you reenter Canada you may bring in, duty-free, 1.14 liters (40 imperial ounces) of wine or liquor *or* 24 12-ounce cans or bottles of beer or ale. If you are 16 or older you may bring in, duty-free, 200 cigarettes and 50 cigars; these items must accompany you.

You may send an unlimited number of gifts worth up to C$60 each duty-free to Canada. Label the package UNSOLICITED GIFT—VALUE UNDER $60. Alcohol and tobacco are excluded.

➤ INFORMATION: **Revenue Canada** (✉ 2265 St. Laurent Blvd. S, Ottawa, Ontario K1G 4K3, ☎ 613/993–0534 or 800/461–9999 in Canada).

ENTERING THE U.K.

From countries outside the EU, including the Bahamas, you may import, duty-free, 200 cigarettes or 50 cigars; 1 liter of spirits or 2 liters of fortified or sparkling wine or liqueurs; 2 liters of still table wine; 60 milliliters of perfume; 250 milliliters of toilet water; plus £136 worth of other goods, including gifts and souvenirs.

➤ INFORMATION: **HM Customs and Excise** (✉ Dorset House, Stamford St., London SE1 9NG, ☎ 0171/202–4227).

D

DISABILITIES & ACCESSIBILITY

LODGING

Most major hotels throughout the Bahamas have special facilities for people with disabilities, in the way of elevators, ramps, and easy access to rooms and public areas. Also, the Bahamas Association for the Physically Disabled has temporary ramps and other portable facilities, including transportation for hire. Call 242/322–2393 for more information and assistance. Here are some suggestions based on a survey conducted by the association:

➤ NASSAU: **Best Western British Colonial Beach Resort** (✉ Box N 7148, ☎ 242/322–3301), **Nassau Marriott Resort & Crystal Palace Casino** (✉ Box N 8806, ☎ 242/327–6200), **Forte Nassau Beach Hotel** (✉ Box N 7756, ☎ 242/327–7711), **Radisson Cable Beach Casino & Golf Resort** (✉ Box N 4914, ☎ 242/327–6000), and **Little Orchard Cottage** (✉ Box N 1514, ☎ 242/393–1297).

➤ PARADISE ISLAND: **Atlantis, Paradise Island** (✉ Box N 4777, ☎ 242/363–3000), **Bay View Village** (✉ Box SS 6308, ☎ 242/363–2555), **Holiday Inn SunSpree Resort** (✉ Box SS 6214, ☎ 242/363–2100), and **Radisson**

Grand Resort (✉ Box SS 6307, ☎ 242/363–2011).

➤ GRAND BAHAMA: **Bahamas Princess Resort & Casino** (✉ Box F 40207, ☎ 242/352–9661) and **Clarion Atlantik Beach** (✉ Box F 42500, ☎ 242/373–1444).

➤ LONG ISLAND: **Stella Maris Marina Inn & Estate** (✉ Box SM 30105, ☎ 242/338–2050 or 800/426–0466).

TIPS AND HINTS

When discussing accessibility with an operator or reservationist, **ask hard questions.** Are there any stairs, inside *or* out? Are there grab bars next to the toilet *and* in the shower/tub? How wide is the doorway to the room? To the bathroom? For the most extensive facilities meeting the latest legal specifications, **opt for newer accommodations,** which are more likely to have been designed with access in mind. Older buildings or ships may offer more limited facilities. Be sure to **discuss your needs before booking.**

➤ COMPLAINTS: **Disability Rights Section** (✉ U.S. Department of Justice, Box 66738, Washington, DC 20035–6738, ☎ 202/514–0301 or 800/514–0301, FAX 202/307–1198, TTY 202/514–0383 or 800/514–0383) for general complaints. **Aviation Consumer Protection Division** (☞ Air Travel, *above*) for airline-related problems. **Civil Rights Office** (✉ U.S. Department of Transportation, Departmental Office of Civil Rights, S-30, 400 7th St. SW, Room 10215, Washington, DC, 20590, ☎ 202/366–4648) for problems with surface transportation.

TRAVEL AGENCIES & TOUR OPERATORS

The Americans with Disabilities Act requires that travel firms serve the needs of all travelers. That said, you should note that some agencies and operators specialize in making travel arrangements for individuals and groups with disabilities.

➤ TRAVELERS WITH MOBILITY PROBLEMS: **Access Adventures** (✉ 206 Chestnut Ridge Rd., Rochester, NY 14624, ☎ 716/889–9096), is run by a former physical-rehabilitation counselor. **Hinsdale Travel Service** (✉ 201 E. Ogden Ave., Suite 100, Hinsdale, IL 60521, ☎ 630/325–1335) is a travel

agency that benefits from the advice of wheelchair traveler Janice Perkins. **Wheelchair Journeys** (✉ 16979 Redmond Way, Redmond, WA 98052, ☎ 206/885–2210 or 800/313–4751), for general travel arrangements.

➤ TRAVELERS WITH DEVELOPMENTAL DISABILITIES: **Sprout** (✉ 893 Amsterdam Ave., New York, NY 10025, ☎ 212/222–9575 or 888/222–9575, FAX 212/222–9768).

DISCOUNTS & DEALS

Shop smart and **compare all your options before making a choice.** A plane ticket bought with a promotional coupon may not be cheaper than the least expensive fare from a discount ticket agency. For high-price travel purchases, such as packages or tours, keep in mind that what you get is just as important as what you save. Just because something is cheap doesn't mean it's a bargain.

LOOK IN YOUR WALLET

When you use your credit card to make travel purchases you may get free travel-accident insurance, collision-damage insurance, and medical or legal assistance, depending on the card and the bank that issued it. American Express, MasterCard, and Visa provide one or more of these services, so **get a copy of your credit card's travel-benefits policy.** If you are a member of the American Automobile Association (AAA) or an oil-company-sponsored road-assistance plan, always **ask hotel or car-rental reservationists about auto-club discounts.** Some clubs offer additional discounts on tours, cruises, or admission to attractions. And don't forget that auto-club membership entitles you to free maps and trip-planning services.

DIAL FOR DOLLARS

To save money, **look into "1-800" discount reservations services,** which use their buying power to get a better price on hotels, airline tickets, even car rentals. When booking a room, always **call the hotel's local toll-free number** (if one is available) rather than the central reservations number—you'll often get a better price. Always ask about special packages or corporate rates.

When shopping for the best deal on hotels and car rentals **look for guar-**

anteed exchange rates, which protect you against a falling dollar. With your rate locked in you won't pay more even if the price goes up in the local currency.

➤ AIRLINE TICKETS: ☎ **800/FLY–4–LESS.**

SAVE ON COMBOS

Packages and guided tours can both save you money, but don't confuse the two. When you buy a package your travel remains independent, just as though you had planned and booked the trip yourself. Fly/drive packages, which combine airfare and car rental, are often a good deal.

JOIN A CLUB?

Many companies sell discounts in the form of travel clubs and coupon books, but these cost money. You must use participating advertisers to get a deal, and only after you recoup the initial membership cost or book price do you begin to save. If you plan to use the club or coupons frequently you may save considerably. Before signing up, find out what discounts you get for free.

➤ DISCOUNT CLUBS: **Entertainment Travel Editions** (✉ Box 1068, Trumbull, CT 06611, ☎ 800/445–4137; $28–$53, depending on destination). **Great American Traveler** (✉ Box 27965, Salt Lake City, UT 84127, ☎ 800/548–2812; $49.95 per year). **Moment's Notice Discount Travel Club** (✉ 7301 New Utrecht Ave., Brooklyn, NY 11204, ☎ 718/234–6295; $25 per year). **Privilege Card International** (✉ 201 E. Commerce St., Suite 198, Youngstown, OH 44503, ☎ 330/746–5211 or 800/236–9732; $74.95 per year). **Sears's Mature Outlook** (✉ Box 9390, Des Moines, IA 50306, ☎ 800/336–6330; $14.95 per year). **Travelers Advantage** (✉ CUC Travel Service, 3033 S. Parker Rd., Suite 1000, Aurora, CO 80014, ☎ 800/548–1116 or 800/648–4037; $49 per year). **Worldwide Discount Travel Club** (✉ 1674 Meridian Ave., Miami Beach, FL 33139, ☎ 305/534–2082; $50 per year family, $40 single).

DRIVING

Remember, like the British, Bahamians **drive on the left side of the road,** which can be confusing because most cars are American with the steering wheel on the left. As a pedestrian, this means that you should **look right before crossing the street** instead of left, as those of us learned who grew up in the States.

➤ AUTO CLUBS: **American Automobile Association** (AAA, ☎ 800/564–6222), in the U.S. **Automobile Association** (AA, ☎ 0990/500600), in the U.K. **Royal Automobile Club** (RAC, ☎ 0990/722722 for membership inquiries, or ☎ 0345/121345 for insurance).

E
ELECTRICITY

Electricity is 120 volts/60 cycles, which is compatible with all U.S. appliances.

F
FERRIES

If you're of an adventurous frame of mind, you can revert to the mode of transportation that islanders used before the advent of air travel: ferries and the traditional mailboats, which regularly leave Nassau from **Potter's Cay,** under the Paradise Island bridge. You may find yourself sharing company with goats and chickens, and making your way on deck through piles of lumber bound for Cat Island, but that's all part of the adventure. Fares vary from $20 to $70 each way, depending on the destination. **Don't plan to arrive or depart punctually;** the flexible schedules can be thrown off by bad weather. Remember, too, that they operate on Bahamian time, which is an unpredictable measure of tempo. You cannot book ahead. In Nassau, check details with the dock master's office at Potter's Cay. You can purchase tickets from the dock master or from the captain or mate just before departure.

G
GAY & LESBIAN TRAVEL

➤ GAY- AND LESBIAN-FRIENDLY TRAVEL AGENCIES: **Advance Damron** (✉ 1 Greenway Plaza, Suite 800, Houston, TX 77046, ☎ 713/682–2002 or 800/695–0880, FAX 713/888–1010). **Club Travel** (✉ 8739 Santa Monica Blvd., West Hollywood, CA 90069, ☎ 310/358–2200 or 800/429–8747, FAX 310/

358–2222). **Islanders/Kennedy Travel** (⊠ 183 W. 10th St., New York, NY 10014, ☎ 212/242–3222 or 800/ 988–1181, FAX 212/929–8530). **Now Voyager** (⊠ 4406 18th St., San Francisco, CA 94114, ☎ 415/626–1169 or 800/255–6951, FAX 415/626– 8626). **Yellowbrick Road** (⊠ 1500 W. Balmoral Ave., Chicago, IL 60640, ☎ 773/561–1800 or 800/642–2488, FAX 773/561–4497). **Skylink Women's Travel** (⊠ 3577 Moorland Ave., Santa Rosa, CA 95407, ☎ 707/585–8355 or 800/225–5759, FAX 707/584–5637) serves lesbian travelers.

H
HEALTH

DIVERS' ALERT

Do not fly within 24 hours of scuba diving.

MEDICAL PLANS

No one plans to get sick while traveling, but since it can happen, **consider signing up with a medical-assistance company.** Members get doctor referrals, emergency evacuation or repatriation, 24-hour telephone hot lines for medical consultation, cash for emergencies, and other personal and legal assistance. Coverage varies by plan, so **review the benefits carefully**.

➤ MEDICAL-ASSISTANCE COMPANIES: **International SOS Assistance** (⊠ Box 11568, Philadelphia, PA 19116, ☎ 215/244–1500 or 800/523–8930; ⊠ Box 466, pl. Bonaventure, Montréal, Québec H5A 1C1, ☎ 514/874–7674 or 800/363–0263; ⊠ 7 Old Lodge Pl., St. Margarets, Twickenham TW1 1RQ, England, ☎ 0181/744–0033). **MEDEX Assistance Corporation** (⊠ Box 5375, Timonium, MD 21094, ☎ 410/453–6300 or 800/537–2029). **Traveler's Emergency Network** (⊠ 3100 Tower Blvd., Suite 1000B, Durham, NC 27707, ☎ 919/490– 6055 or 800/275–4836, FAX 919/ 493–8262). **TravMed** (⊠ Box 5375, Timonium, MD 21094, ☎ 410/453– 6380 or 800/732–5309). **Worldwide Assistance Services** (⊠ 1133 15th St. NW, Suite 400, Washington, DC 20005, ☎ 202/331–1609 or 800/ 821–2828, FAX 202/828–5896).

SUNBATHING

Basking in the sun is one of the great pleasures of a Bahamian vacation; but before abandoning yourself to the tropics, you would be well advised to take precautions against the ravages of sunburn and sunstroke. On a hot, sunny day, even people who are not normally bothered by strong sun should **cover up with a long-sleeve shirt, a hat, and pants or a beach wrap.** These are essential for a day on a boat but are also advisable for midday at the beach. **Carry some UVA/UVB sunblock** (with a sun protection factor, or SPF, of at least 15) for nose, ears, and other sensitive areas such as eyelids, ankles, and so forth; if you're engaging in water sports, be sure the sunscreen is waterproof. Be sure to **drink enough liquids—water or fruit juice preferably**—and avoid coffee, tea, and alcohol. Above all, limit your sun time for the first few days until you become accustomed to the heat. Do not be fooled by an overcast day. Quite often you will get the worst sunburns when you least expect it. The safest hours for sunbathing are 4–6, but even then it is wise to limit exposure to 15–20 minutes.

VACCINATIONS

A vaccination against yellow fever is required if you're arriving from an infected area. Otherwise, no special shots are required before visiting the Bahamas.

I
INSURANCE

Travel insurance is the best way to **protect yourself against financial loss.** The most useful policies are trip-cancellation-and-interruption, default, medical, and comprehensive insurance.

Without insurance you will lose all or most of your money if you cancel your trip, regardless of the reason. It's essential that you **buy trip-cancellation-and-interruption insurance,** particularly if your airline ticket, cruise, or package tour is nonrefundable and cannot be changed. When considering how much coverage you need, look for a policy that will cover the cost of your trip plus the nondiscounted price of a one-way airline ticket, should you need to return home early. Also **consider default or bankruptcy insurance,** which protects you against a supplier's failure to deliver.

Medicare generally does not cover health-care costs outside the United States, nor do many privately issued policies. If your own policy does not cover you outside the United States, **consider buying supplemental medical coverage.** Remember that travel health insurance is different from a medical-assistance plan (☞ Health, *above*).

Citizens of the United Kingdom can buy an annual travel-insurance policy valid for most vacations during the year in which it's purchased. If you are pregnant or have a preexisting medical condition, make sure you're covered.

If you have purchased an expensive vacation, particularly one that involves travel abroad, comprehensive insurance is a must. **Look for comprehensive policies that include trip-delay insurance,** which will protect you in the event that weather problems cause you to miss your flight, tour, or cruise. A few insurers sell waivers for preexisting medical conditions. Companies that offer both features include Access America, Carefree Travel, Travel Insured International, and Travel Guard (☞ *below*).

Always **buy travel insurance directly from the insurance company;** if you buy it from a travel agency or tour operator that goes out of business you probably will not be covered for the agency or operator's default, a major risk. Before you make any purchase, **review your existing health and home-owner's policies** to find out whether they cover expenses incurred while traveling.

➤ TRAVEL INSURERS: **Access America** (✉ 6600 W. Broad St., Richmond, VA 23230, ☎ 804/285–3300 or 800/284–8300), **Carefree Travel Insurance** (✉ Box 9366, 100 Garden City Plaza, Garden City, NY 11530, ☎ 516/294–0220 or 800/323–3149), **Near Travel Services** (✉ Box 1339, Calumet City, IL 60409, ☎ 708/868–6700 or 800/654–6700), **Travel Guard International** (✉ 1145 Clark St., Stevens Point, WI 54481, ☎ 715/345–0505 or 800/826–1300), **Travel Insured International** (✉ Box 280568, East Hartford, CT 06128–0568, ☎ 860/528–7663 or 800/243–3174), **Travelex Insurance Services** (✉ 11717 Burt St., Suite 202, Omaha, NE 68154–

1500, ☎ 402/445–8637 or 800/228–9792, FAX 800/867–9531), **Wallach & Company** (✉ 107 W. Federal St., Box 480, Middleburg, VA 20118, ☎ 540/687–3166 or 800/237–6615). **Mutual of Omaha** (✉ Travel Division, 500 University Ave., Toronto, Ontario M5G 1V8, ☎ 416/598–4083, 800/268–8825 in Canada). **Association of British Insurers** (✉ 51 Gresham St., London EC2V 7HQ, ☎ 0171/600–3333).

L

LANGUAGE

Bahamians speak English with a lilt influenced by their Scottish, Irish, and/or African ancestry. The official language of the Turks and Caicos is also English.

LODGING

Beachfront resort hotels—on Cable Beach and Paradise Island on New Providence Island, and in Lucaya on Grand Bahama Island—are among the most expensive. They also have the widest range of sports facilities, including tennis courts and sailboats. High room rates in many hotels in winter season (slightly less on Grand Bahama than on New Providence) are cut by as much as 30% during the slower May–December period, when managements try to outdo one another with attractive three-day or one-week packages. Prices at hotels away from the beach tend to be considerably lower and are often a better deal because accessible beaches are never far away.

In addition to the apartment suggestions *below,* Out Islands' lodging includes cottages that come with fully equipped kitchens.

APARTMENT AND VILLA RENTALS

If you want a home base that's roomy enough for a family and comes with cooking facilities, **consider a furnished rental.** These can save you money, however, some rentals are luxury properties, economical only when your party is large. Home-exchange directories list rentals (often second homes owned by prospective house swappers), and some services search for a house or apartment for you (even a castle if that's your fancy) and handle the paperwork. Some send an illustrated catalog; others send photographs only of specific properties, sometimes at a charge. Up-front registration fees may apply.

➤ RENTAL AGENTS: **Property Rentals International** (✉ 1008 Mansfield Crossing Rd., Richmond, VA 23236, ☎ 804/378–6054 or 800/220–3332, FAX 804/379–2073). **Rental Directories International** (✉ 2044 Rittenhouse Sq., Philadelphia, PA 19103, ☎ 215/985–4001, FAX 215/985–0323). **Rent-a-Home International** (✉ 7200 34th Ave. NW, Seattle, WA 98117, ☎ 206/789–9377 or 800/488–7368, FAX 206/789–9379). **Vacation Home Rentals Worldwide** (✉ 235 Kensington Ave., Norwood, NJ 07648, ☎ 201/767–9393 or 800/633–3284, FAX 201/767–5510). **Hideaways International** (✉ 767 Islington St., Portsmouth, NH 03801, ☎ 603/430–4433 or 800/843–4433, FAX 603/430–4444) is a travel club whose members arrange rentals among themselves; yearly membership is $99.

HOTELS

For hotel information for the Turks and Caicos Islands, contact the **Turks & Caicos Reservation Service** (☎ 800/282–4753).

M

MAIL

Airmail postcards to the United States, Canada, the United Kingdom, Europe, and South America require a 40¢ stamp. If you're sending an airmail letter, it costs 55¢ per half ounce, 50¢ to the United States and Canada, 60¢ to the United Kingdom, Europe, and South America. The stamps must be Bahamian. Prices from the Turks and Caicos are comparable. Whether or not the term "snail mail" was coined in the Bahamas, you're likely to find that you arrive home long before your postcards do.

MONEY

The U.S. dollar is on par with the Bahamian dollar and is accepted all over the Bahamas; the U.K. pound sterling compares at about 75 pence, and the Canadian dollar at around $1.20. If someone offers you a $3 bill, don't think you're being conned. Bahamian money runs in bills of a half dollar, $1, $3, $5, $10, $20, $50, and $100. The rare $3 bill makes an unusual souvenir.

ATMS

Before leaving home, **make sure that your credit cards have been programmed for ATM use in the Bahamas.** Note that Discover is accepted mostly in the United States. Local bank cards often do not work overseas or may access only your checking account; **ask your bank about a MasterCard/Cirrus or Visa debit card,** which works like a bank card but can be used at any ATM displaying a MasterCard/Cirrus or Visa logo. These cards, too, may tap only your checking account; check with your bank about their policy.

➤ ATM LOCATIONS: **Cirrus** (☎ 800/424–7787). A list of **Plus** locations is available at your local bank.

COSTS

Generally, prices in the Bahamas reflect the exchange rate: They are about the same as in the United States, less expensive than in the United Kingdom, and more expensive than in Canada. A hotel can cost anywhere from $35 a night (for cottages and apartments in downtown Nassau and in the Out Islands) to $145 and up (at the ritzier resorts on Cable Beach and Paradise Island and in Freeport and Lucaya), depending on the season. Add $35 to $50 per person per day for meals. Bus fares in the two main islands, New Providence and Grand Bahama, are cheap. Four-day/three-night and eight-day/seven-night package stays offered by most hotels can cut costs considerably.

CURRENCY EXCHANGE

In the Bahamas, only U.S. cash will be exchanged freely in hotels, stores or restaurants, and since the U.S. currency is accepted throughout, there really is no need to change to Bahamian.

For the most favorable rates, **change money at banks.** Although fees charged for ATM transactions may be higher abroad than at home, Cirrus and Plus exchange rates are excellent, because they are based on wholesale rates offered only by major banks. You won't do as well at exchange booths in airports or rail and bus stations, in hotels, in restaurants, or in stores, although you may find their hours more convenient. To avoid lines at airport exchange booths, **get a small amount of local currency before you leave home**.

➤ EXCHANGE SERVICES: **Ruesch International** (☎ 800/424–2923 for locations). Thomas Cook Currency Services (☎ 800/287–7362 for telephone orders and retail locations).

TRAVELER'S CHECKS

Whether or not to buy traveler's checks depends on where you are headed; **cash works best in the Out Islands, while either cash or traveler's checks are accepted in Nassau and Freeport. Take cash if your trip includes rural areas** and small towns, traveler's checks to cities. If your checks are lost or stolen, they can usually be replaced within 24 hours. To ensure a speedy refund, buy your checks yourself (don't ask someone else to make the purchase). When making a claim for stolen or lost checks, the person who bought the checks should make the call.

N

NEWSPAPERS

You'll get all the Bahamian news and a good idea of what's going on internationally in the *Tribune* and the *Nassau Guardian* on New Providence and in the *Freeport News* on Grand Bahama. But if you want up-to-date news on what's happening around the world, you can also get the *Miami Herald,* the *Wall Street Journal,* and the *New York Times* daily at newsstands.

P

PACKING FOR THE BAHAMAS

The reason you're going to the Bahamas is to get away from all of that big-city suit-shirt-and-tie turmoil, so your wardrobe should reflect the informality of the experience. Aside from your bathing suit, which will be your favorite uniform, take lightweight clothing (short-sleeve shirts, T-shirts, cotton slacks, lightweight jackets for evening wear for men; light dresses, shorts, and T-shirts for women). If you're going during the high season, between mid-December and April, toss in a sweater for the occasional cool

evening. Cover up in public places for downtown shopping expeditions, and save that skimpy bathing suit for the beach at your hotel.

Only some of the more sophisticated hotels require jackets for men and dresses for women at dinner. But there are no such dress rules in any of the Bahamas' four casinos.

Bring an extra pair of eyeglasses or contact lenses in your carry-on luggage, and if you have a health problem, **pack enough medication** to last the entire trip or have your doctor write you a prescription using the drug's generic name, because brand names vary from country to country. It's important that you **don't put prescription drugs or valuables in luggage to be checked**: It might go astray. To avoid problems with customs officials, carry medications in the original packaging. Also, don't forget the addresses of offices that handle refunds of lost traveler's checks.

LUGGAGE

In general, you are entitled to check two bags on flights within the United States and on international flights leaving the United States. A third piece may be brought on board, but it must fit easily under the seat in front of you or in the overhead compartment.

If you are flying between two foreign destinations, note that baggage allowances may be determined not by piece but by weight—generally 88 pounds (40 kilograms) in first class, 66 pounds (30 kilograms) in business class, and 44 pounds (20 kilograms) in economy. If your flight between two cities abroad *connects* with your transatlantic or transpacific flight, the piece method still applies.

Airline liability for baggage is limited to $1,250 per person on flights within the United States. On international flights it amounts to $9.07 per pound or $20 per kilogram for checked baggage (roughly $640 per 70-pound bag) and $400 per passenger for unchecked baggage. Insurance for losses exceeding these amounts can be bought from the airline at check-in for about $10 per $1,000 of coverage; note that this coverage excludes a rather extensive list of items, which is shown on your airline ticket.

SMART TRAVEL TIPS / THE GOLD GUIDE

Before departure, **itemize your bags' contents** and their worth, and label the bags with your name, address, and phone number. (If you use your home address, cover it so that potential thieves can't see it readily.) Inside each bag, **pack a copy of your itinerary.** At check-in, **make sure that each bag is correctly tagged** with the destination airport's three-letter code. If your bags arrive damaged or fail to arrive at all, file a written report with the airline before leaving the airport.

PASSPORTS & VISAS

Once your travel plans are confirmed, **get a passport even if you don't need one to enter the Bahamas**—it's always the best form of ID. It's also a good idea to **make photocopies of the data page**; leave one copy with someone at home and keep another with you, separated from your passport. If you lose your passport, promptly call the nearest embassy or consulate and the local police; having a copy of the data page can speed replacement.

U.S. CITIZENS

For a stay of up to eight months, a passport and visa are not required of tourists with onward/return tickets; a certified birth certificate and two forms of photo identification are sufficient. However, it is a good idea to take your passport for identification. Even an expired passport, if it expired less than five years ago, is a valid form of identification. For additional information, contact the Embassy of the Commonwealth of the Bahamas or the nearest consulate.

CANADIANS

For stays of three weeks or less, Canadian travelers with onward/return tickets do not need a valid passport; a certified birth certificate and two forms of photo identification are sufficient. You do need a valid passport to enter the Bahamas for stays from three weeks to eight months.

➤ INFORMATION: **Passport Office** (☎ 819/994–3500 or 800/567–6868).

U.K. CITIZENS

Citizens of the United Kingdom need only a valid passport to enter the Bahamas for stays of up to eight months.

➤ INFORMATION: **London Passport Office** (☎ 0990/21010) for fees and documentation requirements and to request an emergency passport.

TURKS AND CAICOS

U.S. citizens need some proof of citizenship, such as a birth certificate, plus a photo ID or a current passport. British subjects are required to have a current passport. All visitors must have an ongoing or return ticket.

R

RELIGION

Bahamians are religious people, and you'll find churches representing most faiths on New Providence and the other islands: Anglican, Assembly of God, Baptist, Church of Christ, Church of God, Christian Science, Greek Orthodox, Lutheran, Free Evangelical, Methodist, Presbyterian, Islamic, Jehovah's Witness, Baha'i, and Roman Catholic. For times of services, consult the "What-to-Do" guide available at your hotel desk. Also look for church suppers, which can be a good way to mix with Bahamians.

S

SAFETY

Crime against tourists is relatively unheard of, and, unlike some of the Caribbean countries, the Bahamas has little begging. But take the precautions you would in any foreign country: Be aware of your wallet or handbag at all times, and keep your jewelry in the hotel safe.

SAILING

For information on **sailing** in the Bahamas, ☞ A Mariner's Guide to the Bahamas *in* Chapter 2, Pleasures and Pastimes.

SCUBA DIVING AND SNORKELING

For information on **scuba diving** in the Bahamas, ☞ Diving in Paradise *in* Chapter 2, Pleasures and Pastimes.

Snorkeling requires no special skills, and most hotels that rent equipment have a staff member or, at the very least, a booklet offering instruction in snorkeling basics. There are some steps you can take, however, to make your snorkeling hassle-free. Time often seems to slow and stand still underwater, so wear a water-resistant watch and **let someone on land know when to expect you back.** Wear a T-shirt and **apply sunscreen** to protect your back and the top and backs of your thighs from burning. As with any water sport, **never snorkel alone,** especially if you're out of shape. You don't have to be a great swimmer to snorkel, but occasionally you come up against currents that require stamina.

Remember that taking underwater souvenirs—shells, pieces of coral, or interesting rocks—is forbidden. Beyond the fact that many reefs are legally protected marine parks, the removal of living coral kills the reef and disturbs the delicate undersea ecosystem.

SENIOR-CITIZEN TRAVEL

To qualify for age-related discounts, **mention your senior-citizen status up front** when booking hotel reservations (not when checking out) and before you're seated in restaurants (not when paying the bill). Note that discounts may be limited to certain menus, days, or hours. When renting a car, **ask about promotional car-rental discounts,** which can be cheaper than senior-citizen rates.

➤ EDUCATIONAL TRAVEL PROGRAMS: Elderhostel (✉ 75 Federal St., 3rd floor, Boston, MA 02110, ☎ 617/426–7788).

SHOPPING

There's enough of a savings over U.S. prices (30%–50%, in many cases) to make duty-free shopping enjoyable on New Providence and Grand Bahama. And you'll certainly find exotic merchandise not available back home. Go to Bay Street, Nassau's main thoroughfare, and the side streets leading off it for a wide range of imported perfumes, watches, cameras, crystal, china, and tropical wear. The main shopping areas on Grand Bahama are contained in two tight communities: the exotic **International Bazaar** in Freeport, with shops representing a variety of the world's cultures, and **Port Lucaya Marketplace,** which has strolling musicians and a bandstand where a local group plays. On both islands, be sure to visit the straw markets, where you can bargain for low-priced hats, baskets, place mats, and other handcrafted items.

STUDENTS

To save money, **look into deals available through student-oriented travel agencies.** To qualify, you'll need a bona fide student ID card. Members of international student groups are also eligible.

➤ STUDENT IDs AND SERVICES: Council on International Educational Exchange (✉ CIEE, 205 E. 42nd St., 14th floor, New York, NY 10017, ☎ 212/822–2600 or 888/268–6245, FAX 212/822–2699), for mail orders only, in the United States. **Travel Cuts** (✉ 187 College St., Toronto, Ontario M5T 1P7, ☎ 416/979–2406 or 800/667–2887), in Canada.

➤ HOSTELING: **Hostelling International–American Youth Hostels** (✉ 733 15th St. NW, Suite 840, Washington, DC 20005, ☎ 202/783–6161, FAX 202/783–6171). **Hostelling International–Canada** (✉ 400-205 Catherine St., Ottawa, Ontario K2P 1C3, ☎ 613/237–7884, FAX 613/237–7868). **Youth Hostel Association of England and Wales** (✉ Trevelyan House, 8 St. Stephen's Hill, St. Albans, Hertfordshire AL1 2DY, ☎ 01727/855215 or 01727/845047, FAX 01727/844126). Membership in the U.S., $25; in Canada, C$26.75; in the U.K., £9.30).

T

TAXIS

As in the United States, there are taxis waiting at every airport, all along Bay Street and outside all of the main hotels. At press time, on Grand Bahama and New Providence, the stipulated rates were $2 for two passengers for ¼ mi, 30¢ for each additional ¼ mi. Cabs can also be hired by the hour for $20, and $10 for every additional half hour. In the Out Islands rates are negotiated. Upon arriving, you're likely to find that Bahamian taxi drivers are more loquacious than their U.S. counterparts, so by the time you've reached your hotel, points of interest will have already been explained.

TELEPHONES

The area code for the Bahamas is 242, and you can dial the Bahamas from the U.S. as you would make an interstate call. Within the Bahamas, to make a local call from your hotel room, dial 9, then the number. If your party doesn't answer before the fifth ring, hang up or you'll be charged for the call.

From outside the U.S. and Canada, the country code for the Bahamas is 1. After dialing the appropriate international access code (00 in the U.K.), you dial 1 followed by the 242 Bahamas area code.

LONG-DISTANCE

Before you go, **find out the local access codes** for your destinations. AT&T, MCI, and Sprint long-distance services make calling home relatively convenient, but you may find the local access number blocked in many hotel rooms. First ask the hotel operator to connect you. If the hotel operator balks, ask for an international operator, or dial the international operator yourself. One way to improve your odds of getting connected to your long-distance carrier is to travel with more than one company's calling card (a hotel may block Sprint, for example, but not MCI). If all else fails, call your phone company collect in the United States or call from a pay phone in the hotel lobby.

➤ To Obtain Access Codes: **AT&T** USADirect (☎ 800/874–4000). **MCI** Call USA (☎ 800/444–4444). **Sprint** Express (☎ 800/793–1153).

TIPPING

The usual tip for service, whether from a taxi driver or a waiter, is 15%. Some hotels and restaurants automatically add a 15% gratuity to your bill.

TOUR OPERATORS

Buying a prepackaged tour or independent vacation can make your trip to the Bahamas less expensive and more hassle-free. Because everything is prearranged, you'll spend less time planning.

Operators that handle several hundred thousand travelers per year can use their purchasing power to give you a good price. Their high volume may also indicate financial stability. But some small companies provide more personalized service; because they tend to specialize, they may also be more knowledgeable about a given area.

A GOOD DEAL?

The more your package or tour includes, the better you can predict the ultimate cost of your vacation. Make sure you know exactly what is covered, and **beware of hidden costs.** Are taxes, tips, and service charges included? Transfers and baggage handling? Entertainment and excursions? These can add up.

If the package or tour you are considering is priced lower than in your wildest dreams, **be skeptical.** Also, **make sure your travel agent knows the accommodations** and other services. Ask about the hotel's location, room size, beds, and whether it has a pool, room service, or programs for children, if you care about these. Has your agent been there in person or sent others you can contact?

BUYER BEWARE

Each year consumers are stranded or lose their money when tour operators—even very large ones with excellent reputations—go out of business. So **check out the operator.** Find out how long the company has been in business, and ask several agents about its reputation. **Don't book unless the firm has a consumer-protection program.**

Members of the National Tour Association and United States Tour Operators Association are required to set aside funds to cover your payments and travel arrangements in case the company defaults. Nonmembers may carry insurance instead. Look for the details, and for the name of an underwriter with a solid reputation, in the operator's brochure. Note: When it comes to tour operators, **don't trust escrow accounts.** Although there are laws governing charter-flight operators, no governmental body prevents tour operators from raiding the till. For more information, *see* Consumer Protection, *above.*

➤ Tour-Operator Recommendations: **National Tour Association** (✉ NTA, 546 E. Main St., Lexington, KY 40508, ☎ 606/226–4444 or 800/755–8687). **United States Tour Operators Association** (✉ USTOA, 342 Madison Ave., Suite 1522, New

York, NY 10173, ☎ 212/599–6599, FAX 212/599–6744).

USING AN AGENT

Travel agents are excellent resources. When shopping for an agent, however, you should **collect brochures from several sources**; some agents' suggestions may be skewed by promotional relationships with tour and package firms that reward them for volume sales. If you have a special interest, **find an agent with expertise in that area** (☞ Travel Agents, *below*). Don't rely solely on your agent, who may be unaware of small-niche operators. Note that some special-interest travel companies only sell directly to the public and that some large operators only accept bookings made through travel agents.

SINGLE TRAVELERS

Prices for packages and tours are usually quoted per person, based on two sharing a room. If traveling solo, you may be required to pay the full double-occupancy rate. Some operators eliminate this surcharge if you agree to be matched with a roommate of the same sex, even if one is not found by departure time.

PACKAGES

Like group tours, independent vacation packages are available from major tour operators and airlines. The companies listed below offer vacation packages in a broad price range.

➤ AIR/HOTEL: **American Airlines Fly AAway Vacations** (☎ 800/321–2121). **Certified Vacations** (✉ 110 E. Broward Blvd., Fort Lauderdale, FL 33302, ☎ 954/522–1440 or 800/233–7260). **Delta Dream Vacations** (☎ 800/872–7786). **US Airways Vacations** (☎ 800/455–0123).

THEME TRIPS

➤ FISHING: **Anglers Travel** (✉ 3100 Mill St., #206, Reno, NV 89502, ☎ FAX 702/853–9132). **Cutting Loose Expeditions** (✉ Box 447, Winter Park, FL 32790, ☎ 407/629–4700 or 800/533–4746). **Fishing International** (✉ Box 2132, Santa Rosa, CA 95405, ☎ 707/539–3366 or 800/950–4242, FAX 707/539–1320). **Rod & Reel Adventures** (✉ 3507 Tully Rd., Modesto, CA 95356, ☎ 209/524–7775 or 800/356–6982).

➤ GOLF: **Stine's Golftrips** (✉ Box 2314, Winter Haven, FL 33883-2314, ☎ 813/324–1300 or 800/428–1940, FAX 941/325–0384).

➤ LEARNING: **Earthwatch** (✉ Box 9104, 680 Mount Auburn St., Watertown, MA 02272, ☎ 617/926–8200 or 800/776–0188, FAX 617/926–8532) for research expeditions. **Natural Habitat Adventures** (✉ 2945 Center Green Ct., Boulder, CO 80301, ☎ 303/449–3711 or 800/543–8917, FAX 303/449–3712). **Oceanic Society Expeditions** (✉ Fort Mason Center, Bldg. E, San Francisco, CA 94123-1394, ☎ 415/441–1106 or 800/326–7491, FAX 415/474–3395).

➤ SCUBA DIVING: **Rothschild Dive Safaris** (✉ 900 West End Ave., #1B, New York, NY 10025-3525, ☎ 800/359–0747, FAX 212/749–6172).

➤ VILLA RENTALS: **Villas International** (✉ 605 Market St., San Francisco, CA 94105, ☎ 415/281–0910 or 800/221–2260, FAX 415/281–0919).

➤ YACHT CHARTERS: **Alden Yacht Charters** (✉ 1909 Alden Landing, Portsmouth, RI 02871, ☎ 401/683–1782 or 800/662–2628, FAX 401/683–3668). **Cat Ppalu Cruises** (✉ Box 661091, Miami, FL 33266, ☎ 305/888–1226 or 800/327–9600, FAX 305/884–4214). **Huntley Yacht Vacations** (✉ 210 Preston Rd., Wernersville, PA 19565, ☎ 610/678–2628 or 800/322–9224, FAX 610/670–1767). **Lynn Jachney Charters** (✉ Box 302, Marblehead, MA 01945, ☎ 617/639–0787 or 800/223–2050, FAX 617/639–0216). **The Moorings** (✉ 19345 U.S. Hwy. 19 N, 4th floor, Clearwater, FL 34624-3193, ☎ 813/530–5424 or 800/535–7289, FAX 813/530–9474). **Ocean Voyages** (✉ 1709 Bridgeway, Sausalito, CA 94965, ☎ 415/332–4681 or 800/299–4444, FAX 415/332–7460). **Russell Yacht Charters** (✉ 404 Hulls Hwy., #175, Southport, CT 06490, ☎ 203/255–2783 or 800/635–8895). **SailAway Yacht Charters** (✉ 15605 S.W. 92nd Ave., Miami, FL 33157-1972, ☎ 305/253–7245 or 800/724–5292, FAX 305/251–4408).

TRAVEL AGENCIES

A good travel agent puts your needs first. **Look for an agency that specializes in your destination, has been in** business at least five years, and **emphasizes customer service.** If you're looking for an agency-organized package or tour, your best bet is to choose an agency that's a member of the National Tour Association or the United States Tour Operator's Association (☞ Tour Operators, *above*).

➤ LOCAL AGENT REFERRALS: American Society of Travel Agents (✉ ASTA, 1101 King St., Suite 200, Alexandria, VA 22314, ☎ 703/739–2782, FAX 703/684–8319). **Alliance of Canadian Travel Associations** (✉ Suite 201, 1729 Bank St., Ottawa, Ontario K1V 7Z5, ☎ 613/521–0474, FAX 613/521–0805). **Association of British Travel Agents** (✉ 55–57 Newman St., London W1P 4AH, ☎ 0171/637–2444, FAX 0171/637–0713).

TRAVEL GEAR

Travel catalogs specialize in useful items, such as compact alarm clocks and travel irons, that can **save space when packing.** They also offer dual-voltage appliances, currency converters, and foreign-language phrase books.

➤ MAIL-ORDER CATALOGS: **Magellan's** (☎ 800/962–4943, FAX 805/568–5406). **Orvis Travel** (☎ 800/541–3541, FAX 540/343–7053). **TravelSmith** (☎ 800/950–1600, FAX 800/950–1656).

U

U.S. GOVERNMENT

The U.S. government can be an excellent source of inexpensive travel information. When planning your trip, **find out what government materials are available**.

➤ ADVISORIES: **U.S. Department of State American Citizens Services Office** (✉ Room 4811, Washington, DC 20520); enclose a self-addressed, stamped envelope. Interactive hot line (☎ 202/647–5225, FAX 202/647–3000). Computer bulletin board (☎ 202/647–9225).

➤ PAMPHLETS: **Consumer Information Center** (✉ Consumer Information Catalogue, Pueblo, CO 81009, ☎ 719/948–3334) for a free catalog that includes travel titles.

V

VISITOR INFORMATION

For general information contact these tourist offices before you go. The Bahamas Ministry of Tourism also has a web site on the Internet, featuring maps, photos, and interactive activities that enable you to communicate directly with the ministry. The address is http://www.interknowledge.com/bahamas.

➤ BAHAMAS: **Bahamas Tourist Office** (☎ 800/422–4262, ✉ 8600 W. Bryn Mawr Ave., Suite 820, Chicago, IL 60631, ☎ 773/693–1500, FAX 773/693–1114); (✉ Box 581408, 2050 Stemmons Fwy., Suite 116, World Trade Center, Dallas, TX 75258, ☎ 214/742–1886, FAX 214/741–4118); (✉ Bahama Out Islands Promotion Board, 1100 Lee Wagener Blvd., #204, Fort Lauderdale, FL 33315, ☎ 305/359–8099 or 800/688–4752, FAX 305/359–8098); (✉ 3450 Wilshire Blvd., Suite 208, Los Angeles, CA 90010, ☎ 213/385–0033, FAX 213/383–3966); (✉ 19495 Biscayne Blvd., Aventura, FL 33180, ☎ 305/932–0051, FAX 305/682–8758); (✉ 121 Bloor St. E, Suite 1101, Toronto M4W 3M5, ☎ 416/968–2999, FAX 416/968–6711); (✉ 3, The Billings, Walnut Tree Close, Guildford, Surrey, G1 4UL, U.K., ☎ 01483/448–900, FAX 01483/448–990).

Grand Bahama Tourism Board (✉ 19495 Biscayne Blvd., Suite 809, Aventura, FL 33180, ☎ 305/935–9461, FAX 305/935–9464). **Nassau/Paradise Island Promotion Board** (✉ 19495 Biscayne Blvd., Suite 804, Aventura, FL 33180, ☎ 305/931–1555, FAX 305/931–3005). **Bahamas Tourism Center** (✉ 150 E. 52nd St., New York, NY 10022, ☎ 212/758–2777, FAX 212/753–6531). **Caribbean Tourist Organization** (✉ 20 E. 46th St., New York, NY 10017, ☎ 212/682–0435, FAX 212/697–4258). **Morris-Kevan International Ltd.** (✉ International House, 47 Chase Side, Enfield, Middlesex EN2 6NB, ☎ 0181/364–5188, FAX 0181/367–9949).

W
WHEN TO GO

The Bahamas is affected by the refreshing trade-wind flow generated by an area of high atmospheric pressure covering a large part of the subtropical North Atlantic, so the climate varies little during the year. The most pleasant time is between December and May, when the temperature averages 70°–75°F. It stands to reason that hotel prices during this period are at their highest—around 30% higher than during the less popular times. The rest of the year is hot and humid and prone to tropical storms; the temperature hovers around 80°–85°F.

Remember that the sun is closer to earth the farther south you go. The sun in the Bahamas burns you more quickly than the sun in, say, Baltimore. Stock up on UVA/UVB suntan and sunblock products before you go. These range in SPF 2, for minimal protection, to 34, for complete blocking out. Wear sunglasses because eyes are particularly vulnerable to direct sun and reflected rays.

CLIMATE

What follows are average daily maximum and minimum temperatures for major cities in the Bahamas.

Climate in the Bahamas

NASSAU

Jan.	77F	25C	May	85F	29C	Sept.	88F	31C
	62	17		70	21		74	23
Feb.	78F	26C	June	87F	31C	Oct.	85F	29C
	63	17		73	23		72	22
Mar.	80F	27C	July	89F	32C	Nov.	82F	28C
	64	18		75	24		68	20
Apr.	82F	28C	Aug.	89F	32C	Dec.	79F	26C
	66	19		75	24		64	18

FREEPORT

Jan.	75F	24C	May	85F	29C	Sept.	89F	32C
	60	16		70	21		74	23
Feb.	75F	24C	June	88F	31C	Oct.	85F	29C
	60	16		74	23		71	22
Mar.	78F	26C	July	90F	32C	Nov.	81F	27C
	64	18		75	24		67	19
Apr.	81F	27C	Aug.	90F	32C	Dec.	77F	25C
	67	19		75	24		63	17

GREGORY TOWN

Jan.	77F	25C	May	84F	29C	Sept.	88F	31C
	66	19		72	22		77	25
Feb.	77F	25C	June	86F	30C	Oct.	85F	29C
	65	18		75	24		74	23
Mar.	79F	26C	July	87F	31C	Nov.	81F	27C
	67	19		77	25		71	22
Apr.	82F	28C	Aug.	88F	31C	Dec.	78F	26C
	69	21		77	25		67	20

➤ FORECASTS: **Weather Channel Connection** (☎ 900/932–8437), 95¢ per minute from a Touch-Tone phone.

1 Destination: The Bahamas

IN THE WAKE OF COLUMBUS:
A SHORT HISTORY OF THE BAHAMAS

YOU MIGHT CALL Christopher Columbus the first tourist to hit the Bahamas, although he was actually trying to find a route to the East Indies with his *Niña, Pinta,* and *Santa María.* Columbus is popularly believed to have made his first landfall in the New World on October 12, 1492, at San Salvador, in the southern part of the Bahamas. Researchers of the National Geographic Society, however, have come up with the theory that he may have first set foot ashore on Samana Cay, some 60 mi southeast of San Salvador. The Bahamians have taken this new theory under consideration, if not too seriously; tradition dies hard in the islands, and they are hardly likely to tear down the New World landfall monument on San Salvador.

The people who met Columbus on his landing day were Arawak Indians, said to have fled from the Caribbean to the Bahamas to escape the depredations of the murderous Caribs around the turn of the 9th century. The Arawaks were a shy, gentle breed who offered Columbus and his men their hospitality. He was impressed with their kindness and more than slightly intrigued by the gold ornaments they wore. But the voracious Spaniards who followed in Columbus's footsteps a few years later repaid the Indians' kindness by forcing them to work in the conquistadors' gold and silver mines in the New World; the Bahamas' indigenous peoples were virtually wiped out by 1520. Some Indian words, such as cassava (a vegetable) and guava (a fruit), have been assimilated, and the Spaniards' description of this part of the New World—Baja Mar (shallow sea)—somehow ended up as Bahama.

In 1513 the next Spanish-speaking seafarer stumbled on the Bahamas. Juan Ponce de León had been a passenger on Columbus's second voyage, in 1493. He conquered Puerto Rico in 1508 and then began searching thirstily for the Fountain of Youth. He thought he had found it on South Bimini, but he changed his mind and moved on to visit the site of St. Augustine, on the northeast coast of Florida.

In 1629 King Charles I claimed the Bahamas for England, though his edict was not implemented until the arrival of English pilgrims in 1648. Having fled the religious repression and political dissension then rocking their country, they settled on the Bahamian island they christened Eleuthera, the Greek word for freedom. Other English immigrants followed, and in 1656 another group of pilgrims, from Bermuda, took over a Bahamian island to the west and named it New Providence because of their links with Providence, Rhode Island. By the last part of the 17th century, some 1,100 settlers were trying to eke out a living, supplemented by the cargoes they salvaged from Spanish galleons that ran aground on the reefs. Many settlers were inclined to give nature a hand by enticing these ships onto the reefs with lights.

Inevitably, the British settlers were joined by a more nefarious subset of humanity, pirates and buccaneers like Edward Teach (better known as Blackbeard, he was said to have had 14 wives), Henry Morgan, and Calico Jack Rackham. Rackham numbered among his crew two violent, cutlass-wielding female members, Anne Bonney and Mary Read, who are said to have disconcerted enemies by swinging aboard their vessels topless. Bonney and Read were crafty women, indeed; after being captured, they escaped hanging in Jamaica by feigning pregnancy.

For some 40 years until 1718, pirates in the Bahamas constantly raided the Spanish galleons that carried booty home from the New World. During this period, the Spanish government, furious at the raids, sent ships and troops to destroy the New Providence city of Charles Town, which was later rebuilt and renamed Nassau, in 1695, in honor of King William III, formerly William of Orange-Nassau.

In 1718 King George I appointed Captain Woodes Rogers the first royal governor of the Bahamas, with orders to clean up the place. Why the king chose Rogers for this particular job is unclear—his thinking may well have been that it takes a pirate to know one, for Woodes Rogers had been a privateer. But he did take control of Nassau, hanging eight pirates from trees on the site of what was to become the British Colonial Hotel. Today, a statue of the former governor stands at the hotel entrance, and the street that runs along the waterfront is named after him. Rogers also inspired the saying *Expulsis piratis, restitua commercia* (Piracy expelled, commerce restored), which remained the country's motto until Prime Minister Lynden O. Pindling replaced it with the more appropriate and optimistic Forward, Upward, Onward Together, on the occasion of independence from Britain in 1973.

Although the Bahamas enjoyed a certain measure of tranquillity, thanks to Rogers and the governors who followed him, the British colonies in America at the same time were seething with a desire for independence. The peace of the islanders' lives was to be shattered during the Revolutionary War by a raid in 1778 on Nassau by the American navy, which purloined the city's arms and ammunition without even firing a shot. Next, in 1782, the Spanish came to occupy the Bahamas until the following year. Under the Treaty of Versailles of 1783, Spain took possession of Florida, and the Bahamas reverted to British rule.

THE BAHAMAS were once again overrun, between 1784 and 1789, this time by merchants from New England and plantation owners from Virginia and the Carolinas who had been loyal to the British and were fleeing the wrath of the American revolutionaries. Seeking asylum under the British flag, the Southerners brought their families and slaves with them. Many set up new plantations in the islands, but frustrated by the islands' arid soil, they soon opted for greener pastures in the Caribbean. The slaves they left behind were set free in 1834, but many retained the names of their former masters. That is why you'll find many a Johnson, Saunders, and Thompson in the towns and villages throughout the Bahamas.

The land may have been less than fertile, but New Providence Island's almost perfect climate, marred only by the potential for hurricanes during the fall, attracted other interest. Tourism was foreseen as far back as 1861, when the legislature approved the building of the first hotel, the Royal Vic-

toria. Though it was to reign as the grande dame of the island's hotels for more than a century, its early days saw it involved in an entirely different profit-making venture. During the U.S. Civil War, the Northern forces blockaded the main Southern ports, and the leaders of the Confederacy turned to Nassau, the closest neutral port to the south. The Royal Victoria became the headquarters of the blockade-running industry, which reaped huge profits for the British colonial government from the duties it imposed on arms supplies. (In October 1990, the Royal Victoria Hotel burned down.)

A similar bonanza, also at the expense of the United States, was to come in the 1920s, after Prohibition was signed into U.S. law in 1919. Booze brought into the Bahamas from Europe was funneled into a thirsty United States by rumrunners operating out of Nassau, Bimini, and West End, the community on Grand Bahama Island east of Palm Beach. Racing against, and often exchanging gunfire with, Coast Guard patrol boats, the rumrunners dropped off their supplies in Miami, the Florida Keys, and other Florida destinations, making their contribution to the era known as the Roaring '20s.

Even then, tourists were beginning to trickle into the Bahamas, many in opulent yachts belonging to the likes of Whitney, Vanderbilt, and Astor. In 1929 a new airline, Pan American, started to make daily flights from Miami to Nassau. The Royal Victoria, shedding its shady past, and two new hotels, the Colonial (now the British Colonial Beach Resort) and the Fort Montagu Beach, were all in full operation. Nassau even had instant communication with the outside world: A few miles northwest of the Colonial, a subterranean telegraph cable had been laid linking New Providence with Jupiter, Florida. It took no flash of inspiration to name the area Cable Beach.

One of the most colorful and enigmatic characters of the era came to Nassau in the 1930s. Sir Harry Oakes was a rough-and-ready Canadian who had made his fortune in a gold strike. During the '40s, he built the Bahamas Country Club and developed the Cable Beach Golf Course, a 6,500-yard, par-72 layout that is still in operation; it stands across the street from the Crystal Palace Resort & Casino and the other expensive hotel complexes on Cable Beach. Oakes also built Nassau's first airport in the late '30s to lure the well-heeled and to make commuting easier for the wealthy residents. Oakes Field can still be seen on the ride from Nassau International Airport to Cable Beach.

Oakes was to die in an atmosphere of eerie and mysterious intrigue. On July 8, 1943, his battered and badly charred body was found in his bed. Only his good friend, the late Sir Harold Christie, a real-estate tycoon and one of the most powerful of the Bay Street Boys (as the island's wealthy merchants were called), was in the house at the time. This was a period when all of the news that was fit to print was coming out of the war theaters in Europe and the Far East, but the Miami newspapers and wire services had a field day with the society murder.

Although a gruff, unlikable character, Oakes had no known enemies, but there was speculation that mob hit men from Miami had come over and taken care of him because of his unyielding opposition to the introduction of gambling casinos to the Bahamas. Finally, two detectives brought from Miami pinned the murder on Oakes's son-in-law, Count Alfred de Marigny, for whom the Canadian was known to have a strong dislike. De Marigny was tried and acquitted in an overcrowded Nassau court. Much of the detectives' research and testimony was later discredited. For many years afterward, however, the mysterious and still unsolved crime was a sore point with New Providence residents.

During World War II, New Providence also played host to a noble, if unlikely, couple. In 1936 the Duke of Windsor had forsaken the British throne in favor of "the woman I love," an American divorcée named Wallis Warfield Simpson, and the couple temporarily found a carefree life in Paris and the French Riviera. When the Nazis overran France, they fled to neutral Portugal. Secret papers revealed after the war suggest that the Germans had plans to use the duke and duchess, by kidnapping if necessary, as pawns in the German war against Britain. This would have taken the form of declaring them king and queen in exile, and seating them on the throne when Hitler's assumed victory was accomplished.

Word of the plot might have reached the ears of Britain's wartime prime minister, Winston Churchill, who encouraged King George VI, the duke's younger brother and his successor, to send the couple as far away as possible out of harm's way. In 1939 the duke had briefly returned to England, offering his services to his brother in the war effort. He was given a position of perhaps less import than he had expected, for he and Wallis suddenly found themselves in the Bahamas, with the duke as governor and commander in chief. The Bahamians were nevertheless impressed; a calypso ballad, "Love Alone," was composed in honor of the couple's fairy-tale romance.

CHANGES in the Bahamas' political climate had to wait for the war's end. For more than 300 years, the country had been ruled by whites; members of the United Bahamian Party (UBP) were known as the Bay Street Boys, after Nassau's main business thoroughfare, because they controlled the islands' commerce. But the voice of the overwhelmingly black majority was making itself heard. In 1953 a London-educated black barrister named Lynden O. Pindling joined the opposition Progressive Liberal Party (PLP); in 1956 he was elected to Parliament.

Pindling continued to stir the growing resentment most Bahamians now had for the Bay Street Boys, and his parliamentary behavior became more and more defiant. In 1965, during one parliamentary session, he picked up the speaker's mace and threw it out the window. Because this mace has to be present and in sight at all sessions, deliberations had to be suspended; meanwhile, Pindling continued his harangue to an enthusiastic throng in the street below. Two years later, Bahamian voters threw the UBP out, and Pindling led the PLP into power.

Pindling's magnetism kept him in power through independence from Britain in 1973 (though loyalty to the mother country led the Bahamians to choose to remain within the Commonwealth of Nations, recognize Queen Elizabeth II as their sovereign, and retain a governor-general appointed by the queen). For his services to his nation, the prime minister was knighted by the queen in 1983. His deputy prime minister Clement Maynard received the same accolade in 1989.

In August 1992 there came the biggest political upset since Pindling took power in 1967. His Progressive Liberal Party was defeated in a general election by the Free National Movement party, headed by lawyer Hubert Alexander Ingraham. The 45-year-old former chairman of the PLP and Cabinet member under Pindling had been expelled from the party by Pindling in 1986 because of his outspoken comments on alleged corruption inside the government. Ingraham's continued emphasis on this issue during the 1992 campaign did much to lead to Pindling's defeat and Ingraham's taking over as prime minister.

Today a visitor to the Bahamas can observe a nation with growing prosperity, a steadfast economy, and a stable government. Residents, for the most part, are proud of their country and are actively involved in bettering their own lot—the last complete census showed about 27% of the population was attending school at one level or another. And in the spirit of their national motto—Forward, Upward, Onward Together—they graciously welcome the ever-increasing numbers of outsiders who have discovered their little piece of paradise.

— Ian Glass

WHAT'S WHERE

The Bahamian Islands—with their exquisite white and pink sand beaches, lush tropical landscapes, unsullied waters, and year-round sunshine—couldn't have sprung from the sea in more perfect shape for 20th-century vacationers. The archipelago begins 55 mi off the Florida coast and contains more than 700 islands, approximately 20 of them inhabited, scattered over 100,000 sq mi of the Atlantic.

New Providence Island

Many travelers make New Providence Island—more specifically Nassau, the nation's capital and something of a tourist mecca—their principal stop in the Bahamas. Here you can doze in the sun, bargain at straw markets, dine at fine restaurants, and enjoy sophisticated casino nightlife at plush resorts. Discover the nation's past in the island's historic buildings, forts, gardens, and monuments. Two resort areas, Cable Beach and Paradise Island, are chockablock with luxurious resorts, groomed beaches, water sports aplenty, and a busy nightclub scene.

Grand Bahama Island

Grand Bahama's twin cities, Freeport and Lucaya, may not have the colonial charm of Nassau, but if you want to shop, gamble, or just hang out at the beach—at a slightly lower cost than in the capital—there's no need to go elsewhere. Freeport, which was built in the '60s, has its International Bazaar, where you'll find imported goods at reduced prices. Adjacent to Freeport is Lucaya, where you can swim with dolphins or learn to dive at a world-renowned scuba school. Resorts are split between the two: Freeport's have the best access to shopping, gambling, and golf; Lucaya's sit directly on the beach.

The Out Islands

To escape the crowds and the glittering modernity of New Providence and Grand Bahama, get yourself on a boat or plane to one of the Out Islands, where quiet cays afford a slower-paced, unspoiled way of life. Wander uncluttered beaches and narrow, sand-strewn streets, or lunch in a village where fishermen's neat homes are painted in soft pastel shades and shrouded in brilliantly colored vegetation. The Out Islands' common traits—an abundance of natural beauty and small-town atmosphere—should not disguise their differences, however. You may be surprised by the variety of sites and activities the islands have to offer.

The Abacos

The Abacos, a center for boatbuilding, have attracted sailing and yachting fans over the years because of their translucent waters and excellent marina facilities. If you come without a yacht, take a look at the island's famous striped lighthouse and strap on your fins to explore Pelican Cay, an underwater national park. Marsh Harbour, the third-largest city in the country, is well stocked with restaurants and shops, and resorts dot the Abacos' cays.

Andros

Andros is in fact the largest Bahamian island, and it is flanked by the world's third-largest coral reef—a spectacular, 140-mi-long haunt for underwater creatures, and divers, as a result. On land, the appeal is equally wild, with the little-explored island of forests and swamps having none of the buildup of the more touristed spots. Nonetheless, this is the place where Androsia fabric, a Bahamian version of batik, is made.

The Berry Islands

The tiny cays of the Berry Islands are virtually uninhabited but for seabirds and big-game fishers, who appreciate the proximity to the Tongue of the Ocean and the excellent marinas on Chub and Great Harbour cays.

The Biminis

Deep-sea anglers find bliss in Bimini, for in its waters roam great warriors such as marlin, swordfish, giant tuna, wahoo, sailfish, dolphin, and bonefish. Literary aficionados can follow in the footsteps of Papa himself: In the '30s, Ernest Hemingway chose the Biminis as his favorite getaway, and both his favorite bar and one of his homes are accessible to visitors.

Cat Island

Lush, hilly, off the normal tourist track, this is a tranquil isle of small farms and fishing villages. A few resorts, however, have sprung up to take advantage of a coast ringed with stunning—and usually deserted—beaches.

Crooked and Acklins Islands

Divers, snorkelers, and bonefishers find plenty to keep them busy on these adjoining, very undeveloped islands. Miles of virgin barrier reef seem, so far, to be a well-kept secret, far off the beaten path.

Eleuthera

Eleuthera, one of the best-known Out Islands, is notable for its beaches, surfing, and excellent diving. If you simply want to relax in a quiet seaside setting, opt for the charms of Harbour Island, off the north coast of Eleuthera, with its renowned 3-mi pink-sand beach, some of the Bahamas' most distinctive small hotels, and the New England–style village of Dunmore Town.

The Exumas

These hundreds of little cays are prime cruising ground for yachters, but you might also come to enjoy the charms of several attractive towns, friendly small hotels, Exuma Land and Sea Park (a favorite with snorkelers and bird-watchers), and a 7-mi beach fabled for its seashells.

Inagua

Bird-watchers marvel at the flock of more than 60,000 flamingos that resides in a national park on Inagua, the southernmost of the Bahamian islands. Hundreds of other bird species also make their home in the island's salt flats, which provide much of the raw material for the Morton Salt Company.

Long Island

Two contrasting coastlines make Long Island one of the most scenic Out Island destinations: While the western coast has soft, sandy beaches, the eastern side (never more than 4 mi away on this stretched, skinny strip) falls down to the ocean in the shape of dramatic rocky cliffs.

San Salvador

History may have been made on this little island, the legendary landfall of Christopher Columbus. Today you can visit the marker commemorating the event or dive, snorkel, or fish in the surrounding waters.

The Turks and Caicos Islands

The Turks and Caicos, two groups of islands that lie to the southeast of the Bahamas, are nearly unknown to all but avid divers and seekers of unspoiled beaches. While there's talk of developing the islands along the lines of the Bahamas, for now you'll find all of the beauty but none of the glitz.

NEW AND NOTEWORTHY

Both the Bahamian government and the private sector have been investing time and money to enhance the tourism infrastructure of the islands, and that has paid off. The 1996 year was the biggest ever for tourism in the Bahamas. Service standards have been raised through training programs for those who come in contact with visitors, including police and immigration officers, taxi drivers, tour operators, and hotel workers. On Bay Street, **Nassau**'s main thoroughfare, major landscaping projects are being completed, including new lighting, benches, and repairs to sidewalks and curbs. Shoppers can now hunt for bargains seven days a week, since legislation has been passed to allow stores to open on Sundays. A new Welcome Centre is planned for the dock, and the airport is receiving additional signage and landscaping improvements.

Sun International continues to restore, renovate, and expand its properties, the focal point of which is **Atlantis, Paradise Island,** the sprawling aquatic-theme reinvention of the old Paradise Island Resort & Casino. The Beach Tower wing has received a $3.2 million face-lift. Camp Paradise, an extensive supervised children's program, is now up and running at this family-oriented resort. The facilities and grounds of the 1930s-style **Ocean Club,** treasured for its elegance and sophistication, have been painstakingly restored to the tune of $7.5 million. With the acquisition of **Pirate's Cove Beach Resort** (formerly a Holiday Inn), Sun International now owns nearly 70% of Paradise Island's 826 acres.

Other Paradise Island hotels are also sprucing up and growing: **Club Med** has begun extensive multiphase renovations of its 320 rooms and facilities. **Comfort Suites** is adding 75 rooms (for a total of 225), a tennis court, and another swimming pool.

This large-scale investment in Paradise Island has invoked a new spirit and confidence in Bahamas tourism by other hoteliers. Many major accommodations have been or will soon be undergoing extensive renovations, and some smaller properties are making improvements as well. On Grand Bahama, the formerly government-owned Lucayan Bay Marina Hotel has been bought and transformed into **Pelican Bay,** with a 145-slip marina, a new 11-acre condominium complex, and a hotel in the works. The nearby **Lucayan Beach Resort & Casino** and **Flamingo Beach Resort** (the former Radisson Lucaya Beach Resort) were purchased by Swiss investors who also own and operate Clar-

ion Atlantik Beach Resort. Extensive plans are under way to upgrade these two properties. On Eleuthera, the all-inclusive **Club Eleuthera** at Rock Sound has completed a $7 million renovation and expansion.

Entrepreneur Chris Blackwell, owner of Island Records and several hotels in Miami's South Beach area, has scored big hits with two small Island Outpost properties. Featuring snazzy cabanas, huts, and cottages, these exceptional hotels resemble tropical villages. At delightfully colorful **Compass Point,** on New Providence's Love Beach, the Caribbean fusion cuisine has become so popular that the restaurant has been expanded. In addition, two of Blackwell's nearby private villas are now available for weekly rentals. On Eleuthera's Harbour Island, handsome **Pink Sands** will be gaining an additional cluster of upscale cottages. The success of these distinctive accommodations has prompted Blackwell to broaden his horizons further: Plans are in the works for another village-style hotel on a small island off the coast of New Providence.

Ground has been broken at **Sandals Royal Bahamian Resort & Spa** in Cable Beach for 220 more rooms and suites. **Radisson Cable Beach Resort** is undergoing a $15 million face-lift that will transform it into an all-inclusive playground. The owners of the **Nassau Marriott Resort & Crystal Palace Casino** have bought the elegant Cable Beach **Nassau Beach Hotel,** where guest rooms are slated for a complete renovation. At night, carnival lights still illuminate the **Nassau Marriott,** but this neighboring hotel has spent $30 million to refurbish the former Crystal Palace Resort & Casino. Gone is the garish purple paint, which has been replaced with a neutral sand color, and the public areas, which have been toned down as well, now have stylish Italian tiles, potted plants, and furniture in rich, muted colors.

Other new and improved attractions continue to lure vacationers back to Nassau. **Blue Lagoon Island,** loved for its gorgeous beaches and excellent snorkeling, has added Stingray City. Here in a 3-acre expanse filled with moray eels and schools of colorful fish, you can swim and get up close and personal with a group of friendly stingrays. A **canoeing** operation has opened on peaceful Lake Nancy, along John F. Kennedy Drive. You can paddle out to see a variety of birds, including cranes, ospreys, coots, egrets, and herons, and float along the romantic channel that spills into Lake Killarney, the largest lake on New Providence.

Getting to the Bahamas has become even more convenient and pleasurable. The new joint venture between **Carnival Airlines** and **Paradise Island Airlines** means more flights linking California, northeast cities, and southern Florida with the Bahamas. **Pan Am** has taken over Chalk's seaplane routes that connect southern Florida with Paradise Island, Bimini, and Walker's Cay (the Abacos). Cruise-lovers will be pleased to know that the **Disney Cruise Line** has acquired Gorda Cay, a tiny island in the Abacos that will be used as a playground for daylong stops of the *Disney Magic* and *Disney Wonder.*

FODOR'S CHOICE

Best Beaches

★ **Elbow Cay.** Hugging the Atlantic for about 3 semi-deserted mi, the stark white sand of the beach in Hope Town in the Abacos is a gorgeous sight.

★ **Great Guana Cay.** The 7-mi-long western coast of this cay in the Abacos is a deserted stretch of white sand bordered by palms.

★ **Great Harbour Cay.** Along the length of this 7½-mi strip, you may find your only company to be seabirds.

★ **Harbour Island.** Perhaps the most famous beach in the Bahamas, this 3-mi Eleutheran beach is covered in pink sand, colored by pulverized coral and shells.

★ **Long Island.** Extremely fine, bright white sand edges brilliantly blue water on Cape Santa Maria Beach, on the island's western shore.

★ **Stocking Island.** This delightful little cay off Great Exuma is known for its shelling.

Fun for Kids

★ **Glass-bottom boat trips.** At Prince George Wharf in Nassau, even children who don't swim can take a peek at the underwater world.

★ **Horseback riding.** Ride along Grand Bahama's coast on mounts from the Pinetree Stables in Freeport.

★ **Swimming with dolphins.** The Dolphin Experience in Lucaya, Grand Bahama, can put kids (even the adult variety) in close contact with the sensitive marine mammals.

★ **Waterscape attractions.** The "waterscape" at the Atlantis, Paradise Island resort boasts water slides, a man-made river ride, and a giant aquarium with a glass tunnel running beneath the shark tank.

Great Golf

★ **Cable Beach Golf Club.** This par-72, 7,040-yard course on Cable Beach, in New Providence, is the oldest and most highly regarded course in the Bahamas. It has ponds and small lakes among the back nine holes.

★ **Cotton Bay Club.** This par-72, 7,068-yard course at Rock Sound, Eleuthera, was designed by Robert Trent Jones, who placed two holes on narrow spits of land that effectively turn the Atlantic into a water trap.

★ **Emerald Golf Course.** One of two courses at the Bahama Princess Resort on Grand Bahama (the other is called the Ruby), the par-72, 6,679-yard Emerald was designed by Dick Wilson.

★ **Lucaya Golf and Country Club.** The other Dick Wilson course on Grand Bahama, this 6,824-yarder is the oldest on the island and requires more precision than power.

★ **Paradise Island Golf Club.** This stunning course on the far eastern tip of Paradise Island is surrounded on three sides by the ocean. Designed by Dick Wilson, it clocks in at 6,419 yards and par 72.

★ **Ramada South Ocean Golf Club.** The rolling hills of this 6,707-yard Joe Lee course, considered the best on New Providence Island, are unusual for the Bahamas.

Memorable Dining

★ **Buena Vista.** Fine Continental cuisine is served in one of Nassau's gracious colonial mansions. $$$$

★ **Graycliff.** The elegant ambience is as much a draw as the creative but pricey haute cuisine at this stately home in Nassau that once belonged to a pirate. $$$$

★ **Compass Point.** The blend of Bahamian, Caribbean, and Californian cuisine at this colorful Cable Beach–front hotel is as artfully presented as it is delicious. *$$$*

★ **Luciano's.** Enjoy Italian and French specialties at this attractive spot overlooking the water in Lucaya. *$$$*

★ **Monte Carlo.** Updated French classics, particularly seafood dishes, are the stars of the menu at this Lucayan institution. *$$$*

★ **Runaway Hill Club.** Local chefs whip up culinary masterpieces at this homelike inn on beautiful Harbour Island, off Eleuthera. *$$$*

★ **Coconut Cove Hotel.** The accent is on gourmet Italian, with a dash of Bahamian thrown in for spice, at this cozy beachside hotel just outside George Town, Exuma. *$$*

★ **Guanahani's.** An attractive setting—including a rock garden and waterfall—set the scene for some of Freeport's tastiest Bahamian specialties. *$$*

★ **Poop Deck.** Great Bahamian dishes and a casual, nautical atmosphere keep locals coming back to this Nassau haunt. *$$*

Hideaways in the Out Islands

★ **Cape Santa Maria Beach Resort.** Set on a stunning, 4-mi arc of white sand, this is just about as remote as luxury gets. *$$$$*

★ **Pink Sands.** Chris Blackwell's latest recreation of an old Harbour Island resort on one of the prettiest pink-sand beaches in the Bahamas is truly fabulous—and expensive. *$$$$*

★ **Hope Town Hideaways.** Wonderful Elbow Cay off Great Abaco is the setting for this friendly resort, with fully equipped villas offering total privacy, and several restaurants, stores, and gorgeous beaches a short boat ride away across the harbor. *$$$*

★ **Small Hope Bay Lodge.** This dive resort on Andros is a busy, popular place, but rustic private cottages—as well as the easygoing atmosphere on little-touristed Andros—let you get away from it all. *$$$*

★ **Club Peace and Plenty.** This friendly hotel on Great Exuma Island attracts boaters and anglers, as well as people just looking to relax on nearby Stocking Beach. *$$*

★ **Fernandez Bay Village.** Oceanfront villas with private gardens are situated on one of Cat Island's prettiest coastal stretches. *$$*

Top Resort Hotels

★ **Club Med Columbus Isle.** This deluxe all-inclusive resort sprawls along a luscious beach on the virtually undeveloped island of San Salvador, believed to be Columbus's first landfall in the New World. *$$$$*

★ **Bahamas Princess Resort & Casino.** Two golf courses, a giant casino, and proximity to the International Bazaar shopping arcade make the twin resorts on this property among the most popular in Freeport. *$$$*

★ **Club Fortuna Beach.** One all-inclusive prices covers all meals and activities at this rather secluded, European-owned resort east of Lucaya on Grand Bahama. *$$$*

★ **Lucayan Beach Resort & Casino.** This lush beachfront resort in Lucaya draws guests with its pristine beach, luxurious rooms, ocean views, and proximity to the Port Lucaya Marketplace and the UNEXSO dive school. *$$$*

★ **Nassau Beach Hotel.** This elegant but lively property on New Providence's Cable Beach has great sports' and children's programs. *$$$*

FESTIVALS AND SEASONAL EVENTS

WINTER

DECEMBER➤ The **Sun International Bahamas Open,** an event attracting some of the world's highest-ranked tennis players, is held December 4–10 at the Ocean Club on Paradise Island.

DECEMBER➤ **Christmas Day,** December 25, and **Boxing Day,** December 26, are both public holidays. Boxing Day coincides with the first of the Junkanoo parades.

DECEMBER➤ Green Turtle Cay, Abaco, hosts its annual **New Plymouth Historical Cultural Weekend,** with art exhibits, concerts, and international performing artists on the bill.

DECEMBER➤ **Other annual December doings** are the Beaux Arts Masked Ball and the Night of Christmas Music on Paradise Island and the Junior Junkanoo Parade and Renaissance Singers Concert in Nassau.

JANUARY➤ **Junkanoo** continues its uniquely Bahamian (Mardi Gras–style) festivities welcoming the New Year. More subdued celebrations take place in the Out Islands on January 1, a public holiday.

JANUARY➤ Pomp and pageantry take over when the **Supreme Court** opens in Nassau, a quarterly event.

JANUARY➤ The **New Year's Day Regatta** at Montagu Bay, Nassau, features competition among Bahamian-built sloops, as well as onshore entertainment.

JANUARY➤ The annual **New Year's Day Cruising Regatta** is celebrated at Staniel Cay in the Exumas.

JANUARY➤ The **Annual Mid-Winter Wahoo Tournament** draws anglers in great number to the waters of Bimini.

JANUARY➤ The Bahamas National Trust, the major agency of environmental preservation in the Bahamas, holds an annual **open house** that includes children's activities, garden tours, and a display of indigenous snakes and birds at The Retreat, on Village Road in Nassau.

SPRING

MARCH➤ The annual **Red Cross Fair** in the gardens of Nassau's Government House rounds off the winter social season.

MARCH➤ The annual George Town **Cruising Regatta on Exuma** is a popular sailing event attracting more than 500 visiting yachts for a week of fun and festivities. Cricket season kicks off in March and plays out in late November.

MARCH➤ The annual **International Dog Show & Obedience Trials** are held at the Nassau Botanical Gardens.

MARCH➤ The **Crystal Palace Celebrity Golf Classic** tees off at the Radisson Cable Beach Casino & Golf Resort, and the **Coca-Cola Golf Classic** is played at the South Ocean Golf & Beach Resort, New Providence Island.

MARCH➤ The **Bahamian Out Islands International Game Fish Tournament** is held at Stella Maris Inn on Long Island.

APRIL➤ **Easter,** Good Friday and the following Easter Monday are public holidays.

APRIL➤ George Town, Exuma, hosts the **Out Islands Regatta,** the most important yachting event of the year in the Bahamas.

APRIL➤ The **North Andros Easter Mini Regatta** is at Morgan's Bluff; Eleuthera hosts the **South Eleuthera Sailing Regatta.**

APRIL➤ For duffers, the **Pepsi Cola Open** is played at the Paradise Island Golf Club, Nassau.

APRIL➤ Competition is fierce during the **Annual Bimini Break Blue Marlin Tournament.**

MAY➤ This month brings **billfish tournaments** at Walker's and Treasure cays in the Abacos and at Cat Cay south of Bimini.

MAY➤ The **Long Island Regatta,** Salt Pond, Long Island, features sloop races, a yacht parade, and lots of activity both on and off the water.

MAY➤ The **Nocturne Classic** is played at the Paradise Island Golf & Country Club, and the **Bahamas Princess Grand Bahama Open Championships** take place on the

Princess Emerald & Ruby courses, Freeport.

MAY➤ Bimini, Abaco, Great Harbour Cay, and Treasure Cay all host major **fishing tournaments.**

MAY➤ The **South Caicos Regatta** is held at Cockburn Harbour, South Caicos.

JUNE➤ **Labour Day,** the first Friday of the month, and **Whit Monday** (June 8) are public holidays.

JUNE➤ Yes, more **deep-sea fishing tournaments**: the Bimini Big Five Tournament, the annual Green Turtle Club Fishing Tournament at Green Turtle Cay in the Abacos, and the Big Yard Bonefishing & Bottom Fishing Tournament in Andros.

JUNE➤ Golfers tee off at the **National Open Championships** at the Paradise Island Golf Course.

JUNE➤ Gregory Town is the scene of the **Eleuthera Pineapple Festival,** featuring a Junkanoo parade, crafts displays, tours of pineapple farms, and sports events.

JUNE➤ The four-month-long **Goombay Summer Festival** begins, with street dancing, fairs, beach parties, concerts, arts and crafts shows, and sporting activities.

JULY➤ The Bahamas' most important public holiday falls on July 10— **Independence Day,** which was established in 1973 and marks the end of 300 years of British rule.

Independence Week is celebrated throughout the Bahamas with regattas, boat races, fishing tournaments, and a plethora of parties.

AUGUST➤ **Emancipation Day,** which marks when the English freed Bahamian slaves in 1834, is a public holiday celebrated on the first Monday in August.

AUGUST➤ The annual 10-day **Fox Hill Festival** in Nassau pays tribute to Emancipation with an early morning Junkanoo Rushout (dancing in the streets), music, cookouts, games, and other festivities.

AUGUST➤ The **Cable Beach Amateur Golf Championship** is played at the Radisson Cable Beach Casino & Golf Resort, Nassau.

AUGUST➤ Three annual **regattas** take place, at Andros, Eleuthera, and Cat Island.

AUGUST➤ The Turks and Caicos islands hold their **carnival** during the last days of the month.

SEPTEMBER➤ The **Caribbean Golf Championships** are held at the Lucaya Golf & Country Club.

SEPTEMBER➤ Two legs of the small **B.O.A.T. Tournament,** a fishing contest in Bimini for boats of less than 27 ft, takes place this month.

OCTOBER➤ The first Wednesday marks the fourth and final opening of the year for the **Supreme Court** in Parliament Square.

OCTOBER➤ The **Annual McLean's Town Conch Cracking Contest,** which includes games and entertainment along with good eating, takes place on Grand Bahama Island on October 12.

OCTOBER➤ **Discovery Day,** commemorating the landing of Columbus in the islands in 1492, is observed on October 12, a public holiday.

OCTOBER➤ The **Bahamas Princess Open Tennis Championship** and the **Michelin National Long Driving Championship** for golfers are held at the Bahamas Princess Resort & Casino, Freeport.

OCTOBER➤ The **Shell Bahamas Open** is at the Radisson Cable Beach Casino & Golf Resort, Nassau, and the **Discovery Open** is played at the Paradise Island Golf Club, Nassau.

OCTOBER➤ The **North Andros Community Awareness and Discovery Regatta** is a weeklong event.

NOVEMBER➤ The **Bimini Big Game Fishing Club All Wahoo Tournament** is held in the Biminis.

NOVEMBER➤ The **Bahamas Shell Pro-Am Tournament** is played in Paradise Island, and both the annual **Lucaya International Amateur Golf Championships** and the **Annual Waterford Crystal Tournaments** run at the Lucaya Golf & Country Club, Freeport.

2 Pleasures and Pastimes

A Bahamian Feast

Cashing In: A Casino Gambling Primer

From Sand Shots to Surf-Casting: Other Island Activities

A Mariner's Guide to the Bahamas

Rubbing Shoulders with Bahamians

Scuba Diving in Paradise

WHETHER YOU SET YOUR SIGHTS on the upbeat pleasures of New Providence and Grand Bahama or on mellower Out Island pastimes, the Bahamas won't leave you wanting for activities. If rambunctious revelling is your idea of fun, don't miss the Junkanoo celebrations around the new year. Island music, costumed celebrants, and enough din to wake the dead are all part of this signature Bahamian event. Or take the carnival atmosphere indoors and hit the major islands' blackjack tables, shoot craps, watch the roulette wheel spin, and pull one-armed bandits.

When water and undersea life are as spectacular as they are around the Bahamas, you'd be well advised to spend some time on and under the sea. Astounding dive sites and superb instruction make scuba diving and snorkeling a never-ending series of discoveries. Up on deck, you can discover why Bahamian waters have lured sailors since long before Columbus's time. And of course fishing here is the stuff of legend. Bimini and its waters were among Papa Hemingway's haunts, and as you're trying to haul in that fight-of-a-lifetime marlin, don't be surprised to you find yourself wondering who's been hooked—you or the fish.

A BAHAMIAN FEAST

Restaurants on New Providence (Nassau, Paradise Island, and Cable Beach) and Grand Bahama (Freeport and Lucaya) offer much more variety than do those on the Out Islands. Food ranges from Bahamian home-style to Indian, Chinese, and upscale French and Italian. One night you might be munching conch (pronounced *conk*) fritters and grilled hog snapper at an out-of-the-way local spot, and the next you might be savoring a Grand Marnier soufflé in elegant surroundings. On the Out Islands, simpler cooking predominates, but sophisticated fare is gaining ground, particularly at resorts.

Meat is widely available, but much of it is imported and consequently expensive. Most Bahamian cuisine looks to the sea for produce. Perhaps because it's whispered to be an aphrodisiac, conch finds its way onto many a menu. (It is also valued for the shiny pink interior of its shell, which appears in pendants, bracelets, earrings, brooches, and other ornaments.) The meat turns up in a variety of incarnations, including cracked conch (pounded until tender and fried in seasoned batter), conch salad (raw, marinated in lime juice, with onions and peppers), and conch chowder. You might see fishermen on docks preparing scorched conch, which is eaten straight from the shell after being spiced with hot peppers—said to cure hangovers—salt, and lime.

Grouper is the headline fish, and you can feast on it and other fish from dawn to dusk if you so desire. For breakfast, you might try "boil fish," cooked with salt pork, onions, peppers, and spices, or "stew fish," in a rich brown gravy—both are usually served with grits or mildly sweet johnnycake. For lunch you might move on to steamed fish, cooked in a fragrant tomato base, then sample panfried grouper for dinner. Bahamian lobster, clawless and often called crawfish, is somewhat toothier than its cousins from Maine, but it is no less delicious. Order minced lobster, and the meat will come shredded and cooked with tomatoes, green peppers, and onions.

At lunch and dinner, your entrée will likely be flanked by a generous mound of peas 'n' rice or potato salad with coleslaw. Some local specialties are harder to find, such as turtle steak, wild boar, mutton, crab and rice, pumpkin or okra soup, chicken and dough (dumplings), and the morning eye-opener known as souse—pigs' feet, chicken necks and wing tips, sheep's tongue, or other bits of meat simmered with onions and potatoes in a spicy broth. Salads and other greens are scanty on most local menus. But, particularly at fruit stands, you can find sugarplums, hog plums, sapodillas, pineapples, sea grapes, mangoes, coco plums, soursops, avocados, tangerines, tamarinds, and papayas.

For many, beer is the thirst quencher of choice. Be sure to try locally brewed Kalik, a beer named for the sound of the cowbells played in indigenous Junkanoo music. When you're in the mood for a fruity, rum-based concoction, sip a Goombay Smash, a Bahama Mama, or a Yellowbird.

Bring your meal to a sweet close with guava duff, made by slathering guava jelly on a strip of dough, rolling and boiling it, then pouring white sauce onto warm slices. Bahamians also love benny cake, created by cooking sesame seeds with sugar, and coconut jimmy, chewy dumplings in coconut sauce.

For the most inexpensive local treats, stop in on one of the fund-raising cookouts or parties periodically hosted for different causes on beaches and in Nassau and Freeport churches. The staff at your hotel or local newspapers can provide details.

CASHING IN: A CASINO GAMBLING PRIMER

For a short-form handbook on the rules, the plays, the odds, and the strategies for the most popular casino games—or to decide on the kind of action that's for you and suits your style—read on. You must be 18 to gamble; Bahamians and permanent residents are not permitted to indulge.

There are four glitzy casinos in the Bahamas: two on New Providence Island—the Crystal Palace Casino at Cable Beach and the Paradise Island Casino on Paradise Island—and two on Grand Bahama—the Princess Casino in Freeport and the Lucayan Beach Casino in Lucaya. All have the additional attractions of above-average restaurants, lounges, and colorfully costumed revues. Although a couple of Out Island resorts have received casino licenses, there are no immediate plans to bring gambling to these low-key locales.

The Good Bets
The first part of any viable casino strategy is to risk the most money on wagers that present the lowest edge for the house. Blackjack, craps, video poker, and baccarat are the most advantageous to the bettor in this regard. The two types of bets at baccarat have a house advantage of a little more than 1%. The basic line bets at craps, if backed up with full odds, can be as low as ½%. Blackjack and video poker, at times, can not only put you even with the house (a true 50-50 proposition), but actually give you a slight long-term advantage.

How can a casino possibly provide you with a 50-50 or even a positive expectation at some of its games? First, because a vast number of suckers make the bad bets (those with a house advantage of 5%–35%, such as roulette, keno, and slots) day in and day out. Second, because the casino knows that very few people are aware of the opportunities to beat the odds. Third, because it takes skill—requiring study and practice—to be in a position to exploit these opportunities the casino presents. However, a mere hour or two spent learning strategies for the beatable games will put you light years ahead of the vast majority of visitors who give the gambling industry an average 12% to 15% profit margin.

Baccarat

The most "glamorous" game in the casino, baccarat (pronounced *bah-kuh-rah*) is a version of *chemin de fer,* popular in European gambling halls, and is a favorite with high rollers, because thousands of dollars are often staked on one hand. The Italian word *baccara* means "zero"; this refers to the point value of 10s and picture cards. The game is run by four pit personnel. Two dealers sit side by side in the middle of the table; they handle the winning and losing bets and keep track of each player's "commission" (explained below). The "caller" stands in the middle of the other side of the table and dictates the action. The ladderman supervises the game and acts as final judge if any disputes arise.

HOW TO PLAY

Baccarat is played with eight decks of cards dealt from a large "shoe" (or cardholder). Each player is offered a turn at handling the shoe and dealing the cards. Two two-card hands are dealt, the "player" and the "bank" hands. The player who deals the cards is called the banker, though the house, of course, banks both hands. The players bet on which hand, player or banker, will come closest to adding up to 9 (a "natural"). The cards are totaled as follows: ace through 9 retain face value, while 10s and picture cards are worth zero. If you have a hand adding up to more than 10, the number 10 is subtracted from the total. For example, if one hand contains a 10 and a 4, the hand adds up to 4. If the other holds an ace and 6, it adds up to 7. If a hand has a 7 and 9, it adds up to 6.

Depending on the two hands, the caller either declares a winner and loser (if either hand actually adds up to 8 or 9), or calls for another card for the player hand (if it totals 1, 2, 3, 4, 5, or 10). The bank hand then either stands pat or draws a card, determined by a complex series of rules depending on what the player's total is and dictated by the caller. When one or the other hand is declared a winner, the dealers go into action to pay off the winning wagers, collect the losing wagers, and add up the commission (usually 5%) that the house collects on the bank hand. Both bets have a house advantage of slightly more than 1%.

The player-dealer (or banker) continues to hold the shoe as long as the bank hand wins. As soon as the player hand wins, the shoe moves counterclockwise around the table. Players are not required to deal; they can refuse the shoe and pass it to the next player. Because the caller dictates the action, the player responsibilities are minimal. It's not necessary to know any of the card-drawing rules, even if you're the banker.

BACCARAT STRATEGY

Making a bet at baccarat is very simple. All you have to do is place your money in either the bank, player, or tie box on the layout, which appears directly in front of where you sit at the table. If you're betting that the bank hand will win, you put your chips in the bank box; bets for the player hand go in the player box. (Only real suckers bet on the tie.) Most players bet on the bank hand when they deal, since they "represent" the bank, and to do otherwise would seem as if they were betting "against" themselves. This isn't really true, but it seems that way. In the end, playing baccarat is a simple matter of guessing whether the player or banker hand will come closest to 9, and deciding how much to bet on the outcome.

Blackjack

Blackjack is the most popular table game in the casino. It's easy to learn and fun to play. It involves skill, and therefore presents varying levels of challenge, from beginner to postgraduate. Blackjack also boasts one of the lowest house advantages. Because blackjack is the only table game in the casino in which players can gain a long-term advantage over the house, it is the only game in the casino (other than, to a limited degree, video poker) that can be played professionally. And because blackjack can be played professionally, it is the most written-about and discussed casino game. Of course, training someone to play blackjack professionally is beyond the scope of this guide. Contact the Gambler's Book Club (☎ 702/382–7555) for a catalog of gambling books, software, and videotape, including the largest selection on blackjack around.

HOW TO PLAY

Basically, here's how it works: You play blackjack against a dealer, and whichever of you comes closest to a card total of 21 is the winner. Number cards are worth their face value, picture cards are worth 10, and aces are worth either 1 or 11. (Hands with aces in them are known as "soft" hands. Always count the ace first as an 11; if you also have a 10, your total will be 21, not 11.) If the dealer has a 17 and you have a 16, you lose. If you have an 18 against a dealer's 17, you win (even money). If both you and the dealer have a 17, it's a tie (or "push") and no money changes hands. If you go over a total of 21 (or "bust"), you lose immediately, even if the dealer also busts later in the hand. If your first two cards add up to 21 (a "natural"), you're paid 3 to 2. However, if the dealer also has a natural, it's a push. A natural beats a total of 21 achieved with more than two cards.

You're dealt two cards, either face down or face up, depending on the custom of the particular casino. The dealer also gives herself two cards, one face down and one face up (except in double-exposure blackjack, where both the dealer's cards are visible). Depending on your first two cards and the dealer's up card, you can **stand,** or refuse to take another card. You can **hit,** or take as many cards as you need until you stand or bust. You can **double down,** or double your bet and take one card. You can **split** a like pair; if you're dealt two 8s, for example, you can double your bet and play the 8s as if they're two hands. You can **buy insurance** if the dealer is showing an ace. Here you're wagering half your initial bet that the dealer *does* have a natural; if so, you lose your initial bet, but are paid 2 to 1 on the insurance (which means the whole thing is a push). You can **surrender** half your initial bet if you're holding a bad hand (known as a "stiff") such as a 15 or 16 against a high-up card like a 9 or 10.

BLACKJACK STRATEGY

Playing blackjack is not only knowing the rules—it's also knowing *how* to play. Many people devote a great deal of time to learning complicated statistical schemes. However, if you don't have the time, energy, or inclination to get that seriously involved, the following basic strategies, which cover more than half the situations you'll face, should allow you to play the game with a modicum of skill and a paucity of humiliation:

- When your hand is a stiff (a total of 12, 13, 14, 15, or 16) and the dealer shows a 2, 3, 4, 5, or 6, always stand.

- When your hand is a stiff and the dealer shows a 7, 8, 9, 10, or ace, always hit.

- When you hold 17, 18, 19, or 20, always stand.

- When you hold a 10 or 11 and the dealer shows a 2, 3, 4, 5, 6, 7, 8, or 9, always double down.

- When you hold a pair of aces or a pair of 8s, always split.

- Never buy insurance.

Craps

Craps is a dice game played at a large rectangular table with rounded corners. Up to 12 players can crowd around the table, all standing. The layout is mounted at the bottom of a surrounding "rail," which prevents the dice from being thrown off the table and provides an opposite wall against which to bounce the dice. It can require up to four pit personnel to run an action-packed, fast-paced game of craps. Two dealers handle the bets made on either side of the layout. A "stickman" wields the long wooden "stick," curved at one end, which is used to move the dice around the table; the stickman also calls the number that's rolled and books the proposition bets made in the middle of the layout. The "boxman" sits between the two dealers and oversees the game; he settles any disputes about rules, payoffs, mistakes, and so on.

HOW TO PLAY

To play, just stand at the table wherever you can find an open space. You can start betting casino chips immediately, but you have to wait your turn to be the shooter. The dice move around the table in a clockwise fashion: The person to your right shoots before you, the one to the left after (the stickman will give you the dice at the appropriate time). It's important, when you're the "shooter," to roll the dice hard enough so they bounce off the end wall of the table; this ensures a random bounce and shows that you're not trying to control the dice with a "soft roll."

CRAPS STRATEGY

Playing craps is fairly straightforward; it's the betting that's complicated. The basic concepts are as follows: If, the first time the shooter rolls the dice, he or she turns up a 7 or 11, that's called a "natural"—an automatic win. If a 2, 3, or 12 comes up on the first throw (called the "come-out roll"), that's termed "craps"—an automatic lose. Each of the numbers 4, 5, 6, 8, 9, or 10 on a first roll is known as a "point": The shooter keeps rolling the dice until the point comes up again. If a 7 turns up before the point does, that's another loser. When either the point or a losing 7 is rolled, this is known as a "decision," which happens on average every 3.3 rolls.

But "winning" and "losing" rolls of the dice are entirely relative in this game, because there are two ways you can bet at craps: "for" the shooter or "against" the shooter. Betting for means that the shooter will "make his point" (win). Betting against means that the shooter will "seven out" (lose). (Either way, you're actually betting against the house, which books all wagers.) If you're betting "for" on the come-out, you'd place your chips on the layout's "pass line." If a 7 or 11 is rolled, you win even money. If a 2, 3, or 12 (craps) is rolled, you lose your bet. If you're betting "against" on the come-out, you place your chips in the "don't pass bar." A 7 or 11 loses, a 2, 3, or 12 wins. A shooter can bet for or against himself or herself, as well as for or against the other players.

There are also roughly two dozen wagers you can make on any single specific roll of the dice. Craps strategy books can give you the details on Come/Don't Come, Odds, Place, Buy, Big Six, Field, and Proposition bets.

Roulette

Roulette is a casino game that utilizes a perfectly balanced wheel with 38 numbers (0, 00, and 1 through 36), a small white ball, a large layout with 11 different betting options, and special "wheel chips." The layout organizes 11 different bets into six "inside bets" (the single numbers, or those closest to the dealer) and five "outside bets" (the grouped bets, or those closest to the players).

The dealer spins the wheel clockwise and the ball counterclockwise. When the ball slows, the dealer announces, "No more bets." The ball drops from the "back track" to the "bottom track," caroming off built-in brass barriers and bouncing in and out of the different cups in the wheel before settling into the cup of the winning number. Then the dealer places a marker on the number and scoops all the losing chips into her corner. Depending on how crowded the game is, the casino can count on roughly 50 spins of the wheel per hour.

HOW TO PLAY

To buy in, place your cash on the layout near the wheel. Inform the dealer of the denomination of the individual unit you intend to play (usually 25¢ or $1, but it can go up as high as $500). Know the table limits (displayed on a sign in the dealer area)—don't ask for a 25¢ denomination if the minimum is $1. The dealer gives you a stack of wheel chips of a different color from those of all the other players, and places a chip marker atop one of your wheel chips on the rim of the wheel to identify its denomination. Note that you must cash in your wheel chips at the roulette table before you leave the game. Only the dealer can verify how much they're worth.

ROULETTE STRATEGY

With **inside bets,** you can lay any number of chips (depending on the table limits) on a single number, 1 through 36 or 0 or 00. If the number hits, your payoff is 35 to 1, for a return of $36. You could, conceivably, place a $1 chip on all 38 numbers, but the return of $36 would leave you $2 short, which divides out to 5.26%, the house advantage. If you place a chip on the line between two numbers and one of those numbers hits, you're paid 17 to 1 for a return of $18 (again, $2 short of the true odds). Betting on three numbers returns 11 to 1, four numbers returns 8 to 1, five numbers pays 6 to 1 (this is the worst bet at roulette, with a 7.89% disadvantage), and six numbers pays 5 to 1.

To place an **outside bet,** lay a chip on one of three "columns" at the lower end of the layout next to numbers 34, 35, and 36; this pays 2 to 1. A bet placed in the first 12, second 12, or third 12 boxes also pays 2 to 1. A bet on red or black, odd or even, and 1 through 18 or 19 through 36 pays off at even money, 1 to 1. If you think you can bet on red *and* black, or odd *and* even, in order to play roulette and drink for free all night, think again. The green 0 or 00, which fall outside these two basic categories, will come up on average once every 19 spins of the wheel.

Slot Machines

Around the turn of the century, Charlie Fey built the first mechanical slot in his San Francisco basement. Slot-machine technology has exploded in the past 20 years, and now there are hundreds of different models, which accept everything from pennies to specially minted $500 tokens. The major advance in the game, however, is the progressive jackpot. Banks of slots within a particular casino are connected by computer, and the jackpot total is displayed on a digital meter above the machines. Generally, the total increases by 5% of the wager. If you're playing a dollar machine, each time you pull the handle (or press the spin button), a nickel is added to the jackpot.

HOW TO PLAY

To play, insert your penny, nickel, quarter, silver dollar, or dollar token into the slot at the far right edge of the machine. Pull the handle or press the spin button, then wait for the reels to spin and stop one by one, and for the machine to determine whether you're a winner (occasionally) or a loser (the rest of the time). It's pretty simple—but because there are so many different types of machines nowadays, be sure you know exactly how the one you're playing operates.

SLOT-MACHINE STRATEGY

The house advantage on slots varies widely from machine to machine, between 3% and 25%. Casinos that advertise a 97% payback are telling you that at least one of their slot machines has a house advantage of 3%. Which one? There's really no way of knowing. Generally, $1 machines pay back at a higher percentage than quarter or nickel machines. On the other hand, machines with smaller jackpots pay back more money more frequently, meaning that you'll be playing with more of your winnings.

One of the all-time great myths about slot machines is that they're "due" for a jackpot. Slots, like roulette, craps, keno, and Big Six, are subject to the Law of Independent Trials, which means the odds are permanently and unalterably fixed. If the odds of lining up three sevens on a 25¢ slot machine have been set by the casino at 1 in 10,000, then those odds remain 1 in 10,000 whether the three 7s have been hit three times in a row or not hit for 90,000 plays. Don't waste a lot of time playing a machine that you suspect is "ready," and don't think if someone hits a jackpot on a particular machine only minutes after you've finished playing on it that it was "yours."

Video Poker

Like blackjack, video poker is a game of strategy and skill, and at select times on select machines, the player actually holds the advantage, however slight, over the house. Unlike slot machines, you can determine the exact edge of video poker machines. Like slots, however, video poker machines are often tied into a progressive meter; when the jackpot total reaches high enough, you can beat the casino at its own game. The variety of video poker machines is already large, and it's growing steadily larger. All of the different machines are played in similar fashion, but the strategies are different. This section deals only with straight-draw video poker.

HOW TO PLAY

The schedule for the payback on winning hands is posted on the machine, usually above the screen. It lists the returns for a high pair (generally jacks or better), two pair, three of a kind, a flush, full house, straight flush, four of a kind, and royal flush, depending on the number of coins played—usually 1, 2, 3, 4, or 5. Look for machines that pay with a single coin played: one coin for "jacks or better" (meaning a pair of jacks, queens, kings, or aces; any other pair is a stiff), two coins for two pairs, three for three of a kind, six for a flush, nine for a full house, 50 for a straight flush, 100 for four of a kind, and 250 for a royal flush. This is known as a 9/6 machine—one that gives a nine-coin payback for the full house and a six-coin payback for the flush with one coin played. Other machines are known as 8/5 (8 for the full house, 5 for the flush), 7/5, and 6/5.

You want a 9/6 machine because it gives you the best odds: The return from a standard 9/6 straight-draw machine is 99.5%; you give up only half a percent to the house. An 8/5 machine returns 97.3%. On 6/5 machines, the figure drops to 95.1%, slightly less than roulette. Machines with varying paybacks are scattered throughout the casinos. In some you'll see an 8/5 machine right next to a 9/6, and someone will be blithely playing the 8/5 machine!

As with slot machines, it's always optimum to play the maximum number of coins to qualify for the jackpot. You insert five coins into the slot and press the "deal" button. Five cards appear on the screen—say, 5, J, Q, 5, 9. To hold the pair of 5s, you press the hold buttons under the first and fourth cards. The word "hold" appears underneath the two 5s. You then press the "draw" button (often the same button as "deal") and three new cards appear on the screen—say, 10, J, 5. You have three 5s; with five coins bet, the machine will give you 15 credits. Now you can press the "max bet" button: five units will be removed from your number of credits, and five new cards will appear on the screen. You repeat the hold and draw process; if you hit a winning hand, the proper payback will be added to your credits. Those who want coins rather than credit can hit the "cash out" button at any time. Some machines don't have credit counters and automatically dispense coins for a winning hand.

VIDEO-POKER STRATEGY

Like blackjack, video poker has a basic strategy that's been formulated by the computer simulation of hundreds of millions of hands. The most effective way to learn it is with a video poker computer program that deals the cards on your screen, then tutors you in how to play each hand properly. If you don't want to devote that much time to the study of video poker, memorizing these six rules will help you make the right decision for more than half the hands you'll be dealt:

- If you're dealt a completely "stiff" hand (no like cards and no picture cards), draw five new cards.

- If you're dealt a hand with no like cards but with one jack, queen, king, or ace, always hold on to the picture card; if you're dealt two different picture cards, hold both. But if you're dealt three different picture cards, only hold two (the two of the same suit, if that's an option).

- If you're dealt a pair, always hold it, no matter what the face value.

- Never hold a picture card with a pair of 2s through 10s.

- Never draw two cards to try for a straight or a flush.

- Never draw one card to try for an inside straight.

FROM SAND SHOTS TO SURF-CASTING: OTHER ISLAND ACTIVITIES

In addition to fishing, golf and tennis are major pursuits, and courses, courts, and tournaments abound.

Beaches

Sun, sea, and sand bring most people to the Bahamas. In Nassau, the major Cable Beach and Paradise Island hotels have their own stretches of beach, while hotels on the outskirts are always near public beaches, such as Love Beach and Saunders Beach on the north shore, and Adelaide Beach on the south. On Grand Bahama, only the Lucaya hotels have their own private beaches. If you're staying in Freeport you'll have access to public spots like Xanadu Beach, Taino Beach, and the long strip at Williams Town, all local favorites. The Out Islands are similarly brimming with beautiful beaches. One of the most intriguing is the pink-sand beach at Harbour Island, off Eleuthera.

The calm, leeward, western sides of most islands have the safest and most popular swimming beaches. There are no big waves, little undertow, and the buoyant salt water makes staying afloat almost effortless. The windward, or Atlantic, sides of islands are a different story, and even strong, experienced swimmers should exercise caution here. For novices, ocean waves are powerful and can be dangerous, and unseen currents, strong undertows, and uneven, rocky bottoms are only more perilous. Some beaches post signs or flags to alert swimmers to water conditions, but few—even those at the best hotels—are protected by lifeguards. Swim at your own risk.

Fishing

This country is an angler's dream. Light tackle, heavy tackle, fly-fishing, deep-sea fishing, reef fishing, flats fishing, fishing for blue marlin, bonefish—you name it. Fishing in the Bahamas starts in the waters of Bimini off the Florida coast and ends at the southernmost island, Inagua, on the northern edge of the Caribbean. Tournaments pop up all over the Out Islands during the year—Bimini alone has a dozen. Many Out Island hotels offer money-saving fishing packages.

Golf

Golfers will find some enticing courses, most of them with refreshing sea views. The 18-hole, par-72, championship courses on New Providence and Paradise islands are all spectacularly beautiful and will put your swing to the test. Cable Beach Golf Course is on West Bay Street in Nassau, across the boulevard from the Radisson Cable Beach Resort. The course at South Ocean Beach and Golf Resort, an elegant spot on the island's south coast, is secluded and scenic. A third course, Paradise Island Golf Course & Club, covers most of the east end of Paradise Island. All three courses are open to the public, and instruction is available. A fourth course, at the Lyford Cay Golf Club, is only available to members and their guests. There are also four courses on Grand Bahama. Paradise Island and Freeport host tournaments annually. PGA championship golf returned to the Bahamas in November 1995, with the initiation of the annual Paradise Island Invitational Pro-Am Tournament.

Although your choices for teeing off on the Out Islands are more limited, you'll still find some appealing courses: one in Treasure Cay, Great Abaco; another at the Cotton Bay Club in Rock Sound, Eleuthera (the once-upscale hotel is closed, but the golf course is now open to the public); and a nine-holer on Great Harbour Cay, Berry Islands.

Tennis

New Providence has more than 80 courts, Grand Bahama has about 40, and many of the Out Islands, including Eleuthera, Exuma, and the Abacos, are also in on the racket. Each year, Paradise Island sponsors the **Bahamas International Tennis Open,** and the **Freeport Tennis Open** is held on Grand Bahama.

A MARINER'S GUIDE TO THE BAHAMAS

Seafarers who navigate around the Bahamian islands can retrace the historical routes of Christopher Columbus, Juan Ponce de León, Blackbeard the Pirate, and rumrunners from the United States during the

Prohibition years. The Bahamas is only 55 mi from Florida across the Gulf Stream. Many first-time visitors are deeply impressed by the striking color and clarity of its waters. Veteran yachtsmen gauge the depth of the water by its color. The deep blues of the Gulf Stream fade into lighter blues and brilliant turquoises as boaters come closer to the Bahamian shores.

Crossing the Gulf Stream

The Gulf Stream crossing from Florida to the Bahamas, either on your own boat or a chartered one, is a delight. Most of south Florida's major marinas offer private charters to the Bahamas (usually yachts, from 35 to 60 ft); these boats generally carry from four to six people and may run from $100 to $150 per person per day. Knowing your boat and its capabilities is necessary.

The average northward drift of the Gulf Stream is 2½ knots, which means that if you're heading from Miami or Fort Lauderdale to Bimini, you would set your course a little south of where you want to land. If you figure that your crossing will take three hours, you would set your course for a point about 7½ nautical miles south of Bimini. If you estimate it will take four hours, head for a spot 10 nautical miles south. The Gulf Stream commands and deserves respect. The combination of the northerly flow with a wind out of the northern quadrant can whip up the waters to an extremely uncomfortable pitch. So pick a calm day for your first crossing.

If you're making the crossing with slow-moving, trawler-type craft, begin at midnight or in late evening. This will bring you into Bahamian waters at daybreak, when navigating through the shallower waters is easier. Most yachters try to avoid arriving at dusk, because darkness falls swiftly in the Bahamas. Keep in mind that crossing at night should also be approached with care and a keen eye for slow-moving tankers and tugs with long invisible cables that tow barges, sometimes as far as a mile behind.

If you are reluctant to make that first crossing alone, consider the Bahama Boating Flings. This series of group crossings from south Florida to Bimini or Freeport is sponsored and organized by the Bahamas Ministry of Tourism, the Bahamas Sports and Aviation Center, and the Marine Industries Association of South Florida. One "Fling" usually runs from the Palm Beach area to Freeport. These gatherings of up to 30 boats at least 22 ft in length rendezvous at a Fort Lauderdale marina and cross as a group with an experienced leader. Outings last three or four days, although many skippers stay on after the initial crossing, cruise a little on their own, and catch a later group crossing for the return to Florida. For more information or applications, contact **Bahamas Sports and Aviation Center** (✉ 1 Turnberry Pl., 19495 Biscayne Blvd., Suite 809, Aventura, FL 33180-2321, ☎ 305/932–0051 or 800/327–7678).

Ports of Entry

When entering Bahamian waters, you must clear customs and immigration at the first designated port of call. Fly a yellow quarantine flag to indicate plans to check in. The captain must fill out Maritime Declaration of Health and Inward reports, listing all crew members and passengers, who must have proof of citizenship. Birth certificates, passports, and voter registration cards constitute proof—driver's licenses do not. A cruising permit will be issued for the boat, good for up to six months. It must be shown when requested by government officials; requests can be frequent, particularly if drug smuggling is suspected.

Only the boat's captain can go ashore until the boat and passengers have cleared customs and immigration.

The following are Bahamian ports of entry: **The Abacos:** Grand Cay, Green Turtle Cay, Marsh Harbour, Sandy Point, Spanish Cay, Treasure Cay, and Walker's Cay. **Andros:** Andros Town, Congo Town, Fresh Creek, Nicholl's Town, and San Andros. **The Berry Islands:** Chub Cay and Great Harbour Cay. **The Bimini Islands:** Alice Town, Big Game Fishing Club, and Government Dock, South Bimini. **Eleuthera:** Governor's Harbour, Hatchet Bay, Harbour Island, and Rock Sound. **The Exumas:** George Town. **Grand Bahama Island:** Freeport, Lucaya, Xanadu Marina, and West End. **Inagua:** Matthew Town. **Long Island:** Stella Maris. **New Providence Island:** All marinas. **Ragged Island:** Duncan Town. **San Salvador:** Cockburn Town.

Island-Hopping

The Bahamian islands fringe the edges of two major, and several smaller, sand banks. The Little Bahama Bank is bordered on the south by Grand Bahama Island, and on the east and north by the Abaco chain. The Great Bahama Bank is a vast area of shallow water split by a deep trench called the Tongue of the Ocean. Along the western side of the Tongue lies Andros, the largest of the Bahamian islands, and a spectacular barrier reef, the third longest in the world.

Across the Great Bahama Bank to the northwest is Bimini, usually the first landfall for boaters coming from Florida. At the top of the Great Bahama Bank is Great Isaac Island. Farther to the east is Great Stirrup Cay, the northern end of the Berry Islands chain. Most cruise ships use the beacons of Great Isaac and Great Stirrup to guide them to Nassau on the island of New Providence. Smaller boats generally cross the bank from Cat Cay or Gun Cay south of Bimini to Chub Cay, at the foot of the Berry Islands, before crossing the Tongue of the Ocean to Nassau.

Northeast of Nassau is Eleuthera, with Spanish Wells and Harbour Island off its north coast. East of Nassau, the long Exuma chain stretches along the western edge of Exuma Sound, another large and deep body of water within the Great Bahama Bank. Cat Island separates the sound from the Atlantic Ocean to the east. Long Island marks Exuma Sound's lower end and stretches southeast to the Crooked Island Passage. Crooked Island and Acklins Island form their own little bank, as does Mayaguana to the east. To the south, Great and Little Inagua represent the last Bahamian port of call for boats heading down to the Caribbean.

Three small islands—Rum Cay, Conception Island, and San Salvador—lie out in the Atlantic, east of the northern tip of Long Island. Possibly the most obscure island in the country is Cay Lobos, a speck just 20 mi off the northern coast of Cuba. The Cay Sal Bank, which includes the Damas Cays and Anguilla Cays, lies in the middle of the Florida Straits and is also considered part of the Bahamas archipelago.

You'll find the most extensive boating facilities on New Providence and Grand Bahama. However, serious sailors tend to head to the empty sandy shores and drowsy settlements of the Out Islands, which are stunning in their pristine beauty.

THE ABACOS

The Abacos, a chain of islands in the northeastern Bahamas, offer superb cruising grounds. Marinas and services for yachtsmen range from rugged and rustic to high-tech facilities, with more of the latter than the former. Walker's Cay at the top of the Abacos is about 55 mi northeast of West End at the tip of Grand Bahama Island, and it's also a 55-mi crossing from Palm Beach. Many cruising yachtsmen coming from the north opt for the 110-mi route from the Fort Pierce–Vero Beach area to Walker's Cay.

Walker's Cay and its neighbor, Grand Cay, the late president Richard M. Nixon's hideaway, represent the contrasts in facilities available for yachtsmen. Walker's Cay has a high-class, 75-slip, full-service marina, a 2,500-ft paved airstrip, and extravagant hotel comforts. Grand Cay, on the other hand, is a ramshackle settlement of about 200 people and four times that many dogs of mixed breed, called Bahamian potcakes. These potcakes wander and sleep on the cracked, meandering sidewalks of the community by day and howl by night. Yachtsmen will find both the people and the dogs friendly and the anchorage off the community dock adequate. Double anchors are advised to handle the harbor's tidal current.

Heading south from Walker's Cay and Grand Cay, you will pass (and maybe want to stop and explore by dinghy) a clutch of tiny cays and islets, such as Double Breasted Cays, Roder Rocks, Barracuda Rocks, Miss Romer Cay, Little Sale Cay, and Great Sale Cay. Great Sale Harbour provides excellent shelter. Snorkeling in the shallows along the mangroves of these cays can be a rewarding experience—you may encounter graceful manta rays and eagle rays, basking sand sharks, and perhaps a school of small barracuda on the prowl. In the same area, you'll find other small islands, including Carter Cay, Moraine Cay, Umbrella Cay, Guineaman Cay, Pensacola and Allan's cays (which are now virtually one island since a hurricane filled in the gap between them) and the Hawksbill Cays. Most offer varying degrees of lee anchorage. Fox Town, due south of Hawksbill Cay on the western tip of Little Abaco, is the first refueling stop for powerboats traveling east from West End.

A narrow causeway joins Little Abaco to Great Abaco, where the largest community at the north end is Cooper's Town. Visitors here can stock up on supplies of groceries, hardware, marine parts, liquor, and beer. The settlement also has a coin laundry, a telephone station, a few small restaurants, bakeries, and a resident doctor. Green Turtle Cay has excellent yachting facilities at White Sound to the north and Black Sound to the south. The Green Turtle Club dominates the northern end of White Sound, while Bluff House, halfway up the sound, has docks on the inside and a dinghy dock below the club on the bank side.

Green Turtle Cay's New Plymouth will remind you of Cape Cod, with its pastel clapboard cottages flanking the narrow lanes. The New England–style ambience comes honestly, for many of the 400 or so residents are direct descendants of original 18th-century Loyalist settlers. The town also offers some little bars and restaurants, well-stocked stores, and a wide range of services, including a post office and a medical clinic.

South of New Plymouth on Great Abaco's mainland stands the Treasure Cay Hotel Resort and Marina, a sophisticated but relaxed international resort with a marina and one of the finest and longest beaches in the area. Another New England–style charmer lies a little to the south: Man-O-War Cay, a boatbuilding settlement of Loyalist descent. This island, with the 60-slip Man-O-War Marina, is devoid of cars, beer, liquor, and women in skimpy bikinis. It is well worth a visit for its friendly inhabitants and the wide variety of canvas goods made and sold here.

The most photogenic lighthouse in the Bahamas sits atop Elbow Cay. This spectacular red-and-white candy-stripe beacon signals the harbor opening to Hope Town, with more New England–style architecture. This pretty islet has a little of everything, including three marinas, a selection of restaurants, inns, markets, shops, bakeries, and even a museum.

Boats also make their way to two less developed neighboring islands: Guana Cay, with a 22-slip marina, and Spanish Cay, with 70 slips.

Back on Great Abaco, you'll find the most populous settlement in the Abacos at Marsh Harbour, which has plenty of facilities for yachters. These include the modern (and growing) 160-slip Boat Harbour Marina, a full-service operation on the east side of the island. The other side of town has additional marinas, including the 75-slip Conch Inn Marina, Marsh Harbour Marina and its 60 slips, and a couple of smaller facilities.

ANDROS

The largest link in the Bahamas's chain, yet among the least developed, Andros has a 20-slip marina at the Lighthouse Yacht Club in Andros Town. This island lures fishing enthusiasts to its superb bonefish flats, and divers can't get enough of the sprawling barrier reef just offshore.

THE BERRY ISLANDS

The clarity of Bahamian waters is particularly evident when you cross the Great Bahama Bank from the Bimini area along the Berry Islands on the way to Nassau. The depth of the waters here is seldom more than 20 ft. Grass patches and an occasional coral head or flattish coral patch dot the light sand bottom. Starfish abound, and you can often catch a glimpse of a gliding stingray or eagle ray. You might spot the odd turtle, and if you care to jump over the side of the boat with a mask, you might also pick up a conch or two in the grass.

In the upper Berry Islands, Great Harbour Cay, which was closed for a few years, has returned to the yachting fold with an 80-slip, full-service marina that can handle boats up to 150 ft. Accessible now through an 80-ft-wide channel from the bank side, Great Harbour Cay has one of the most pristine beaches in the Bahamas running along its east side. Chub Cay, about 75 mi from Bimini and 35 mi northwest of Nassau, is a semiprivate club with public facilities that include a full-service, 90-slip marina and a 50-room hotel.

THE BIMINI ISLANDS

The Biminis are the initial taste of the Bahamas for most visiting boaters. The ghost of Ernest Hemingway still haunts the island of North Bimini, where the writer stayed and played in the late '30s. The Compleat Angler Hotel serves as a veritable museum to the Hemingway mystique, though the current loud music at the hotel bar some nights might not be to Papa's taste.

The Biminis, which also include South Bimini, Gun Cay, and Cat Cay to the south, offer several good yachting facilities. The Bimini Big Game Fishing Club, a first-class, full-service marina with 100 slips, serves as headquarters for many of the spring and summer billfish tournaments. Bimini's Blue Water Marina offers 32 modern slips and usually hosts the annual Hemingway billfish tournament. Brown's Hotel and Marina, with 22 slips and a full line of services, is another popular hangout for yachters, fishermen, and divers. Weech's Dock, immediately north of Brown's, has 15 slips and a few waterfront rooms available. The Native Fishing Tournament remains one of the more vibrant events on the Bimini calendar; it's a nonstop party. If you come here during this August blowout, be prepared to lose some sleep.

Yachters will enjoy the excellent fishing opportunities along the eastern edge of the Gulf Stream. The bonefishing on the flats in this area is unsurpassed. However, you should talk to local residents about where to fish. Some of the shoal and reef areas can be tricky, especially for someone unfamiliar with the Bahamas.

ELEUTHERA

Harbour Island, off the northern coast of Eleuthera, is one of the Bahamas' most scenic islands. This petite beach-edged cay is where you'll find friendly Dunmore Town, a historic New England–style village filled with pastel cottages enclosed by white picket fences. Harbour Island has a surprisingly wide selection of restaurants, at some of the Bahamas' best small hotels as well local dining spots. Valentine's Yacht Club & Marina, with 39 slips, is particularly lively on weekend nights. The waterfront Reach Grill and the second-story Reach Up deck make wonderful vantage points for sunset watching while dining or drinking. In a quieter area outside town, the 32-slip Harbour Island Club & Marina invites boaters to cool off in the tiny seaside plunge pool and relax at the handsome alfresco bar.

THE EXUMAS

The Exuma island chain, stretching south and east along the western rim of Exuma Sound, may be the finest cruising area in the Bahamas. In the Upper Exumas, at the anchorage between Allan's and Leaf cays, a nature wonderland lies only about 32 mi out of Nassau. The nightly cacophony of birdcalls here could shatter crystal. On a morning visit to Leaf Cay, you might discover iguanas, oversize lizards that measure up to 3 ft long. These curious critters come to the beach when travelers arrive, but you're advised not to feed them. They have sharp teeth and might mistake a hand for food. Iguanas, protected by Bahamian law, must not be killed, captured, or exported.

The Exuma Cays National Land and Sea Park, from Wax Cay to Conch Cay, is a protected area worth visiting, although no fishing is allowed. On Little Wax Cay dwells the Bahamas' only indigenous mammal, the hutia. This nocturnal animal, about the size of a rabbit, is also protected by law. The west side of Hawksbill Cay offers lonely beaches, while Warderick Wells to the south is reputed to be haunted by the ghosts of hymn-singing choral groups, though there has never been any record of habitation on the island.

George Town, on Great Exuma in the lower end of the island chain, is generally the final destination of yachters cruising the Exumas. The Tropic of Cancer runs through the middle of this small community, which offers excellent anchorages and businesses that carry supplies necessary for yachters. Stocking Island, just a mile offshore of George Town, has a coastline of exquisite beaches and thick coconut groves.

GRAND BAHAMA ISLAND

Grand Bahama Island offers a wide variety of boating opportunities from West End all the way around to Deep Water Cay. Xanadu Beach Marina has 400 ft of dockage and 77 slips, and it provides dockside valet service. The Running Mon Marina, a half mile to the east, has 66 slips and serves as the base for a deep-sea fishing fleet that serves most of the hotels in the Freeport and Lucaya area. Inside Bell Channel at Lucaya, the 150-slip, full-service Lucayan Marina features complimentary ferry service across the harbor to the nearby Lucayan Beach Resort & Casino. Tucked in behind the bustling Port Lucaya Marketplace, the 100-slip Port Lucaya Marina boasts a broad range of water sports, including waterskiing, diving, snorkeling, jet skiing, and paddleboating.

About 6 mi east of the Bell Channel is the opening to the Grand Lucayan Waterway, a man-made channel that cuts through the island to

Dover Sound on the north side. Designed mainly for powerboats, the waterway is limited by fixed bridges with 27-ft clearances, but it does cut considerable time off cruising to the northern Abacos for boats coming from Fort Lauderdale or Miami. At the east end of Grand Bahama, the Deep Water Cay Club has a few slips, 18 rooms, a small dive operation, and bonefishing opportunities.

LONG ISLAND

Stretching some 80 mi in length yet never more than 4 mi across, Long Island treats boaters to seemingly endless beach-trimmed coasts. The topography here is more varied than on most Bahamian islands. Boaters anchored in shallow bays look out to undulating hills, rugged sea cliffs, and quiet sandy shores. Near the airport at the southern end, 15-slip Stella Maris Resort & Marina hosts parties in an eerie cave and safely guides scuba divers over a reef teeming with sharks.

NEW PROVIDENCE ISLAND

From Chub Cay to Nassau, the sailing route goes across the mile-deep Tongue of the Ocean. The Paradise Island Light welcomes yachters to Nassau Harbour, which is open at both ends. The harbor can handle the world's largest cruise liners; sometimes as many as eight will be tied up at one time. The looming Paradise Island Bridge bisects the harbor connecting the resort island to Nassau. It has a high-water clearance of 70 ft, so sailboats with taller masts heading for the marinas east of the bridge must enter the harbor from the east end. East Bay Yacht Basin and part of the Hurricane Hole Marina are the only boating facilities west of the bridge. Beyond the bridge on the Nassau side of the harbor lie several full-service marinas, including Nassau Yacht Haven, Bayshore Marina, Brown's Boat Yard, and the Nassau Harbour Club.

Across the harbor, Hurricane Hole, with 57 slips, guards the Paradise Island end of the bridge. The Nassau Yacht Club and Royal Nassau Sailing Club are at the eastern opening of the harbor. At the western end of New Providence, Lyford Cay, a posh development for the rich and famous, features an excellent marina.

SAN SALVADOR

Ever since Columbus first reached these shores in 1492, visitors have been sailing to quiet San Salvador (☞ "In Search of Columbus" *in* Chapter 7). Around the island, various monuments commemorate Europe's discovery of the existence of the New World. Riding Rock Inn, long known for its exceptional scuba diving program, has a 20-slip marina. Nearby, the newer Club Med Columbus Isle, elaborately decorated with Asian, African, and Pacific art and artifacts, is one of the Bahamas' most luxurious resorts.

Regattas

Both powerboats and sailboats participate in regattas, held throughout the year, out of most of the islands. Some of the most prominent are the **Nassau Cup Yacht Race** in February; the **Out Islands Regatta** at Exuma in April; the **Long Island Regatta** in May; the **Bahamas Princess Regatta Week** and **Regatta Time** at Marsh Harbour, Great Abaco, both in June; **Green Turtle Regatta Week** at Green Turtle Cay, in the Abacos, in July; and the annual regattas at Andros and Cat Island, both in August (☞ Outdoor Activities and Sports *throughout* Chapter 4).

Chartering a Boat in the Bahamas

If you are not coming to the Bahamas in your own boat or one that you have chartered, a few other cruising options are available. Most resorts have crewed charter boats available for deep-sea fishing or bonefishing. Some have small rental boats for day cruising. Import duties for boats and boat parts are 7½% on boats from 30 to 100 ft and as much as 5% on boats over 100 ft.

Several bareboat charter companies serve the islands. **Swift Yacht Charters** (☎ 800/866–8340) or **Tropical Diversions** (☎ 800/343–7256) will match you up with the best boat for your needs. Or call any of the following directly: **Abaco Bahamas Charters** (☎ 800/626–5690), in Hope Town on Elbow Cay, has a fleet of 10 sailboats from 30 to 44 ft. In Marsh Harbour on Great Abaco, **Sun Sail Services** (☎ 410/280–2553 or 800/327–2276) has a 26-boat fleet of 30- to 51-ft sailboats, plus a powerboat. Also in Marsh Harbour, the **Moorings at Conch Inn** (☎ 242/367–4000) can arrange charters. **Eleuthera Charters** (☎ 242/335–0186 or 800/446–9441), in Hatchet Bay on Eleuthera, has several privately owned 36- to 45-ft sailboats, catamarans, and trawlers for bareboating or with partial crew.

RUBBING SHOULDERS WITH BAHAMIANS

Two of the best ways to meet islanders are the Junkanoo festival—the ultimate Bahamian bash—and the People-to-People Programme, where you'll have an open opportunity to converse with those who call this country home.

Junkanoo and Goombay

Much of the Bahamians' music carries echoes of African rhythms, Caribbean calypso, English folk songs, and their own hearty Goombay beat. Nowhere is the Bahamians' zest for life more exuberantly expressed than in the Junkanoo celebrations held yearly on Boxing Day (the day after Christmas) and New Year's Day.

The origin of the word "Junkanoo" is hazy. One apocryphal legend has it that an African chieftain named John Canoe loved to indulge in wild parties. Whatever its provenance, Junkanoo—which can be likened in its uninhibited and frenzied activities only to Carnival in Rio de Janeiro and Mardi Gras in New Orleans—is a time when raucous masked revelers, dressed in costumes representing everything from dragons to bats, fill the streets, playing goatskin drums, clanging cowbells, and shrieking whistles. Junkanoo, in fact, has become an organized festival, with teams of participants with names such as the Valley Boys, the Saxon Superstars, the Fox Hill Congos, and the Vikings vying for prizes for best float, best theme, and best costumes. The celebration gets more imaginative, more colorful, and noisier every year.

Goombay is similar to Junkanoo, but it is not quite as frenetic. It runs throughout the summer, with festivals on Wednesday evenings on Nassau's Bay Street. Goatskin drummers and dancers wearing shimmering costumes perform, with the added contribution of the Royal Bahamas Police Band.

People-to-People Programme

The free People-to-People Programme, which allows visitors to get a more intimate glimpse of Bahamian life, continues to be a popular social event in the islands. Residents of New Providence, Grand Bahama, Eleuthera, the Exumas, the Abacos, the Biminis, and San Salvador volunteer to host tourists. Coordinators try to match visitors with Bahamians who have similar interests; your hosts may show you around their town, invite you to attend a church service or community event, or even ask you into their home for a meal. People-to-People also sponsors an afternoon tea at Government House on the last Friday of each month (Jan.–Aug.) and arranges tropical weddings that, at 50 to 60 each month, have become one of the most successful aspects of the program.

Coordinators ask that potential participants contact the **People-to-People Unit** (☎ 242/326–5371) or a Bahamas tourist office in the United States two to three weeks before their visit. However, arrangements can sometimes be made with short notice, so if you're already in the islands, go to a Nassau or Freeport Tourist Information Centre or ask at your hotel's events desk.

SCUBA DIVING IN PARADISE

By Gordon Lomer

Few places in the world offer a wider variety of diving opportunities than the Bahamas—wrecks and reefs, blue holes and drop-offs, sea gardens and shallow shoals can all be found here. In fact, one of the most famous scuba schools and NAUI (National Association of Underwater Instructors) centers in the world is UNEXSO (Underwater Explorers Society), in Lucaya, Grand Bahama. For the most stunning peek at the watery underworld, head to the less crowded Out Islands, where many hotels offer economical dive packages.

Before You Dive

While scuba (which stands for **s**elf-**c**ontained **u**nderwater **b**reathing **a**pparatus) looks and is surprisingly simple, phone your physician before your vacation and make sure that you have no condition that should prevent you from diving. A full checkup is an excellent idea, especially if you're over 30.

Learning to dive with a reputable instructor is a must. In addition to training you how to resurface slowly enough to avoid "the bends"— a painful and potentially fatal condition caused by the accumulation of nitrogen bubbles in the bloodstream—a qualified instructor can teach you to read dive tables, the charts that calculate how long you can safely stay at certain depths. Many resorts offer short courses consisting of two to three hours of instruction on land and time in a swimming pool or waist-deep water to get used to the mouthpiece and hose (known as the regulator) and the mask. A shallow 20-ft dive from a boat or beach, supervised by the instructor, follows. Some resorts offer a five-day concentrated certification course. Since it can be dangerous to travel on a plane for 24 hours after diving, you should schedule both your diving courses and travel plans accordingly.

Successful completion of an introductory course may prompt you to do further course work to earn a certification card—often called a C-card—from one of the major accredited diving organizations: NAUI, CMAS (Confederation Mondiale des Activités Subaquatiques, which translates into World Underwater Federation), NASE (National Association of Scuba Educators), or PADI (Professional Association of Diving Instructors). PADI offers a free list of training facilities; write to them at 1251 East Dyer Road, #100, Santa Ana, CA 92705.

Dive Operators

Most dive resorts in the Bahamas are members of the Bahamas Diving Association and will require a certification card (C-card) for tank and regulator rentals. A card is not required for refills, but the tanks must show hydrostatic test marks not more than five years old. For information on specific dive operators, *see* Outdoor Activities and Sports in the individual chapters.

Dive Sites

With more than 700 islands, the Bahamas offers literally thousands of dive sites within its crystal-clear waters. The local dive shops and operations, while geared for regularly scheduled dives or personalized custom diving, are willing and generous in offering correct and precise directions to many dive sites. In some cases, they will even give you the coordinates of a location. Unless you and your navigational equipment are extremely sharp, however, you could miss a site by 100 yards or so, which would still give you a lot of seabed to search. Some sites, of course, are obvious; you won't need a local guide to show you a sunken ship that stands 25 ft out of the water, and drop-offs aren't that hard to spot. Local experts, however, will know the best places to dive, the drop-offs, the safest places to drop an anchor, and even the best time of day for the dive.

ABACOS

Ocean Holes (Hole-in-the-Wall, 45–100 ft). To the southwest of Hole-in-the-Wall are several ocean holes starting at 100 ft. They have not been fully explored yet. Closer to shore are several prolific reefs at about 45 ft.

Pelican Cay Land and Sea Park (Marsh Harbour, 10–30 ft). This 2,000-acre preserve is under the protection of the Bahamas National Trust. It contains a full range of marine life. It's excellent for novice divers, snorkelers, and photographers.

USS *Adirondack* (Man-O-War Cay, 20 ft). This wreck from the Civil War lies among a host of cannons on the outside of the reef. The coral heads off Man-O-War are large and spectacular and have a wide variety of coral and fish life.

ANDROS

Andros, the largest island in the Bahamas, probably has the largest number of dive sites in the country. With the third-longest barrier reef in the world (behind those of Australia and Belize), the island offers about 100 mi of drop-off diving into the Tongue of the Ocean. Uncounted numbers of blue holes are forming in the area; in some places, these constitute vast submarine/subterranean networks.

The Barge (Fresh Creek, 55–70 ft). An old landing craft was sunk about 30 years ago. Now encrusted with coral, it has become home to a group of groupers and a blizzard of tiny silverfish. There is a fish-cleaning station where miniature cleaning shrimp and yellow gobies clean grouper and rockfish by swimming into the mouths and out the gills of the larger fish, picking up food particles. It's excellent subject matter for close-up photography.

Blue Holes (Fresh Creek, 40–100 ft; North Andros, 40–200+ ft; South Bight, 40–200 ft). Blue holes are named both for their inky-blue aura when viewed from above and for the light-blue filtered sunlight that is still visible from 180 or 200 ft down. Some include huge cathedral-like interior chambers with stalactites and stalagmites, offshoot tunnels, and seemingly endless corridors. Others have distinct thermoclines (temperature changes) between layers of water or are subject to tidal flow. The dramatic Fresh Creek site provides an insight into the complex Andros cave system; there isn't much coral growth but plenty of midnight parrot fish, big southern stingrays, and some blacktip sharks. Similar blue holes are located all along the barrier reef, including several at Mastic Point in the north and the ones explored and filmed off South Bight.

Over the Wall (Fresh Creek, 80–185 ft). This split-level dive takes novices to the 80-ft ledge and experienced divers to a pre–Ice Age beach at 185 ft. The wall is covered with black coral and a wide variety of tube sponges.

THE BIMINI ISLANDS

Atlantis (North Bimini, 10–40 ft). Divers and scientists argue over what might be evidence of an ancient civilization in the shallow waters west of North Bimini. Huge blocks form a 300-ft-long rectangle, which some scientists think could be a former roadbed. The foundations measure 30 ft across, and a few of the stones are 16 ft square. Radioactive tests indicate, according to one scientist, that this area was above water 5,000 years ago. Others, however, scoff.

Piquet Rock (Gun Cay, 5–20 ft). Wreck debris from a Spanish galleon includes ballast rocks, cannonballs, and ribs; it has produced brass spikes and other artifacts. A fish-cleaning station for grouper and jewfish and many coral and sponge stands can be found here.

Sapona (South Bimini, 15–20 ft). This landmark wreck of a concrete-and-steel ship is of historical interest. A hapless victim of two hurricanes, it has served as a rock carrier, bootleg liquor warehouse, and World War II bombing target. Home for hundreds of tiny tropical fish, it makes a particularly fascinating night dive, with lights playing mysteriously through the openings from hold to hold.

THE EXUMAS

Every conceivable sort of diving, virtually all at little-explored sites, is available in the Exumas. While the diving is uniformly good, it is recommended that you seek the advice of local guides at any of the marinas.

Exuma Cays National Land and Sea Park (North/Central Exumas, 10–200 ft). This 7-mi-wide fish and bird sanctuary runs 22 mi from Wax Cay Cut to Conch Cut and is administered by the Bahamas National Trust. The many dive sites in the park include the full range of coral stands—brain, elkhorn, staghorn, and oscillating corals reaching almost to the surface. A wide variety of drop-off sites are located in Exuma Sound.

Stocking Island Cave (George Town, 10–80 ft). This tunnel, about 12 ft wide and 8 ft high throughout, has been explored several hundred feet back into the island. From the mouth, ablaze with schools of milling fish, the cave dips and rises, reaching 80 ft at its deepest. Fish swim upside down on the ceiling, and the walls are covered with an orange spongelike substance. Lifeline and lights are needed. This is for experienced divers only.

Thunderball Grotto (Staniel Cay, 10–20 ft). Nature made this spot, a grotto inside one of three rocks north of the Staniel Cay Yacht Club, spectacular. It is pierced by eerie shafts of light from holes in the roof of the partially submerged cave (at low tide, snorkelers can enter two of the eight openings without submerging). Stalactites creep down the limestone walls, and there are coral and sponge growths usually found only at deep drop-offs.

GRAND BAHAMA ISLAND

Grand Bahama Island offers some fascinating diving sites near the West End. An extensive reef system runs along the edge of the Little Bahama Bank from Mantinilla Shoals down through Memory Rock, Wood Cay, Rock Cay, and Indian Cay. Sea gardens, caves, and colorful reefs rim the bank all the way from the West End to the Freeport/Lucaya area and beyond.

Angels' Camp (Lucaya, 35–50 ft). About 1¼ mi off Lucayan Beach, this medium reef is a scattering of small coral heads surrounding one large head. They are covered with gorgonians, as well as with sponge life, and are the habitat for a nation of angelfish.

Indian Cay Light (West End, 30–80 ft). Several reefs off Indian Cay Light form a vast sea garden with schools of grunts, snapper, chub, and tiny tropical fish. Royal grammas are everywhere, and the rare Atlantic long-nose butterfly fish is common.

Pygmy Caves (Lucaya, 80 ft). These caves near Angel's Camp are formed by overgrown ledges and cuts in the reef, the edges and undersides of which are covered with colorful sponges.

Theo's Wreck (Freeport/Lucaya, 100 ft). This 230-ft steel freighter, sunk as a dive site in 1982, is perched on its side on the edge of the Grand Bahama ledge. The stern hangs out over the 2,000-ft drop-off. Divers can sit on the poop and rudder and contemplate the deep blue abyss below.

Zoo Hole (West of Lucaya, 35–185 ft). This large hole in the ocean floor starts at 35 ft. At 75 ft are the entrances to two huge caverns—explored to 185 ft—both of which contain schools of large angelfish, cobia, crabs, and a plethora of shells.

NEW PROVIDENCE ISLAND

Lost Ocean Hole (East of Nassau, 40–195 ft). This elusive (and thus exclusive) hole is aptly named because it is difficult to locate. The rim of the 80-ft opening in 40 ft of water is dotted with coral heads and teeming with small fish—grunts, margate, and jacks—as well as larger pompano, amberjack, and sometimes nurse sharks. Divers will find a thermocline at 80 ft, a large cave at 100 ft, and a sand ledge at 185 ft that slopes down to 195 ft.

Lyford Cay Drop-Off (West of Nassau, 40–200+ ft). Starting from a 40-ft plateau, the cliff plummets almost straight into the inky blue mile-deep Tongue of the Ocean. The wall offers endless varieties of sponges, black coral, and wire coral. Along the wall, grunts, grouper, hogfish, snapper, and rockfish abound. Off the wall are pelagic game fish, such as tuna, bonito, wahoo, and kingfish.

Rose Island Reefs (Nassau, 5–35 ft). The series of shallow reefs along the 14 mi of Rose Island are popular with locals on weekends and visitors on scheduled dives. The coral is varied, though the reefs are showing the effects of the heavy traffic. Plenty of tropical fish make these reefs home.

3 New Providence Island

Nassau and Paradise Island are the big hitters in the Bahamian lineup. Along with dozing in the sun, you can bargain at the Straw Market, dine at fine restaurants, gamble at casinos, and explore the nation's historic buildings, forts, gardens, and monuments. Opulent resort areas tout groomed beaches, water sports aplenty, and a busy nightclub scene.

Updated by
Jessica
Robertson and
Allyson Major

NEW PROVIDENCE ISLAND, now home to two-thirds of all Bahamians, has in the course of its history weathered the comings and goings of lawless pirates, Spanish invaders, and slave-holding British Loyalists who fled the United States after the Revolutionary War. The island housed Confederate blockade-runners during the Civil War and hosted rum-runners during Prohibition. Despite this polyglot past, however, New Providence remains most influenced by England, which sent its first royal governor to the island in 1718. Although black Bahamians won control of the government in 1967 and independence six years later, the British influence continues to this day.

Nassau is the Bahamas' capital and transportation hub, as well as the country's banking and commercial center. While businesspeople take advantage of bank secrecy laws that rival those made famous by Switzerland and enjoy the absence of income, sales, and inheritance taxes, most visitors need look no farther than Nassau's many duty-free shops for proof of the island's commercial vitality. This fortuitous combination of tourist-friendly enterprise, tropical weather, and British ambience—all a mere 35-minute flight from Miami—has not gone unnoticed: A constant flow of planes from all over the United States and, to a lesser extent, from Canada and Europe, arrives daily at Nassau International Airport. Meanwhile, each year more than 1 million visitors—passengers on more than 20 cruise ships—arrive at Nassau's Prince George Wharf, on short trips from Florida or as the final stop on Caribbean cruises.

Cruise-ship passengers and overnight visitors alike enjoy exploring Nassau's Bay Street shops and its busy Straw Market, where women weave their magic on hats and baskets. A mile or so east of town, under the Paradise Island Bridge, Potter's Cay Dock is another colorful scene: Out-Island sloops bring catches of fish and conch (say *konk*), open-air stalls carry fresh fruit and vegetables, and street vendors sell local foods. If the daytime bustle of old Nassau isn't enough, the tropical entertainment in nightclubs and the action at the island's two casinos can take you into the wee hours of the morning.

Most overnight visitors venture just beyond downtown Nassau to Cable Beach and Paradise Island, two areas that offer plush hotels, unfettered beach access, and proximity to casinos. Cable Beach, a crescent-shape stretch of sand west of Nassau, is rimmed by low-rise luxury resorts and the Crystal Palace Casino. While the environment is neither secluded nor pristine, all Cable Beach hotels provide easy access to the beach and to the casino. Many of Cable Beach's attractions are also popular with locals, so you won't feel too removed from the day-to-day life of average Bahamians staying there.

The island's other vacation enclave, Paradise Island, takes the opposite tack. A high, arched bridge just east of Nassau links New Providence and Paradise islands. This resort community, long considered the unspoiled alternative to Cable Beach's glitz, has been reinvented. Sun International (the corporation behind South Africa's legendary Sun City, among other resorts) invested over $150 million in phase one of a major development plan that includes three of the island's properties. The Paradise Island Resort & Casino, long the island's centerpiece, has been transformed into an aquatic-theme wonderland called Atlantis, Paradise Island; the grounds, guest rooms, and clubhouse at the Ocean Club have been renovated, but the resort's classic style and elegance have been maintained. Though the new developments have certainly added to the overall hustle and bustle, the island hasn't lost its famous serenity. Long expanses of beach and clear, blue-green waters appeal to yachters, anglers, divers, water-skiers, parasailers, and windsurfers. Landlubbers can choose among three golf courses, fabulous beaches, and abundant tennis courts.

EXPLORING NEW PROVIDENCE ISLAND

You could easily while away your vacation days and nights exclusively at the pools, beaches, sports activities, and entertainment of Nassau, Cable Beach, and Paradise Island's resorts and hotels. To make the most of your visit to this island, though, explore downtown Nassau's historic buildings and shops, too. Wear comfortable shoes. Bay Street and its side streets are usually crowded, particularly in the afternoon, and walking can be a somewhat slow and hot-footed process.

Tourist action is concentrated on the northeastern side of New Providence. If you have the time, you can make your way around the rest of this 7-by-21-mi island in a day, including occasional stops for beautiful beaches, local cuisine, and historic sites. The terrain is flat, and getting around is quite easy. Renting a car is your best bet—or pick up a scooter for a more adventurous ride. Either way, drive on the left-hand side of the road. Remember to pick up a copy of a New Providence map at your hotel desk. Most have the entire island on one side and a detailed downtown Nassau plan on the other.

Numbers in the text correspond to numbers in the margin and on the Nassau and Paradise Island, and New Providence Island maps.

A Good Tour

In a day, you can take in most of the markets, gardens, and historical sites of **Nassau** ①–⑭ or Paradise Island. Likewise, set aside a half-day or more for excursions out to Lake Nancy for a few hours of canoeing, a trip to the **Commonwealth Brewery** ㉝ or the **Bacardi Distillery** ㉟, some exploring at **The Caves** ㉛, or to make a circuit of the east end of the island, stopping in at the gardens of **The Retreat** ㉑.

Rawson Square, with its statue of Sir Mil Butler, the first Bahamian governor-general, is a good starting point in the heart of downtown Bay Street. Pick up any brochures and maps at the Ministry of Tourism information booth on the northern side. Now head west along the north side of famous Bay Street—save your shopping for later, as your new-found treasures will prove cumbersome along the way. And by all means leave time for the **Straw Market,** just west of Market Street—and remember that vendors expect you to barter for goods. Continue west to the **Pompey Museum** ③ for a quick trip into the slave days of old Nassau. Follow the bend at Navy Lion Road past the historic **British Colonial Hotel** ④ on West Bay Street.

Continue along West Bay, up along the Western Esplanade beach for a spectacular view of the ocean and the harbor.

If you've packed a sense of adventure, stray west to make your next stop lunch and a bite of culture at **Arawak Cay** ㉘, which lies a few minutes farther along West Bay Street on the north side. Pull up a stool at any one of the brightly painted native shacks and grab a bite of fried snapper or a bowl of conch salad. Wash it down with a cold Kalik or some potent "sky juice" (gin and coconut water).

Once you've filled up, hop across West Bay and take in some more history, not to mention a fantastic view, at **Fort Charlotte** ㉕.

Head east along West Bay to West Street, then turn south and take in the quaint Bahamian homes lining the street. Stop in at St. Francis Xavier Church, and then turn left onto West Hill Street. Note Villa Doyle, a historic old home, scheduled to be converted into a national art gallery, and continue eastward.

Walk across Blue Hill Road onto Duke Street and snap a picture with Christopher Columbus, who graces the entrance to the **Government House** ⑥ grounds.

Head north onto George Street and on the right at the first junction is the regal **Christ Church Cathedral** ⑦. From the cathedral, turn east on King Street then south along Market Street, where you can take a short tour of the pink **Balcony House Museum** ⑧, typical of turn-of-the-century Bahamian architecture. Check to see if there is local artists' work on display at the **Central Bank of the Bahamas** ⑨ across the street, then after a peek continue east until you reach Frederick Street. Trinity Methodist Church is on the corner. On Shirley Street, turn east, past Charlotte and Parliament streets to the public library. Once upon a time this was a jail housing the island's scoundrels.

Follow Shirley Street farther east until you get to Elizabeth Avenue. Head south, and you'll find the **Queen's Staircase** ⑪—hand cut out of limestone—and **Fort Fincastle** ⑫ and the **Water Tower,** the highest point on the island.

When you're finished at the fort, backtrack along Elizabeth Avenue and Shirley Street to Bank Lane. Stop to take in the buildings at **Parliament Square** ⑭, then return to Rawson Square to get a close-up look at the floating hotels, the surrey horses, and the hair-braiding stand.

From here, you can catch a bus at Navy Lion Road (at the western end of Bay Street) to Cable Beach for some gambling or a show, or take a taxi east to Paradise Island, where you can take in **Atlantis, Paradise Island** ⑯ and the **Cloisters** ⑰, then spend some time working on your tan.

TIMING

This tour will take up the better part of a day. If the fare on Arawak Cay isn't to your liking, there are any number of other good restaurants along the route. In order to keep your bearings, remember that Bay Street and Shirley Street run east to west, and just about all other streets link them running north to south.

Nassau

In Nassau, the nation's capital and the bustling city for which New Providence is best known, reminders of the island's British heritage are everywhere—in the pomp and ceremony and bewigged judges that attend the opening of Supreme Court sessions; in the discipline of the policemen meticulously attired in starched white jackets, red-striped trousers, and pith helmets; and in the tradition of driving on the left side of the road. Behind the walls fronting the city's narrow streets are shuttered, colonial-style buildings with sculpted shrubbery as well tended as any you might find in an English garden.

Nassau's sheltered harbor bustles with cruise ship activity. Just one block from the waterfront, colorful Bay Street bustles with commercial activity. Shops angle for tourist dollars with fine imported and locally handcrafted goods at duty-free prices, and Straw Market vendors bargain for the same dollars with straw goods, T-shirts, and jewelry at a fraction of those prices. Nassau's historic sites are centered around downtown and can be toured on foot or by scooter or horse-drawn carriage.

Sights to See

★ ❽ **Balcony House Museum.** This charming 18th-century landmark—an islandy pink-and-white two-story house aptly named for its free-standing balcony—is the oldest wooden residential structure in Nassau. Originally, the house was constructed with American cedar, its architecture suggesting that it was built by ship's carpenters. Later, a mahogany staircase, believed to have been salvaged from a ship during the last century, was installed. In its present state, the furnishings and design of Balcony House Museum recapture the elegance of a bygone era. ⊠ *Market and Bay Sts.,* ☎ *242/326–2566/8.* ☒ *Donation recommended.* ⊘ *Mon., Wed., Fri. 10–1 and 2–4.*

❹ **British Colonial Hotel.** The imposing building at the corner of Bay and Cumberland streets is the island's oldest and most revered hostelry. Fondly dubbed "the B.C.," this six-story, pink-and-white structure was once an outpost of the British Empire, a dowager on a par with Singapore's Raffles or Hong Kong's Peninsula hotels. The original structure, built in 1899 on the site where Fort Nassau stood from 1696 to 1837, was destroyed by fire in 1921. Rebuilt and reopened in 1923 as the New Colonial Hotel, it was the kind of serene place where bonneted ladies crooked their pinkies when they lifted their teacups. Now, it's run by Best Western and flags of five nations flutter at the main entrance; a fine statue of Woodes Rogers recalls the hotel's colorful history. ⊠ *1 Bay St.,* ☎ *242/322–3301.*

❾ **Central Bank of the Bahamas.** The Central Bank of the Bahamas functions as the government's official arm monitoring and regulating the country's financial institutions. The cornerstone of the building itself was laid by Prince Charles on July 9, 1973, during the country's Independence celebrations, and the bank was opened by Queen Elizabeth II in February 1975. Throughout the year, art exhibits in the lobby display the country's best in all media. ⊠ *Frederick and Bay Sts.,* ☎ *242/322–2193.*

★ ❼ **Christ Church Cathedral.** It was not until Christ Church Parish became a cathedral in 1861 that Nassau became a city. Anglican services are now held daily in the grand Cathedral, which is open to the public during regular hours. The stained-glass windows that encompass the cathedral are worth the short walk off the main thoroughfare. The east windows depict the Crucifixion in the center panel and the Empty Tomb and the Ascension in the two side panels. Then, take a leisurely stroll through the small Gardens of Remembrance, where roses bloom, and tombstonelike plaques adorn the walls, offering a living history of the old city. ⊠ *George St.*

⓬ **Fort Fincastle.** A paddle-wheel steamer–shaped structure built in 1789 to serve as a lookout post for marauders trying to sneak into the local harbor, this fort is at the top of the Queen's Staircase (☞ *below*). The view of most of Nassau and the harbor from the 126-ft-tall water tower is quite spectacular. The tower, more than 200 ft above sea level, is the highest point on the island. ⊠ *Top of Elizabeth Ave. hill near Shirley St.* ☒ *Guided tours 50¢.* ⊘ *Fri.–Wed. 8–5.*

★ ❻ **Government House.** The official residence of the governor-general of the Bahamas since 1801 is an imposing pink-and-white building at the intersection of Market and Duke streets. Its most notable occupants were the Duke and Duchess of Windsor, who made it their home during World War II. This distinguished mansion is an excellent example of the mingling of Bahamian-British and American Colonial architecture. Its graceful columns and broad, circular drive could be found in Virginia or the Carolinas; but its pink color and distinctive white quoins are typically

Nassau and Paradise Island

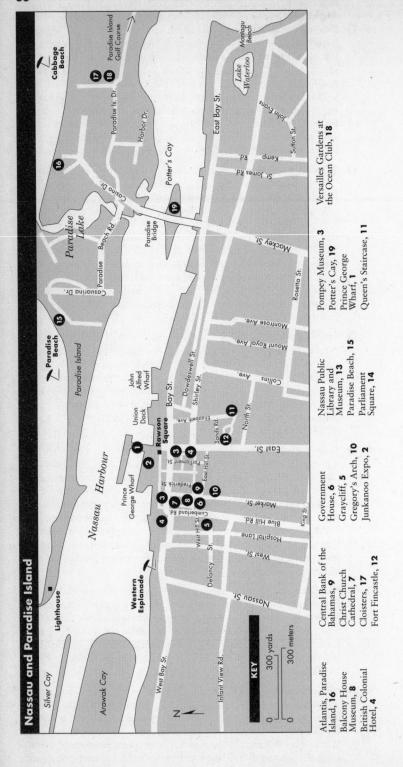

Silver Cay

Arawak Cay

Lighthouse

Paradise Beach

Paradise Island

Cabbage Beach

Paradise Island Golf Course

Montagu Beach

Nassau Harbour

Prince George Wharf

Western Esplanade

Paradise Lake

Casuarina Dr.

Beach Rd.

Paradise Beach Rd.

Harbor Dr.

Paradise Is. Dr.

Potter's Cay

Casino Dr.

Paradise Bridge

Lake Waterloo

East Bay St.

John Evans

Sutton St.

Kemp Rd.

St. James Rd.

John Alfred Wharf

Union Dock

Bay St.

Rawson Square

Dowdeswell St.

Shirley St.

Elizabeth Ave.

Sands Rd.

East St.

North St.

Collins Ave.

Mount Royal Ave.

Montrose Ave.

Rosetta St.

Mackey St.

Prince George Wharf

Frederick St.

Parliament St.

East Hill St.

Market St.

Cumberland Rd.

Blue Hill Rd.

King St.

Hospital Lane

West Hill St.

West St.

Delancy St.

Nassau St.

West Bay St.

Infant View Rd.

N

KEY

0   300 yards
0   300 meters

Atlantis, Paradise Island, **16**
Balcony House Museum, **8**
British Colonial Hotel, **4**

Central Bank of the Bahamas, **9**
Christ Church Cathedral, **7**
Cloisters, **17**
Fort Fincastle, **12**

Government House, **6**
Graycliff, **5**
Gregory's Arch, **10**
Junkanoo Expo, **2**

Nassau Public Library and Museum, **13**
Paradise Beach, **15**
Parliament Square, **14**

Pompey Museum, **3**
Potter's Cay, **19**
Prince George Wharf, **1**
Queen's Staircase, **11**

Versailles Gardens at the Ocean Club, **18**

Bahamian. (Quoins are cross-laid cornerstones reaching to the full height of a building's walls, and they are found on many old Bahamian homes and public buildings.) Notice, too, the shutters—wooden louvers that completely enclose the large upper and lower verandas—that are designed to keep out the tropical sun and are typically seen on many well-preserved old mansions in Nassau. Halfway up the white steps that lead to the entrance of the stately building is an imposing statue of Christopher Columbus, dressed ostentatiously in plumed hat and cloak and looking as if he were preparing to make his entrance at the Court of Ferdinand and Isabella. Here you can also catch the spiffy, flamboyant **Changing of the Guard ceremony**, which takes place every other Saturday morning at 10. The star of the pomp and pageantry is the Royal Bahamas Police Force Band, the members of which are decked out in white tunics, red-striped navy trousers, and spiked, white pith helmets with red bands; the drummers sport leopard skins. ⊠ *Duke St.,* ☎ *242/322–7500 for changes in ceremony schedule.*

❺ **Graycliff.** The gracious Graycliff, across the street from Government House, was once a stately home. Now it is one of Nassau's classiest small hotels and restaurants (☞ Dining *and* Lodging, *below*). This superb example of Georgian Colonial architecture dates from the mid-1700s. It is said that it was built by a Captain Graysmith, a privateer whose vessel was named the *Graywolf*. The landmark's colorful history includes its use as an officers' mess by the British West Indian garrison. It also acquired a certain notoriety during the rum-running days of Prohibition. Until the 1970s, Graycliff was the private winter home of the Earl and Countess of Dudley. ⊠ *W. Hill St.,* ☎ *242/322–2796.*

❿ **Gregory's Arch.** Named for John Gregory (royal governor from 1849 to 1854), this arch, at the intersection of Market and Duke streets, separates downtown from the "over-the-hill" neighborhood of **Grant's Town,** where much of Nassau's population lives. Grant's Town was laid out in the 1820s by Governor Lewis Grant as a settlement for freed slaves. There was a time when visitors would enjoy late-night mingling with the locals over rum drinks in the small, dimly lit bars of Grant's Town. Nowadays, tourists should exhibit the same caution they would if they were visiting impoverished areas of a large city.

❷ **Junkanoo Expo.** At the entrance to the wharf in an old customs warehouse you'll find exhibits of the fantastic costumes that revelers wear during the annual Bahamian Junkanoo celebration. Junkanoo parades, similar to those that take place elsewhere during Mardi Gras or Carnival, are held in the early morning hours on Boxing Day (the day after Christmas) and on New Year's Eve. ⊠ *Prince George Wharf,* ☎ *242/356–2731.* ☞ *$1.* ☼ *Daily 9–5:30.*

⓭ **Nassau Public Library and Museum.** This octagonal building near Parliament Square was the Nassau Gaol (a British spelling for *jail*), circa 1797. You're welcome to pop in and browse. The small prison cells are now lined with books. The museum has an interesting collection of historic prints and old colonial documents. ⊠ *Shirley St. between Parliament St. and Bank La.,* ☎ *242/322–4907.* ☞ *Free.* ☼ *Mon.–Thurs. 10–8, Fri. 10–5, Sat. 10–4.*

★ ⓮ **Parliament Square.** Nassau is the seat of the national government. The Bahamas Parliament is comprised of two houses—a 16-member Senate (Upper House) and a 40-member House of Assembly (Lower House)—and a ministerial cabinet headed by a prime minister. Parliament Square's pink, colonnaded government buildings were constructed during the early 1800s by Loyalists who came to the Bahamas from North Carolina. The buildings were patterned after the southern Colonial architecture of New Bern, the early capital of North Carolina. The Square is dominated by a statue of the young Queen Victoria that was erected on her birthday, May 24, in 1905. In the immediate area are a half dozen magistrates' courts (open to the public). Behind the House of Assembly is the **Supreme Court;** its four-times-a-year opening ceremonies (held the first weeks of January, April, July, and October) recall similar wigs and mace-bearing pageantry at the Houses of Parliament in London. The Royal Bahamas Police Force Band is usually on hand for the event. ⊠ *Bay St.,* ☎ *242/322–7500, 242/356–7591 for information on Supreme Court ceremonies.* ☞ *Free; obtain pass at door to view session.* ☉ *Weekdays 10–4.*

❸ Pompey Museum. Named for a rebel slave who lived on the Out Island of Exuma in 1830, this museum opened in 1992. In the 1700s, slave auctions took place in what is now the museum building. Exhibits focus on the issues of slavery and emancipation and highlight the works of local artists, such as Amos Ferguson, whose delightfully simplistic folk-art canvases depict religious, natural, and "ole story" themes. ⊠ *Bay and George Sts.,* ☎ *242/326–2566 or 242/326–2568.* ☞ *$1.* ☉ *Weekdays 10–4:30, every other Sat. 10–1.*

❶ Prince George Wharf. Parliament Square is the first view that cruise passengers encounter after they tumble off the ships berthed at Prince George Wharf. Up to a dozen gigantic cruise ships can be in port at any one time. They stop at Nassau either on short jaunts from Miami or during weeklong cruises to Caribbean islands. The wharf received a $2.5 million face-lift in 1996, and phase II—completion date not announced—will add island shops, an audiovisual information center, and a footbridge from the Straw Market on Bay Street to the wharf. ⊠ *Waterfront at Rawson Sq.*

⓫ Queen's Staircase. During the late 18th century, slaves carved these 65 steps (originally there were 66) into a solid limestone cliff. The staircase was later named to honor the 65-year reign of Queen Victoria. It's at the top of Elizabeth Avenue hill, off Shirley Street.

Paradise Island

The graceful, arched Paradise Bridge ($2 toll for rental cars and motorbikes; free to bicyclists and pedestrians), 1 mi east of Nassau's Rawson Square, leads to the extravagant, tranquil world of Paradise Island.

Until 1962 it was known as the largely undeveloped Hog Island. A&P heir Huntington Hartford changed the name when he built the island's first resort complex. Although several huge high-rise resorts have been built since then, much of the island remains untamed and pristine. The north shore is lined with white-sand beaches and turquoise seas. The protected south shore is a haven for yachts. Aptly renamed, the island *is* a paradise for beach lovers, boaters, and fun lovers.

Paradise Island is conducive to walking and bicycling because it's flat and compact. A free casino shuttle bus makes frequent rounds, picking up passengers at major hotels as well as anywhere along the route. It's a good way to get from place to place on a hot day.

Sights to See

★ ⓰ Atlantis, Paradise Island. Just across the Paradise Island Bridge, Casino Drive leads directly to Atlantis, its surrounding 14 acres of unparalleled waterscape, and the famed Café Martinique—James Bond ate here in *Thunderball* (☞ Dining, *below*). The huge complex is home to restaurants, glitzy shopping malls, a cabaret theater, an outdoor aquarium complete with an underwater tunnel with sharks looming above, and a 30,000-sq-ft casino with slot machines, roulette wheels, and black-jack tables. The "Sunsation" cabaret show is billed as something the whole family can enjoy, with native dancers moving to the beat of trop-ical island rhythms. The casino is fairly relaxed and uncrowded dur-ing the afternoon; shirtless, barefoot, or otherwise scantily covered sightseers are not welcome. At night, people are inclined to dress up. ⊠ *Casino Dr.,* ☎ *800/363–3000.* ⊙ *Daily 24 hrs.*

★ **⑰** **Cloisters.** At the top of the **Versailles Gardens** (☞ *below*) stand the re-mains of a 14th-century French stone monastery that were imported to the United States in the '20s by newspaper baron William Randolph Hearst. Forty years later, grocery-chain heir Hartford bought the Clois-ters and had them installed on their present commanding site. At the center is a graceful, contemporary, white marble statue called *Silence,* by U.S. sculptor Dick Reid. Daily, tourists take or renew wedding vows under the delicately wrought gazebo overlooking Nassau Har-bour. The cloister is one of four that have ever been removed from French soil. ⊠ *Paradise Island Dr.*

⑮ **Paradise Beach.** One of the most beautiful stretches of white sand to be found anywhere in New Providence is at the end of Casuarina Drive. You can enjoy the beach for a $3 fee that includes towels and changing rooms.

⑲ **Potter's Cay.** At this charming spot underneath the Paradise Bridge, sloops bring in fish and conch, which fishermen clean on the spot and sell to local residents and hotel chefs. Vegetables, herbs, and native limes are sold at nearby stalls, along with locally grown pineapples, papaya, and bananas. If you don't have the facilities or the know-how to han-dle the preparation of the tasty conch—getting the diffident creature out of its shiny pink shell requires boring a hole at the right spot to sever the muscle that keeps it entrenched—you'll find a stall selling local delicacies such as conch salad.

⑱ **Versailles Gardens.** At the Ocean Club, once owned by Huntington Hartford, fountains and statues of luminaries and legends (such as Napoléon and Josephine, Franklin Delano Roosevelt, David Living-stone, Hercules, and Mephistopheles) adorn the terraced lawn, known as the Versailles Gardens. It is a favorite locale for weddings. **Cloisters** (☞ *above*) brought over from France grace the top of the gardens. ⊠ *Ocean Club, Paradise Island Dr.,* ☎ *242/363–3000.*

Eastern New Providence

The eastern end of New Providence Island is predominantly residen-tial, although there are some interesting historical sites and fortifica-tions here. From East Bay Street, just beyond Paradise Bridge, it's a short, scenic drive to East End Point—about 20 minutes, depending on traffic.

Sights to See

㉔ **Blackbeard's Tower.** On a hill near the easternmost point of New Providence, this edifice is dismissed by the more pragmatic people of Nassau as the remains of an old stone water tower. The more roman-tic insist it was used by the piratical Edward Teach, a.k.a. Blackbeard, as a lookout for Spanish ships ripe for plundering. The best thing about the place, in the end, is its view of Nassau and its harbor. ⊠ *East-ern Rd.*

⑳ **Fort Montagu.** The oldest of the island's three forts, Montagu was built in 1741 of local limestone to repel Spanish invaders. The only action

New Providence Island

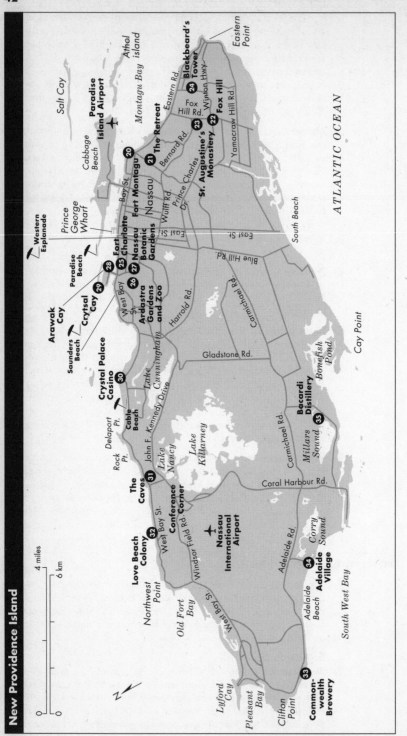

Salt Cay

Athol Cay

Paradise Island Airport

Montagu Bay Island

Cabbage Beach

Eastern Point

Blackbeard's Tower

Eastern Rd.

Fox Hill Rd.

Winton Hill Rd.

24

23

22

Fox Hill

The Retreat

Bernard Rd.

Yamacraw Hill Rd.

St. Augustine's Monastery

Prince Charles Dr.

20

21

Fort Montagu

Nassau

Bay St.

Wulff Rd.

East St.

East St.

South Beach

ATLANTIC OCEAN

Prince George Wharf

Western Esplanade

Paradise Beach

Fort Charlotte

Nassau Botanic Gardens

25

27

28

Ardastra Gardens and Zoo

26

29

West Bay St.

Blue Hill Rd.

Arawak Cay

Saunders Beach

Crystal Cay

Harrold Rd.

Carmichael Rd.

Gladstone Rd.

Cay Point

Crystal Palace Casino

30

Lake Cunningham

John F. Kennedy Drive

Lake Nancy

Lake Killarney

Bacardi Distillery

35

Millars Sound

Bonefish Pond

Delaport Pt.

Rock Pt.

Cable Beach

31

The Caves

Coral Harbour Rd.

Carmichael Rd.

Corry Sound

Conference Corner

32

West Bay St.

Love Beach Colony

Northwest Point

Old Fort Bay

Windsor Field Rd.

Nassau International Airport

Adelaide Rd.

34

Adelaide Village

Adelaide Beach

South West Bay

West Bay St.

Lyford Cay

Pleasant Bay

Clifton Point

33

Common-wealth Brewery

4 miles

6 km

0

0

N

it saw, though, was when it was occupied for two weeks by rebel American troops—among them a lieutenant named John Paul Jones— seeking arms and ammunition during the Revolutionary War. The fortification is well maintained, and though there are no guided tours, you are welcome to wander around. A broad public beach stretching for more than a mile beyond the fort looks out on Montagu Bay, where many international yacht regattas and Bahamian sloop races are held annually. ⊠ *East of Bay St. on Eastern Rd.* ☜ *Free.*

㉒ Fox Hill. Legend has it that it took a week for the original news of freedom—from the shackles of slavery—to reach the community here back in 1834, which is why Fox Hill Day comes one week after the rest of the island celebrates Emancipation Day. So on the second Tuesday in August, this little community on Fox Hill Road has its own annual festival, celebrating with island music, down-home cooking, arts-and-crafts booths, and gospel singing.

㉑ The Retreat. Nearly 200 species of exotic palm trees stand on the 11 acres of tropical gardens known as the Retreat. Half-hour tours are given at noon Tuesday, Wednesday, and Thursday. This is also the headquarters of the Bahamas National Trust. ⊠ *Village Rd.,* ☎ *242/393– 1317.* ☜ *$2.* ☉ *Weekdays 9–5.*

㉓ St. Augustine's Monastery. This Romanesque home of the Bahamas' Benedictine brothers was built in 1946 by a monk named Father Jerome, who is also famed for his carvings of the Stations of the Cross on Cat Island's Mt. Alvernia, the highest point (206 ft) in the Bahamas. He is buried there, at the top of the mountain, in a hermitage that he built. The St. Augustine buildings overlook beautiful gardens, and the monks will be pleased to give you a tour of their home—including their own bakery, where you can buy their homemade guava jelly. ⊠ *Fox Hill Rd.*

Western New Providence and South Coast

Starting from downtown Nassau, West Bay Street follows the coast west past the glamorous resorts and classy residential neighborhoods of Cable Beach, then past popular Love Beach to Northwest Point. Just beyond is Lyford Cay, the most exclusive residential area on the island. Old-money pioneers started settling the cay four decades ago, and along with its 200-odd houses there is a private golf course for residents. Your experience of Lyford Cay is likely to be voyeuristic at best—an entrance gate wards off all but residents and friends.

Much of the interior and southwestern coast of New Providence is undeveloped, and the coastal scenery and long, low stretches of palmetto and pine forest are picturesque. The loop around the west and south coasts of the island can be done in a couple of hours by car or scooter; however, you'll probably prefer to take time out for lunch and a swim along the way.

Sights to See

㉞ Adelaide Village. This small community on the southwest coast of New Providence sits almost on the ocean. It was first settled during the early 1800s by blacks who had been captured in their African homes and loaded aboard slave ships bound for the New World. They were rescued on the high seas by the British Royal Navy. The first group of liberated slaves reached Nassau in 1832. Today, only a few dozen families live in Adelaide. They raise vegetables and chickens and inhabit well-worn, pastel-painted wooden houses, sheltered in bougainvillea and other vegetation. The village has a primary school, some little grocery stores, and a tiny bar. On the beach, you might find a patient old man huddled over a table with conch shells for sale. He is rarely disturbed, for few tourists come this way. ⊠ *Southwest Rd.*

28 Arawak Cay. Known to locals as "The Fish Fry," Arawak Cay is one of the best places to get a delicious bite of a Bahamian delicacy, knock back a locally brewed Kalik beer, chat with the locals, or play a game of dominoes. Pastel-color shacks, many of which have long outworn the name, line the perimeter of the large fairgrounds. No trip to the islands would be complete without a taste of conch. At Arawak Cay, take your pick of the vendors, and order up a cracked conch (beaten, breaded, and fried), fresh conch salad (diced with onions, cucumbers, and tomatoes in a lime marinade with a touch of bird pepper), or fried fish. Head to Goldies Enterprises on the western side and give his famous Sky Juice (a potent gin and coconut water concoction) a try.

To get to Arawak Cay, head west along Bay Street, follow the main road around the Best Western British Colonial Hotel, and continue west. Pass Western Esplanade beach on the north shore, then Fort Charlotte on the south side of the street, and the cay is on the north side of the T-junction of West Bay and Chippingham Road.

26 Ardastra Gardens and Zoo. The flamingo is the national bird of the Bahamas, and you'll see plenty of them at these gardens, renowned for the parade of pink, spindly legged, marching birds that perform daily at 11, 2, and 4. The 5 acres of tropical greenery and flowering shrubs also include an aviary of rare tropical birds, tame boa constrictors, and other exotic animals from different parts of the world. ⊠ *Near Ft. Charlotte and Chippingham Rd.,* ☎ *242/323–5806.* ⊠ *$10.* ⊙ *Daily 9–4:30.*

35 Bacardi Distillery. Visitors are welcome to tour this facility, established in 1962, and sample a range of its well-known rum products at the Visitors Pavilion. Reservations are recommended for tours. ⊠ *Bacardi and Carmichael Rds.,* ☎ *242/362–1412.* ⊠ *Free.* ⊙ *Mon.–Thurs. 9:30– 4, Fri. 9:30–3.*

31 The Caves. Large limestone caverns that the waves have sculpted over the aeons are said to have sheltered the early Arawak Indians. Just beyond the caves is **Conference Corner,** where President John F. Kennedy, Canadian Prime Minister John Diefenbaker, and British Prime Minister Harold MacMillan planted trees to commemorate their summit meeting in Nassau in 1962. ⊠ *W. Bay St. and Blake Rd.*

33 Commonwealth Brewery. Kalik, Nassau's own tasty beer, is brewed here. The local beverage has become so popular that it has lent its name to a lilting chant sung during the Junkanoo parades. Free tours, which include a tasting, are available by appointment only. ⊠ *Clifton Pier and Southwest Rd.,* ☎ *242/362–4789.*

29 Crystal Cay. To say that you can't miss Crystal Cay (it used to be called Coral Island) is an understatement. Its Observation Tower soars 100 ft above the surface of the ocean. This 16-acre marine extravaganza occupies the entire island, which is linked to Arawak Cay and the mainland by a bridge. You can descend a winding staircase to a depth of 20 ft below the water's surface to observe denizens of the deep, such as turtles, stingrays, moray eels, and starfish. The tower has two viewing decks and a gift shop. In the adjacent **Marine Park,** the Reef Tank is the world's largest man-made living reef, where you have a 360-degree view of coral, sponges, tropical fish, and other forms of sea life. At the nearby Shark Tank, predators native to the Caribbean can be observed both from an overhead deck and from windows around the tank. All together, the Marine Gardens Aquarium has 24 aquariums that tell the story of life on the reef. You can also enjoy nature trails with tropical foliage, waterfalls, and exotic trees. Flamingos occupy another area of the park. Shark, turtle, and other feeding times are announced daily. The boat to Coral Island shuttles visitors between Woodes Rogers Dock (near the Straw Market) in downtown Nassau and Silver Cay three times daily, except Thursdays. ⊠ *Silver Cay,* ☎ *242/328–1036.* ▨ *$16.* ⊘ *Mon.–Sat. 9–5:30.*

★ ③⓪ **Crystal Palace Casino.** You can try your luck at baccarat, blackjack, roulette, craps, and Caribbean stud poker or simply settle for the slots—there's plenty to keep you entertained in the Caribbean's largest casino, including a sports book where you can place bets on all your favorite sports—professional and collegiate. When you've had enough gaming, stroll through the shopping mall that connects the casino with the Radisson Cable Beach Hotel. Display cases on the upper level exhibit very good examples of Junkanoo art, the Bahamian craft that comes into play during the lavish Boxing Day and New Year's Day festivities. ⊠ *Nassau Marriott Resort, Cable Beach, Nassau,* ☎ *242/327–6200.* ⊘ *Daily, tables 9 AM–4 AM, slots 24 hrs.*

★ ②⑤ **Fort Charlotte.** This imposing fort was built during the late 18th century and comes complete with a waterless moat, drawbridge, ramparts, and dungeons. Lord Dunmore, the builder, named the massive structure in honor of George III's wife. At the time, some called it Dunmore's Folly because of the staggering expense of building it—which came to eight times more than was originally planned. (Dunmore's superiors in London were less than ecstatic when they saw the bills, but he managed to survive unscathed.) Ironically, no shots were ever fired in anger from the fort. It is about 1 mi west of central Nassau. ⊠ *W. Bay St. at Chippingham Rd.* ▨ *Free.* ⊘ *Local guides conduct tours daily 8–4.*

③② **Love Beach Colony.** Near the northwest corner of New Providence, one of the loveliest stretches of beach on the island is lined with expensive private homes. On the side of the road, you'll notice a sign for music lessons; local celebrity and guitarist Chris Fox offers instruction for $15 an hour from his Love Beach home. Farther up the road, a partially hidden pink house named Capricorn is owned by singer Julio Iglesias. About 1 mi off Love Beach are 40 acres of coral and sea fan, with forests of fern, known as the **Sea Gardens.** The clear waters are a favorite with snorkelers. Glass-bottom boats with guides make frequent excursions to the Sea Gardens from Prince George Wharf. ▨ *Boat fare $10 per person.*

②⑦ **Nassau Botanic Gardens.** Six hundred species of flowering trees and shrubs, a small cactus garden, and two freshwater ponds with lilies, water plants, and tropical fish cover 18 acres. The many trails that wind through the gardens are perfect for leisurely strolls. The Botanic Gardens are across the street from Ardastra Gardens and Zoo (☞ *above*). ⊠ *Near Ft. Charlotte and Chippingham Rd.,* ☎ *242/323–5975.* ▨ *$1.* ⊘ *Weekdays 8–4:30.*

BEACHES

New Providence is blessed with stretches of white sand studded with palm and sea-grape trees. Some of the beaches are small and crescent shape, while others stretch for miles. Right in downtown Nassau, you'll find the **Western Esplanade.** It sweeps west from the British Colonial Hotel on Bay Street, and has rest rooms, a snack bar, and changing facilities. Just past the bridge that leads to Coral Island is **Saunders Beach,** a popular weekend rendezvous spot for locals. On Paradise Island, **Paradise Beach,** at the far western tip of the island, is an exquisite stretch of sand, with facilities, but you'll pay $3 for the privilege of getting your tan there. Three-mile-long **Cabbage Beach** rims the entire north coast of Paradise Island. It begins at the Atlantis, Paradise Island, lagoon and continues to Snorkelers Cove.

Cable Beach, so-named because it is the location of the first telephone cable connecting the Bahamas to Florida, is on the north shore of New Providence about 3 mi west of downtown Nassau. Luxury resorts line much of this beautiful, broad swath of white sand, and there is public access. Just west of Cable Beach is a rambling pink house on the Rock Point promontory, where much of the 1965 Bond film *Thunderball* was filmed. Tiny, crescent-shape **Caves Beach** is beyond Cable Beach on the north shore, about 7 mi from downtown just before the turnoff on Blake Road that leads to the airport. **Love Beach** is a snorkeler's favorite, on the north shore beyond Caves Beach, about 20 minutes from town. It's technically the domain of Love Beach residents, but they aren't inclined to shoo away anyone. On the south shore, drive down to **Adelaide Beach,** at the end of Adelaide Village, for sand that stretches down to Coral Harbour. The people who live at the east end of the island tend to flock to **South Beach,** at the foot of Blue Hill Road on the south shore.

DINING

Over the past few years, with the escalation of Bahamian tourism and the subsequent growth of Cable Beach and Paradise Island hotels and their in-house restaurants, the preparation of meals at the better dining spots has become as sophisticated as you'll find in any leading U.S. city. European chefs brought in by the top restaurants on the island have trained young Bahamians in the skills of fine cuisine. Artfully prepared dishes with delicate sauces incorporate local seafood. Gourmet French, Chinese, Indian, Mexican, Creole, Northern Italian, and Polynesian fare have also become available on menus. Fish is often the most economical dining choice, because meats often have to be imported from the United States.

You can still get traditional Bahamian fare—peas 'n' rice, conch (chowder, fritters, and cracked), Bahamian lobster (crayfish), "stew" or "boil" fish, freshly caught red snapper, grouper fingers, and for dessert guava duff—at more than two dozen restaurants around Nassau and its environs, and it would be a shame not to try some native dishes in local restaurants. Island chefs, banded together in the Bahamian Culinary Association, have also developed a new Bahamian cuisine. This innovative cooking style relies on local products not generally used before, such as coconut, tamarind, wild spinach, and a pepper-sour sauce made of limes and red-hot bird peppers. The chefs have even come up with something new to do with conch, the popular national shellfish: The red parts of fresh conch are sliced very thin, dipped in a special sauce, and—voilà—conch sushi!

Following the trend that is sweeping the Caribbean, many of the Cable Beach and Paradise Island resorts are offering special package rates—including meals. The advantage is, of course, that you know up front exactly what your vacation will cost, with no surprises upon checkout or back home when the credit-card bill arrives. A disadvantage is that you feel tied to your resort at mealtime. With its 12 restaurants serving as many kinds of cuisines, Atlantis, Paradise Island, offers meal plans where guests and nonguests alike can dine at various venues for $42–$69 per person per day, or $99 per day for a family of four—a significant savings.

CATEGORY	COST*
$$$$	over $30
$$$	$20–$30
$$	$15–$20
$	under $15

per person for a three-course meal, excluding drinks and 15% gratuity

Nassau

$$$$ ✗ **Buena Vista.** High on a hill above Nassau's harbor, this serene
★   restaurant sits secure in its reputation as one of Nassau's dining institutions, and draws a loyal local clientele. Open for nearly 30 years, it occupies what was once a rambling private home built in the early 1800s. Tuxedoed waiters serve guests at tables laid with china, crystal, and silver; a pianist who can sing in five languages serenades diners nightly with show tunes and ballads. You can sit in the main dining room, the more intimate Victoria Room, or the Garden Patio room with its enclosed greenhouse setting and enormous ceiling skylight. The menu features Continental cuisine and Bahamian seafood specialties. You may want to begin with escargot or cream of garlic soup; exemplary entrées include grouper à la Bimini, and fillet of Dover sole simmered in white wine, cream, and mustard sauce and topped with shrimp. Be sure to leave room for cherry cheesecake or for Mrs. Hauck's Orange Pancakes, a house specialty crepe dessert since it was created in 1946 by Buena Vista's original owner. ⊠ *W. Hill and Delancy Sts., Nassau,* ☎ *242/322–2811. AE, DC, MC, V. No lunch.*

$$$$ ✗ **Graycliff.** Located in a mid-18th-century Colonial mansion that
★   was once the private home of a pirate, this magnificent restaurant has seven dining areas—among them the original dining room with a chandelier and an impressive mahogany table, the original library which overlooks the garden, and an outdoor dining section. Period furniture, French doors, soft piano music, and solicitous service set the mood for European cuisine with a Bahamian touch. Consider the cold appetizer called Chiffonade Tiède: smoked goose, wild boar pâté, pickled papaya, thinly sliced truffles, and Bahamian chilies in coriander sauce. Other dishes on the menu are just as unusual. Kings, celebrities, and other rich and famous patrons frequent Graycliff. Don't be surprised, then, that dinner for two might easily cost $300, not including wine. (Owner Enrico Garzaroli values his wine collection—which he keeps in a cellar underneath the building—at over $8 million. The more than 175,000 bottles are a sight worth seeing, and a trip to the cellar can likely be arranged if you ask in advance.) The ambience may justify the prices, but the food, while excellent, is not as consistently superb as it once was. ⊠ *W. Hill St. at Cumberland Rd., Nassau,* ☎ *242/322–2796. AE, DC, MC, V.*

$$$$ ✗ **Sun And . . .** All the superlatives have long been exhausted for this
★   culinary oasis, generally dubbed the best restaurant in Nassau. You're sure to see Bahamian moguls wining and dining their clients here; and if you came to Nassau hoping to catch sight of an international superstar, this is the place to look. Crossing the drawbridge of the converted 19th-century estate brings you to an enclosed garden area, with its rock pool and fountain, where you dine under the stars. Try the roast rack of spring lamb for two, braised duckling with raspberry sauce, or sautéed grouper in puff pastry. Keep in mind while feasting, though, that you'll be denying yourself heaven if you don't follow with one of Belgian owner-chef Ronnie Deryckere's six incomparable soufflés, which range from almond amaretto to guava. The restaurant is nearly impossible to find by accident and almost as difficult to find with directions, so take a taxi or bring a map. ⊠ *Lakeview Rd. and E. Shirley*

New Providence Dining

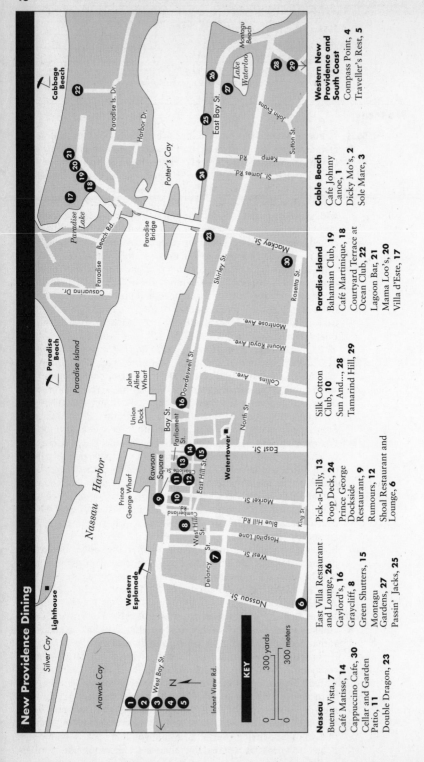

KEY

300 yards
300 meters

Silver Cay

Arawak Cay

Lighthouse

Nassau Harbor

Western Esplanade

Paradise Beach

Paradise Island

Cabbage Beach

Prince George Wharf

Union Dock

John Alfred Wharf

Rawson Square

Paradise Lake

Paradise Bridge

Potter's Cay

Lake Waterloo

Montagu Beach

West Bay St.

Infant View Rd.

Nassau St.

Delancy St.

West St.

West Hill St.

Hospital Lane

Blue Hill Rd.

Cumberland Rd

Market St.

King St.

Parliament St.

Charlotte St.

East Hill St.

Bay St.

East St.

North St.

Collins Ave.

Mount Royal Ave.

Montrose Ave.

Shirley St.

Mackey St.

Rosetta St.

Dowdeswell St.

Watertower

Casuarina Dr.

Paradise Beach Rd.

Paradise Is. Dr.

Harbor Dr.

East Bay St.

John Evans

Kemp Rd.

St. James Rd.

Sutton St.

Nassau
Buena Vista, **7**
Café Matisse, **14**
Cappuccino Cafe, **30**
Cellar and Garden Patio, **11**
Double Dragon, **23**

East Villa Restaurant and Lounge, **26**
Gaylord's, **16**
Graycliff, **8**
Green Shutters, **15**
Montagu Gardens, **27**
Passin' Jacks, **25**

Pick-a-Dilly, **13**
Poop Deck, **24**
Prince George Dockside Restaurant, **9**
Rumours, **12**
Shoal Restaurant and Lounge, **6**

Silk Cotton Club, **10**
Sun And..., **28**
Tamarind Hill, **29**

Paradise Island
Bahamian Club, **19**
Café Martinique, **18**
Courtyard Terrace at Ocean Club, **22**
Lagoon Bar, **21**
Mama Loo's, **20**
Villa d'Este, **17**

Cable Beach
Café Johnny Canoe, **1**
Dicky Mo's, **2**
Sole Mare, **3**

Western New Providence and South Coast
Compass Point, **4**
Traveller's Rest, **5**

St., Nassau, ☎ *242/393–1205. AE, D, MC, V. Closed Aug., Sept., and Mon. No lunch.*

$$$ ✕ **Café Matisse.** The walls of this mostly Italian restaurant are, as you might expect, hung with the works of its namesake French painter. Consider starting with thin slices of veal with tuna and caper sauce, then dive into risotto with mushrooms, or scallops on a bed of spinach with ginger and shallots, or roasted lobster with green cabbage. The pasta is all freshly made, and you'll find five varieties of pizza on the menu, including one topped with local seafood. Dress up for dinner and choose a candlelit table inside or dine alfresco in the ground-floor garden. Cigar smokers gravitate to the second-floor veranda. The small tables here also draw people for after-dinner drinks. There is a daily happy hour from 5 to 7. ✉ *Bank La. and Bay St., behind Parliament Sq.,* ☎ *242/356–7012. AE, D, MC, V. Closed Sun.*

$$$ ✕ **Cellar and Garden Patio.** You'll find two different dining experiences here, depending on your preference to eat inside among more traditional surroundings or outside on a covered patio encircled with greenery. In the alfresco locale, lazily rotating ceiling fans are suspended from beams of white latticework. The subdued indoor dining room has Bahamian decor with varnished wood tables and bar. Seafood is the specialty, with a menu that features conch chowder, grouper, lobster tail, grilled snapper, and cracked conch. Other items, which especially appeal to the local lunchtime business crowd, include quiches and roast-beef sandwiches. ✉ *2 Charlotte St., at Bay St., Nassau,* ☎ *242/ 322–8877. AE, MC, V. Closed Sun.*

$$$ ✕ **East Villa Restaurant and Lounge.** This dimly lit restaurant, elegantly appointed with Chinese statuettes and aquariums awash with exotic fish, has become quite a success since it opened in 1991. The Chinese-Continental menu includes such luscious entrées as Canton lobster, *hung shew* (walnut chicken), and steak *kew* (cubed prime fillet served with baby corn, snow peas, water chestnuts, and choice vegetables). Local sentiment is that the lamb chops are otherworldly. Spicy Szechuan and Mandarin specialties can be ordered mild, medium, or hot. A short taxi ride from Paradise Island or downtown Nassau, this is perfect if you're seeking something a little different. ✉ *E. Bay St. near Nassau Yacht Club, Nassau,* ☎ *242/393–3377. AE, MC, V.*

$$$ ✕ **Gaylord's.** In late 1995 Nassau's culinary scene got a lot spicier with the opening of this Indian restaurant. In a handsome historic building that dates back to the 1870s and was once a private home, decorative plates, sculpture, and other Indian works of art are attractively displayed around the two dining areas, and draped silk adorns ceilings. Whet your appetite with a Gaylord Special, a cocktail made from tropical juice and rum, then tuck into the tandoori chicken, vegetable curry, or a *roti* (nan bread stuffed with chicken or minced lamb). Dishes are seasoned from mild to hot, according to your tolerance of fire. ✉ *Dowdeswell and Bay Sts.,* ☎ *242/356–3004. AE, MC, V. No lunch weekends.*

$$$ ✕ **Montagu Gardens.** Certified 100% Angus beef and fresh native seafood—flame-grilled and seasoned with home-mixed spices—are the specialties at this romantic restaurant. Located in an old Bahamian mansion on Lake Waterloo, the dining room is surrounded by a walled courtyard and lovely gardens. Besides steak and seafood, menu selections include chicken, lamb, lobster, pasta, and ribs. A favorite dessert is Mud Pie. Excellent service adds a fine touch to the dining experience. Montagu Gardens is next door to Club Waterloo, one of the town's trendy nightspots, making the restaurant a popular place to eat before going next door to boogie off those calories. ✉ *E. Bay St., 1 mi east of Paradise Bridge,* ☎ *242/394–6347. AE, MC, V. Closed Sun.*

$$$ ✕ **Silk Cotton Club.** Featuring live music several nights a week—mellow jazz standards, bebop, and blues set the tone—this is one of Nas-

sau's newest and liveliest places to dine. House specialties include French bread served with roasted garlic and olive oil, chicken breast in cream-and-wine sauce, pasta primavera, and, for dessert, Bahamian guava duff. On Fridays and Saturdays, when the bar is busiest, an after-hours light menu is available. ⊠ *Market St. near Bay St. Straw Market,* ☏ *242/356–0955. MC, V. Closed Sun. and Mon. No lunch.*

$$ ✕ **Green Shutters.** Shades of Fleet Street! In a Bahamian house dating from 1782 just two blocks south of Bay Street, this British-style pub is a cozy wood-paneled hangout, popular with locals. Traditional English fare—bangers and mash, fish-and-chips, shepherd's pie, and steak-and-kidney pie—shares the menu with island favorites such as cracked conch and Bahamian crayfish tail. Beer on draught is imported directly from England. ⊠ *48 Parliament St.,* ☏ *242/325–5702. AE, MC, V. Closed Sun.*

$$ ✕ **Pick-a-Dilly.** You might just stumble on this festive eatery while strolling downtown. The best time to stop in is late afternoon, when the outdoor Daiquiri Bar is jumping and the Schizos (half-banana, half-strawberry daiquiris) are flowing. Drinks and free hors d'oeuvres whet your appetite for the tasty dinner fare you'll find here. The restaurant, part of a bed-and-breakfast owned by Bill and Jennifer Stack, serves zesty specialties that include fresh fish, pasta, burgers, and sandwiches. There is live music some weekends. ⊠ *18 Parliament St., at Bay St.,* ☏ *242/322–2836. Reservations not accepted. AE, MC, V. Closed Sun.*

$$ ✕ **Poop Deck.** Coiled rope wraps around beams and railings, life pre-
★ servers hang on walls, and port and starboard lights adorn the newel posts of this favorite haunt of Nassau residents. The restaurant is located a quick eight-minute cab ride from the center of town just east of the Paradise Island bridge. Tables on the large waterfront deck have a beautiful view of the harbor and bridge. Excellent Bahamian-style seafood, along with friendly service and a comfortable atmosphere, keeps regulars coming back. Expect spicy dishes with names like Mary's grouper and Rosie's chicken, and an extensive wine list. Save room for guava duff, that warm, layered Bahamian assemblage, and a calypso coffee spiked with secret ingredients. ⊠ *E. Bay St. near Nassau Yacht Haven Marina, ¼ mi east of bridge,* ☏ *242/393–8175. AE, MC, V.*

$$ ✕ **Prince George Dockside Restaurant.** Besides location, this Bay Street restaurant has the advantage of a very diverse menu—the Italian, Bahamian, Greek, and American entrées are all tasty and filling, though some have a bit more zing than others. Broiled shrimp stuffed with crabmeat is a winner, as is the devilishly indulgent guava duff. Prices vary as much as the cuisine: generally, it is worth it to spend a little more. You can dine inside amidst potted palm trees or on the spacious terra-cotta patio with a partial view of Prince George Wharf. ⊠ *Bay St. west of Rawson Sq.,* ☏ *242/322–5854. AE, MC, V. Closed Sun.*

$$ ✕ **Rumours.** Mahogany, brass, and polished high-back chairs gleam at this spacious new restaurant and wine bar. The food is mainly Bahamian, featuring staples such as cracked conch and grouper fingers. You'll also find old reliables like shrimp scampi, steak, burgers, and sandwiches. See if you can get the bartender to divulge the secret ingredients in a Rumours Delight, the house special—it's green! This dining spot is another Nassau addition that attracts cigar aficionados. ⊠ *Charlotte and Bay Sts.,* ☏ *242/323–2925. AE, D, MC, V.*

$$ ✕ **Tamarind Hill.** Colorful, primitive Caribbean paintings and murals, indoor and outdoor dining, and a guitar duo on weekends create a casual island atmosphere. The food is excellent and reasonable. Homemade soups are a specialty, along with pastas and fresh seafood. Try the warm chicken breast salad with raspberry dressing, grouper marinated in ginger-lime cream, or gourmet vegetarian pizza. ⊠ *Village Rd. near Shirley St.,* ☏ *242/393–1306. AE, MC, V. No lunch.*

$ ✕ **Cappuccino Cafe.** This deli and specialty shop lies a little off the beaten tourist path, but it's the perfect port of call for those who wish to see a bit of "real" Nassau. There are clutches of indoor and outdoor tables at which to enjoy a frothy cappuccino, and a fountain burbles in the corner. Classical music harmonizes nicely with the red-and-white, European-style decor. Try the sophisticated sandwiches made with top-quality Angus beef, smoked salmon, and fine cheeses; peruse liquors, chocolates, teas, and coffees ranging from the superior to the obscure; or order one of the exquisitely prepared picnic baskets. Just give the staff a few hours' notice, and they'll accommodate with a feast to go. The café is open from brunch through Happy Hour. ⊠ *Royal Palm Mall, Mackey St.,* ☎ *242/394–6332. AE, MC, V. Closed Sun.*

$ ✕ **Double Dragon.** Come to this informal haunt for its array of Cantonese, Hunan, Szechuan, and Mandarin dishes. Try chicken with black bean sauce or, if you like it hot, shredded beef Szechuan style. Or go for the chef's specialties: shrimp and scallops or honey-garlic chicken. Delivery is free in the downtown area with a $20 purchase. ⊠ *Bridge Plaza Commons, Mackey St., on the Nassau side of Paradise Bridge,* ☎ *242/393–5718. AE, MC, V. No lunch weekends.*

$ ✕ **Passin' Jacks.** On the top floor of the Nassau Harbour Club, this semicircular restaurant with a wraparound porch affords a stunning view of the passing parade of harbor traffic. Generous portions of Bahamian favorites—cracked conch, peas 'n' rice, and fresh broiled grouper—at reasonable prices make this a local favorite. There are also burgers, salads, fajitas, and a children's menu. ⊠ *E. Bay St., ½ mi east of Paradise Bridge, Nassau,* ☎ *242/394–3245. AE, MC, V.*

$ ✕ **Shoal Restaurant and Lounge.** Saturday morning at 9, you'll find hordes of hungry Bahamians digging into boiled fish and johnnycake, the specialty of the house. A bowl of this peppery local dish, filled with chunks of boiled potatoes, onions, and grouper, may keep you coming back to this dimly lit, basic, and off-the-tourist-beat "Ma's kitchen," where standard Bahamian dishes, including peas 'n' rice and cracked conch, are staples. Mutton can be hard to find locally, but if it suits your taste buds, you'll find it here, curried. ⊠ *Nassau St. between Meadow St. and Poinciana Dr.,* ☎ *242/323–4400. AE, MC, V.*

Paradise Island

$$$$ ✕ **Bahamian Club.** A clubby British atmosphere prevails in this dimly
★ lit restaurant, where walls are lined with dark oak and overstuffed chairs and banquettes are upholstered in leather. Impeccable table-side service heightens the enjoyment. Starters include Dungeness crab cakes or a selection from the raw bar. Meat is the specialty of the house—grilled T-bone steak, veal chop, roast prime rib, and chateaubriand for two—but that is no reason to avoid the rest of the menu. Grilled swordfish steak, yellowfin tuna, salmon fillet, and other fresh seafood dishes are all prepared with finesse. And do leave room for a piece of homemade pecan pie with bourbon caramel sauce. Dinner is accompanied by soft piano music; between courses, couples can share a waltz on the small dance floor. ⊠ *Atlantis, Paradise Island,* ☎ *242/363–3000, ext. 6508. AE, DC, MC, V. No lunch.*

$$$$ ✕ **Café Martinique.** Limestone walls and huge etched-glass windows
★ that overlook a lagoon distinguish the fin de siècle setting of this renowned, elegant, very romantic restaurant. Plan on a leisurely meal, but if you are short on time, the accommodating staff can hasten the process a bit. The classic French cuisine and innovative seafood specialties are consistently above average, but not all things on the menu are equal. The escargots bourguignonne, chilled melon soup with champagne, and Caesar salad (prepared table-side) are especially good

beginnings. Both roasted rack of lamb with assorted vegetables and duckling à l'orange are skillfully assembled and presented. Café Martinique's Soufflés are out of this world, but you must order them before your main course as they take an hour to prepare. Try the soufflé Arlequin: half chocolate, half Grand Marnier, and all heaven. Sunday brunch is also exceptional. ⊠ *Atlantis, Paradise Island,* ☎ *242/363–3000. Reservations essential. Jacket required. AE, DC, MC, V. Closed Sun. No lunch.*

$$$$ ✕ **Courtyard Terrace at Ocean Club.** An elite clientele congregates here
★ to indulge in refined dining under the stars, accompanied by the music of a calypso combo. With its Wedgwood place settings, Irish linen napery, lighted fountains, and adjacent sculpture gallery, this is one of the most romantic garden settings in the Bahamas. The varied treats of a carefully orchestrated menu emphasize the lighter side of Continental cuisine. Sample the grilled Muscovy duck breast with raspberry coulis, free-range chicken with crab hash and two-color bell pepper sauce, or indulge in chateaubriand for two. Alfresco dining begins at twilight, and if the weather doesn't cooperate, dinner is served indoors. Service is superb. ⊠ *Ocean Club,* ☎ *242/363–2501. Reservations essential. Jacket required. AE, DC, MC, V. No lunch.*

$$$$ ✕ **Mama Loo's.** Caribbean-Chinese delights are the order of the evening at this dinner-only restaurant in Atlantis. The intimate dining room is done in an *Out of Africa* motif, with torchlight chandeliers, rattan wingback chairs, and island artwork with a jungle theme. Go Chinese and pick seafood stir-fry, crispy fish, cashew chicken, or Hong Kong orange beef; opt for Caribbean and choose Jamaican jerk pork tenderloin, *bifteck* (steak) à la Creole, or shrimp curry. For dessert, pineapple spring rolls with rum crème anglaise are a tease. ⊠ *Atlantis, Paradise Island,* ☎ *242/363–3000. AE, MC, V. Closed Mon. No lunch.*

$$$ ✕ **Villa d'Este.** Noble Italian cuisine is graciously served in a trendy trattoria setting, accompanied by classical guitar music. The room is attractively appointed with dark wood, upholstered chairs, and an impressive fresco on the ceiling. The antipasto display is effective in whetting the appetite for such dishes as baked grouper with a pine-nut crust, fettuccine with tomato and crabmeat, or veal saltimbocca—and lobster ravioli deserves honorable mention. Follow up with dessert pastries if the spirit takes you. ⊠ *Atlantis, Paradise Island,* ☎ *242/363–3000. AE, DC, MC, V. No lunch.*

$$ ✕ **Lagoon Bar.** One of the concepts behind the Atlantis resort is to "bring the water into the hotel," and nowhere is that more exemplified than at this restaurant—to reach the open-air, gazebo-style dining terrace you walk through an underwater glass tunnel running directly beneath the Predator Lagoon, where the sight of sharks looming above your head may make you hurry toward your own food. Clam chowder, salads, fresh shellfish, and deli sandwiches are staples on the limited menu. ⊠ *Atlantis, Paradise Island,* ☎ *242/363–3000. AE, MC, V.*

Cable Beach

$$$$ ✕ **Sole Mare.** The combination of fine food, excellent service, elegant
★ decor, and a lovely view make this classy Italian restaurant on the second floor of the Casino Tower a delight. Start off with a selection of imported meats and cheeses from the antipasti cart. Pasta, with usual and unusual sauces and fresh pecorino Romano cheese grated tableside, is offered in half or full portions. Entrées include tender veal scallopini alla marsala, grilled tenderloin of beef with green peppercorn sauce, lobster *fra diavolo,* and several other delicious possibilities. Leave room for dessert (tiramisu, anyone?) and a cup of espresso. ⊠

Nassau Marriott Resort & Crystal Palace Casino, Cable Beach, ☎ 242/
327–6200, ext. 6861. AE, MC, V. Closed Mon. No lunch.

$$$ ✕ **Dicky Mo's.** The nautical decor lets you know that seafood is the
star of the show at this Bahamian restaurant, one of Cable Beach's
newest. With fishnets, glass buoys, and portholes, the indoor dining
area resembles a ship—or you can dine outside. Popular menu items
include conch fritters and conch chowder, stone crab claws, broiled or
panfried grouper, minced lobster (cooked with herbs and spices in a
tomato sauce), and a seafood platter (fried in a light tempura batter).
Friendly staff and the live Bahamian music (every night except Mon-
day) create a festive atmosphere. ✉ *Next to the Radisson Cable Beach
Casino & Golf Resort.* ☎ 242/327–7854. AE, MC, V.

$ ✕ **Cafe Johnny Canoe.** This crowded restaurant gets its name from Ba-
hamian folklore. Johnny Canoe is said to be the name of the first black
man to set foot on the island after slavery was abolished. His name is
the supposed origin of "Junkanoo," and a mini-Junkanoo show winds
among the tables on weekend nights year-round. With a spacious out-
door seating area and a menu of traditional Bahamian fare—cracked
conch and grouper fillet—as well as burgers, chicken, ribs, and trop-
ical drinks, this has become a favorite casual night out for locals and
tourists. Conch salad—a dish reputed to enhance a man's virility—is
a spicy way to start your meal, and grilled seafood entrées are also ex-
cellent. ✉ *Next to the Forte Nassau Beach Hotel,* ☎ 242/327–3373.
AE, MC, V.

Western New Providence and South Coast

$$$ ✕ **Compass Point.** The trendy restaurant at this cheery resort is a real
★ winner. The design and decor follow the Junkanoo and eco-friendly
themes of the village of cabanas and cottages that make up the resort.
Surf literally laps against the seawall that supports the outdoor dining
terrace, so the ocean view is unparalleled both day and night. And the
menu consists of a selection of appetizing food that mixes Bahamian,
Caribbean, and Californian cuisines. Light and satisfying jerk chicken
salad is a lunchtime treat—or opt for fresh fish, pasta, gourmet pizza,
or a steak sandwich. Dinner entrées include roasted Bahamian lobster
tail with Thai herbs, or rack of lamb with a guava-and-roasted-garlic
glaze. The wine list is extensive, and you can eat indoors or alfresco.
✉ *Compass Point Resort, W. Bay St., Gambier,* ☎ 242/327–4500. AE,
MC, V.

$$ ✕ **Traveller's Rest.** Traveller's has the reputation of serving some of
the best seafood on the island. This relaxed family restaurant with a
great ocean view opened in the early 1970s and is a favorite among
Bahamians. A fresh seafood dinner served just steps from the beach is
a real treat—conch, grouper, and crawfish are the big hitters. Dine out-
side or in, and toast the sunset with a fresh-fruit banana daiquiri—a
specialty of the house. Take-out service is available if you're on the road—
or prefer eating at the beach. ✉ *W. Bay St., Gambier,* ☎ 242/327–
7633. AE, MC, V.

LODGING

New Providence Island is fortunate to have an extensive range of ho-
tels, from quaint, family-owned guest houses, where you can rent a room
for $50 a night, to the megaresorts at Cable Beach and on Paradise
Island, which cater to the $175-a-night-and-up group.

The homey, friendly little spots will probably not be on the beach—
though the walk to the beach will rarely be far—and you'll have to go
out to eat unless you have access to a kitchen (in which case you'll have

no problem picking up groceries at one of the local supermarkets). On the flip side, your stay is likely to be relaxing, low-key, and less removed from everyday Bahamian life. The plush resorts are big and beautiful, glittering and splashy, or simply chic. In any case, these big, top-dollar properties generally offer more amenities than you expect, a selection of dining options, and a full roster of sports and entertainment. The battle for the tourist dollar rages unceasingly between Cable Beach and Paradise Island, where hotels are continually being developed and refurbished. All of this competition, of course, encourages the operators to offer a wide variety of vacation packages, with enticements such as free snorkeling gear, free scuba lessons, or free admission to a Las Vegas–style revue.

If you're trying to choose between Cable Beach and Paradise Island for accommodations, there is, in general, a broader choice of beaches on Paradise Island and a more intimate atmosphere in which to stroll around and explore attractions such as the Cloisters. Cable Beach hotels tend to be noisier and more active, and as a guest you are more likely to stick to you own hotel and beach; when you leave, it's usually to explore and shop in downtown Nassau.

A tax ranging from 8% to 10%, representing resort and government levies, is added to your hotel bill. Some hotels also add a gratuity charge of between $2.50 and $4 per person, per day, for the housekeeping or pool staff.

The prices below are based on high season (winter) rates. Expect to pay between 15% and 30% less off-season in most resorts. In general, the best rates are available through packages, which almost every hotel offers. Call the hotel directly or ask your travel agent.

CATEGORY	COST*
$$$	over $155
$$	$95–$155
$	under $95

All prices are for a standard double room during high season, excluding tax and service charge.

Nassau

$$$ ☒ **Graycliff.** This Georgian Colonial landmark, built over 250 years ago by a prosperous retired pirate named Captain John Howard Graysmith, sits on a small hill overlooking Nassau and the harbor. It was also the home of Lord Dunmore, the first governor of the Bahamas. Over the years, Graycliff has welcomed into its chambers the Duke and Duchess of Windsor, press baron Lord Beaverbrook, Aristotle Onassis, the Beatles, and King Olaf of Norway. Today, the small elegant hotel includes 12 guest suites—each huge and uniquely decorated with a combination of turn-of-the-century period pieces and modern amenities— and receives annual accolades from travel magazines. Thick terry robes, modern bathrooms, and bottles of springwater enhance guest comfort. The on-site gourmet restaurant of the same name (☞ Dining, *above*) is one of the premier places to dine on the island, and Continental breakfast is included in the room rate. Though the grounds are not large, they are enveloped in tropical foliage, with graceful palms, small statues of cherubs, and a circular fountain. Graycliff best suits those who enjoy excellent service and being immersed in a setting that exudes an ambience of a more genteel time, while remaining amid the bustle of downtown Nassau. ☒ *Box N 10246, W. Hill St.,* ☎ *242/322–2796 or 800/633–7411. 9 rooms, 5 suites. Restaurant, bar, pool, sauna, health club. AE, DC, MC, V.*

Nassau and Paradise Island Lodging

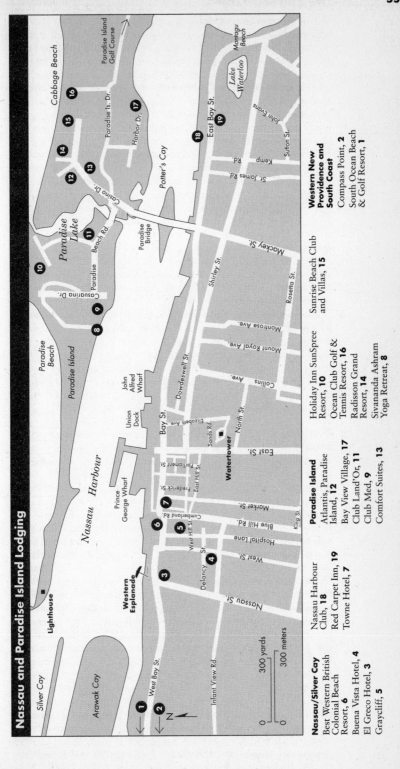

Silver Cay

Arawak Cay

Lighthouse

Nassau Harbour

Cabbage Beach

Paradise Island Golf Course

Montagu Beach

Lake Waterloo

Paradise Beach

Paradise Island

Paradise Lake

Potter's Cay

Paradise Bridge

John Alfred Wharf

Union Dock

Prince George Wharf

Western Esplanade

Watertower

West Bay St.

Infant View Rd.

Nassau St.

West St.

Delancy St.

Blue Hill Rd.

Hospital Lane

Cumberland Rd.

West Hill St.

Frederick St.

East Hill St.

Parliament St.

Bay St.

Market St.

King St.

East St.

Sands Rd.

Elizabeth Ave.

Dowdeswell St.

North St.

Collins Ave.

Mount Royal Ave.

Montrose Ave.

Shirley St.

Mackey St.

Rosetta St.

Sutton St.

Kemp Rd.

St. James Rd.

John Evans

East Bay St.

Casuarina Dr.

Paradise Beach Dr.

Casino Dr.

Harbor Dr.

Paradise Is. Dr.

0   300 yards
0   300 meters

Nassau/Silver Cay
Best Western British
Colonial Beach
Resort, **6**
Buena Vista Hotel, **4**
El Greco Hotel, **3**
Graycliff, **5**

Nassau Harbour
Club, **18**
Red Carpet Inn, **19**
Towne Hotel, **7**

Paradise Island
Atlantis, Paradise
Island, **12**
Bay View Village, **17**
Club Land'Or, **11**
Club Med, **9**
Comfort Suites, **13**

Holiday Inn SunSpree
Resort, **10**
Ocean Club Golf &
Tennis Resort, **16**
Radisson Grand
Resort, **14**
Sivananda Ashram
Yoga Retreat, **8**

Sunrise Beach Club
and Villas, **15**

**Western New
Providence and
South Coast**
Compass Point, **2**
South Ocean Beach
& Golf Resort, **1**

$$ ☑ **Best Western British Colonial Beach Resort.** This towering pink bastion was built in 1922 on the site of historic Fort Nassau—at separate times the home of Blackbeard the Pirate, American sailors, and the British Royal Navy. Today, there's a swimming pool and garden where the fort's lookout towers were. Situated on 8 beachfront acres in the heart of downtown Nassau, guests benefit from an in-town location—shopping, restaurants, and transportation are right at the front door—and the amenities of a tropical resort—gardens, a private beach, water sports, tennis, and a great harbor view are out the back. Accommodations in all categories are basically the same; the view determines price. Some rooms have an ocean view; others overlook bustling Bay Street and the Straw Market. The well-maintained beach is also a good place to watch cruise ships steam to and from Prince George Wharf. The Palm Patio Bar is a popular meeting place with an upbeat atmosphere. There's live Bahamian music on weekends, a Tropical Drink Tasting event, and other organized social activities. Value for the dollar is stressed. Nonmotorized water sports, such as sailing and windsurfing, are free to guests. Deep-sea fishing and scuba diving are available on-site. ☒ *Box N 7181, 1 Bay St., Nassau,* ☎ *242/322–3301 or 800/528–1234,* ℻ *242/322–2286. 219 rooms. 2 restaurants, lounge, pool, 3 tennis courts, basketball, volleyball, beach, snorkeling, windsurfing, boating, fishing. AE, D, DC, MC, V.*

$ ☑ **Buena Vista Hotel.** This agreeable 19th-century plantation house— its Spanish name means "fine view"—is set amid a beautiful 3-acre garden high on a hill, a half mile from downtown Nassau. The two-story building is better known as an elegant place to dine (☞ Dining, *above*) than as a spot to stay. The five guest rooms—each named after a tropical flower—are spacious and decorated with a contemporary sense of old-world charm. There is no pool; the public beach is a 10-minute walk away. ☒ *Box N 564, Delancy St., Nassau,* ☎ *242/322–2811,* ℻ *242/322–2286. 5 rooms. Restaurant, bar. AE, DC, MC, V.*

$ ☑ **El Greco Hotel.** Pleasant Greek owners create an ambience more in keeping with a cozy guest house than a hotel. The two-story, white-and-sand-color building is ideally located just minutes from the center of town. Rooms surround a central courtyard and pool and are decorated in a mélange of soothing, old-fashioned earth tones. The resulting atmosphere is quiet, and seems to appeal, primarily, to a European crowd. The on-site Vesuvio's restaurant serves Italian food. Across the street from the hotel are the public Western Esplanade beach and two popular nightclubs: Enigma, and Cocktails and Dreams. ☒ *Box N 4187, W. Bay St.,* ☎ *242/325–1121. 26 rooms. Restaurant, pool, baby-sitting. AE, MC, V.*

$ ☑ **Nassau Harbour Club.** Built in 1961 and long known for its two restaurants, which feed hungry mariners at all hours, this establishment is often mistakenly overlooked as a good place to sleep. Rooms have personal touches and are decorated in tropical pastels. Each has a white tile floor, and some offer a tiny balcony overlooking either the pool or the harbor. Locals and tourists alike gather at the downstairs Cudabay bar to watch big football games and sit outside on the deck overlooking the harbor. Up the spiral wooden staircase is Passin' Jack's, which serves Bahamian fare for breakfast, lunch, and dinner. Handily situated on the main road into town, the Harbour Club is popular with international sailing aficionados and the hordes of students on spring break who make it an annual base—all of which makes it, though a convenient place to stay, not one to seek for peace and quiet. ☒ *Box SS 5755, East Bay St., Nassau,* ☎ *242/393–0771,* ℻ *242/393–5393. 44 rooms, 16 2-bedroom suites. Restaurant, bar, pool, dock. AE, D, MC, V.*

$ ☑ **Red Carpet Inn.** This comfortable, modern hotel complex is far enough off the beaten path to provide a sense of island solitude, yet close enough to the action that you won't miss out on a thing. Opened in 1992, Red Carpet Inn has large, clean rooms with soft floral decor. The two two-story wings of rooms open up to a lush garden courtyard. Rooms in the eastern wing have large balconies or patios overlooking tropical fauna, and a few have kitchenettes with a microwave or stove and limited flatware. The Barn Bar and Restaurant serves Bahamian and American fare daily, as does the more casual, poolside El Rancho Restaurant and Bar. It's just a short walk to an upscale shopping center, and the sandy white beaches of Paradise Island are a quick taxi ride away. Rates remain the same year-round, and children under 12 accompanied by a parent stay free. ⊠ *Box SS 6233, East Bay St., Nassau,* ☎ *242/393–7981,* FAX *242/393–9055. 40 rooms. 2 restaurants, 2 bars, pool. AE, D, MC, V.*

$ 🏨 **Towne Hotel.** African parrots and white cockatoos in cages greet guests as they enter this pleasant, no-frills hostelry favored by business travelers, shoppers, and others who want to be only a block away from the heart of town. Rooms have cream-colored tile floors, pink-and-white Formica furniture, and ceiling fans. For families, five junior suites provide space for spreading out. The mostly American and Canadian clientele enjoys the roof sundeck, with a Ping-Pong table, and the Talking Stick Bar, where backgammon matches take place. There's a small pool and a nightly happy hour. ⊠ *Box N 4808, 40 George St.,* ☎ *242/322–8451,* FAX *242/328–1512. 46 rooms. Restaurant, bar, lounge, pool. AE, MC, V.*

Paradise Island

$$$ 🏨 **Atlantis, Paradise Island.** After $150 million worth of renovations,
★ and $375 million more on the horizon, Atlantis is trying to appeal to upscale families as a sort of theme-park-cum-resort-hotel. As its name implies, the overriding theme of this incredible property is water—for swimming, snorkeling, and observing marine life, as well as for mood and effect. All in all, more than 3.2 million gallons of seawater are recycled four times daily to maintain the resort's six exhibit lagoons, 100-plus species of tropical fish, and 800 ft of cascading waterfalls. Seagrapes Tunnel, a man-made replica of the island's coral caves, snakes through the property and permits an underwater view of the marine life that inhabits the lagoons. A 90-ft rope suspension bridge swings over the Predator Lagoon, which is home to sharks, barracuda, and stingrays in a natural environment. The River Ride is a ¼-mi man-made river in which you can wade, swim, or float on a tube as the artificial current takes you along. Most guest rooms at this huge resort are in either the Coral Towers or the Beach Tower. The Reef Club is a VIP section of 92 luxurious rooms with concierge service. Sixty-four more one-bedroom suites are located in four private low-rise "villas" facing the pool area. The aquatic theme extends to all the rooms, which are decorated in warm coral and sea-green colors. Camp Paradise is a supervised program that keeps the youngsters busy. A dine-around meal plan allows guests to eat breakfast and dinner at any of the resort's 12 restaurants. Numerous sporting activities are available, and there is plenty of nightlife on the premises: the Joker's Wild Comedy Club, the Atlantis Showroom, and the Sports Bar to name a few. An expansion project, scheduled to be completed by the spring of 1998, will add a hotel replicating ancient ruins, with six restaurants, three lounges, several intimate bars, and 2 million more gallons of saltwater fish habitats, freshwater pools, waterfalls, and rivers. ⊠ *Box N 4777, Nassau,* ☎ *242/363–3000,* FAX *242/363–3524. 1,147 rooms. 12 restaurants, 12 bars, 4 pools, beauty salon, 18-hole golf course, 9 tennis courts, health club, jogging, beach, snorkeling, windsurfing, boating, shops,*

*casino, nightclub, baby-sitting, children's programs, travel services, car
rental. AE, DC, MC, V.*

$$$ 🏨 **Bay View Village.** Guests socialize around three pools at this 4-acre
condominium resort, with lush tropical landscaping (including several
varieties of hibiscus and bougainvillea) and an intimate atmosphere.
Choose among one- and two-bedroom apartments and two- and three-
bedroom villas, all of which are spacious, clean, comfortable, and
equipped with satellite TV, hair dryers, and a full kitchen with a micro-
wave. All rooms have private balconies or garden terraces; penthouse
apartments have roof gardens and a view of the harbor. Units do not
have telephones, and there's no restaurant—only a poolside snack bar
and a minimarket. There's no private beach, but Cabbage Beach is only
a 10-minute walk away. If you prefer to ride, the casino shuttle costs
50¢ and will drop you off beachside. A golf course is 1½ mi away. ⊠
Box SS 6308, Nassau, ☎ *242/363–2555,* FAX *242/363–2370. 30 units
and villas. Bar, snack bar, kitchenettes, 3 pools, tennis court, baby-sit-
ting, coin laundry. AE, MC, V.*

$$$ 🏨 **Club Land'Or.** Translating to "land of gold," this three-story time-
share hotel has one-bedroom villas that include full kitchens, bathrooms
with shower, living rooms, and patios that overlook the lagoon, the
gardens, or the pool. The units are billed to accommodate four people, but they seem better suited to couples. The Blue Lagoon restaurant has a panoramic view of the island. There's also an attractive
courtyard on the premises. A variety of special guest activities are
planned throughout the week. ⊠ *Box SS 6429, Nassau,* ☎ *242/363–
2400. 72 rooms. 2 restaurants, 2 bars, pool, baby-sitting, laundry service. AE, DC, MC, V.*

$$$ 🏨 **Club Med.** The originators of the all-inclusive, don't-pay-anything-
after-you've-left-home concept have created another winner on this is-
land. When you stay here, literally everything but your drinks is
included in the price: all water sports, including windsurfing, snorkel-
ing, and sailing; golf lessons, a chipping green, and driving range; a
tennis program; water and land exercise classes; all meals at a choice
of three restaurants (with unlimited wine, beer, and soft drinks); and
a daily program of group activities led by a team of enthusiastic or-
ganizers. The 21-acre compound has a lush look, with meandering paths
bordered by swaying casuarina trees and graceful palms, a huge salt-
water swimming pool set within a Gothic garden, and long stretches
of green lawn. Half of the rooms were enlarged and renovated in 1996
with an art deco motif. The other no-frills rooms—with white cane fur-
niture and white tile floors—reflect the simplicity you'll find here.
Forget Club Med's "swinging singles" reputation: This village is pop-
ular with parents traveling without their kids (under 12s are not al-
lowed), honeymooners, and others over 25 years old—with an almost
even mix of couples and singles. In fact the only real swinging being
done here is on the 20 Har-Tru clay tennis courts, which are a big draw
at this resort; the 2½-hour intensive tennis clinics with optional video
analysis attract all levels of players. ⊠ *Box N 7137, Nassau,* ☎ *242/
363–2640 or 800/258–2633,* FAX *242/363–3496. 312 rooms. 3 restau-
rants, 2 bars, 2 saltwater pools, 19 tennis courts, beach, nightclub. AE,
MC, V.*

$$$ 🏨 **Comfort Suites.** This three-story pink-and-white hotel caters to hon-
eymooners with its competitively priced packages. The 222 cozy ju-
nior suites have sitting areas with sofa beds and are decorated in pinks,
blues, and whites, with ceiling fans and wildlife prints. All units have
coffeemakers, hair dryers, in-room safes, and minibars. New suites also
have refrigerators and microwaves. Guests can use pool and beach facilities, a health spa, tennis courts, and restaurant signing privileges at
Atlantis, Paradise Island, across the street. There's also free Continental

breakfast, a swim-up bar, and poolside lunch for those who want to stay on site. Three-mile-long Cabbage Beach is just a hop, skip, and jump away. Baby-sitting is available on property, and kids can enroll at Camp Paradise at Atlantis. ⊠ *Box SS 6202, Nassau,* ☎ *242/363–3680 or 800/228–5150,* FAX *242/363–2588. 222 junior suites. Restaurant. AE, D, DC, MC, V.*

$$$ 🏨 **Holiday Inn SunSpree Resort.** Situated in a woodsy setting on a crescent of private beach at Pirates Cove, this 17-story resort—the tallest in the Bahamas—offers reasonably priced accommodations and a number of special programs for families. The cheerfully modern rooms have deep turquoise, seashell pink, and mauve tropical decor. A 90-ft-long replica of the pirate ship *Bonny Anne* dominates the enormous pool area and serves as a pool bar. The free Captain Kid's Day Camp (ages 4–12) keeps children occupied, as does the Pirate's Den game room and video arcade. On the weekends, parents are given an opportunity to dine alone while kids enjoy special evening activities. Tennis tournaments, calisthenics, volleyball, and tugs-of-war are fun for the entire family. Offerings at the water-sports center (an independent concession) are comprehensive and include scuba-diving lessons, parasailing, and the use of aquatrikes. ⊠ *Box SS 6214, Nassau,* ☎ *242/363–2100 or 800/234–6835,* FAX *242/363–3386. 480 rooms, 85 suites. 3 restaurants, 2 bars, pool, 2 tennis courts, exercise room, beach, snorkeling, jet skiing, parasailing, baby-sitting, children's programs, travel services, car rental. AE, DC, MC, V.*

$$$ 🏨 **Ocean Club Golf & Tennis Resort.** Once the private hideaway of A&P
★ heir Huntington Hartford, and more recently the secluded Bahamian getaway of the rich and famous of the world, this resort provides the most understated elegance you'll find on Paradise Island. A quiet, tasteful mood is apparent in the lounge with its antique furniture, in the lovely courtyard and fountains, and in the 35-acre terraced Versailles Gardens and 14th-century French Cloister. The spacious and stylishly decorated rooms have private verandas, high ceilings, and a color scheme of soft green, peach, and gold. Each room is furnished with carved or hand-stenciled furniture, as well as a 27-inch TV. Luxurious marble bathrooms have double sinks, bidet, iron and ironing board, plush terry towels and robes. Both rooms and verandas have ceiling fans, which add a period look. The property's four suites and five two-bedroom villas each have an extra large bathtub. The Ocean Club resembles an exclusive country club, with manicured grounds, tennis courts, and crystal-clear pool. Shuttle service is available to the golf course. Guests lounging on the magnificent ocean beach are provided with small flags alongside their chaise longues to signal watchful waiters that they would like a drink or a snack. Luncheon is served at the Clubhouse and the Beach Bar and Grill. The open-air Courtyard Terrace is a particularly romantic dining spot in the evening, and the indoor restaurant is equally charming. ⊠ *Box N 4777, Ocean Club Dr., Nassau,* ☎ *242/363–2501 or 800/321–3000,* FAX *242/363–2424. 49 rooms, 5 villas and 4 suites. 3 restaurants, 3 bars, pool, 18-hole golf course, 9 tennis courts, beach, snorkeling, windsurfing, boating, baby-sitting, laundry service. AE, DC, MC, V.*

$$$ 🏨 **Radisson Grand Resort.** Besides being particularly magnificent (even by Bahamian standards), the stretch of beach on which this hotel sits provides easy access to the casino next door, as well as to secluded coves and forest trails. Since it's also very near the Paradise Island bridge, guests are only about a mile or so from restaurants and shops in Nassau proper. Every room overlooks the water from its own small triangular balcony and comes equipped with a minibar. Decor includes shades of muted gray, green-and-white-striped curtains, and tropical prints. Big spenders opt for the enormous Penthouse, with stained-glass

windows, a wraparound terrace, two Jacuzzis, and a price tag of $5,000 a night. Colorful island-motif murals add to the festive feeling around the pool, where a live combo plays Caribbean and pop tunes in the afternoons. Evening dining takes place at the elegant Rotisserie dining room, which overlooks the water and features everything from catch-of-the-day to hamburgers. Later, go to Le Paon, for dancing. In summer and during the Easter and Christmas holiday seasons, the Radisson's Activity Center organizes plenty of special events for children. A lending library and bicycle rentals are also available. ⊠ *Box SS 6307, Nassau,* ☎ *242/363–3500 or 800/325–3535,* FAX *242/363–3193. 360 rooms. 4 restaurants, 3 bars, lounge, pool, 4 tennis courts, beach, bicycles, nightclub, baby-sitting, meeting rooms, travel services. AE, DC, MC, V.*

$$ 🖫 **Sunrise Beach Club and Villas.** The privacy and charm of this re-
★ laxing, low-rise family resort lures its mostly European clientele back year after year. Set right on the beach, the property is lushly landscaped with coconut palms, fragrant bougainvillea, colorful hibiscus, and crotons. The gardeners behind the glorious flora are co-owners Heinrich Kloihofer and his son, Heinz-Robert, who is also the Austrian consul to the Bahamas. Two pools—one multilevel with a waterfall and covered grotto—sustain the ambience. What makes this resort so interesting, though, is the eclectic architectural mix: one-bedroom town houses with spiral staircases leading to an upstairs bedroom, two-bedroom apartments, and three-bedroom villas. All accommodations have a fully equipped kitchen or kitchenette, a king-size bed in the master bedroom with a ceiling-to-floor mirrored headboard, and a patio. Rooms are decorated in subdued tropical colors. On arrival, you will find complimentary breakfast groceries in the refrigerator, and you can take a shuttle to stores to shop for food. ⊠ *Box SS 6519, Nassau,* ☎ *242/363–2234 or 800/451–6078,* FAX *242/363–2308. 35 1-, 2-, and 3-bedroom units. Restaurant, bar, kitchenettes, 2 pools, baby-sitting, laundry service. AE, D, DC, MC, V.*

$ 🖫 **Sivananda Ashram Yoga Retreat.** Founded in 1967 as a yoga vacation spot, this retreat continues to hold its group meditations twice daily, its yoga breathing, relaxation, and exercise classes, and its workshops in various New-Age disciplines. Lodgings range from semiprivate accommodations in 35 cottages on the beach and in palm groves to dormitory-style rooms in the main building. Bringing your own tent and camping on the property at a reduced rate is another option. There is no pool, but the property borders on a pristine stretch of sandy beach. Most rooms and all washroom facilities are shared, and a rising bell wakes you at 5:30 AM. You are expected to maintain silence from 10 PM to 8 AM; nonvegetarian food, nonprescription drugs, alcohol, and tobacco are forbidden on the premises. Two vegetarian meals are served daily and are included in the rates. ⊠ *Box N 7550, Nassau,* ☎ *242/363–2902. 64 rooms. Restaurant. AE, MC, V.*

Cable Beach

$$$ 🖫 **Nassau Beach Hotel.** With a tasteful elegance and colonial style for which it has been known since it was built in the 1940s, this venerable Cable Beach mainstay exudes a cheerful, gracious air. Its three wings, painted Bahama pink with white trim, are set amidst 10 acres of gardens, fountains, and scenic walkways. The lobby and lounging areas are smart and welcoming, decorated in corals and greens with sofas and chairs arranged in cozy circular groupings. A talking parrot also sits in the lobby to greet guests and preen for attention. All rooms have balconies, but views vary: Some face the half-mile strip of sandy beach, while others overlook neighboring buildings. Mahogany furniture and print spreads in deep colors give rooms an elegant look. Guests have

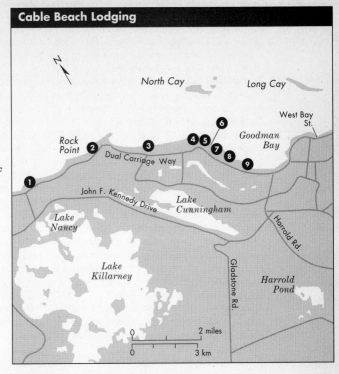

Cable Beach Lodging

use of all nonmotorized water-sports equipment, including Windsurfers, sailboats, paddleboats, and snorkeling equipment. Tennis clinics are available. Guests can opt for the all-inclusive Palm Club program, which includes all meals and drinks in the room rate. The hotel has a variety of indoor and outdoor restaurants on-site, as well as a shopping arcade. The Crystal Palace Casino is next door, and the Cable Beach Golf Course is across the street. ⊠ *Box N 7756, Nassau,* ☎ *242/327–7711 or 800/225–5843,* ℻ *242/327–7615. 411 rooms. 7 restaurants, 3 bars, pool, 6 tennis courts, exercise room, snorkeling, windsurfing, boating, baby-sitting. AE, DC, MC, V.*

$$$ ▦ **Nassau Marriott Resort & Crystal Palace Casino.** As soon as you set sight on this hotel, the reason behind the name becomes, shall we say, crystal clear. The large structure, with its glistening windows, is unlike any other on the island. By night its five towers are illuminated, and each floor is lit with a different color, making the entire hotel look like a giant rainbow reflecting on the ocean. The interior is equally glitzy, and a comprehensive sign system helps you find your way around the massive resort. Eighty percent of the rooms overlook the water, and 100 elegantly appointed corner suites have as much as 180-degree ocean views. Guest rooms are furnished in light oak, with deep-green and white carpets, peach and tan floral comforters, and local art hanging on the walls. The Crystal Club, consisting of three concierge floors at the top of the Casino Tower, house 30 spectacularly decorated supersuites—Galactica, Casablanca, Santa Fe, Kyoto, and others—available at spectacular rates ($550–$2,000 per night). The resort has its own palm-fringed beach and lagoon for swimming, sunbathing, and water sports. The health club has top-notch equipment and daily aerobics classes, youngsters are well taken care of in the Marriotter Kids Klub program, and of course the 35,000-sq-ft Crystal Palace Casino provides even further adult diversion. There is also a 20-shop mall on site.

⊠ *Box N 8306, Nassau,* ☎ *242/327–6200 or 800/222–7466,* ℻ *242/327–6308. 870 rooms, 100 suites, 30 supersuites. 12 restaurants, 5 bars, pool, 18 tennis courts, beach, dive shop, snorkeling, water slide, windsurfing, boating, shops, recreation room, theater, baby-sitting, children's programs, meeting rooms. AE, DC, MC, V.*

$$$ ⚏ **Radisson Cable Beach Casino & Golf Resort.** This luxury high-rise property is ideal for those who want to be smack in the middle of Cable Beach action. Connected by a shopping arcade to Crystal Palace Casino, the hotel fairly buzzes with activity. In the lobby lounge, there's usually live music or a happy hour in progress. Daytime options include dance lessons by the pool, beach volleyball, free scuba lessons, and plenty of activities for kids. Guests get special rates at the hotel's challenging 18-hole Cable Beach Golf Club. At night, choices range from gourmet dining at Italia, enchiladas at Tequila Pepe's, beach parties, and revues to—of course—gambling at the adjoining casino. All rooms have balconies and face either the beach and pool or gardens. Management is currently pumping $15 million into the property—renovating guest rooms, upgrading the outdoor area, expanding the pool area to include lagoons, improving restaurants, and adding an observation deck to the atrium lobby. The resort offers a plan called "Splash" that includes meals, beverages, activities, greens fees, and taxes. ⊠ *Box 4914, Nassau,* ☎ *242/327–6000 or 305/932–0222,* ℻ *242/327–6987. 700 rooms. 4 restaurants, 3 bars, pool, 18-hole golf course, 18 tennis courts, health club, racquetball, squash, beach, snorkeling, boating, bicycles, shops, baby-sitting, children's programs, meeting rooms. AE, DC, MC, V.*

$$$ ⚏ **Sandals Royal Bahamian Resort & Spa.** This all-inclusive luxury resort for couples only is spread over 13 beautifully landscaped acres on Cable Beach. Formerly Le Meridien Royal Bahamian, this regal resort centers around a pink-and-white Georgian-style manor with stately columns and Romanesque statues. It is the chain's first entry in its "Royal" collection of resorts, which present an elegant environment and spa facilities. Accommodations are in posh villas with views of the ocean, garden, or pool. Each of the spacious guest rooms is opulently furnished with king-size, custom-crafted mahogany four-poster beds, separate sitting rooms, marble baths, and stocked bars. In addition to a "Wellness Clinic," the spa offers "Treatments for Two." A state-of-the-art fitness club is located in the resort's penthouse. You can dine in any of four gourmet restaurants, and spa cuisine is an option in each. Nightly entertainment takes place in the resort's amphitheater. ⊠ *Box CB 15005, Cable Beach, Nassau,* ☎ *242/327–6400,* ℻ *242/327–1894. 196 rooms. 2 bars, pool, 2 tennis courts, basketball, croquet, exercise room, volleyball, beach, dive shop, snorkeling, windsurfing, boating, waterskiing, dance club, recreation room, meeting rooms. AE, MC, V.*

$$ ⚏ **Breezes Bahamas.** Right on Cable Beach, this SuperClubs property offers couples and singles over 16 years old a moderately priced package plan that includes accommodations, entertainment, all meals (even snacks) and unlimited beverages, a host of scheduled land and water sports, airport transfers, and taxes. Breezes will even include a wedding in a tropical garden gazebo or atop a three-tiered sand wedding cake, if you're so inclined. And no tipping is allowed. The open-air lobby alone is a veritable entertainment center, with a bar, pool tables, fitness center, stage for nightly entertainment, and a pile of beanbag chairs for watching the large-screen TV. Ping-Pong tables are installed by the pool, and on the beach you can get instruction on a trampoline and circus-quality flying trapeze. In the heat of summer, five freshwater pools are available for cooling off, or you could forego the effort of a dive and sunbathe on a deck chair planted in a misting pool. Inside, large, modern rooms are pleasant but ordinary, which caters to guests' presumed interest in action and entertainment over plush surroundings. Meals are served buffet-style in the Tropical Terrace dining room. Pastafari restaurant is open for dinner, Italian style. The Pool Grill has snacks and refreshments during the day. Evening activities include local musical entertainment, beach parties, theme nights, toga parties, karaoke, pajama parties, dance contests, and cabaret. Guests must wear an identification wristband throughout their stay. ⊠ *Box CB 13049, Nassau,* ☎ *242/327–5356,* ℻ *242/327–5155. 400 rooms. 3 restaurants, 4 bars, snack bar, 5 pools, 3 tennis courts, basketball, health club, jogging, volleyball, beach, windsurfing, boating, bicycles, billiards, dance club. AE, MC, V.*

$$ ▨ **Casuarinas of Cable Beach.** In 1977, Eleutheran native Nettica Symonette, who had previously worked for Paradise Island developer Dr. Axel Wenner-Gren and in Nassau hotel management, bought 1½ acres of land on Cable Beach. The land contained only a guardhouse and an abandoned residence, but she parlayed her original investment into a seven-building hotel-restaurant—more rustic than most of the resorts in the area—that she named after the casuarina trees dotting the property. Casuarinas has two restaurants: the upscale Round House (the rehabilitated guardhouse) and Albrion's, famous for the Friday night, $12 all-you-can-eat Bahamian buffet. Rooms are decorated in tropical greens, yellows, and tans, along with wicker furniture, plush couches, and beige tile floors. Rooms have balconies overlooking the pool or lush tropical gardens. The family atmosphere—five of Nettie's seven children work here—makes guests feel at home and keeps them coming back. The small resort overlooks the Atlantic Ocean and is a great location for snorkeling, but white-sand beaches are a 10-minute walk away. A free casino shuttle runs every hour from 10 AM to 2 AM, and a public bus stop is located right outside the front door. ⊠ *Box N 4016, Nassau,* ☎ *242/327–7921. 78 rooms, some with kitchens. 2 restaurants, 2 bars, lounge, 2 pools, tennis court, beach, baby-sitting. AE, D, DC, MC, V.*

$$ ▨ **Guanahani Village.** The substantial, well-furnished accommodations at this time-share resort are perfect for young families or groups of friends traveling together. Tiled three-bedroom luxury villas, oceanfront or garden-side, sleep six comfortably, up to eight using roll-aways. Each unit has oversize rooms filled with stylish glass and wicker furniture, a delightful secluded patio, and a fully equipped kitchen, cable television, washers and dryers, and dishwashers. Room telephones connect through the hotel switchboard. On the down side, the property seems a bit overpriced considering that there's no restaurant on site and that maid service is included only if you're staying for more than a week. There is a tennis court and a pool. The beach is a 10-minute walk away, even though the property is on the ocean. ⊠ *Box N CB 10977, Nassau,* ☎ *242/327–7962,* ℻ *242/327–5059. 35 units. Snack bar. MC, V.*

$$ ▨ **West Wind II.** Privacy is the lure at this resort of cozy time-share
★ villas situated at the west end of Cable Beach, 6 mi from downtown. Each two-bedroom, two-bath condominium has modern island decor, a fully stocked kitchen, and a living room. Balconies or patios overlook the gardens or the poolside. It's not plush, and the maid comes to visit only once a week, but the reasonable prices and relaxed atmosphere make it wonderful for families or groups on a budget. The pleasant, quiet location—off the road amid manicured lawns and pruned gardens—offers children the freedom to play outdoors. The spectacular sea view somewhat compensates for the tiny and very windy beach. Lunch is the only meal served on premises, but there's a grocery store and myriad restaurants nearby on the Cable Beach strip. A bus stop and taxi stand are right outside. A beachside barbecue with a calypso band is held every Monday night, and a harbor cruise is planned

for Wednesday nights. ⊠ *Box N 10481, Nassau,* ☎ *242/327–7211 or 242/327–7019,* ℻ *242/327–7251. 54 villas. Snack bar, 2 pools, 2 tennis courts, beach, snorkeling, boating, baby-sitting, laundry service, travel services. MC, V.*

$ ☷ **Orange Hill Beach Inn.** If you prefer down-home coziness over glitz and glamour, then this is the place to stay. Judy Lowe, British owner and Nassau resident for over 20 years, makes sure that guests are treated like family. Orange Hill has built a reputation as an inexpensive alternative for honeymooners and scuba divers. It hosts more than 100 Bahamian-style weddings a year, mainly for American and European couples. The owner makes all local arrangements and handles legal and civil formalities through the Ministry of Tourism. Arrangements are also made for scuba divers. This is not the place for resort lovers: It's a 20-minute drive from town and 15 minutes from the casinos. A pleasant roadside beach, however, is only 300 ft from the inn, which is perched on a hilltop overlooking the ocean. Rooms and apartments vary considerably in size. None are spacious, but all have either a balcony or a patio with a view of the pool, ocean, or tropical gardens, and some rooms have a kitchenette. The dining room, where breakfast and dinner are served, has oval windows swathed in turquoise fabric. The international menu changes daily. Guests get to know one another by hanging out in a cozy lounge equipped with a television and VCR, video library, and jigsaw puzzles. None of the rooms has a phone, but guests are welcome to use one of several lines on the premises. ⊠ *Box N 8583, Nassau,* ☎ *242/327–7157,* ℻ *242/327–5186. 32 rooms. Restaurant, bar, pool. AE, MC, V.*

Western New Providence and South Coast

$$$ ☷ **Compass Point.** Hotelier and recording-studio mogul Chris Black-
★   well has scored a hit with this cheerful beachfront property 20 minutes west of downtown Nassau. To call the accommodations colorful is an understatement: Designer Barbara Hulanicki incorporated 39 brilliant Junkanoo colors to transform the clapboards and architectural details of this tiny town of handcrafted wooden bungalows into a feast for the eyes. Opened in early 1995, the seven one- and two-bedroom cottages, four one-bedroom huts, and five cabanas are steps from sand and surf and connected by winding pathways. Some structures are duplex and on stilts, some are octagonal, some immediately face the ocean, with decks where you can catch the morning sun or an evening breeze. All rooms have bare wood walls and furnishings covered in handmade batik, king- or queen-size beds, a personal sundeck, kitchenettes or refrigerator, coffeemaker, TV/VCR, fax machine, and CD player. The property has its own stretch of sand, but stunning Love Beach—which is great for snorkelers—is right next door. Waterskiing, jet skiing, snorkeling, diving, and deep-sea fishing are all available. An open-air bar overlooks the oceanfront swimming pool. The excellent restaurant is right on the waterfront. ⊠ *Box 13842, W. Bay St., Gambier, Nassau,* ☎ *242/327–4500 or 800/688–7678,* ℻ *242/327–3299. 18 rooms. Restaurant, bar, pool, tennis court, beach, dive shop. AE, MC, V.*

$$$ ☷ **South Ocean Golf & Beach Resort.** In a style reminiscent of a colo-
★   nial plantation, the main building of this most serene and secluded of New Providence getaways, 40 minutes southwest of town, is dressed with white columns and ornate balconies. The casual, open-air-feeling interior is graced with wicker chairs, bright tropical prints, and plenty of mahogany. Guest rooms are cheerfully decorated with wicker valances and chairs, colorful bedspreads and paintings, and tile floors. Each unit has a patio that opens onto the gardens or a balcony that overlooks the pool. The finest accommodations are across the road on

either side of the beach club. Called Great Houses (with such flowery appellations as Frangipani, Hibiscus, and Oleander), these oceanfront luxury rooms are filled with Queen Anne chairs, four-poster beds covered with cheerful country-French bedspreads, bleached Mediterranean-tile floors, whirlpool baths, and three sets of fully screened mahogany doors that open onto a private beachfront patio or balcony. Pink jitneys drive you to the 18-hole PGA-rated golf course (the most challenging on the island), the four tennis courts (two lit for night play), the beach club, and Stuart Cove's Dive South Ocean facility. You can take advantage of free tennis and golf clinics, an array of water-sports activities, and dancing at the Flamingo Club; and there is a nightly one-man calypso band. Popular with divers, golfers, and honeymooners, this full-service resort has a kids center but no casino, and no dazzling evening shows. Public bus service runs into town for $1.75 round-trip, and another bus to Paradise Island costs $10 round-trip. ⊠ *Box N 8191, Nassau,* ☎ *242/362–4391 or 800/228–9898. 268 rooms. 2 restaurants, 3 bars, snack bar, 2 pools, 18-hole golf course, 4 tennis courts, beach, dive shop, snorkeling, boating, baby-sitting. AE, DC, MC, V.*

NIGHTLIFE AND THE ARTS

The Arts

Dundas Center (☎ 242/393–3728) on Mackey Street, is Nassau's performing arts theater. Plays, musicals, ballets, and other performances by local and out-of-town artists are produced and staged throughout the year.

Casinos

Leave your black tie at home, for these are hardly intimate European gaming houses, and attire reflects the casual atmosphere. You have to be at least 21 years old to gamble; Bahamians and permanent residents are not permitted to indulge.

Crystal Palace Casino (☎ 242/327–6200), at the Nassau Marriott Resort on Cable Beach, is the largest casino in the Bahamas. Its 35,000-sq-ft gaming floor has 850 slot machines, craps, baccarat, blackjack, roulette, Big Six, and face-up 21. There's a Sports Book facility for sports betting, equipped with one 70-inch and eight 35-inch television screens which air live sporting events. Both VIPs and low-limit bettors have their own areas. Casino gaming lessons are available for beginners. At press time, Sun International had just announced a major, $375 million expansion to include 50,000 sq ft of casino space, which would incorporate the views, sounds, and light of the Bahamas' tropical environment. The new casino is slated to have more than 1,100 slots and 70 gaming tables. The project should be completed by the spring of 1998. The casino is open from 10 AM to 4 AM weekdays, 24 hours on weekends; slots are open 24 hours every day.

Paradise Island Casino (☎ 242/363–3000) at the Atlantis, Paradise Island resort, is a 30,000-sq-ft, world-class casino with more than 800 slots, as well as baccarat, blackjack, roulette, and craps tables. The Salon Privé is reserved for high-stakes players. Slot tournaments and complimentary gaming lessons are available daily. Tables are open from 10 AM to 4 AM daily; slots, 24 hours.

Nightlife

Before Nassau blossomed as a tourist mecca, Peanuts Taylor's, on Bay Street, was the only nightclub for after-dark frolicking with locals. Now the Cable Beach and Paradise Island resorts have their own flashy clubs, bistros, and discos where residents and visitors alike come to enjoy a variety of late-night entertainment. The attire for attending these soirees is typically as casual as the atmosphere, though some clubs require dressier duds.

Nassau

Club Waterloo (✉ E. Bay St., ☎ 242/394–0163) is a popular disco, with five bars and nonstop dancing Monday through Saturday until 4 AM (no live band on Monday). Try the world-famous Waterloo Hurricane, a tropical mixture of rums and punches.

Cudabay (✉ E. Bay St., ☎ 242/393–0771), on the lower floor of the Nassau Harbour Club, draws locals and visitors during happy hour and Monday night football games.

New Culture Club (✉ Nassau and W. Bay Sts., ☎ 242/356–6266), with its checkered dance floor and cosmopolitan feel, is where locals and visitors go to dance the night away to disco and island sounds from 10 PM to 4 AM Wednesday, Thursday, and weekends. Women dance free on Wednesday and Sunday, and Happy House runs from 6 to 8 on Friday.

Silk Cotton Club (✉ Market and Bay Sts., ☎ 242/356–0955), just 30 paces from the hustle and bustle of Bay Street, is a small gem of a jazz and blues house. Daddy Long Legs, known far and wide for his contortionist moves as well as his music, plays a few nights. The jazz club is open Tuesday–Saturday from 7 PM to 2 AM, Sunday from 7 PM to midnight and serves lunch Tuesday–Friday.

Paradise Island

Atlantis Showroom (☎ 242/363–3000) at the Atlantis, Paradise Island resort has a late-night revue, Sunsation, a family entertainment spectacular with magic acts, acrobats, and an international cast. Shows are presented twice each night. One night each week, a musical headliner substitutes for one of the shows. It's open Tuesday–Saturday.

Joker's Wild Comedy Club (☎ 242/363–3000) at the Atlantis, Paradise Island complex is just off the casino floor. It features mostly American comedians Tuesday–Saturday.

Le Paon (☎ 242/363–2011) at the Radisson Grand Resort gets its groove on every Friday and Saturday night from about 7 PM to 3 AM. Everybody boogies to the mix of oldies, calypso, and disco tunes. Thursday night is open mike at the karaoke machine.

Oasis Lounge (☎ 242/363–2400) at Club Land'Or on Paradise Island presents live calypso music nightly 7 PM–midnight in a romantic setting overlooking the lake.

Cable Beach

King & Knights (☎ 242/327–5321) at the Nassau Beach Hotel showroom is a native show featuring world-famous King Eric and his Knights. The show is the only one of its kind on the island with steel drums, unbelievable limbo feats, fire dancing, Bahamian music, and song and dance. Dinner is at 7 PM, followed by shows at 8:30 and 10:30 Tuesday–Saturday. One show is held Sunday and Monday at 8:30, and on Friday and Saturday after the show, you can stay and dance till the wee hours of the morning.

Palace Theater (☎ 242/327–6200) at the Nassau Marriott Resort on Cable Beach presents a lavish Las Vegas–style revue—Jubilation—with state-of-the-art special effects, dancers in elaborate headdresses and rhinestone costumes, a magic act, comedy, and a Junkanoo grand finale. The 800-seat dinner theater is open nightly except Mondays.

Rock N Roll Café (☎ 242/327–7639) next to the Forte Nassau Beach Hotel on Cable Beach plays oldies, goodies, and karaoke daily from noon 'til 2 AM. The main bar is a favorite with entertainers who often stop by for a burger and brew when in town. Walls are covered with rock memorabilia. Sports events are shown on the giant-screen and satellite TVs located throughout the club.

Zoo Nightclub (☎ 242/322–7195) is Nassau's largest indoor nightclub. Five regular bars, a sports bar, and a VIP lounge keep the drinks coming while party animals dance the night away to popular music. Out back, reggae tunes flood the night, often played by a live band.

OUTDOOR ACTIVITIES AND SPORTS

Boating

Boaters arriving in Nassau with their own vessels should note that Paradise Bridge, which bisects Nassau Harbour, has a high-water clearance of 70 ft, so sailboats with taller masts heading for marinas east of the bridge must enter the harbor from the east end. East of the bridge on the Nassau side of the harbor are Nassau Yacht Haven, Bayshore Marina, Brown's Boat Yard, and the Nassau Harbour Club, all full-service marinas. The Nassau Yacht Club and Royal Nassau Sailing Club are at the harbor's eastern opening. East Bay Yacht Basin and part of the Hurricane Hole Marina are boating facilities located west of the bridge. Hurricane Hole has 45 slips and is on the Paradise Island side of the bridge.

Kids love the concept of sitting in a row on a rubber banana and bouncing along behind a motorboat. The going rate is about $10 per person for a 15-minute **banana boat ride.** Ride the big banana at Sea & Ski Ocean Sports at the Radisson Grand Resort (☎ 242/363–3370), Flash at the Nassau Beach Hotel (☎ 242/327–7711, ext. 6590), and Funsea at the Radisson Cable Beach (☎ 242/327–6000, ext. 6315).

Bowling

There's an alley with 20 lanes called the **Village Lanes** (⌂ Village Rd., ☎ 242/393–2277). A game costs $2.75 from 9:30 to 5; $3 after 5 PM, and $2.50 after 10 PM. You can rent shoes for $1, and there's a snack bar and lounge.

Canoeing

For a relaxing adventure, travel out to Lake Nancy for an afternoon of canoeing. Owner and operator Craig Ferguson rents two-person canoes for $10 per person, per hour. Lake Nancy is 700 ft wide by 2,100 ft long, and the brackish water is a mere 3 ft deep. A narrow opening in the mangrove thicks leads to the massive Lake Killarney, the largest lake in New Providence. Turtles, snapper, and tilapia swim around the canoes, and osprey, egrets, warblers, cranes, poor Joes, and white crown pigeons fly overhead. Afterward, traipse along the nature trail and obstacle course where flora and fauna are clearly identified, and obstacles offer a challenge at every turn. Beverages and snacks are served from a rustic green shack, and hamburgers, hot dogs, and steaks are cooked up on a barbecue. ⌂ *John F. Kennedy Dr.,* ☎ *242/356–4283.*

Fishing

The waters here are generally smooth and alive with all sorts of species of game fish, which is one of the reasons the Bahamas has more than 20 fishing tournaments open to visitors every year. A favorite spot just west of Nassau is the Tongue of the Ocean, so called because it looks like that essential organ when viewed from the air. The channel stretches for 100 mi. For boat rental, parties of two to six will pay $300 or so for a half day, $600 for a full day.

For fishing charters, try the **Charter Boat Association** (☎ 242/363–2335 or 242/393–3739 after 6), with 17 boats available, or one of the following: **Brown's Charters** (☎ 242/324–1215), **Chubasco Charters** (☎ 242/322–8148), **Hurricane Hole Marina** (✉ Paradise Island, ☎ 242/363–3600), and **Nassau Yacht Haven** (☎ 242/393–8173).

Fitness Clubs and Spas

Nassau offers a number of health clubs and gyms for those in the mood for an indoor workout or some spa pampering—an energizing alternative to shopping on an overcast day. Most are stocked with the latest high-tech machinery, including stair climbers, treadmills, and exercise bikes, and offer aerobics and step classes. If you plan to stay in the area for a stretch, check into the several-day or weekly package rates available at many clubs.

Atlantis, Paradise Island Fitness Center (☎ 242/363–3000) has treadmills, exercise bikes, and saunas. Use of the facilities is free to guests. Massages are also available for a fee.

Gold's Gym (✉ Bridge Plaza, ☎ 242/394–4653) offers aerobics, step, and cardio funk classes and has top-of-the-line fitness equipment, a juice bar, and a nursery. Fees start at $8 per day.

Palace Spa (☎ 242/327–6200) in the Crystal Palace complex and adjoining the Radisson Cable Beach is a full-service gym with all the amenities and aerobics classes. Exercise bikes face the water, and the spa has stair machines and excellent showers. Pamper yourself at the relaxing Jacuzzi and sauna. Fees are $8 per day and $30 per week for Nassau Marriott and Radisson guests, $10 and $35 for nonguests.

Windermere (✉ E. Bay St., ☎ 242/393–8788) offers a variety of luxurious, ultramodern spa treatments such as hydrotherapy and salt glows as well as top-quality facials, massages, manicures, and pedicures. There is also a small, exclusive training center. Daily rates for training equipment and steam, sauna, and shower facilities are $20.

Golf

Cable Beach Golf Club (7,040 yards, par 72) is the oldest and most highly regarded golf course in the Bahamas. Don't let the front nine here lull you into false complacency. If you do, the back nine will surprise you with longer holes and considerably more water hazards. The course is owned by the Radisson Cable Beach Casino & Golf Resort. ✉ *Box N 4914, Nassau,* ☎ *242/327–6000 or 800/451–3103.* ⛳ *18 holes, guests $55, nonguests $65; 9 holes, $35/$45; mandatory electric cart, $60/$40; clubs, $25.* ☉ *Daily 7–5:30, summer; last tee-off at 3:30 in winter.*

Paradise Island Golf Club, designed by Dick Wilson, is an attractive and challenging 6,805-yard, par-72 course with 70 sand traps and water hazards, among them the Atlantic Ocean. The championship course is surrounded by the ocean on three sides, which means that winds can get stiff. Staff pros are available for lessons and clinics. ⊠ *Box N 4777, Nassau,* ☎ *242/363–3925 or 800/321–3000 in the U.S.* ⚑ *18 holes $86, 9 holes $70, electric carts included. Clubs $20.* ☉ *Daily tee-off times 7–4, driving range daily 7:30–4:30.*

South Ocean Beach & Golf Resort (6,707 yards, par 72), on the secluded southern part of New Providence, is the newest course to surrender its divots to visiting players. Narrow fairways are a notable feature. ⊠ *Box N 8191,* ☎ *242/362–4391 or 800/223–6510.* ⚑ *18 holes: guests $55, nonguests $70 (rates include cart and greens fees). Clubs $15.* ☉ *Weekdays 7:30–5:30, weekends 7–5:30.*

Horseback Riding

Happy Trails Stables offers guided hour-long trail rides through remote wooded areas and beaches on the southwestern coast of New Providence. Courtesy round-trip bus transportation from hotels is provided (about an hour each way). Tours are limited to 10 persons, there is a 200-pound weight limit; and children must be at least eight years old. ⊠ *Coral Harbour,* ☎ *242/362–1820 or 242/323–5613.* ⚑ *$50 per person.* ☉ *Mon.–Sat.*

Parasailing

Atlantis, Paradise Island (☎ 242/363–3000) offers six minutes of floating above the beach for $30.

Sea & Ski Ocean Sports at the Radisson Grand Resort (☎ 242/363–3370) lets you jump off a platform and into the skies for five to seven minutes for $40; $45 for 10 to 12 minutes.

Sea Sports Ltd. on Cable Beach in the Nassau Marriott Resort (☎ 242/327–6058) charges $30 for a six-minute parachute ride, and $50 for a 10- to 12-minute flight.

Sailing

Funsea at the Radisson Cable Beach (☎ 242/327–6000, ext. 6315) rents Hobie Cats for $37 per hour, Sunfish $22 per hour, and gives hourly lessons for $25.

Sea & Ski (☎ 242/363–3370) on Paradise Island rents Hobie Cats for $35 per hour and Sunfish for $20 per hour.

Scuba Diving and Snorkeling

New Providence Island has several popular dive sites and a number of dive operators who offer regular trips. The Rose Island Reefs are close to Nassau Harbour, and the wreck of the steel-hulled ship *Mahoney* is just outside the harbor. Lost Ocean Hole is an 80-ft opening east of Nassau. Gambier Deep Reef, off Gambier Village about 15 minutes west of Cable Beach, goes to a depth of 80 ft. Sea Gardens is off Love Beach on the northwest shore beyond Gambier. Lyford Cay Drop-off, at the west end of New Providence, is a cliff that plummets into the Tongue of the Ocean. The South Side reefs are great for snorkelers as well as divers because of the shallowness of the reefs.

Diving operations are plentiful in Nassau. Most hotels have dive instructors who teach short courses, followed the next day by a reef trip. Many small operations have sprung up in recent years in which experienced divers with their own boats run custom dives for one to five people. A lot of these are one-person efforts. In many cases, the custom dive will include a picnic lunch with freshly speared lobster or fish cooked over an open fire on a private island beach.

Bahama Divers Ltd. (☎ 242/393–1466 or 800/398–3483) has two 42-ft custom dive boats that make separate trips for beginners and experienced divers. PADI certification courses are available, and there's a full line of scuba equipment for rent. Destinations are drop-off sites, wrecks, coral reefs and gardens, and an ocean blue hole. A video is taken of each dive. The three-hour trips leave twice a day; transportation is provided between hotels and the dock.

Dive Dive Dive, Ltd. (☎ 242/362–1143 or 242/362–1401) offers free scuba lessons at the Radisson Cable Beach pool. Resort courses, dives to walls and reefs, night dives, and shark dives are all available at this PADI facility. Transportation is provided.

Dive Nassau Bahamas (☎ 242/356–5170) at Bay and Deveaux streets in Nassau will teach you to dive in 80 minutes. They also offer specialty certification courses taught by PADI instructors. Dive trips explore magnificent reefs, walls, wrecks, and the Lost Blue Hole. Prices include equipment and transportation.

Stuart Cove's Dive South Ocean (☎ 242/362–4171) at the South Ocean Beach & Golf Resort on the island's south shore offers scuba instruction, rents scuba and snorkel equipment, and runs dive trips to the south shore reefs twice a day, at 9:30 and 1:30. Shark dives and day trips to the Exuma Cays (where you dive the Highbourne Cay Wall, snorkel conch for lunch, and feed the iguanas on Allan's Cay), Andros (for the blue holes and shark dives), and the Berry Islands are also available.

Sun Divers Ltd. (☎ 242/325–8927) at the Best Western British Colonial Beach Resort offers half-day shallow or deep-dive trips, as well as night dives, with all gear provided. Trips leave at 9 and 1.

Spectator Sports

Among other imperishable traditions, the British handed down to the Bahamians such sports as soccer, rugby, and cricket—that languid game whose players occupy such positions on the field as silly midon, third slip, long leg, and square leg. (It is absolutely essential that someone versed in the rules of the game and long on patience accompany you.) Cricket is played at Haynes Oval, baseball at Queen Elizabeth Sports Center, rugby at Winton Estates, and softball at Clifford Park. For information on **spectator sports,** call the Ministry of Tourism (☎ 242/322–7500) or check the local papers for sports updates and calendars to find out what's going on and when.

Squash

Village Club (☎ 242/393–1760) charges $8 per hour for play on its courts, with a $1.50 charge for racket rental and $3.50 for balls.

Tennis

Fees quoted at hotel courts are for nonguests.

Atlantis, Paradise Island (☎ 242/363–3000, ext. 6118) offers the largest tennis complex on the island. You can play on any of its 12 clay courts for $5 per hour.

Best Western British Colonial Beach Resort (☎ 242/322–3301) has three hard courts, on which night play can be arranged. The charge is $5 for use of the courts, with no time limit.

Nassau Beach Hotel (☎ 242/327–7711) charges $5 per person for unlimited play on its six Flexipave courts.

Radisson Grand Resort (☎ 242/363–3500) on Paradise Island has four lighted asphalt courts and charges $15 per hour, with a $5 racket-rental fee. Half-hour lessons cost $20 and one hour is $40.

Sun Spree Holiday Inn (☎ 242/326–2100) on Paradise Island offers four asphalt courts and charges $3 per hour.

Waterskiing

Sea & Ski Ocean Sports at the Radisson Grand Resort (☎ 242/363–3370) charges $30 for 3½ mi of riding the wake.

Windsurfing

Sea & Ski Ocean Sports at the Radisson Grand Resort (☎ 242/363–3370) rents sailboards for $20 per hour.

SHOPPING

New Providence shopping is centered on Bay Street, in downtown Nassau, although there are some shops just over the bridge on Paradise Island and in the large resort shopping arcades. You'll find duty-free prices on imported items, such as crystal, linens, watches, cameras, sweaters, leather goods, and perfumes. Prices rival those in other duty-free destinations, generally 25% to 50% less than back home. Wandering around Nassau's Straw Market, between Bay Street and the waterfront, is an experience in itself; you'll be tempted by the stacks of inexpensive straw hats, boxes, and baskets, as well as T-shirts, wood carvings, and doodads that vendors have accumulated. Bargaining is expected.

Although some shops will be happy to mail bulky or fragile items home for you, they won't deliver purchases to your hotel, plane, or cruise ship. Business hours for most shops are Monday through Saturday 9 to 5. Drugstores and the Straw Market are open on Sundays. Recently passed legislation permits Bay Street stores to be open on Sundays when cruise ships are in port, although most still opt to remain closed.

Most of Nassau's Bay Street shops are between Rawson Square and the British Colonial Hotel and on the side streets leading off Bay Street. However, many stores are beginning to pop up on the eastern end of the main shopping thoroughfare. You can bargain at the Straw Market, but prices in shops are fixed. And do observe the local dress customs when you go shopping: Shorts are acceptable, beachwear is not.

Incidentally, if you've checked into one of the major Cable Beach or Paradise Island resorts, you'll find branches of many of the top Bay Street shops. Prices at the branches are the same as at the Bay Street stores.

Markets and Arcades

The **Straw Market,** midway along Bay Street, is a main attraction of old Nassau for good reason: It is one of the world's largest such markets. Hundreds of people, mostly women, hawk their wares—brightly colored, hand-decorated straw hats and bags, baskets and totes, mats and slippers, wall hangings, and dolls. You'll also find necklaces and bracelets strung with shells, sharks' teeth, and bright beans, berries, or pods; clothing; original oils, prints, and wood carvings by local artists; and shells and coral harvested from Bahamian waters. Bargaining with vendors is part of the fun—all prices are negotiable.

Don't forget the little arcades off Bay Street. **Colony Place** features arts and crafts. The **Nassau Arcade** has the Bahamas' Anglo-American bookstore (☏ 242/325–0338). The **Prince George Plaza** has 14 shops with varied wares and a rooftop restaurant. A few blocks east of Rawson Square, at the **Moses Plaza Arcade,** you can shop for Mexican trinkets, fancy lingerie, and gifts.

Specialty Shops

Antiques, Arts, and Crafts

Balmain Antiques (⊠ Bay St., ☏ 242/323–7421) has an impressive collection of Bahamian artwork and antique maps, prints, and bottles, as well as a 434-year-old atlas.

Charlotte's Gallery (⊠ Charlotte St., ☏ 242/322–6310) is nonprofit and sells only local art—everything from small prints and ceramic tiles to full-size original oil paintings.

Green Lizard (⊠ Prince George Plaza, Bay St., ☏ 242/356–5103) is home to a delightful cornucopia of handmade wind chimes and other native and imported gift items, including that most famous of Bahamian inventions, the hammock.

Island Tings (⊠ Bay St., ☏ 242/326–1024) sells the best in authentic Bahamian-made arts and crafts, foods, aromatherapy notions, and clothing. Look for a Bahamian-style quillow (a quilt that you can fold up into a pillow), island-style stained glass, or little jars of pepper jelly, guava jam, or sapodilla, all local delicacies. Stock changes often as new treasures are discovered.

Plait Lady (⊠ E. Bay St., ☏ 242/356–5726), an islandy store if ever there was one, displays and sells hundreds of straw goods, as well as the Androsia print. Variety is nearly unlimited, and an authentic straw workshop is located in the back of the store. Custom order a straw bag with your own personal logo on it.

China, Crystal, and Silver

Bernard's (⊠ Bay St., ☏ 242/322–2841) carries Wedgwood, Royal Copenhagen, Royal Doulton, Baccarat, and Lalique items.

Little Switzerland (⊠ Bay St., ☏ 242/322–8324) sells silver items, pottery, and figurines.

Marlborough Antiques (⊠ Bay St., ☏ 242/328–0502) specializes in English furniture and bric-a-brac. You can also find Bahamian art, rare books, European glassware, Victorian jewelry, and unusual greeting cards and notepaper.

Scottish Shop (⊠ Charlotte St., ☏ 242/322–4720) sells St. Andrew and Highland bone china, as well as Scottish stoneware.

Cigars

Cigars have become quite the rage along Bay Street. And there is no doubt that the impressive displays of Cuban cigars, handpicked and imported by Bahamian merchants, lure aficionados to the Bahamas for cigar sprees. Beware, however, that some merchants on Bay Street and elsewhere in the islands are selling counterfeits—whether knowingly or not. If the price seems too good to be true, chances are it is. Check the wrappers, feel to ensure that there is a consistent fill before you purchase, and chances will be good that you won't get burned. A number of stores along the main shopping strip do stock only the best authentic Cuban stogies.

Caripelago (✉ Bay St., ☎ 242/326–3568) does carry cigars—venture through the myriad Caribbean wares toward the aroma of island coffees to the rear of the store and you'll find a somewhat limited but nonetheless authentic display of Cubanos housed in coconut palm frond briefcases. Grab a cappuccino to go with your smoke.

Pink Flamingo Trading Company (✉ Bay St., ☎ 242/322–7891), on its second floor, houses the best coffee, tea, and cigar bar in the Bahamas. It stocks the world-renowned La Casa del Havanas Cuban stogies. It is noted in general for its upbeat atmosphere and great service, and downstairs for T-shirts with exclusive designs and swimsuits, as well as interesting souvenirs, gadgets, and gizmos.

Pipe of Peace (✉ Bay St., ☎ 242/325–2022)—keep a lookout for the giant wooden pipe out front—is a conduit for a wide variety of cigars, pipes, and cigarettes, including all major Cuban cigars and a variety from other countries. A video showing what to look out for when buying a cigar plays continuously at the cigar counter.

Fashion

Clothing is no great bargain in Nassau, but many stores sell fine English imports. Perhaps the best local buy is brightly batiked Androsia fabric—available by the yard or sewn into sarongs, dresses, and blouses.

Bonneville Bones (✉ Bay St., ☎ 242/328–0804) is a handsome full-service men's store that sells everything from jeans and T-shirts to gorgeous lightweight Perry Ellis suits.

Fendi (✉ Bay St., ☎ 242/322–6300) occupies a magnificent old building and carries the Italian house's luxury line of handbags, luggage, watches, jewelry, shoes, and more.

Girls From Brazil (✉ Bay St., ☎ 242/323–5966) has a large selection of reasonably priced swimwear along with matching colorful wraps and casual evening wear at its two Bay Street locations.

Mademoiselle Ltd. (✉ Bay St., ☎ 242/322–1530) has 19 shops throughout the Bahamas (many in hotel arcades) and stocks a variety of women's clothing; be sure to check out their Androsia fashions.

National Hand Prints (✉ Mackey St., ☎ 242/393–1974) is well stocked with Bahamian fabrics, shirts, and dresses.

Jewelry, Watches, and Clocks

Coin of the Realm (✉ Charlotte St., ☎ 242/322–4862) has Bahamian coins and native conch pearls in various jewelry settings.

John Bull (✉ Bay St., ☎ 242/322–3328), established in 1929, and magnificently decorated in its latest incarnation behind a Georgian-style facade, fills its complex with Tiffany & Co., Cartier, and other boutiques that carry cultured pearls from Mikimoto and costume jewelry by Monet, Nina Ricci, and Yves Saint Laurent.

Little Switzerland (✉ Bay St., ☎ 242/322–8324) is the place to buy watches by Tag-Heuer, Omega, Borel, Swiss Army, and more. They also carry European sapphires and diamonds, as well as Spanish pieces of eight in settings.

Perfumes

Body Shop (✉ Bay St., ☎ 242/326–7068) sells the company's internationally acclaimed line of all-natural body lotions, shampoos and conditioners, and makeup. The products feature secrets inspired by remote communities around the world. The Body Shop also offers a perfume bar where you can have your fragrance of choice added to bath or massage oils.

Cameo (✉ Bay St., ☎ 242/322–1449) sells Swiss La Prairie sun and skin-treatment products.

John Bull (✉ Bay St., ☎ 242/322–3328) is where you'll find fragrances by Chanel, Yves Saint Laurent, and Estée Lauder.

Little Switzerland (✉ Bay St., ☎ 242/322–8324), one of the Caribbean's largest duty-free retailers, stocks French, Italian, and U.S. fragrances, skin-care products, and bath lines.

Perfume Bar (✉ Bay St., ☎ 242/322–3785) exclusively carries the best-selling French fragrance, Boucheron, and the Clarins line of skin-care products.

Perfume Shop (✉ Bay and Frederick Sts., ☎ 242/322–2375) is a land-mark perfumery that offers knowledgeable service and the broadest selection of imported perfumes and fragrances in the Bahamas.

Miscellaneous

Animal Crackers (✉ Prince George Plaza, ☎ 242/325–1887) sells colorful JAMZ clothing, cool cards, and every kind of stuffed animal imaginable. It's a jungle inside.

Cody's Record and Video Store (✉ Bay St., E. Bay St., and George St., ☎ 242/325–8834) has the best selection of tapes and CDs of island calypso, soca, reggae, and Junkanoo music in its three locations.

Island Shops (✉ Bay St., ☎ 242/322–4183) sells travel guides, novels, paperbacks, gift books, and international magazines. Take a peek at the "Bahamian Books" section, where you'll find texts on everything from poetry to politics.

Linen Shop (✉ Bay St., ☎ 242/322–4266) sells fine embroidered Irish linens and lace.

NEW PROVIDENCE ISLAND A TO Z

Arriving and Departing

By Plane

AIRLINES

Flights listed below originate in the United States. If you are arriving from the United Kingdom, the best option is to fly to Miami and transfer to one of the numerous carriers listed below for the final leg to Nassau.

Air Canada (☎ 800/776–3000) flies from Montreal and Toronto.

American Airlines (☎ 800/433–7300) has flights from Dallas/Fort Worth, Chicago, Houston, Atlanta, Los Angeles, and nonstop from New York City.

American Eagle, its subsidiary, flies 16 times a day from Miami and also serves the Abacos, Exumas, and other destinations in the Out Islands.

Bahamasair (☎ 242/377–5505 or 800/222–4262), the national carrier, has daily flights from Miami, Fort Lauderdale, and Orlando. The airline also flies to all of the Out Islands.

Carnival Air Lines (☎ 242/377–6449 or 800/722–2248) flies from New York, Newark, Cleveland, Fort Lauderdale, Pittsburgh, Philadelphia, and Cincinnati.

Comair (☎ 800/354–9822) flies from Orlando and also serves the Out Islands.

Delta (☎ 800/221–1212) is one of the busier carriers, with daily flights from Atlanta, Fort Lauderdale, New York City, and Orlando.

Gulf Stream International (☎ 242/377–4314 or 800/992–8532) has service from Fort Lauderdale or Miami.

Paradise Island Airlines (☎ 242/363–2845 or 305/359–8043) flies daily from Miami, Fort Lauderdale, and West Palm Beach exclusively into Paradise Island Airport.

US Airways (☎ 242/377–8887 or 800/622–1015) flies in daily from Charlotte, NC; **US Airways Express** leaves from Fort Lauderdale, Miami, and West Palm Beach.

AIRPORTS

Nassau International Airport (☎ 242/377–7281), located by Lake Killarney, 8 mi west of Nassau, is served by an increasing number of airlines.

Paradise Island Airport (☎ 242/363–2845) is at the east end of Paradise Island and a very short drive from the island's resorts.

BETWEEN THE AIRPORT AND HOTELS

No bus service is available from Nassau International Airport to New Providence hotels, except for guests on package tours. A taxi ride from the airport to Cable Beach costs about $14; to Nassau, $16; and to Paradise Island, $23 (this includes the causeway toll of $2). In addition, drivers expect a 15% tip. (☞ Getting Around, *below*, for taxi companies.)

By Ship

Nassau is a port of call for a number of cruise lines, including **Carnival Cruise Lines, Disney Cruise Lines, Dolphin/Majesty Cruise Lines, Kloster/Norwegian Cruise Line, Premier Cruise Lines,** and **Royal Caribbean Cruise Line** (☞ Cruising *in* the Gold Guide). Ships dock at Prince George Wharf, right in downtown Nassau.

Getting Around

By Bus

Frequent **jitney (bus) service** is available around Nassau and its environs, though this is not the preferred form of travel, as drivers typically adhere to their own set of road rules. These buses can be hailed at bus stops and go to hotels, Cable Beach, public beaches, and residential areas for 75¢, exact change. When you're ready to return to your hotel from downtown Nassau, you'll find jitneys congregated and leaving one by one from Navy Lion Road between Bay Street and Woodes Rogers Walk. Bus service runs throughout the day until 7 PM.

Guests staying at major hotels on Cable Beach can take the free **Cable Beach Casino Shuttle,** which starts at the Crystal Palace Casino every hour beginning at 6 PM and stops at every hotel along the beachfront. The last bus leaves the casino at 2 AM. A free **Atlantis, Paradise Island Casino Express Shuttle** takes a circular route around the island hourly starting at 8 AM and ending at the Paradise Island Casino. The shuttle stops at the major hotels en route or you can flag it down.

By Car

For exploring at your leisure, you'll want to have a car. Rentals are available at Nassau International Airport, downtown, on Paradise Island, and at some resorts. Plan to pay $45–$80 a day, $250–$480 a week, depending on the type of car. At press time, gasoline cost $2.50 a gallon. Remember to drive on the left.

Avis Rent-A-Car has branches at the Nassau International Airport (☎ 242/326–7121), on Paradise Island at the Pirates Cove Holiday Inn (☎ 242/363–2061), on West Bay Street (☎ 242/322–2889), and downtown near the British Colonial Hotel (☎ 242/326–6380).

Budget has offices at the Nassau International Airport (☎ 242/377–9000) and the Paradise Island Airport (☎ 242/363–3095).

Dollar Rent-a-Car can be found at Nassau International Airport (☎ 242/377–7231), at the Radisson Cable Beach (☎ 242/377–6000, ext. 6220), on Paradise Island (☎ 242/325–3716), and downtown on Marlborough Street near Cumberland St. (☎ 242/325–3716).

Teglo Rental Cars (✉ Mt. Pleasant Village, ☎ 242/362–4361) is a local rental agency with offices near Cable Beach.

By Scooter

Two people can ride around the island on a motor scooter for $30 a half day or $40–$45 for a full day, plus a $10 deposit. Helmets for both driver and passenger and insurance are mandatory and are included in the rental price. Many hotels have scooters on the premises. You can also try **Fathia Investment** (☎ 242/326–8329) at Prince George Wharf. Once again, remember to drive on the left.

By Surrey

Beautifully painted horse-drawn carriages with fringes on top (the animals wear straw hats) will take as many as four people around Nassau at a rate of $5 per person for a 25-minute ride; don't hesitate to bargain. Most drivers give a very comprehensive tour of the Bay Street area, pointing out all of the points of interest and offering an extensive history lesson.

By Taxi

Taxis are generally the best and most convenient way of getting around New Providence. Fares are fixed by the government at $2 for the first ¼ mi, plus 30¢ for each additional ¼ mi. You can also hire a car or small van for sightseeing for $20–$23 an hour; it's $30 for seven-passenger limo taxis. There is a $2 charge for each additional passenger over two. It is customary to tip taxi drivers 15%.

Bahamas Transport (☎ 242/323–5111 or 242/323–5112) has radio-dispatched taxis, as do **Li'l Murph & Sons** (☎ 242/325–3725) and the **Taxi Cab Union** (☎ 242/323–4555). There are stands at **Nassau Beach Hotel** (☎ 242/327–7865) on Cable Beach and **Paradise Taxi Co.** (☎ 242/363–3211) on Paradise Island.

By Water Taxi

Water taxis operate during daylight hours (usually 9–5) at 20-minute intervals between Prince George Wharf and Paradise Island. The one-way cost is $2 per person.

Opening and Closing Times

Banks are open on New Providence Island Monday–Thursday 9:30–3 and Friday 9:30–5. They are closed on weekends. Principal banks on the island are Bank of the Bahamas, Bank of Nova Scotia, Barclays Bank, Canadian Imperial Bank of Commerce, Chase Manhattan Bank, Citibank, and Royal Bank of Canada.

Shops are open Monday–Saturday 9–5; the Straw Market is also open on Sunday. By law, Bay Street shops are permitted to open on Sundays if cruise ships are in port, but the main thoroughfare remains all but deserted on Sundays.

Contacts and Resources

Embassies

U.S. Embassy Consular Section (⊠ Mosmar Bldg., Queen St., ☎ 242/322–1181).

Canadian Consulate (⊠ Shirley Street Shopping Plaza, Shirley St., ☎ 242/393–2123).

British High Commission (⊠ Bitco Bldg., East and Shirley Sts., ☎ 242/325–7471).

Emergencies

Ambulance (☎ 242/322–2221).

Drug Action Service (☎ 242/322–2308) can provide prescription drugs.

Hospitals: Princess Margaret Hospital (⊠ Shirley St., ☎ 242/322–2861) is government-operated; Doctors Hospital (⊠ Shirley St., ☎ 242/322–8411) is private.

Police or Fire (☎ 919).

Guided Tours

More than a dozen local operators provide tours of New Providence Island's natural and commercial attractions. Some of the many possibilities include sightseeing tours of Nassau and the island; glass-bottom boat tours to Sea Gardens; and various cruises to offshore cays, all starting at $12. A full day of ocean sailing will cost around $60. In the evening, there are sunset and moonlight cruises with dinner and drinks ($35–$50) and nightlife tours to casino cabaret shows and nightclubs ($28–$45). Tours may be booked at hotel desks in Nassau, Cable Beach, and Paradise Island or directly through one of the tour operators listed below, all of which offer knowledgeable guides, and a selection of tours in air-conditioned cars, vans, or buses.

CRUISES

Calypso I and *II* (⊠ Box N 8209, Nassau, ☎ 242/363–3577) offer cruises to a private island for swimming and snorkeling. The $45 cost includes lunch, two frozen daiquiris, and nonmotorized water sports.

Flying Cloud (☎ 242/393–1957) runs half-day catamaran cruises at 9:30 and 2 that for $35 include two drinks, dry snacks, and snorkeling; for $30, sunset cruises include hors d'oeuvres. A five-hour Sunday cruise, departing at 10 AM, is $50 and includes unlimited rum punch. All trips include complimentary round-trip transportation from hotels.

Topsail Yacht Charters' (☎ 242/393–0820 or 242/393–5817) *Wind Dance, Riding High,* and *Liberty Call* leave from the British Colonial Hotel Dock for a variety of sailing, snorkeling, and champagne cruises. All-day cruises cost $49; champagne-cocktail cruises $35.

EXCURSIONS

Commercial tour operators offering similar tours and prices include **Bowtie Tours** (⊠ Box N 8246, ☎ 242/325–8849), **Happy Tours** (⊠ Box N 1077, ☎ 242/323–5818), **Majestic Tours** (⊠ Box N 1401, ☎ 242/322–2606), **Playtours Ltd.** (⊠ Box N 7762, ☎ 242/322–2931), and **Richard Moss Tours** (⊠ Box N 4442, ☎ 242/393–2753).

HORTICULTURAL TOURS

The lofty casuarina trees that bend with the wind, the palms used to make umbrella-like thatched beach huts, yucca used in making hedges, sisal used in making rope, and jumbey trees, which have medicinal value—all are part of the Bahamian landscape. If you would like to know more about the island's flowers and trees, the **Horticultural So-**

ciety of the Bahamas meets at 10 AM at the homes of members on the first Saturday of each month. The Society can arrange field trips.

SPECIAL-INTEREST TOURS

Atlantis Submarines (☎ 242/327–3740) nose around the coral reefs and shipwrecks in air-conditioned comfort. Tours ($68) last about three hours (actual time aboard the sub is 50 minutes) and include an island tour and the cruise to the dive site.

Dolphin Encounters (☎ 242/363–1653 or 242/363–1003) can be experienced on Blue Lagoon Island (Salt Cay), just east of Paradise Island. During the two-hour *Close Encounter,* ($30 per person) you can sit on a platform with your feet in the water while dolphins play around you. Trainers are available to answer questions. If you wish, you can wade in the waist-deep water to get up close and personal with them. *Swim-with-the-Dolphins* ($85 per person) allows you to actually swim with these friendly creatures for about 30 minutes. Programs are educational, and each includes a 15-minute informational talk. They're also very popular, so make reservations as early as possible. Programs are available daily, 8 AM–5:30 PM, and the cost includes transfers from your hotel and the boat ride to the island.

Hartley's Undersea Walk (☎ 242/393–8234) takes you for a stroll on the ocean floor. Special helmets protect hair, eyeglasses, and contacts while allowing you to see the fish and flora. Hartley's yacht, the *Pied Piper,* departs daily at 9:30 and 1:30 from the Nassau Yacht Haven on East Bay Street.

WALKING TOURS

A walking tour around **Historic Nassau,** arranged by the Tourist Information Office at Rawson Square, is offered Monday through Saturday by advance arrangement. The cost is $2. Call ahead for information and reservations at 242/326–9781.

Visitor Information

The **Ministry of Tourism** (✉ Box N 3701, Nassau, ☎ 242/322–7500, FAX 242/328–0945) is located on Bay Street. Its Tourism Help Line (☎ 242/325–4357 or 242/326–4357) is an information source that operates from 8:30 AM to 11:30 PM daily. The ministry also operates information booths at Nassau International Airport (☎ 242/377–6833), open daily from 8:30 AM to 11 PM, and at Rawson Square (☎ 242/326–9781 or 242/326–9772), open daily from 8:30 AM to 5 PM. Ask about Bahamahosts, specially trained tour guides who will talk to you about island history and culture and pass on their individual and imaginative knowledge of Bahamian folklore.

The Ministry of Tourism's **People-to-People Programme** (☎ 242/326–9781) is designed to let a Bahamian personally introduce you to the Bahamas. By pre-arrangement through the ministry, you can spend a day with a Bahamian family with similar interests to learn local culture firsthand or enjoy a family meal. It's best if you make arrangements—through your travel agent or by calling direct—prior to your trip. (This is not a dating service!)

4 Grand Bahama Island

Grand Bahama's twin cities, Freeport and Lucaya, may not have the colonial charm of Nassau, but if you want to shop, gamble, or just relax at the beach—at slightly lower cost than in the capital—there's no need to go elsewhere. Beyond the ever-expanding Freeport-Lucaya region most of the eastern and western parts of the 96-mi-long island remain comparatively untouched—a seemingly endless, flat swath of casuarina, palmetto, and pine trees rimmed by long stretches of open beach and broken only by inlets and small fishing villages.

Updated by
Jessica
Robertson &
Allyson Major

GRAND BAHAMA, the fourth-largest island in the Bahamas after Andros, Eleuthera, and Great Abaco, lies only 55 mi off Palm Beach, Florida. The ever-warm waters of the Gulf Stream lap its shores from the west, and the Great Bahama Bank protects it on the east. The island was largely undeveloped until four decades ago, when a sudden boom transformed it into a popular and economically successful Bahamas tourist destination second only to Nassau.

In 1492, when Columbus set foot on the Bahamian island of San Salvador, Grand Bahama was already well populated. Skulls found in caves on Grand Bahama attest to the existence of the Lucayans, a peaceable tribe, who were constantly fleeing the more bellicose Caribs. The skulls show that the Lucayans were flat-headed. According to anthropologists, Lucayans flattened their babies' foreheads with boards to strengthen them, the object being to make them less vulnerable to the cudgels of the Caribs, who were cannibals.

Spanish conquistadors visited the island briefly in the early 16th century. They used the island as a watering hole but dismissed it as having no commercial value and went on their way. During the 18th century, Loyalists settled on Grand Bahama to escape the wrath of American revolutionaries who had just won the War of Independence. When Britain abolished the slave trade early in the 19th century, many of the Loyalists' former slaves settled here as farmers and fishermen.

Grand Bahama took on new prominence in the Roaring '20s, when the western end of the island, along with neighboring Bimini, became a convenient jumping-off place for rumrunners ferrying booze to Florida during Prohibition. But it was not until the 1950s that American financier Wallace Groves envisioned the grandiose future of Grand Bahama. Groves had been involved in the lumber business on Grand Bahama and Abaco. In fact, the harvesting of pine trees was Grand Bahama's major industry at the time. Groves's dream was to establish a tax-free port for the shipment of goods to the United States, a plan that also involved the building of a city.

On August 5, 1955, largely due to Groves's efforts and those of British industrialist Sir Charles Hayward, the government signed the Hawksbill Creek Agreement (named after a body of water on the island), which set in motion the development of a planned city and established the Grand Bahama Port Authority to administer a 200-sq-mi area near the center of the island. Settlers were given tax concessions and other benefits. In return, the developers would build a port, an airport, a power plant, roads, waterways, and utilities. They would also promote tourism and industrial development.

What evolved are the cities of Freeport and Lucaya. They are separated by a 4-mi stretch of East Sunrise Highway, though no one is quite sure where one community ends and the other begins. A modern industrial park has developed west of Freeport and close to the harbor. Companies such as Syntex Pharmaceuticals and Uniroyal have been attracted here because there is no corporate, property, or income tax and no customs duties or excise taxes on materials used for export manufacturing. In return, these companies hire local workers and have become involved in community activities and charities.

Most of Grand Bahama's commercial activity is concentrated just inland in Freeport, this island country's second-largest city. On average, about one-third of the roughly 3.5 million people who come to the Bahamas visit Freeport and neighboring waterfront Lucaya. They are drawn by two bustling casinos, resort hotels offering close to 2,900 rooms, two large duty-free shopping complexes, and a variety of activities on land and sea. Each day several thousand cruise-ship passengers arrive at Freeport Harbour from the Florida ports of Miami, Fort Lauderdale, Cape Canaveral, and Palm Beach. The harbor, a privately owned enterprise, currently accommodates up to 13 cruise ships at a time. Work is ongoing to expand the port's container facilities, generating millions of dollars in new business, hundreds of new jobs, and increased residential development throughout the island.

On Grand Bahama you can also enjoy the solitude of its hinterlands. Three sights fairly close to Freeport are definitely worth visiting: the 100-acre Rand Nature Centre, the Garden of the Groves, and the Lucayan National Park. The island's golf courses host tournaments throughout the year. Surrounding waters lure anglers from around the world to participate in deepwater fishing tournaments. The island is also popular with scuba divers, particularly because it is the home of the Underwater Explorers Society (UNEXSO), the world-famous diving school.

EXPLORING GRAND BAHAMA ISLAND

You won't find traces of colonial history on Grand Bahama; this is a newly developed island with a modern look, feel, and attitude. The main attractions here are relaxation and fun—the beach, water sports, boats, duty-free shops, casinos, and nightclubs. The natural world has been drawing interest as well—the island has lovely parks and gardens to explore, and eco-friendly tours are available.

Numbers in the text correspond to numbers in the margin and on the Freeport-Lucaya and the Grand Bahama Island maps.

A Good Tour

Grand Bahama is the only planned island in the Bahamas—this results in areas that are well laid out, but quite a distance apart. Getting around in Freeport-Lucaya is very straightforward, and both the **International Bazaar** ② and the **Port Lucaya Marketplace** ⑦ can easily be walked. But to get a look at some of the more remote areas, consider renting a car and and dispersing stops at a few sights over two days. And bring lunch for a picnic, as you won't find many restaurants along the way to tie you over until evening.

The **Garden of the Groves** ⑬ on Midshipman Road is a beautiful, serene place to start the day. Photo opportunities greet you at each turn, and the quaint, little hilltop church is a must see in Grand Bahama.

At this point, it's beach time. Turn onto the East Sunrise Highway to Casuarina Bridge. Continue along Casuarina Drive, turn right at the first roundabout and travel south until you hit **Barbary Beach,** so secluded that you'll rarely see another person.

Continue the adventure in the afternoon with a trip to **Lucayan National Park** ⑭, home of the wondrous Ben's Cave. To get to the park, return to Casuarina Drive and go left onto the Grand Bahama Highway and continue about 10 mi along the pine barren road. The park is on the left, and you'll find adequate parking. Across the road is a boardwalk trail that meanders about a mile to Gold Rock Creek.

Another side trip will take you to the western end of the island. Once again, make sure that you have a full tank of gas and a picnic and drinks on hand.

From the International Airport, take Airport Road to Queen's Highway and follow it until you get to Eight Mile Rock. The scenery is positively rural compared to the buzzing city of Freeport that you've left behind. Life moves at a slower pace. Find your way to a beach out here or strike up a conversation with locals. Relax—take out your camera for a few photographs while you are away from the city.

After taking all this in, get back on Queen's Highway and head west to Holmes Rock. West End is chock full of history—it served as a base for gun-runners in the U.S. Civil War and for bootleggers during the days of Prohibition.

Toward the end of the road is the Straw Market, souvenir stores, and of course, the Chicken Nest, ideal for a home-style meal.

If going all of the way out to West End sounds appealing, you could continue out Queen's Highway for a sundowner at the somewhat unkempt **Star Restaurant & Bar** ⑪ before heading back into town.

TIMING

To drive straight out to the farthest points on this tour, allow about 30 minutes to drive out to Lucayan National Park east of Freeport, 45 minutes to get to the Star Restaurant & Bar.

Freeport

Freeport, the second-largest city in the Bahamas, is an attractive, planned city of broad boulevards, modern shopping centers, and convenient tourist facilities. The airport is just a few minutes from downtown, and the harbor not too much farther. Freeport is the center of commercial activity in Grand Bahama, and it is a tax-free port. It's also home to a number of resort hotels and two championship golf courses. Tourists flock to the International Bazaar for duty-free shopping, and to the Princess Casino, next door, to try their luck.

Sights to See

❸ **Goombay Park Straw Market.** Here dozens of Bahamian vendors display an endless selection of straw goods: handbags, place mats, hats, baskets, and more. You'll also find T-shirts, mahogany and native-pine carvings, and costume jewelry. Don't be shy about haggling over prices. The vendors will be surprised if you don't. ☒ *Behind International Bazaar entrance, no phone.* ☉ *Daily 10–6.*

❻ **Hydroflora Gardens.** Plant enthusiasts and other nature lovers should plan to spend some time at this lovely sight, where a member of the Victor family takes you on "the most educational garden tour in Freeport," accompanied by classical music. Hydroflora Gardens was developed on the concept of hydroponics, plant cultivation without soil. The Bahamas' primarily limestone soil provides the perfect natural laboratory. Wander through trails blooming with native flora. Learn about medicinal and biblical plants, especially as they pertain to Bahamian history and culture. If the fruit trees are bearing their seasonal crop, you might get to taste a mango or guava guaranteed to be bursting with homegrown flavor. ☒ *E. Beach Dr. and E. Sunrise Hwy.,* ☏ *242/352–6052.* ☉ *Mon.–Sat. 9–5.*

★ ❷ **International Bazaar.** If the cobbled lanes and jumble of shops and restaurants in this 10-acre complex built in 1967 look like something from a Hollywood soundstage, that's not surprising: It was designed by special-effects artist Charles Perrin. At the entrance stands a 35-ft torii arch, a red-lacquered gate that is a traditional symbol of welcome in Japan. More than 100 shops, lounges, and restaurants representing goods and cuisines from 25 countries line the narrow walkways.

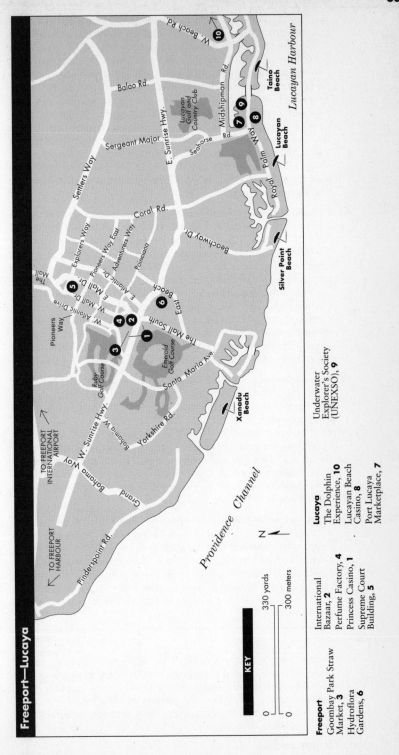

Freeport—Lucaya

KEY

0   330 yards
0   300 meters

Freeport
Goombay Park Straw
Market, **3**
Hydroflora
Gardens, **6**

International
Bazaar, **2**
Perfume Factory, **4**
Princess Casino, **1**
Supreme Court
Building, **5**

Lucaya
The Dolphin
Experience, **10**
Lucayan Beach
Casino, **8**
Port Lucaya
Marketplace, **7**

Underwater
Explorer's Society
(UNEXSO), **9**

You can purchase—at 20% to 40% below U.S. prices—silver and emeralds from South America, French perfumes, Spanish leather, brass from India, Chinese jade, African carvings, tailored clothes from Hong Kong, Thai silks, Irish linens, English china, and caftans from Turkey. **Colombian Emeralds International,** in the South American section of the bazaar, offers a free tour of its jewelry factory. You can watch craftspeople fashion gold, silver, and gemstones into rings, bracelets, and pendants. Freeport is home base for this company, though you'll find its shops scattered throughout the Caribbean. A simple emerald set in a 14-karat-gold ring may cost about $100, but most pieces start at $300. The choice of ethnic restaurants is almost as varied as the shops. ⊠ *W. Sunrise Hwy. and Mall Dr.,* ☎ *242/352–5464 for Colombian Emeralds International.* ⊡ *Free.* ⊗ *Mon.–Sat. 10–6, tours of Colombian Emeralds Mon.–Sat. 10–1 and 2–5.*

❹ Perfume Factory. The quiet and elegant Perfume Factory is housed in a restored pink-and-white 18th-century Bahamian mansion—the kind built by Loyalists transplanted to the Bahamas after the American Revolution. The interior resembles a tasteful drawing room. This is the home of Fragrance of the Bahamas, a company that produces popular perfumes, colognes, and lotions using the scents of jasmine, cinnamon, gardenia, spice, and ginger. Bahamian women conduct free tours of the mixology laboratory, where you are invited to blend your own creations, choosing from 30 different scents. You can sniff mixtures until they hit on the right combination, then bottle, name, and take the personalized perfume home for a $30 charge. ⊠ *Behind International Bazaar on access road,* ☎ *242/352–9391.*⊗ *Weekdays 10–5:30, Sat. 11–4.*

★ ❶ Princess Casino. Gamblers are attracted here in droves to try their hand at the 250 nickel, quarter, dollar and five-dollar slots, blackjack, and other gambling temptations (☞ Nightlife and the Arts, *below*). Place a bet on your favorite NFL, NBA, NHL, NCAA basketball, boxing, and baseball teams at the casino's new Sports Book tucked at the rear of the bustling casino. The Princess Casino is part of the Bahamas Princess Resort & Casino, a Freeport landmark with a distinctive Moorish-style dome that straddles both sides of Mall Drive and is adjacent to the International Bazaar. ⊠ *W. Sunrise Hwy.,* ☎ *242/352–6721, 800/422–7466 in the U.S.* ⊗ *Daily 9* AM*–3:30* AM.

❺ Supreme Court Building. This striking building was completed in 1994 to honor the visit of Queen Elizabeth II to the island. The design—bright pink stucco with white trim and green shutters—reflects the old British colonial architecture more common to Nassau than Freeport. The Bahamian legal system is guided by British law; on workdays, you can catch a glimpse of local lawyers in robes and wigs. Visitors are welcome to observe court in session. ⊠ *Mall Dr.,* ☎ *242/351–4275.* ⊗ *Weekdays 9–4:30.*

Lucaya

Lucaya, on the southern coast of Grand Bahama and just east of Freeport, was developed as the island's resort center. It has evolved into a comfortable residential area with large resort hotels, a fine sandy beach, marina facilities, a championship golf course, and a beachfront casino. Port Lucaya is a tourist mecca, with dozens of shops, restaurants, and a straw market.

Sights to See

★ ❿ The Dolphin Experience. A close encounter with a pod of Atlantic bottle-nosed dolphins is waiting for you at Sanctuary Bay, about 2 mi east of Port Lucaya. This is the world's largest dolphin facility. A

ferry takes you from Port Lucaya to the bay to observe and photograph the animals. If you don't mind getting wet, you can sit on a
partially submerged dock or stand waist deep in the water, and one
of these friendly creatures will swim up and touch you. The program
started in 1987, when five dolphins were captured and trained to interact with people. Later, the animals were trained to head out to sea
and swim with scuba divers on the open reef. A two-hour dive program is available. If you really get hooked on these affectionate animals, you can enroll in an all-day program and work with the
trainers in different aspects of the dolphin program. Buy tickets for
the Dolphin Experience and the dive program through UNEXSO, at
Port Lucaya. The program is very popular, so make reservations as
early as possible. ⊠ *UNEXSO, Port Lucaya,* ☎ *242/373–1250 or
800/992–3483,* FAX *242/373–8956.* ☜ *2-hr program $29, 8-hr pro-
gram $159, 2-hr dive $105.* ⊙ *Daily 9–5.*

★ ❽ **Lucayan Beach Casino.** Those who love the gaming tables won't want
to miss a visit to this small casino. It's part of the Lucayan Beach Resort & Casino (☞ Nightlife and the Arts, *below*), across from the Port
Lucaya Marketplace. ⊠ *Lucayan Beach Resort, Royal Palm Way,* ☎
242/373–7777. ⊙ *Daily 9 AM–4 AM.*

★ ❼ **Port Lucaya Marketplace.** The town of Lucaya's capacious shopping
complex—a dozen low-rise, pastel-painted buildings with tropical-
colonial architecture influenced by that of traditional island homes—
is on the waterfront 4 mi east of Freeport and across the street from
several major hotels. Among the 100 or so establishments is a wide
variety of waterfront restaurants and bars, and shops that sell clothes,
crystal and china, watches, jewelry, and perfumes. Small wooden stalls
dot the area, where vendors offer rejuvenating fresh-fruit drinks (with
or without alcohol). Local artists hawk their wares, and you can watch
wood-carvers as they hew animals and human faces out of native mahogany, ebony, and wild tamarind. The walkways have small, well-kept
gardens of hibiscus and croton. Just beyond the Port Lucaya Marketplace is a straw market, festooned mainly with T-shirts, that looks like
the entire community's weekly wash hanging out to dry. The centerpiece of Port Lucaya Marketplace is **Count Basie Square,** named after
Freeport's own King of Jazz, Count Basie. The square features a
bougainvillea-covered bandstand where live bands, steel bands, and
gospel singers often play Bahamian music. On balmy weekend evenings,
families—locals and tourists—gather to make new friends and greet
old. Kids of all ages form conga lines and do the limbo around the square.
⊠ *Sea Horse Rd.,* ☎ *242/373–8446.* ⊙ *Mon.–Sat. 10–6.*

★ ❾ **Underwater Explorers Society (UNEXSO).** One of the world's most re-
spected diving facilities, UNEXSO welcomes more than 12,000 individuals from around the world each year and trains more than 3,000
of them in scuba diving. Nearby Treasure Reef, where more than $2
million in Spanish treasure was discovered in the '60s, is one of the
school's premier dive sites. UNEXSO's facilities include an 18-ft-deep
training tank with observation windows, a recompression/decom-
pression chamber, and the Museum of Underwater Exploration. UN-
EXSO also has educational courses and specialized training for
experienced divers seeking upgraded or specialized certification. Visit
the extensive dive shop, where you can talk to instructors, pick up
brochures, and meet other divers. ⊠ *On the wharf at Port Lucaya
Marketplace,* ☎ *242/373–1244 or 800/992–3483.* ☜ *3-hr resort
course and 1 dive $89, snorkeling trip (includes mask, fins, and
snorkel) $18.* ⊙ *Daily 8–6.*

Beyond Freeport-Lucaya

Grand Bahama Island gets quite narrow at picturesque West End, once the capital of Grand Bahama and still home to many of the island's first settlers. Along the one main road that is just inches from the water, you'll see fishing boats moored opposite the colorful houses where the fishermen live. Islanders come here to buy fresh fish; and if there's a hankering in the crowd for a conch salad, one of the fishermen will surely pop into his house for the necessary ingredients to whip one up. Local vendors also sell native meals, such as fried grouper and peas 'n' rice.

Little seaside villages, with houses painted in bright blue and pastel yellow, dot the landscape between Freeport and West End. Many of these island settlements—Russell Town, Pinder's Point, and William's Town—are more than 100 years old. Their names derive from the surnames of the original homesteaders, and the tiny settlements are largely populated by descendants of these founders. Mr. Bartlett and Mr. Martin still live in their respective namesake hamlets of Bartlett Hill and Martin's Town.

The East End is the "back-to-nature" side of Grand Bahama. The road east from Lucaya is long, flat, and straight. It cuts through endless pine forest to reach McLean's Town, the end of the road. Curly-tailed lizards, raccoons, pelicans, and other native creatures populate this underdeveloped part of the island.

Underwater is home to wild dolphins, colorful coral formations, and other tropical marine life.

Sights to See

★ ⓬ **Bahamas National Trust Rand Nature Centre.** These 100 acres, just minutes from downtown Freeport, include a half mile of winding trails designed to show off the 130 types of native plants, including 20 species of wild orchids. One variety, the *vanilla correlli* is found nowhere else in the world. A flock of flamingos, the national bird of the Bahamas, also adds local interest. On site, you might observe a Cuban emerald hummingbird sipping the nectar of a hibiscus, or a Bahama woodstar, which is even tinier. You may even see a raccoon, an animal introduced to the island during the rum-running days of the 1920s and 1930s. In the room reserved for learning aids and exhibits, you can see three species of native boa constrictors, among other native and introduced animals. On the grounds themselves, don't miss the Lucayan Village Exhibit; completed in 1995 by a staff of volunteers, this is a reconstruction of one of the small villages believed to have been inhabited by the original Lucayans. The reserve is named for philanthropist James H. Rand, the former president of Remington Rand, who donated a hospital and library to the island. ⊠ *E. Settlers Way,* ☎ *242/352–5438.* ✇ *$5.* ☉ *Mon.–Sat. 9–4, guided nature walks at 10 and 2.*

★ ⓭ **Garden of the Groves.** This lush, 12-acre botanical paradise was a $3.5 million project cultivated in 1973 and named for American financier and pioneer developer Wallace Groves and his wife, Georgette, the founders of Freeport. The grounds are peaceful, with trickling fountains and forceful waterfalls that empty into a sleepy stream where ducks wade. There are some 10,000 varieties of Bahamian flora, including fruit trees, ferns, flowering plants, and exotic species, each clearly labeled for identification. One path gives way to a picture-perfect chapel on a hill, surrounded by manicured hedges and a rose garden. It is a replica of Grand Bahama's first church and offers a peaceful sanctuary for reflection. Beyond another pathway lies a hidden hibiscus garden—a favorite spot on the island for weddings. Snacks and drinks are available

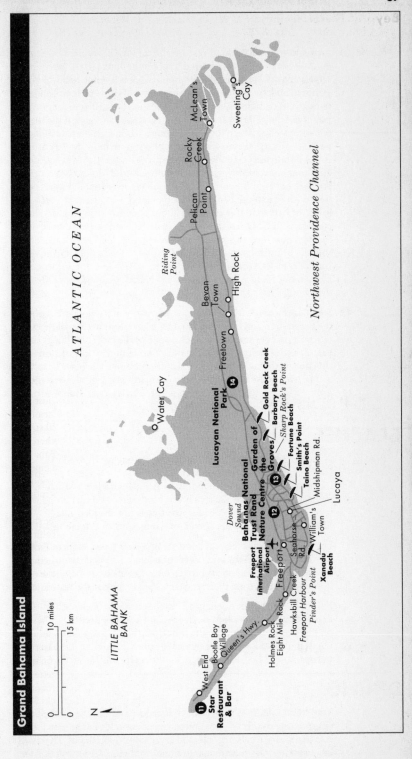

in an adjoining café. ⊠ *Midshipman Rd. and Magellan Dr.,* ☎ *242/352–4045.* ☒ *$5.* ◷ *Weekdays 9–4, weekends and holidays 10–4.*

★ ⑭ **Lucayan National Park.** Trails and elevated walkways wind through a natural forest of wild tamarind and gumbo-limbo trees, past an observation platform, a mangrove swamp, what is believed to be the largest explored underwater cave system in the world (it's 7 mi long), and sheltered pools containing rare marine species. This 40-acre seaside land preserve, some 20 mi east of Lucaya, contains examples of the island's five ecosystems. A sign near the entrance has a large map detailing the park's distinctive features, which enables you to find your way around. A spiral staircase descends into Ben's Cave—an eerie world of crumbly limestone and a freshwater pool with fish. Burial Mound Cave, nearby, is where bones of the early Lucayan Indians were found. Expert divers who wish to explore beneath the caves (and who aren't put off by the horde of bats that visit en masse about once a year in August) should contact UNEXSO (☞ *above*). Across the road, a boardwalk winds through pine forest and mangrove swamp to Gold Rock Beach, an absolutely beautiful, usually deserted strand of white sand and aquamarine ocean. ⊠ *Grand Bahama Hwy., no phone (for information, contact the Rand Nature Centre,* ☎ *242/352–5438).* ◷ *Daily, daylight hrs.*

★ ⑪ **Star Restaurant & Bar.** A dilapidated, two-story wooden building at the far western end of Grand Bahama Island, looking for all the world like part of a ghost town, the Star is one of the oldest buildings on the island, and is thought to be the oldest hotel. It saw lots of furtive action during the rum-running days of Prohibition. The place hasn't had a stay-over guest in years, but you can still get a drink here and eat grouper fingers at the small restaurant. ⊠ *Bayshore Rd., West End,* ☎ *242/346–6207.* ◷ *Daily 10–4.*

BEACHES

Some 60 mi of magnificent, uncluttered stretches of sand extend between Freeport-Lucaya and McLean's Town, the isolated eastern end of the island. Most are used only by people who live in adjacent settlements along the way. Lucaya hotels have their own beaches and watersports activities; guests at Freeport hotels are shuttled free to places like **Xanadu,** a mile-long stretch of white sand, and **Taino** beaches.

Local residents have their favorites. At **William's Town,** south of Freeport (off East Sunrise Hwy. and down Beachway Dr.) and east of Xanadu Beach, the sandy solitude is broken only by the occasional intrusion of horseback riders from Pinetree Stables passing by at the water's edge.

East of Freeport, three delightful beaches run into one another—**Taino Beach, Smith's Point, Fortune Beach,** and **Barbary Beach.** Farther east on the island, at the end of the trail from the Lucayan National Park, you'll find **Gold Rock Creek,** which is only a 20-minute drive from the Lucaya hotels. Locals drive here on the weekends for picnics.

DINING

You'll find hundreds of options in Freeport and Lucaya, including elegant dining rooms at large hotels, charming cafés by the water, poolside snack bars, local hangouts, and familiar fast-food chains. The choices of cuisine are varied, with menus often combining Continental, American, and Bahamian fare. Freeport's International Bazaar is worth exploring for exotic fare, such as Indian or Japanese. Wednesday evenings, there's a native fish fry at Smith's Point, east of Lucaya (taxi drivers know the way), where you can sample fresh seafood—conch, grouper, barracuda—cooked outdoors at the beach. It's a great opportunity to meet local residents, and at about $7 per person, it's also a bargain!

In general, the restaurants on Grand Bahama Island cannot be rated as highly as those in New Providence; only a handful of establishments in Freeport and Lucaya could be considered fine dining. However, a meal in Freeport usually costs less than a comparable one in Nassau. Prices on menus often include three courses—an appetizer or salad, an entrée, and a dessert.

CATEGORY	COST*
$$$	over $30
$$	$20–$30
$	under $20

*per person for a three-course meal, excluding drinks, service, and 15% tip

Freeport

$$$ ✕ **Crown Room.** This French-Continental restaurant is tucked in a corner of the Bahamas Princess Casino, away from the bustle of the gaming tables. Rose-colored, beveled-glass mirrors alternating with coral wall panels adorn the intimately lighted dining room. High-back French colonial chairs and white Italian smoked-glass chandeliers add to the atmosphere, and light jazz plays in the background. This is a pleasant place for celebrating a casino win, even if the tables are a bit too close together. Specialties of the house include escargots in basil sauce, a Caesar salad prepared table-side, and lobster casino (chunks of lobster sautéed with a cream and cognac sauce)—worth the splurge. The Crown's rack of lamb will more than satisfy meat lovers. ✉ *Bahamas Princess Casino,* ☎ *242/352–7811 or 242/352–6721, ext. 54. Reservations essential. Jacket required. AE, MC, V. Closed Sun., Mon. No lunch.*

$$$ ✕ **Ruby Swiss European Restaurant.** Popular with both locals and tourists since it opened in 1986, this restaurant offers generous portions, excellent service, and musical entertainment. Potted artificial ficus trees strung with twinkling lights add to the festive mood, and burgundy drapes add a touch of elegance to the large dining room. Although you can have a nice evening here, the ambience isn't exactly conducive to romance. The extensive Continental menu features 14 different seafood dishes and more than 17 beef offerings; the wine list's 50-odd varieties cover six countries. Menu specialties include steak Diane (thinly sliced steak flavored with cognac), fondue bourguignonne (prepared with filet mignon), and desserts flambéed at the table. Snacks are served until 5 AM, making this a good place to come after the casino. ✉ *W. Sunrise Hwy. and Atlantic Dr. across from Bahamas Princess Tower,* ☎ *242/352–8507. Reservations essential. AE, DC, MC, V. No lunch Sat. or Sun.*

$$–$$$ ✕ **Rib Room.** This establishment resembles an English hunting lodge with its long narrow rooms, rough-hewn timber ceiling, wood and brick walls, red leather chairs, and tartan carpet. Come here when you're in the mood for a generous portion of prime rib, steak, or surf and turf. Some prices are high, but a good deal is the special three-course meal, served from 6 to 7, which includes appetizer, entrée, dessert, and coffee for $26 per person. ✉ *Princess Country Club, Bahamas Princess Resort & Casino,* ☎ *242/352–6721, ext. 59. Reservations essential. Jacket required. AE, DC, MC, V. Closed Tues., Wed. No lunch.*

$$ ✕ **Guanahani's.** Named after the Lucayan Indian word for the island
★ of San Salvador, this spot has three dining rooms separated by Moorish arches. The rest of the decor is predominantly Bahamian, featur-

Freeport—Lucaya Dining

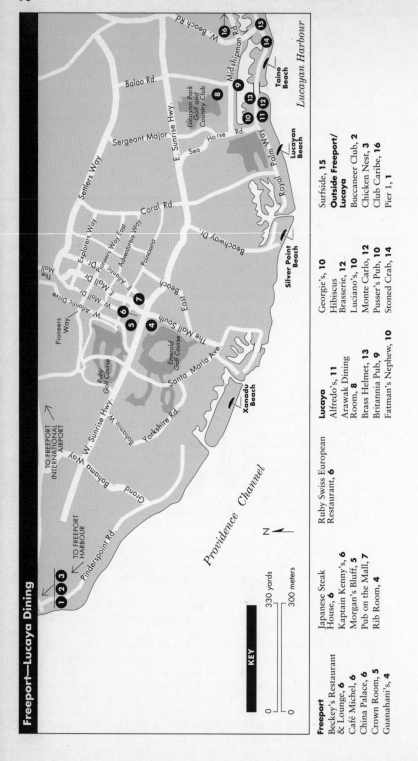

Freeport

Beckey's Restaurant & Lounge, **6**
Café Michel, **6**
China Palace, **6**
Crown Room, **5**
Guanahani's, **4**

Japanese Steak House, **6**
Kaptain Kenny's, **6**
Morgan's Bluff, **5**
Pub on the Mall, **7**
Rib Room, **4**

Ruby Swiss European Restaurant, **6**

Lucaya

Alfredo's, **11**
Arawak Dining Room, **8**
Brass Helmet, **13**
Britannia Pub, **9**
Fatman's Nephew, **10**

Georgie's, **10**
Hibiscus Brasserie, **12**
Luciano's, **10**
Monte Carlo, **12**
Pusser's Pub, **10**
Stoned Crab, **14**

Surfside, **15**

Outside Freeport/ Lucaya

Buccaneer Club, **2**
Chicken Nest, **3**
Club Caribe, **16**
Pier 1, **1**

KEY

0   330 yards
0   300 meters

N

ing a high cedar-and-cypress wooden ceiling, potted palms, laminated wood tables, and high-back rattan chairs. The menu includes steak, ribs, chicken, fish, lobster tail, and shrimp—grilled, blackened, or barbecued. All à la carte dinners come with a dessert of hot-fudge fondue, served with a large plate of sliced fresh fruits. The Bahamian chef also makes a good conch chowder, an island favorite. And if you dine before 6:30 PM, you can take advantage of the special—choose from five main courses for only $15 per person. Reserve a window table to look out on the lighted rock garden and waterfall. ⊠ *Princess Country Club, Bahamas Princess Resort & Casino,* ☎ *242 352–6721, ext. 56. AE, DC, MC, V. Closed Thurs., Fri. No lunch.*

$$ ✕ **Morgan's Bluff.** The cheerful, relaxed ambience of this family-style seafood restaurant, named after 17th-century pirate Sir Henry Morgan, is enhanced by nautical decor: A collage of colorful sails is suspended from the ceiling and a row of red neon "portholes" decorates a wall. Look for the menu's array of tasty island specialties, such as conch chowder, conch fritters, Bahamian lobster tail, blackened redfish, and fresh grouper sautéed in lemon, butter, and spices. ⊠ *Princess Tower, Bahamas Princess Resort & Casino,* ☎ *242/352–9661. AE, MC, V. Closed Mon. and Tues. No lunch.*

International Bazaar (Freeport)

$$ ✕ **Kaptain Kenny's.** Lobster traps and hunks of driftwood hang from the ceiling and walls of this popular place to meet and eat. One of the oldest and most interesting buildings in Freeport has been carefully remodeled to create a half-museum, half-Disneyland atmosphere—check out Freeport's Walk of Fame, just outside the entrance, with imprints of such luminaries as Cliff Robertson, Hank Aaron, Lou Rawls, and a smattering of soap-opera stars who signed the names of their characters. Inside, gnarled wood tables are inlaid with parchment treasure maps. Outside, on the spacious wood patio, diners and drinkers can listen to live music—and dancing is "always permissible." Despite all the trappings, however, this is not a form-over-content operation: Seafood is first-rate. Grouper, the house specialty, is prepared three ways—panfried, stuffed, and papillote (baked in parchment) with shrimp. Pizza with various toppings is also on the menu. ⊠ *International Bazaar,* ☎ *242/351–4759. AE, MC, V.*

$$ ✕ **Pub on the Mall.** You have three options here. The Prince of Wales Lounge, an authentic English-style pub, serves fish-and-chips, kidney pie, and three types of ale; early- and late-bird specials, served 5–7 and 10–11, include salad, entrée, dessert, and coffee for $7.95. The Baron's Hall Grill Room provides a medieval setting: Banners, coats of arms, and a tapestry of King Richard the Lionhearted cover the walls. The diverse menu includes a satisfying Angus beef and *coquilles St. Jacques* (scallops). A third restaurant, Silvano's, serves fine homemade cannelloni and fettuccine in a circular dining room with a striking red ceiling and paintings of Italian cities. ⊠ *Ranfurly Circus opposite International Bazaar,* ☎ *242/352–2700 for Prince of Wales Lounge, 242/352– 5110 for Baron's Hall Grill Room, 242/352–5111 for Silvano's. AE, MC, V.*

$–$$ ✕ **Japanese Steak House.** Experience a taste of Japan in a tropical climate as the chefs prepare chicken, seafood, and marbled Kobe steaks in a fast-paced, sizzling hibachi show right at your table. Two rooms, separated by sliding paper screens, are gracefully decorated with umbrellas, fans, and red and gold lanterns. In the room at the back, you can sit on the floor Japanese style. At the front room's long tables, set for groups of 10 or more, you sit with other diners. All of the hibachi meals include soup, salad, vegetables, and rice with the entrée. The à la carte menu is more expensive, but you can save money by ordering the early-bird dinner special—for $19.95 you can choose from four complete hibachi meals. ⊠ *International Bazaar,* ☎ *242/352–9521. AE, MC, V. No lunch.*

$ ✕ **Beckey's Restaurant & Lounge.** This popular eatery opens at 7 AM and may be the best place in town to fuel up before a full day of shopping or gambling. Its diner-style booths and bright lighting provide a basic backdrop for the inexpensive menu of traditional Bahamian and American food, from conch salad and minced lobster tail to fried chicken or a BLT; pancakes, eggs, and special Bahamian breakfasts— spicy "boil" fish, "stew" fish, or chicken souse, with johnnycake or grits—are served all day. In the afternoons, you'll find a mixed crowd enjoying drinks and people-watching on the bustling patio. ⊠ *International Bazaar,* ☎ *242/352–8717 or 242/352–5247. No credit cards.*

$ ✕ **Café Michel.** This unpretentious bistro provides a relaxed place to snack or have a light meal alfresco. The 20-odd outside tables, with their festive red umbrellas and tablecloths, are placed in an ideal people-watching location just off the Bazaar's main promenade. The small, indoor restaurant offers a no-frills, coffee-shop atmosphere with 11 tables. The menu includes both American and Bahamian dishes, and the rotating specials menu always offers at least one tasty and filling bargain. ⊠ *International Bazaar,* ☎ *242/352–2191. AE, MC, V.*

$ ✕ **China Palace.** Good Cantonese and Szechuan cuisine, along with some American-style offerings, can be sampled at this lively restaurant whose striking red-and-green exterior resembles a mandarin palace. You enter by walking up a flight of stairs adorned with dragons and Chinese characters. The dining room is tastefully decorated with delicate statues in wall niches and screens that hide the kitchen doors. An early bird special dinner (soup, appetizer, entrée, and dessert) is available for only $9.75 per person. Happy hour is 4–6; tropical drinks with names like Bahamian Scorpion and Bali Daiquiri are served. ⊠ *International Bazaar,* ☎ *242/352–7661. AE, MC, V.*

Lucaya

$$$ ✕ **Arawak Dining Room.** This lovely restaurant at the Lucaya Golf & Country Club has a wall of windows that allows a spectacular 180-degree view of the golf course and directly overlooks one of the island's talked-about attractions, the Balancing Boulders of Lucaya waterfall. Fine French cuisine with a Bahamian flair is served at lunch and dinner. Freshly made coconut layer cake and other delectable pastries are on display at the entrance to whet your appetite for dessert after such delicious entrées as salmon poached in champagne sauce. Jazz accompanies dinner on weekend evenings and brunch on Sunday afternoons. Guests of the Clarion Atlantik Beach, which owns the property, are provided with free shuttle service. ⊠ *Lucaya Golf & Country Club,* ☎ *242/373–1066 or 242/373–1067. Reservations essential. Jacket required. AE, MC, V. No dinner Sun.*

$$$ ✕ **Luciano's.** One of the best places for fine dining on the island, this
★ sophisticated Port Lucaya restaurant concentrates on Continental cuisine, prepared and served under the expert eye of owner Luciano Guindani, who formerly ran the Arawak Dining Room at the Lucaya Country Club. The large dining area overlooks the waterway; its modern decor uses halogen lamps and abstract paintings. You can't go wrong with the house specialty, veal Luciano, which is embellished with shrimp, lobster, and a spicy cream sauce. ⊠ *Port Lucaya Marketplace,* ☎ *242/373–9100. AE, MC, V.*

$$$ ✕ **Monte Carlo.** The pride and joy of the Lucayan Beach Resort, this
★ distinguished establishment offers gracious Continental cuisine with a

Gallic accent. The restaurant was once called Les Oursins, French for "sea urchins," and sea-urchin shells have been cleverly modeled into the light fixtures; elegant floral prints decorate the walls of the refined burgundy-color dining room. Some of the recommended dishes include chateaubriand *bouquetière* (garnished with "bouquets" of vegetables) for two, rack of lamb, and Bahamian-style lobster tail. ⊠ *Lucayan Beach Resort & Casino,* ☎ *242/373–7777. AE, MC, V.*

$$ ✕ **Alfredo's.** This intimate, strictly Italian restaurant on the Clarion Atlantik Beach accommodates only 36 people at a time. Inside, white wicker chairs speak of the restaurant's informality. One wall is painted with a mural of an elaborate garden with marble pillars, and the arched ceiling resembles the blue-and-white sky of a perfect spring day. Try the linguine with Bahamian lobster or the fillet of sole poached in white wine with scampi. ⊠ *Clarion Atlantik Beach,* ☎ *242/373– 1444 or 800/622–6770. AE, MC, V. No lunch.*

$$ ✕ **Britannia Pub.** This jovial, British-style bar-restaurant, founded in 1968, comes complete with mock-Tudor decor, a beamed ceiling, and the inevitable dartboards. Locals and tourists alike enjoy English beer at the bronze-surfaced bar. Because one of the owners, Takis Telecano, is Greek, the menu offers several non-British dishes, such as shish kebab and moussaka, along with traditional English fare and the requisite Bahamian seafood. ⊠ *King's Rd., Bell Channel,* ☎ *242/373– 5919. AE, MC, V.*

$$ ✕ **Stoned Crab.** This comfortable, informal local favorite, with its 14-story pyramid-shape roof, faces one of the island's loveliest stretches of sand, Taino Beach. The scrumptiously sweet, fist-size stone crabs are locally caught, as are the lobsters. Whether panfried, grilled, or steamed, the grouper here is delicious. In fair weather, you can enjoy a delightful ocean view from the outdoor patio. ⊠ *Taino Beach,* ☎ *242/373–1442. AE, MC, V. No lunch.*

$–$$ ✕ **Hibiscus Brasserie.** In the Lucayan Beach Resort, close to the casino, ★ this simple coffee shop serves reliably, good food at reasonable prices. The breakfast and lunch menu combines standard American selections and island fare, such as chicken souse. For dinner, try another special Bahamian creation—perhaps well-seasoned conch chowder, red pea soup, cracked conch, or minced lobster. ⊠ *Lucayan Beach Resort & Casino,* ☎ *242/373–7777. AE, D, MC, V.*

$–$$ ✕ **Surfside.** This deceptively low-key restaurant sits on stilts atop Taino Beach (complimentary transportation is provided from your hotel). Its bare-bones decor—faded blue-and-gray color scheme, wooden electrical spools for tables—is more than made up for by its colorful clientele. The kitchen is somewhat unreliable, but the cracked conch and lobster are popular staples. There is a daily happy hour from 5:30 to 6:30. Dinner here entitles you to discount admission to the "native show" at the Yellowbird nightspot, including transportation. ⊠ *Taino Beach,* ☎ *242/373–1814. MC, V.*

$ ✕ **Brass Helmet.** The name is embodied in the timeworn metal diving helmet displayed on an aged wooden crate, amid other antique diving gear. To give you the feeling of being in the depths, colorful underwater videos play continually on a large-screen TV. Diners get a kick out of the fierce-looking life-size shark that has "burst" through one of the walls at this casual restaurant above the UNEXSO dive operation. The cracked conch is delicious here, along with Jamaican beef or chicken patties, and steak. Wash it all down with a Hammerhead, if you dare: It's made with both light and dark rum, apricot brandy, vodka, and fruit punch. ⊠ *Upstairs from UNEXSO, Port Lucaya Marketplace,* ☎ *242/373–2032. AE, D, MC, V.*

$ ✕ **Fatman's Nephew.** Owner Stanley Simmons named his restaurant for the two rotund uncles who taught him the restaurant trade. One of the better spots to dine in Port Lucaya, this relaxed place serves substantial Bahamian fare. The best seating is on the L-shaped outdoor terrace overlooking the waterway and marina. The menu is somewhat limited, but the value for the price can't be beat. Try the Southern-style ham hocks, cracked conch, or curried beef. For the less adventurous, the menu also includes the standard American burger. ✉ *Port Lucaya Marketplace,* ☎ *242/373–8520. AE, MC, V.*

$ ✕ **Georgie's.** Stop in at this pleasant, casual spot for happy hour and snacks or dinner. Conch fritters, lobster, and grouper are among the specialties. Get a table outside and watch the scene while you sip a fruity drink or a Kalik beer. The early-bird special, 5–8 PM, offers lobster tails for $9.95 and grouper fingers or cracked conch for $7.95, and all dishes come with peas 'n' rice. ✉ *Port Lucaya Marketplace,* ☎ *242/373–8513. AE, MC, V.*

$ ✕ **Pusser's Pub.** One of several Pusser's establishments located around the Caribbean, this amiable pub is right on the Port Lucaya waterfront. It derives its name from the term applied to the daily rum ration that used to be issued to sailors in the British Navy by the "Pusser" (slang for "Purser"). The nautical decor incorporates antique copper measuring cups and ersatz Tiffany lamps suspended from a wood-beam ceiling. Locals swap tall tales and island gossip with tourists as they people-watch and drink Pusser's Painkillers, which are graded by strength from 2 to 4, depending on the quantity of Pusser's rum in the mix. The outside terrace is the most popular area for dining; also outside is a daiquiri bar that serves drinks and ice cream. Solid English fare is favored, such as shepherd's pie, fisherman's pie, and steak-and-ale pie. Other recommended dishes include double-cut lamb chops, Bahamian lobster tail, and strip sirloin. ✉ *Port Lucaya Marketplace,* ☎ *242/373–8450. AE, DC, MC, V.*

Outside Freeport-Lucaya

$$$ ✕ **Buccaneer Club.** The oldest restaurant on the island, this festive place on the way to the West End, a 20-minute drive from Freeport, features good Bahamian and Swiss cuisine in a rustic chalet setting. Barbecued dishes are also served at lunch. You may wish to time your arrival to toast the sunset from the uncluttered 1 mi-long beach nearby. Beach parties—a Pirate's Buffet of salad, conch fritters, barbecued fish and ribs—take place Wednesday and Sunday evenings. The restaurant provides courtesy transportation if you're without a car. ✉ *Deadman's Reef,* ☎ *242/349–3794. Reservations essential. AE, MC, V. Closed Mon.*

$$ ✕ **Club Caribe.** This small, attractive beachside haunt is an ideal spot to unwind. Relax with a Bahama Mama drink, or dine on the local fare, such as minced Bahamian lobster, grouper, or steamed pork chops. Free transportation is available to and from your hotel. ✉ *Mather Town, off Midshipman Rd.,* ☎ *242/373–6866. Reservations essential. AE, MC, V.*

$$ ✕ **Pier 1.** You actually do walk the plank to get to this rustic, windswept
★ eatery on stilts, where you can observe the cruise-ship activity of Freeport Harbour or watch the sunset over cocktails. Not surprisingly, the pleasant dining area can become crowded with cruise passengers seeking a scrumptious sample of island seafood (including fresh oysters) and Bahamian cooking before returning to shipboard dining. Baby shark, prepared a half-dozen-plus ways—sautéed with garlic, stuffed with crabmeat and cheese, or over linguine with Provençale sauce are a few—is the specialty of the house; you can watch the denizens of the deep in the shark pool alongside the restaurant. Aquariums dot the restaurant, and when the sun goes down it's feeding time: Fish seem to appear out of nowhere to put on a show in which dozens of sharks

and, if you're lucky, even a barracuda named Charlie appear. Uwe Nath, the German-born host, entertains guests with stories about sharks and other fish. ⊠ *Freeport Harbour,* ☎ *242/352–6674. AE, MC, V. No lunch Sun.*

$ ✕ **Chicken Nest.** About 10 mi west of the Buccaneer Club (☞ *above*), in the West End, this is a simple pop-in-for-lunch place. The no-nonsense menu includes cracked conch, and you can shoot pool while you wait for your order. ⊠ *Bayshore Rd.,* ☎ *242/346–6440. No credit cards. Closed Mon.*

LODGING

Generally speaking, hotel rates tend to be lower in Grand Bahama Island than in Nassau, Cable Beach, and Paradise Island. You can choose among Grand Bahama's approximately 3,500 rooms and suites, ranging from attractive one- and two-bedroom units in sprawling resort complexes to practical apartments with kitchenettes to comfortable rooms in economy-oriented establishments. The higher-price hotels in Freeport and Lucaya, some of which date back 30 years, have managed to maintain their appeal to guests through continual renovation over the years. Small apartment complexes and time-sharing rentals are economical alternatives, especially if you're planning to stay for more than a few days. If being on the beach is important, Lucaya hotels and the Xanadu offer beach access, and UNEXSO—Freeport's scuba central—is within easy walking distance. Gambling and shopping are also close by. If your priorities focus less on the beach and more on gambling, golf, and shopping, you will probably enjoy being right in Freeport, where hotels provide complimentary transportation to the beach.

All of the larger hotels offer honeymoon packages, and several offer special three-, four-, or seven-day money-saving packages to golfers, gamblers, scuba divers, and other vacationers. Families will find that almost every hotel, even the small economy type, offers baby-sitting services. Some also allow children under 12 to stay in a room for free and will even provide a crib or roll-away bed at no extra charge.

An 8% tax is added to your hotel bill, representing resort and government levies. Rates between April 15 and December 14 tend to be 25%–30% lower than those during the rest of the year.

CATEGORY	COST*
$$$	over $125
$$	$85–$125
$	under $85

All prices are for a standard double room, excluding tax and service charge.

Freeport

$$$ ⚅ **Bahamas Princess Resort & Casino.** Two sister resorts separated by
★ a boulevard—and sharing two 18-hole championship golf courses, a beach club, and a 20,000-sq-ft Moorish-style domed casino—make up this complex. Service, on the whole, is good. An activities hostess coordinates a daily schedule of events and games for both children and adults. Shoppers appreciate the fact that the International Bazaar is next door. Those who prefer the beach over a pool, however, must take a free shuttle bus (running every half hour) to the resort's beach club, which several other hotels use as well. There, you'll find waterskiing, parasailing, and the gamut of water sports—all of which can be arranged through the hotel. And you can elect a dining plan that provides charg-

ing privileges at nine restaurants. Special packages are available to honeymooners and to golfers—who show up in force every January for the Crystal Pro-Am tournament. The resort also offers an all-inclusive package deal, which, for a fee added to standard room rates and airfare, provides three meals at any of seven wide-ranging restaurants, unlimited drinks all day long, a golf clinic, tennis lessons and other activities, admission to the resort's Las Vegas–style review, and kids' enrollment in Camp Sea Shells.

Princess Tower. Next door to the casino, this 400-room, 10-story building is the quieter of the two properties because its guests are usually gambling. Its dramatic, Moorish-style design includes turrets, arches, and a dazzling white dome. Portuguese tiles in bright colors, soaring Moorish arches, and a 28-ft ceiling, give the lobby an exotic air. Despite the grand architecture, it's a casual hub of activity, especially at happy hour when a small band plays Bahamian music. The large guest rooms, however, are strictly contemporary—decorated in beige, mauve, and turquoise, with mirrored closets, framed watercolor prints, and oak-wash wood furniture. An in-house cable hospitality network, with all sorts of resort and island information, was recently installed in rooms. High rollers may want to opt for the lavish Princess Suite, for $950 a night, which comes with every conceivable amenity, including a baby grand piano.

Princess Country Club. This 565-room property, across the street from the Princess Tower, attracts a lively, mixed crowd of serious golfers, families, and couples who enjoy sports. Tiered swim-through waterfalls cascade from a man-made rock formation that rises from the center of an enormous pool. Sipping a tropical concoction at the lively John B. Bar or sampling the lobster tail at Guanahani's are among the evening pursuits in the always-buzzing pool area, which is ringed by Ping-Pong tables. Eight two- and three-story guest-room wings radiate outward like the spokes of a wheel from the circular deck around the pool area. The comfortable rooms in wings 2, 4, 7, and 9 have modern vanities and baths, emerald-green carpets, muted floral-print bedspreads and drapes, beige wallpaper, and oak-wash wood furniture. Wings 1, 3, and 8 offer rooms with plain wood furniture and tile floors instead of carpeting. Standard rooms have an outdoor entryway, while the Superior class rooms open up into a closed, air-conditioned hallway. Two full wings have been converted to time-share kitchen apartments under the name Princess Vacation Club International. ⊠ *Box F 2623, Freeport,* ☎ *242/352–9661 or 242/352–6721, 800/223–1818 in the U.S.,* FAX *242/352–6842. 965 rooms (including 35 suites). 9 restaurants, 6 bars, room service, 2 pools, 2 beauty salons, hot tub, sauna, 2 18-hole golf courses, 9 tennis courts, exercise room, jogging, dance club, theater, playground, travel services. AE, DC, MC, V.*

$$–$$$ 🏨 **Xanadu Marina and Beach Resort.** This high-rise is still best re-
★   membered as one of the final hideaways of billionaire Howard Hughes. The resort—situated only a few minutes from town—has a pink exterior, with hot-pink trim and turquoise balconies which overlook either the small pool, marina, parking lot, or beach. Rooms are cheerful and tropical, with a soothing color scheme of sea-foam green and peach. The Escoffier Room, named after a 19th-century culinary genius, provides the perfect setting for a romantic dinner. The beach, a three-minute walk away, is dotted with coconut palms and flanked on both sides by thick stands of Australian pines. Here, water sports and beach volleyball are available. Nighttime activities include a fish fry on the beach on Wednesday and Friday nights. ⊠ *Box F 2438, Freeport,* ☎ *242/352–6782 or 800/772–1227,* FAX *242/352–5799. 189 rooms.*

Freeport—Lucaya Lodging

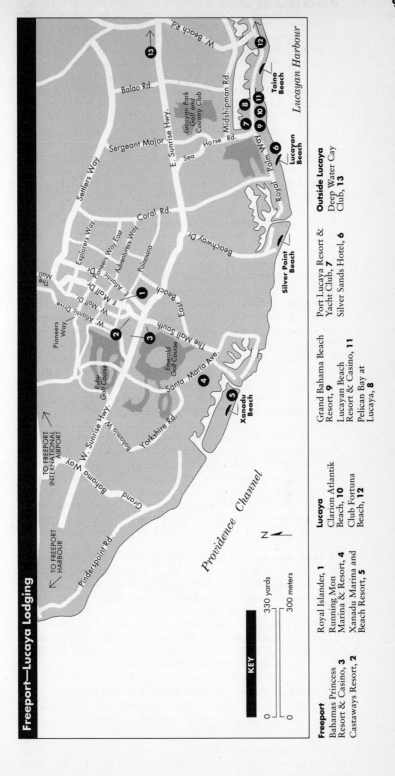

Freeport
Bahamas Princess Resort & Casino, **3**
Castaways Resort, **2**

Royal Islander, **1**
Running Mon Marina & Resort, **4**
Xanadu Marina and Beach Resort, **5**

Lucaya
Clarion Atlantik Beach, **10**
Club Fortuna Beach, **12**

Grand Bahama Beach Resort, **9**
Lucayan Beach Resort & Casino, **11**
Pelican Bay at Lucaya, **8**

Port Lucaya Resort & Yacht Club, **7**
Silver Sands Hotel, **6**

Outside Lucaya
Deep Water Cay Club, **13**

Restaurant, 3 bars, pool, beauty salon, 3 tennis courts, beach, dock, fishing, baby-sitting, meeting room. AE, DC, MC, V.

$$ 🏨 **Running Mon Marina & Resort.** Each room in this waterfront resort has a view of the 66-slip marina. Built in 1991, the two-story, pink stucco hotel with natural wood decking is located away from the action. Water quietly lapping against cabin cruisers docked at the marina punctuates the peaceful atmosphere. Guest rooms are decked out in soothing corals and aqua and island prints, light woods, wicker, and rattan. One luxurious suite has a king-size bed, kitchen, dining room, living area, two baths, a walk-in closet, and a Jacuzzi. Boat owners will appreciate the haul-and-launch facility, on-site mechanics, and repair services. Deep-sea fishing charters can be arranged through the dockmaster. Mainsail, the resort's only restaurant and lounge, overlooks the marina channel. ✉ *Box F 42663, 208 Kelly Court, Freeport,* ☎ *242/352–6834 or 800/315–6054,* 📠 *242/352–6835. 32 rooms. Restaurant, bar, refrigerators, pool, dive shop, fishing, meeting room, travel services. AE, D, MC, V.*

$ 🏨 **Castaways Resort.** About as close to the action as you can get, this four-story budget hotel is next to the International Bazaar and a short walk away from the Bahamas Princess Casino. Kaptain Kenny's, a popular (and often noisy) nightspot, is just next door. This is not the most attractive hotel Freeport has to offer, but it has the basic amenities, is secure, and has a great location for shoppers and gamblers. The hotel's two buildings are connected by walkways over somewhat barren garden courtyards. The large lobby includes a boutique, a souvenir shop, four tour operators, and a small video-game room. Sun worshipers can find some privacy on the large pool's sundeck or take the free shuttle to Xanadu Beach, which the Bahamas Princess guests also use. The average-size, motel-style rooms vary in price according to location; the most expensive, on the ground floor near the pool, have open decks. Furnishings are tropical against white, peach, or bright blue walls. Children under 12 can stay in rooms at no additional charge, and a colorful playground is located next to the pool, which has a volleyball net for pickup games. Every night but Sunday, fire-eaters and limbo dancers perform in a popular "native" show at the hotel's Yellow Bird nightclub. Monday-night manager's cocktail parties include free drinks, hors d'oeuvres, and prizes. The Flamingo Restaurant specializes in Bahamian and American food. ✉ *Box F 2629, Freeport,* ☎ *242/352–6682,* 📠 *242/352–5087. 130 rooms. Restaurant, 2 bars, pool, nightclub. AE, DC, MC, V.*

$ 🏨 **Royal Islander.** This motel-style property is near the International Bazaar and the Princess Casino, and provides free scheduled shuttle service to Xanadu beach. Its 100 rooms have light wood furnishings, framed pastel prints, and tile floors on the lower level or carpet upstairs, where no-smoking rooms are available. An inviting white-and-pastel lobby faces the spacious pool area, which includes a snack bar, Ping-Pong tables, and a poolside performance space where "native" shows take place on Mondays, Wednesdays, and Fridays from 4 to 7 PM. There is also a show at the hotel's Royal Crown Restaurant at 6:30 on Tuesdays, Thursdays, and Saturdays. ✉ *Box F 2549, Freeport,* ☎ *305/ 476–5000 or 800/327–2005,* 📠 *242/351–3546. 100 rooms. Dining room, snack bar, pool, Ping-Pong, travel services. AE, D, MC, V.*

Lucaya

$$$ 🏨 **Clarion Atlantik Beach.** The exterior of the area's only high-rise re-
★   sort does not do the hotel any justice. From the outside, the Atlantik Beach is imposing and appears out of place in its tropical setting. Inside, however, the small lobby is plush and inviting, and large rooms

In case you want to be welcomed there.

We're here to see that you're always welcomed at establishments everywhere. That's why millions of people carry the American Express® Card – for peace of mind, confidence, and security, around the world or just around the corner.

do more

Cards

In case you're running low.

We're here to help with more than 118,000 Express Cash locations around the world. In order to enroll, just call American Express before you start your vacation.

do more

Express Cash

And just in case.

We're here with American Express® Travelers Cheques and Cheques *for Two*.® They're the safest way to carry money on your vacation and the surest way to get a refund, practically anywhere, anytime.
Another way we help you...

do more ®

Travelers Cheques

are tucked in nooks and crannies in the maze of hallways. This 16-story Swiss-owned and -managed resort is particularly popular with couples and attracts a European clientele. In typical European style, all rooms have a separate sitting room of some kind, where the remote-control television is housed, away from the bedrooms. Drapes and bedspreads are in soft mauves and greens, and palm-tree prints. Suites on the seventh and tenth floors open onto the ocean or bay. The higher up your room, the better your view of the Atlantic Ocean or Port Lucaya and the Grand Lucaya Waterway. Honeymooners will enjoy the romantic, island-theme decor of the spacious one-bedroom bi-level suites. Two-bedroom apartments, complete with full-service kitchens, feel like a home away from home. The hotel has a friendly staff and a relaxed ambience and never feels crowded, even in high season. Outside, lush vegetation and palm trees line a tile walkway that leads to an Olympic-size pool, a sundeck, and a Jacuzzi overlooking the private beach. In addition, a complete water-sports facility and the only windsurfing school on the island are located on the premises. Guests get a special rate on greens fees at the hotel-owned Lucaya Golf and Country Club. The Port Lucaya Marketplace is across the street, and the Lucayan Beach Resort & Casino is next door. ⊠ *Box F 531, Freeport,* ☎ *242/373–1444 or 800/622–6770,* ℻ *242/373–7481. 123 rooms, 52 suites. 2 restaurants, 2 bars, snack bar, pool, beauty salon, massage, 18-hole golf course, 2 tennis courts, health club, beach, meeting rooms. AE, DC, MC, V.*

$$$ 🖫 **Club Fortuna Beach.** This Italian-run resort has been a bit of a European secret since its 1992 opening. Increased marketing in recent years has brought more American vacationers, but you're still most likely to hear languages other than English as you stroll around the grounds. Popular with couples and families, the club provides a casual, low-stress, all-inclusive getaway—one price covers meals, unlimited drinks, taxes, tips, and activities, such as water sports, bicycling, tennis, boccie, volleyball, archery, table tennis, and aerobics. Club Fortuna Beach is a rather isolated enclave—8 to 10 mi from town—so to get around, you'll need to rent a car, take a taxi, or ride one of the hotel's bikes. A vast private beach bustles with activity day and night. Golf, gambling excursions, and UNEXSO diving and dolphin experiences can be arranged through the hotel at extra cost. Meals are served buffet-style in the huge, natural wood, gazebo-style dining pavilion. The rooms are simple and pleasant, with unpainted pine furniture, clay tile floors, framed island prints, and small balconies that overlook the beach. ⊠ *Box F 42398, Freeport,* ☎ *242/373–4000 or 800/847–4502,* ℻ *242/373–5555. 204 rooms. Restaurant, pool, 2 tennis courts, boccie, exercise rooms, beach, boating, waterskiing. AE, D, MC, V.*

$$$ 🖫 **Lucayan Beach Resort & Casino.** The grounds of this 16-acre com-
★ plex with low-rise buildings now have a tropical look to complement the stone exterior walls and red-and-white lighthouse tower that has become a Lucayan landmark. The resort's 2-mi-long stretch of pristine sand has kept guests coming back for years; there's also a sundeck and large pool area, shaded by sea-grape and palm trees. Comfortable North Wing rooms, replete with marble baths, cable television, in-room safe, and direct-dial phones, open onto an outside corridor. Balconies, alas, are barely large enough to step out on. High rollers opt for the Lanai Wing rooms, which are next to the casino and have large patios and superb views of the ocean. Every room in the resort has a view of the sea, the bay, or the wide canal leading into the bay. The staff here is friendly, and daily sporting activities are organized for children and adults. In the evening, you can dine at Monte Carlo, the French restaurant (☞ Dining, *above*), or gamble at the 20,000-sq-ft beachfront casino. The complex is adjacent to the Port Lucaya Marketplace and the UNEXSO

diving school. One aspect of the future of the resort remains in limbo as the Swiss group that controls the Atlantik Beach Hotel and the Grand Bahama Beach Resort tries to take over. They hope to have invested more than $20 million in the property by 1998. ✉ *Box F 40336, Freeport-Lucaya,* ☎ *242/373–7777 or 800/772–1227,* 🖷 *242/373–6916. 243 rooms (including 10 suites). 5 restaurants, 5 bars, pool, beauty salon, 4 tennis courts, beach, casino, meeting rooms. AE, MC, V.*

$$$ 🏨 **Pelican Bay at Lucaya.** Pelican Bay opened its native mahogany lobby doors to its first guests in November 1996, and the newly constructed Danish-style resort offers the romance of the Caribbean with European design and Bahamian hospitality. Earthy shades of green, gray, rust, and mustard distinguish one town house–type section of the resort from the next. The cozy reception area is furnished with a mahogany front desk, cushioned wicker seats, and paintings of Bahamian island scenery. The three-level resort consists of 48 tropically designed rooms equipped with satellite television, direct-dial telephones, personal in-room safes, coffeemakers, and mini-refrigerators. Stare endlessly at the ever-changing tides and sunsets from your room's full private wooden-railed balcony, which overlooks the pool and whirlpool area, canal, and marina. Pelican Bay is next door to UNEXSO, which makes it a popular stay for divers. Only steps away from the myriad shops, restaurants, and entertainment offered at Port Lucaya Marketplace, the resort is also across the street from a casino, magnificent beaches, and water-sports activities. A ferry runs between Pelican Bay and Lucayan Marina Village from 8 AM to 11 PM. The resort's helpful, friendly staff enhance its pristine image. ✉ *Box F 42654, Freeport-Lucaya,* ☎ *242/373–9550,* 🖷 *242/373–9551. 48 rooms. Restaurant, snack bar, pool, hot tub, coin laundry. AE, MC, V.*

$$ 🏨 **Grand Bahama Beach Resort.** This sprawling four-story resort, with its beautifully manicured grounds, lined with coconut palms and sea-grape trees, reopened in February 1996 with 200 of its rooms completely refurbished. Ongoing renovations will improve a total of 500 deluxe rooms, a new pool and enhanced beach area, jogging and Rollerblade tracks, lighted tennis courts, and a pavilion to be used for exhibitions and events. The large pool has an ocean view and is located next to a kiddie pool and a bright, fun playground. Inside, rooms are spacious and tastefully decorated with soft, tropical teals and pinks, befitting an island getaway. Most rooms have a full-size private balcony—some with a breathtaking ocean view—while others overlook tropical gardens. Quiet and simple, yet comfortable, this resort is adjacent to the bustling activities of Port Lucaya. And it is ideal for ocean lovers and divers—right on the beach, and a short walk from UNEXSO. ✉ *Box F 2469, Freeport,* ☎ *242/373–1333 or 800/333–3333,* 🖷 *242/373–2396. 500 rooms. 2 restaurants, 2 bars, snack bar, pool, beauty salon, 2 tennis courts, dance club, playground, meeting rooms. AE, DC, MC, V.*

$$ 🏨 **Port Lucaya Resort & Yacht Club.** Next door to the Port Lucaya Marketplace, and equipped with its own 50-slip marina, this full-service resort opened in 1993. Golf carts transport guests and luggage to its 10 pastel buildings, which are arranged in a decahedron around the Olympic-size swimming pool, Jacuzzi, restaurant, and garden. The 160 rooms are styled as standard, superior, and deluxe and have garden, pool, or marina views. Decorated with rattan furniture, tile floors, large wall mirrors, and light tropical patterns, they are among the most appealing rooms in town. At night, the celebratory sounds of Port Lucaya Marketplace spill into buildings 7, 8, 9, and 10, and guests can enjoy the festivities from their balconies; for those who prefer peace to partying, buildings 1–6 are very quiet. Buildings 5 and 6 are strictly no-smoking. Marina activities are operated by the Port Lucaya Ma-

rina, and special rates are offered to hotel guests. Daily breakfast and dinner buffets at the restaurant are accompanied by Bahamian music. ⊠ *Box F 2452, Freeport,* ☎ *242/373–6618 or 800/582–2921,* 🗚 *242/373–6652. 157 rooms, 3 suites. Restaurant, 2 bars, pool, dock, laundry service. AE, MC, V.*

$–$$ ⊡ **Silver Sands Hotel.** This modest-looking hotel has more to offer than is apparent at first glance. The lobby is bright and cheerful, with a tile floor and bamboo furnishings, but the guest rooms are the most pleasant surprise: All have two full beds, a dining area, a full-size kitchen, and a private balcony. Upper-level rooms have dramatically slanting ceilings with skylights. Shades of beige and ivory, complemented by an island print, finish the look. Another plus is the beach—although you have to walk down a narrow path past a cesspool to get to it, this sandy stretch remains one of the nicest in the area. ⊠ *Box F 2385, Freeport,* ☎ *242/373–5700,* 🗚 *242/373–1039. 164 studio and 1-bedroom apartments. Snack bar, pool, 2 tennis courts, beach, snorkeling, meeting room. AE, MC, V.*

Outside Freeport-Lucaya

$$ ⊡ **Deep Water Cay Club.** If you want to get away from it all, this prop-
★ erty offers a handful of adequately furnished guest cottages scattered along the beach of a private island. Daily activities center on the main lodge, which houses the dining room, a self-service bar, and a tackle shop. The diversions here are lounging on the beach, diving, boating, and fishing—you can get in some of the best bonefishing in the Bahamas— and there's a 20-mi barrier reef nearby. The resort has its own airstrip, into which you fly from West Palm Beach. ⊠ *1515 Perimeter Rd., West Palm Beach, FL 33406,* ☎ *242/353–3073 or 407/684–3958. 18 rooms in 10 cottages. Restaurant, bar, pool, croquet. No credit cards.*

Time-Sharing

A number of condominiums in Freeport-Lucaya have become involved in time-sharing operations. Contact any of the following for information about rentals. For information about other time-share houses, apartments, and condominiums, check with the Grand Bahama Island Tourism Board (☞ Grand Bahama Island A to Z, *below*).

Bahama Reef (⊠ Box F 2695, Freeport, ☎ 242/373–1151). Eleven one-bedroom units and a three-bedroom penthouse face a canal 3½ mi from the beach. Visitors have access to bicycles and motorboats.

Coral Beach (⊠ Box F 2468, Freeport, ☎ 242/373–2468). A five-minute cab ride from the activity of Port Lucaya, these spacious, slightly weathered rooms are for budget-conscious travelers.

Freeport Resort & Club (⊠ Box F 2514, Freeport, ☎ 242/352–5371). The apartments here are in a woodsy setting close to the International Bazaar and the Bahamas Princess Casino.

Lakeview Manor Club (⊠ Box F 2699, Freeport, ☎ 242/352–2283). These one- and two-bedroom apartments are adjacent to the fairway of the fifth hole of the Ruby Golf Course.

Mayfield Beach and Tennis Club (⊠ Box F 458, Freeport, ☎ 242/352–9776). The rentals here consist of apartments that share a pool and tennis court on Port-of-Call Drive at Xanadu Beach.

Ocean Reef Resort and Yacht Club (⊠ Box F 898, Freeport, ☎ 242/373–4661). These three-bedroom, three-bath apartments are situated close to the International Bazaar, the Bahamas Princess Casino, and golf courses. The resort has a marina and a pool.

Princess Vacation Club International (⊠ Box F 684, Freeport, ☎ 242/352–3050). Located on the grounds of the landmark Bahamas Princess Resort & Casino, these converted time-shares are right in the middle of the action.

NIGHTLIFE AND THE ARTS

The Arts

Freeport Players' Guild (☎ 242/373–8400), a nonprofit repertory company, produces four plays a year at the 400-seat Regency Theatre during its September–June season.

Grand Bahama Players (☎ 242/352–4406), a local amateur group, produces two or more plays each year by Bahamian, West Indian, and North American playwrights.

Casinos

Whatever day and night activities are offered in Freeport and Lucaya, there's no doubt that the Princess Casino and the Lucayan Beach Casino are among the island's top attractions. They contain a dizzying array of slot machines, craps and blackjack tables, roulette, and baccarat to amuse novices and high rollers alike. Beginners can request a gaming guide, which explains the rules of each game, from the casino manager. Both casinos have nightly entertainment with live music. Drinks are free to table or slots players; those not gaming have to pay. At both casinos, slots are open from 9 AM until 3 AM or so; tables open at 10 AM. There's no specific dress code, although bathing suits and bare feet are not permitted. You must be at least 18 years of age to go into the casino, and residents of the Bahamas are not permitted to gamble. Photography is prohibited.

Lucayan Beach Casino, where dreams are shattered or come true, has 544 superslots, poker and video blackjack, and other assorted games. Novices are invited to take free gaming lessons at the casino at 11 AM and 7 PM. The casino bar offers two-for-one drinks from 4 to 7 PM and a live band on weekends. ⊠ *Lucayan Beach Resort, Royal Palm Way,* ☎ *242/373–7777.* ☉ *Daily 9 AM–4 AM.*

Princess Casino packs its 20,000 sq ft with 492 slot machines, 26 blackjack tables, seven craps tables, four roulette wheels, six Caribbean poker games, and one minibaccarat. A sports book for betting on sports was recently added, enlivening the atmosphere a bit. An elevated circular bar is a great place from which to watch both casino action and live bandstand area entertainment. ⊠ *Bahamas Princess Resort & Casino, W. Sunrise Hwy.,* ☎ *242/352–6721, 800/422–7466 in the U.S.* ☉ *Daily 9 AM–3:30 AM.*

Nightlife

For evening and late-night entertainment, Grand Bahama delivers calypso music, discos, live music for dancing at hotel lounges, and lavish Las Vegas–style sequins-and-feathers revues. Nightclubs are open generally from 8 or 9 PM until 3 AM. Major hotels organize their own late-night entertainment.

Bahamas Princess Country Club has the recently expanded John B. outdoor lounge and disco every night but Sunday and a Goombay show, with live local music and dinner, on Saturday. ⊠ *Bahamas Princess Resort & Casino,* ☎ *242/352–6721.* ☉ *Lounge and disco nightly 9–2; doors open for Goombay show Sat. and Wed. at 6.*

Bahamas Princess Towers presents the Sultan's Tent, where singer and entertainer Marvin Henfield dazzles the hotel crowd with his glittering outfits, stunning impersonations, and expert all-request sets. ⊠ *Bahamas Princess Resort & Casino,* ☎ *242/352–9661.* ◷ *Shows Fri.–Wed. at 9.*

Casino Royale Show Room presents a twice-nightly extravaganza, with glamorous costumes, dancing, and novelty acts. ⊠ *Bahamas Princess Resort & Casino,* ☎ *242/352–6721.* ◷ *Shows at 8:30 and 10:45; closed Mon.*

Joker's Wild Supper & Show Club features an exciting "native" show that includes limbo dancing, a fire-eater, island dancers, steel drum music, and a climactic Junkanoo finale. Enjoy dinner and the show or just the show. ⊠ *Midshipman Rd., Lucaya,* ☎ *242/373–7765.* ◷ *Dinner at 7, show at 9; closed Sun.*

Port Lucaya Marketplace has become one of the liveliest places to be after dark, with live entertainment and calypso music at Count Basie Square which is bordered by three popular hangouts, The Corner Bar, Kaptain Kenny's Rum Runners, and The Pub at Port Lucaya. ⊠ *Sea Horse Rd., no phone.* ◷ *Daily from 10.*

Veranda Bar overlooks the pool at the Clarion Atlantik Beach and has piano music nightly except Sunday. ⊠ *Clarion Atlantik Beach,* ☎ *242/373–1444.* ◷ *Daily 6–11.*

Yellow Bird Showroom has one of Grand Bahama's best "native" shows, with calypso, limbo, and fire dancers. ⊠ *Castaways Resort,* ☎ *242/352–6682.* ◷ *Wed.–Mon. from 8.*

OUTDOOR ACTIVITIES AND SPORTS

Banana Boating

Bahamas Sea Adventures (⊠ On the beach in front of Clarion Atlantik Beach, Lucaya, ☎ 242/373–3923) lets you ride the banana for 10 minutes for $10. A favorite for the kids, this ride involves straddling a huge rubber banana and bumping along behind a motorboat.

Boating and Fishing

Charters

Boat charters cost about $300 a half day, $600 all day. Bahamian law limits the catching of game fish to six dolphinfish, kingfish, or wahoo per person per day.

Reef Tours (⊠ Bayside, Port Lucaya Marketplace, ☎ 242/373–5880) offers sportfishing on four custom boats; equipment is provided for free. All vessels are licensed, inspected, and insured. Trips run from 8:30 to 12:30 and from 1 to 5, weather permitting; full-day trips are also available. Reservations essential.

Running Mon Marina (⊠ Kelly Ct., Freeport, ☎ 242/352–6834) has daily half- and full-day deep-sea fishing charters. Equipment is included, as is free pickup and return to and from all Freeport hotels. Reservations are essential.

Marinas

Deep Water Cay Club (⊠ Off eastern coast of Grand Bahama Island, ☎ 242/359–4831) has slips for boats of guests, for its small dive operation, and for bonefishing charters.

Lucayan Marina Village (✉ Midshipman Rd., Port Lucaya, ☎ 242/373–8888) features complimentary ferry service to the Lucayan Beach Resort; it has 150 slips.

Port Lucaya Marina (✉ Bayside, Port Lucaya Marketplace, ☎ 242/373–9090) offers a broad range of water sports and has 100 slips for vessels up to 150 ft. If you arrive in your own boat, you're permitted courtesy docking here while you shop or dine at the Port Lucaya Marketplace.

Running Mon Marina (✉ Kelly Ct., Freeport, ☎ 242/352–6834) has 66 slips and serves as the base for a deep-sea fishing fleet. Marina facilities include gas and diesel fuel service, boatyard and on-site mechanics, a 40-ton travel lift (the only one on the island), water and power hookups, marina store, laundry facilities, showers, and rest rooms. The boatyard operates Monday–Friday from 7 AM to 6 PM and on Saturday from 7 to noon. The marina is open daily from 7 to 7.

Xanadu Marina and Beach Resort (✉ Dundee Bay Dr., Freeport, ☎ 242/352–3811) offers 400 ft of dockage plus 77 slips and provides dockside valet service.

Bowling

Sea Surf Lanes (✉ Queen's Hwy., ☎ 242/352–5784) has eight lanes and a snack shop.

Fitness Centers

Bahamas Princess Resort & Casino (✉ W. Sunrise Hwy., ☎ 242/352–6721) has an independently owned small fitness area open to guests and nonguests, with a Universal gym, bicycles, aerobics and jazz classes, a sauna, massages, and facials.

Olympic Fitness Center (✉ Clarion Atlantik Beach, ☎ 242/373–1444) has Universal machines, weights, and fitness classes. Nonguests can use the facilities for a small fee.

YMCA Scandinavian Fitness Centre (✉ E. Atlantic Dr. and Settler's Way, ☎ 242/352–7074) offers weights, machines, and aerobics classes.

Golf

The four championship golf courses (two are located at the Bahamas Princess Resort & Casino) are a major attraction on Grand Bahama Island. Annual events at the Lucaya Golf & Country Club include European Golf Weeks, Caribbean Golf Championships, the Lucaya International Amateur Championship, and the Lucaya Golf & Country Club Pro-Am. The Bahamas Princess Resort & Casino hosts the Bogey Bash Golf Tournament and the Nat Moore Invitational Golf Tournament.

Bahamas Princess Resort & Casino has two 18-hole PGA-rated championship courses: the 6,750-yard Ruby designed by Joe Lee and the 6,679-yard Emerald designed by Dick Wilson—both par-72. A pro shop is also available to visitors. ✉ *W. Sunrise Hwy.,* ☎ *242/352–9661.* ▥ *Greens fees for 18 holes: guests $60, nonguests $65 (shared electric cart included). Club rental $21.*

Fortune Hills Golf & Country Club is a nine-hole, par-36, PGA-rated, 3,453-yard championship course—a Dick Wilson and Joe Lee design—with a restaurant, a bar, and a pro shop. ✉ *E. Sunrise Hwy.,* ☎ *242/373–4500.* ▥ *9 holes $24, 18 holes $38 (cart included). Clubs: 9 holes $10, 18 holes $15.*

Lucaya Golf & Country Club, designed in 1962 by Dick Wilson, is a dramatic 6,824-yard, par-72, 18-hole course currently rated one of the top three courses in the Caribbean. The 18th hole has a double lake and cascading waterfalls, dubbed "The Balancing Boulders of Lucaya." There's a cocktail lounge, the Arawak Dining Room, and a pro shop. ⊠ *Lucaya Beach,* ☎ *242/373–1066.* ⊠ *18 holes $63 (shared electric cart included). Club rental $20.*

Horseback Riding

Pinetree Stables runs trail and beach rides Tuesday–Sunday three times a day; all trail rides are accompanied by an experienced guide. Visitors have a choice of English or western saddles. Private lessons, including jumping and dressage, can be arranged. ⊠ *Beachway Dr.,* ☎ *242/373–3600.* ⊠ *1½-hr beach ride $35.*

Parasailing

Bahamas Sea Adventures (⊠ Lucaya, ☎ 242/373–3923), on the beach in front of the Clarion Atlantik Beach, is a privately run organization that features five- to seven-minute parachute rides for $25.

Sailing

Bahamas Sea Adventures (⊠ Lucaya, ☎ 242/373–3923) has boats of various size for rent. A Hobie Cat costs $30 per hour, a Sunfish, $25.

Paradise Watersports (⊠ Xanadu Beach, ☎ 242/352–3887) rents Hobie Cats for $25 per hour; Sunfish are $20 with a $25 deposit. Lessons are $35 per hour.

Scuba Diving

Grand Bahama Island has some fascinating dive sites near the West End. An extensive reef system runs along the edge of the Little Bahama Bank from Mantinilla Shoals down through Memory Rock, Wood Cay, Rock Cay, and Indian Cay. Sea gardens, caves, and colorful reefs rim the bank all the way from the West End to Freeport-Lucaya and beyond. Some of the main dive sites around the island include **Theo's** Wreck, a 230-ft steel freighter that was sunk in 1982 near Freeport; **Angel's Camp,** a reef about 1¼ mi off Lucayan Beach, offering a scattering of small coral heads surrounding one large head; **Pygmy Caves** (in the same area as Angel's Camp), formed by overgrown ledges that cut into the reef; **Zoo Hole,** west of Lucaya, with huge caverns at 75 ft containing various types of marine life; and **Indian Cay Light,** on the West End, featuring several reefs that form a vast sea garden. Grand Bahama Island is also home of UNEXSO, considered one of the finest diving schools in the world.

Caribbean Divers (⊠ Running Mon Marina, ☎ 242/372–6834), and **Bell Channel Inn,** opposite Port Lucaya (☎ 242/351–6272 or 242/373–9111) offer guided tours, instruction, and equipment rental.

UNEXSO (Underwater Explorers Society) (⊠ Box F 2433, Bayside, Port Lucaya Marketplace, ☎ 242/373–1244, 305/351–9889, or 800/992–3483), a world-renowned scuba-diving facility, provides full equipment for rental, 15 guides, and seven boats, as well as NAUI and PADI certification. Underwater cameras are available for rent, or you can have a dive videotaped for you for $35. A standard three-dive package costs $89; a 20-dive package is $299. Special underwater destinations include Shark Junction and Ben's Cavern. UNEXSO is known for its work with Atlantic bottle-nosed dolphins; open-water dives with the center's animals or standing in a pool and touching them are options. For dolphin encounters, reservations should be made well in advance. Many hotels and tour companies in the area offer scuba and snorkeling packages through this top-notch organization.

Xanadu Undersea Adventures (⊠ Xanadu Beach Resort, ☎ 242/352–3811 or 800/327–8150) offers a resort course for $79; shark dives and night dives are also available.

Sea Kayaking

Sea Kayaking Nature Trip (⊠ Queen's Cove, ☎ 242/373–2485) is a six-hour voyage through the shallow waters along Grand Bahama's north shore. Spot blue heron, crabs, fish, and other marine life as you paddle silently through mangrove creeks. A picnic lunch is served on a deserted island. Trips last from 9 to 3, and children must be at least 10 years old to participate. The cost is $60, with lunch and round-trip transportation from your hotel included.

Snorkeling

Aside from dive shops, a number of tour operators offer snorkeling trips to nearby reefs.

Pat & Diane (⊠ Freeport, ☎ 242/373–8681), with offices in front of the Clarion Atlantik Beach Hotel, takes snorkelers to a shallow reef three times a day on 1¾-hour cruises (drinks included) for $18.

Tennis

The island has more than 50 courts, many lighted for night play. All courts are hard surface unless otherwise noted.

Club Fortuna has two lighted courts on its property. ⊠ *Churchill Beach,* ☎ *242/373–4000.* ☜ *Guests free.*

Lucayan Beach Resort & Casino has four lighted courts on its property. ⊠ *Royal Palm Way,* ☎ *242/373–7777.* ☜ *$5 per hr.*

Princess Country Club has nine courts, with five of them lighted for night play. ⊠ *W. Sunrise Hwy.,* ☎ *242/352–6721.* ☜ *$5 per hr, $10 per hr for night play.*

Silver Sands Hotel has two courts. ⊠ *Royal Palm Way,* ☎ *242/373–5700.* ☜ *Guests free, nonguests $5 per hr.*

Xanadu Beach Resort's three clay courts are all lighted for night play. ⊠ *Sunken Treasure Dr.,* ☎ *242/352–6782.* ☜ *Guests free, nonguests $5 per hr during the day; guests and nonguests $10 per hr for night play.*

Waterskiing

Paradise Watersports (⊠ Xanadu Beach, ☎ 242/352–2887) lets you ski the waves for about 1½ mi, which costs $15; a half-hour lesson is available for $35.

Windsurfing

Bahamas Sea Adventures (⊠ Lucaya, ☎ 242/373–3923) rents Windsurfers for $20 per hour; lessons cost $15 per hour. It's located on the beach in front of the Clarion Atlantik Beach resort.

Clarion Atlantik Beach (⊠ Royal Palm Way, ☎ 242/373–1444) carries 18 boards. Fees are $150 per week or $10 per hour; private lessons are $25.

Paradise Watersports (✉ Xanadu Beach, ☎ 242/352–2887) rents sailboards for $15 an hour, with a $25 deposit; lessons run $30.

SHOPPING

In the hundreds of stores, shops, and boutiques in the International Bazaar in Freeport and at the Port Lucaya Marketplace, you can find duty-free goods costing up to 40% less than what you might pay back home. You'll have to use your own judgment in considering more precious items such as Mexican silver or Chinese jade. Don't try to haggle with shopkeepers, except at the straw markets. At the several perfume shops in the Bazaar and at Port Lucaya, fragrances can often be purchased at a sweet-smelling 30% below U.S. prices. The straw market at Port Lucaya is a huge warren of stalls where vendors expect you to bargain for straw goods, T-shirts, and souvenirs.

Shops in Freeport and Lucaya are open Monday–Saturday from 10 to 6. Stores may stay open later in Port Lucaya.

Markets and Arcades

Goombay Park Arts & Crafts (✉ Behind International Bazaar, no phone) is a straw market consisting of dozens of brightly painted booths resembling little wooden houses.

International Arcade (✉ Connects the International Bazaar and the Princess Casino, no phone) has its own collection of smart shops, primarily branches of stores found at the adjacent International Bazaar, including Colombian Emeralds International, Fendi, The Leather Shop, and Parfum de Paris.

International Bazaar (✉ W. Sunrise Hwy. and E. Mall Dr., ☎ 242/352–2828) should be your first stop for the best bargains on fine imported goods, exotic items, and international fashions. This 10-acre complex consists of an array of shops displaying imports from 25 different countries.

Port Lucaya Marketplace (✉ Sea Horse Dr., ☎ 242/373–8446) has 75 boutiques and restaurants housed in 12 quaint pastel-color buildings in an attractive harborside setting. Free entertainment is provided by local musicians, who often perform at the bandstand in the afternoons and evenings.

Regent Centre (✉ Explorers Way between E. Mall Dr. and W. Mall Dr., no phone) will satisfy your shopping fever with its 60 stores in three mall buildings. This is where local people do their shopping, but you'll also find branches of shops that sell mainly duty-free items, such as the Leather Shop and B. H. L. Duty-Free Liquor Supermarket.

Specialty Shops

Antiques
Old Curiosity Shop (✉ International Bazaar, ☎ 242/352–8008) carries old English clocks, lithographs, brass, and silver objets d'art.

China and Crystal
Island Galleria (✉ International Bazaar and Port Lucaya Marketplace, ☎ 242/352–8194) carries china and crystal by Waterford, Wedgwood, Aynsley, Orrefors, and Coalport.

Lladro Gallery (✉ International Bazaar, ☎ 242/352–2660) specializes in Lladro figurines and Swarovski and Waterford crystal.

Midnight Sun (⊠ International Arcade, ☎ 242/352–9515) is the place to go for gift items by Royal Worcester, Stratton, Daum, and Lalique; you can also purchase Hummel figurines. A life-size troll greets customers at the doorway. Pat his well-worn bald head for good luck.

Fashion

Androsia House (⊠ Port Lucaya Marketplace, ☎ 242/373–8384) sells brightly colored batik fabrics and fashions handmade on the island of Andros.

Gemini (⊠ International Bazaar, ☎ 242/352–4809) specializes in shoes and clothing.

London Pacesetter Boutique (⊠ International Bazaar, ☎ 242/352–2929) has a good selection of swimwear and beachwear, including Reef sandals.

Jewelry and Watches

Colombian (⊠ International Bazaar and Port Lucaya Marketplace, ☎ 242/352–5380) purveys a line of Colombia's famed emeralds.

Colombian Emeralds International (⊠ International Bazaar, International Arcade, and Port Lucaya Marketplace, ☎ 242/352–5464) is *the* place to find diamonds, rubies, sapphires, and gold jewelry; the best brands in watches, including Tissot, Omega, and Citizen, are also available here. The exterior of the stylish shop is decorated with the plaster faces of Aztec gods.

John Bull (⊠ International Bazaar, ☎ 242/352–7515) is famous for its selection of exclusive watches (including Rolex), jewelry, perfumes, cameras (including Nikon and Minolta), and gifts. It also has a Tiffany & Co. boutique.

Leather Goods

Fendi Boutique (⊠ International Bazaar and International Arcade, ☎ 242/352–7908) specializes in Italian leather goods of the same name.

Gucci Boutique (⊠ International Bazaar, ☎ 242/352–4580) patterns its leather creations with its highly recognizable logo. Roman columns and statues of warriors make for a unique shopping experience.

Leather Shop (⊠ International Bazaar and International Arcade, ☎ 242/352–5491) sells HCL, Vitello, Land, and Fendi handbags, shoes and briefcases.

Unusual Centre (⊠ International Bazaar, ☎ 242/352–3994) carries eelskin leather and peacock feather goods.

Perfumes

Les Parisiens Perfumes (⊠ International Bazaar, ☎ 242/352–5380) stocks Giorgio products and the latest scents from Paris.

Oasis (⊠ International Bazaar, International Arcade, and Port Lucaya Marketplace, ☎ 242/352–5923) is a complete pharmacy where you can choose from a selection of French perfumes; it also sells cosmetics, jewelry, and leather goods.

Parfum de Paris (⊠ International Bazaar, International Arcade, and Port Lucaya Marketplace, ☎ 242/352–8164) offers the most comprehensive range of French fragrances on the island.

Perfume Factory (⊠ International Bazaar, ☎ 242/352–9391) sells a large variety of perfumes, lotions, and colognes by Fragrance of the Bahamas. A product called Guanahani was created to commemorate the 500th anniversary of Christopher Columbus's first landfall in the New World, Pink Pearl actually contains conch pearls, and Sand cologne for men has a small amount of island sand in each bottle. You can also create your own scent.

Miscellaneous

Intercity Records (✉ International Bazaar and Port Lucaya Marketplace, ☎ 242/352–8820) is the place to buy records, tapes, and CDs of that Junkanoo, reggae, and soca music that served as a soundtrack for your vacation. Tapes cost $8–$10 and CDs are $20 each, which are not bargain prices, but island music is not always easy to find back home.

Photo Specialist (✉ Port Lucaya Marketplace, ☎ 242/373–7858) carries an extensive range of photo and video equipment and repairs cameras.

Souvenirs of Paradise (✉ International Bazaar, ☎ 242/352–2947) sells the usual souvenir items with Bahamian appeal.

UNEXSO Dive Shop (✉ UNEXSO, Port Lucaya Marketplace, ☎ 242/373–1244) sells everything water-related, from swimsuits to state-of-the-art dive equipment to computers.

Ye Olde Pirate Bottle House (✉ Port Lucaya Marketplace, ☎ 242/373–2000) is an unremarkable souvenir shop, but the adjoining museum, dedicated to the history of bottles, is worth the $3 admission.

GRAND BAHAMA ISLAND A TO Z

Arriving and Departing

By Plane

Freeport International Airport (☎ 242/352–6020) is located just off Grand Bahama Highway, about six minutes from downtown Freeport and about 10 minutes from Port Lucaya.

American Eagle (☎ 800/433–7300) serves Freeport from Miami, with American Airlines connections from a range of U.S. cities.

Bahamasair (☎ 242/352–8341 or 800/222–4262) serves Freeport International Airport with flights from Fort Lauderdale and Miami, as well as via Nassau.

Comair (☎ 800/354–9822) serves Freeport daily from Fort Lauderdale as Delta's international partner airline.

Delta (☎ 800/221–1212) serves Freeport from Orlando only.

Laker Airways (☎ 305/653–9471) provides charter service from Fort Lauderdale, Chicago, Hartford, Cleveland, Cincinnati, Richmond, and Raleigh/Durham.

BETWEEN THE AIRPORT AND HOTELS

No bus service is available between the airport and hotels. Metered taxis meet all incoming flights, and the driver will charge about $8 to take you to Freeport; $12 to Lucaya.

By Ship

Freeport is the port of call for numerous cruise lines, including Carnival Cruise Lines, Celebrity Cruises, Discovery Cruises, Dolphin & Majesty Cruise Line, Premier Cruise Lines, and Sea Escape Cruise Lines (☞ Cruising *in* The Gold Guide, *above*).

BETWEEN THE HARBOR AND FREEPORT

Taxis meet all cruise ships. With six to eight passengers per cab, the driver will charge $3 per person to the International Bazaar, and $4 per person to Port Lucaya. An individual passenger will be charged by the meter; the trips will cost about $10 and $12, respectively.

Getting Around

By Bicycle

Flat Grand Bahama is perfect for bicycling, with its broad avenues and long, straight stretches of highway. Be sure to wear sunblock and carry a bottle of water. Bicycle rentals are inexpensive, starting at about $10 a day. Try **Castaways Resort** (⊠ W. Mall Dr. and International Bazaar, ☎ 242/352–6682), **Princess Country Club** (⊠ W. Sunrise Hwy. and The Mall S, ☎ 242/352–6721), and **Princess Tower** (⊠ W. Sunrise Hwy., ☎ 242/352–9661). **Club Fortuna Beach Resort** (⊠ Churchill Beach, ☎ 242/373–4000) has bicycles available for free use by guests.

By Bus

Buses are an inexpensive way to travel the 4 or 5 mi between downtown Freeport and Port Lucaya Marketplace. Many privately owned buses travel around downtown Freeport and Lucaya for a fare of 75¢.

By Car

If you plan to drive around the island, you'll find it more economical to rent a car than to hire a taxi. Automobiles may be rented at the Freeport International Airport and at individual hotels at a cost of $65 a day and up; gas is about $2.50 a gallon. Local car-rental companies include **Avis Rent-A-Car** in Freeport (☎ 242/352–7666), in Lucaya (☎ 242/373–1102), and at the airport (☎ 242/352–7675); **Bahama Buggies** in Lucaya (☎ 242/325–8750) has bright pink and teal open jeeps for rent; **Dollar Rent-A-Car** at the airport (☎ 242/352–9308) and at the Clarion Atlantik Beach & Golf Resort (☎ 242/373–1444); **National Car Rental** at the airport (☎ 242/352–9308) and at the Xanadu (☎ 242/352–6782); **Sears Rent-A-Car** at the airport (☎ 242/352–8841) and at the Clarion Atlantik Beach Resort (☎ 242/373–4938); and **Star Rent-A-Car** (☎ 242/352–5953) at the airport.

By Scooter

Grand Bahama's flat terrain and straight, well-repaired roads make for good scooter riding. Rentals start at about $35 a day. Helmets are required and provided. Contact **Princess Country Club** (⊠ W. Sunrise Hwy. and The Mall S, ☎ 242/352–6721), **Clarion Atlantik Beach** (⊠ Royal Palm Way, ☎ 242/373–1444), and **Princess Tower** (⊠ W. Sunrise Hwy., ☎ 242/352–9661). Cruise-ship passengers can also rent motor scooters in the Freeport Harbour area.

By Taxi

Limos are commonly used as taxis in Grand Bahama, and they translate ordinary transportation into an experience—what a way to arrive at the casino! Taxi fares are fixed by the government at $2 for the first ¼ mi and 30¢ for each additional ¼ mi regardless of whether the taxi that picks you up is a regular-size cab, van, or stretch limo. Taxi companies in Freeport include **Freeport Taxi Co., Ltd.** (⊠ Old Airport Rd., ☎ 242/352–6666), **Austin and Sons** (⊠ Queen's Hwy., ☎ 242/352–5700), and **G. B. Taxi Union** (⊠ Freeport International Airport, ☎ 242/352–7101).

Opening and Closing Times

Banks on Grand Bahama are generally open Monday–Thursday 9:30–3 and Friday 9:30–5. Some of the major banks on the island include Bank of the Bahamas, Bank of Nova Scotia, Barclays Bank, and Royal Bank of Canada.

Shops are usually open Monday–Saturday 10–6, although they sometimes close earlier on Thursday, Friday, and Saturday. Straw markets and pharmacies are open on Sunday.

Contacts and Resources

Emergencies

Ambulance (☎ 242/352–2689 or 242/352–6735).

American Express (☎ 242/352–4444) is located in the Regent Centre downtown. It is open weekdays 9–1 and 2–5. For lost cards, ☎ 800/327–1267.

Bahama Air Sea Rescue (☎ 242/352–2628).

Fire Department (☎ 242/352–8888).

Hospital. The government-operated Rand Memorial Hospital (⊠ E. Atlantic Dr., ☎ 242/352–6735) has 74 beds.

Police (☎ 919).

Guided Tours

Tours can be booked through the tour desk in your hotel lobby, at tourist information booths, or by calling one of the tour operators listed below.

AIR TOURS

You can take short airplane flights around Grand Bahama, to Nassau, or to some of the nearby Out Islands on **Taino Air** (⊠ Freeport, ☎ 242/352–8885).

EXCURSIONS

A Grand Bahama day trip will take you to the major attractions on the island at a cost of $12 to $18 per person for an approximate three-hour tour. A glass-bottom-boat tour, which visits offshore reefs and sea gardens, starts at $15. If you're interested in a trip to the Garden of the Groves, expect to pay about $10. A tour of the historic West End costs $16.

For evening entertainment, a dinner cruise will cost around $40. Nightclub tours are about $20.

You can even take a day trip to New Providence Island that includes round-trip air transportation, a sightseeing tour of Nassau, a visit to Paradise Island, and shopping on Bay Street. Such a package will cost about $175.

The following tour operators on Grand Bahama offer a combination of the tours described above, and several of them have desks in major hotels: **Bahamas Travel Agency** (⊠ Box F 3778, ☎ 242/352–3141), **Bain's Travel Service** (⊠ Box F 42045, ☎ 242/352–3861 or 800/372–6963), **Executive Tours** (⊠ Box F 2509, Mercantile Bldg., ☎ 242/352–8858), **International Travel & Tours** (⊠ Box F 850, ☎ 242/352–9311), **Reef Tours Ltd.** (⊠ Box F 2510, Port Lucaya, ☎ 242/373–5880), **Sun Island Tours** (⊠ Box F 2585, ☎ 242/352–4811), and **Sunworld Travel and Tours** (⊠ Box F 2631, ☎ 242/352–3717).

SPECIAL-INTEREST TOURS

***Deepstar* Submarine.** If you want to see what goes on in the depths of the ocean but don't necessarily want to take up scuba diving, this 45-passenger submarine dives to 100 ft, and you'll get a panoramic underwater view through the completely transparent acrylic hull. The *Deepstar* is moored about 1½ mi offshore. You transfer by ferry from the UNEXSO dock in Port Lucaya. ⊠ *Bayside, Port Lucaya Market-*

place, ☎ *242/373–7934.* 🎫 *3 2-hr voyages $49.* ☯ *Daily voyages at 10, 11, and 1:30, weather permitting.*

East End Adventure. This land-and-sea guided ecotour includes a trip to the Lucayan National Park and a Jeep ride along pristine beaches and through dense pine forests to Sweeting's Cay. Snorkeling, catch-and-release fishing, and a speedboat ride are included. A Bahamian lunch is served on a nearby deserted island called Lightbourne's Cay. ⊠ *Freeport,* ☎ *242/373–6662.* 🎫 *Daylong tours $100.* ☯ *Trips depart at 8 AM and return at 6 PM.*

Seaworld Explorer. If you don't want to go too far underwater, this semisubmarine does not submerge. You descend into the hull of the boat and observe sea life in air-conditioned comfort from a vantage point 5 ft below the surface. The vessel departs from Port Lucaya and travels to Treasure Reef. ⊠ *Bayside, Port Lucaya Marina, Port Lucaya,* ☎ *242/373–7863.* 🎫 *1½-hr voyage $29.* ☯ *Daily trips at 10, 11:30, 1:30, and 3.*

Visitor Information

Grand Bahama Island Tourism Board (☎ 242/352–8044, FAX 242/352–7840) has its main office and a separate tourist information center near the entrance to the International Bazaar in **Freeport.** Branch offices are located at the **Freeport International Airport** (☎ 242/352–2052), the **Harbour Cruiseship Port** (☎ 242/351–4277), and **Port Lucaya** (☎ 242/373–8988). Ask about Bahamahosts, specially trained tour guides who will talk to you about island history and culture and pass on their individual and imaginative knowledge of Bahamian folklore. Tourist offices are open Monday through Saturday, 9 to 5:30 (the airport office is also open on Sunday).

5 The Out Islands

To escape the crowds and the glittering modernity of New Providence and Grand Bahama, get yourself on a boat or plane to one of the Out Islands, where quiet cays afford a slower-paced, unspoiled way of life. Wander uncluttered beaches and narrow, sand-strewn streets, or lunch in a village where fishermen's neat homes are painted in soft pastel shades and shrouded in brilliantly colored vegetation.

Updated by
Rachel
Christmas
Derrick

THE QUIET, SIMPLER WAY OF LIFE of the Bahama Out Islands, sometimes referred to as the Family Islands, is startlingly different from the fast-paced glitz and glitter of Nassau and Freeport. On the dozen or so islands outside of New Providence and Grand Bahama that are equipped to handle tourists, you leave the sophisticated nightclubs, casinos, bazaars, and shopping malls behind. If you love sports and the outdoors, however, you'll be in fine shape: Virtually all the Out Islands have good to excellent fishing, boating, and diving, and you'll often have endless stretches of beach all to yourself. For the most part, you won't find hotels that provide the kind of costly creature comforts taken for granted in Nassau and Freeport—although this is changing with the development of luxury resorts like Pink Sands on Harbour Island and Club Med–Columbus Isle on San Salvador. Accommodations in the Out Islands are generally more modest lodges, rustic cottages, and small inns with balustraded balconies, many without telephones and TV (inquire when making reservations if these are important to you). The meals in your hotel are usually cooked by a local, with freshly caught fish, conch, or chicken and peas 'n' rice being the staple diet. On some of the more remote islands, making a phone call to friends back home, or receiving one, may require an extra trip to the local BaTelCo telephone station.

Along with the utter lack of stress on an Out Islands holiday, you'll also find largely unspoiled environments. Roughing it in Inagua, for example, is a small price to pay for the glorious spectacle of 60,000 pink flamingos taking off into the bright blue sky. And a day of sightseeing can mean little more than a stroll down narrow, sand-strewn streets in fishing villages, past small, pastel-color homes where orange, pink, and bright-red bougainvillea spill over the walls. The taverns are tiny and usually noisy with chatter, and you can make friends with locals over a beer and a game of pool or darts much more quickly than you would in the average stateside cocktail lounge. Nightlife may involve listening to a piano player or a small village combo in a clubhouse bar, or joining the crowds at a local disco playing everything from R&B to calypso.

The Out Islands were once the domain mostly of yachters and private plane owners; the tourist who discovered a favorite hideaway on Andros, Eleuthera, or in the Exumas would cherish it and return year after year to find the same faces as before. But the islands are slowly becoming more and more popular, largely because of increased airline activity. By the same token, the frequency of air service may play a part in your choice of destination. Most islands are served from Nassau or Florida daily; others may only have a couple of incoming and outgoing flights a week. If you want to sample an Out Island without feeling completely cut off, you may want to choose a slightly busier spot that is closer to the mainland United States, such as Bimini, Eleuthera, or Great Abaco Island. If you go farther away from the mainland, to a place like Cat Island or San Salvador, you'll feel much more like you're getting away from it all.

Pleasures and Pastimes

Dining

For the most part, hotels in the Out Islands serve a combination of Bahamian, Continental, and American cuisine. independent restaurants are often family-run and focus on homestyle dishes. You'll notice that there is little variety from one local dining spot to the next. It is each cook's special flair that creates a loyal following. Fish, always on the menu, is almost certain to be very fresh. Grouper cooked almost any way is delicious, but the Bahamian specialty, boiled fish (with tomatoes and spices), is especially good. Conch and lobster are prepared in a variety of ways, all of them tasty. Side dishes are generally peas 'n' rice, potato salad, and coleslaw—often all three in the same meal.

Because much of the food is imported, eating out in the Bahamas is expensive, even on the less developed islands. Entrées will run anywhere from $10 to $30 per person and drinks aren't cheap. A service charge of 15% is virtually always added to your bill. Lobster, which is found all over the islands, costs the same as a New York strip steak, which has to be imported.

Although some Out Island resorts are operated solely on the European Plan (no meals included), most offer the Modified American Plan (breakfast and dinner) for prices ranging from $17 to $40, plus 15% gratuity, in addition to room rates. Occasionally the Full American Plan (breakfast, lunch, and dinner) will be available. Look for the abbreviations EP, MAP, and FAP at the end of most resort reviews in this chapter for indication of which plan or plans the property offers.

CATEGORY	COST*
$$$$	over $35
$$$	$25–$35
$$	$15–$25
$	under $15

per person, excluding drinks and service

Lodging

The small hotels of the Out Islands are mostly owner-operated, which ensures a personal touch, such as owners greeting you in the bar for cocktails in the evening. Some accommodations even use an honor bar system—mix your own and sign for it—so you really feel at home. Many hotels specialize in the sports of fishing or diving—such as Bimini Blue Water or Bimini Big Game Fishing Club on Bimini and Small Hope Bay Lodge on Andros—and offer packages which may include airfare, accommodations, meals, and a number of fishing or diving trips. There are also self-contained resorts, which offer their own sports facilities, such as the Club Med on Eleuthera and on San Salvador. When you make a reservation, be sure to find out if the hotel has any special packages.

Although accommodations may be small and out of the way, don't expect your Out Island vacation to be inexpensive. The islanders have to import almost everything; produce and other goods coming by mail boat can arrive spoiled or broken. This means $6 hamburgers and gasoline at $2.50 to $3 per gallon—for residents and for you. A pack of cigarettes will run you more than $5—here's your chance to quit! Still, it's hard to put a price on the total escape these resorts have to offer. What would you pay for a powdery pink beach that stretches for miles with no footprints but your own? Or water so clear that snorkeling makes you feel like you're flying? Or a seafood dinner harvested the same day? Part of the price you pay may be the lack of in-room phones, TVs, or air-conditioning, but you may find that those conveniences aren't so important in paradise.

The Out Island Promotion Board can also help you find a house to rent. Properties of all sizes and prices are available, and monthly rentals may be as much as one-third less than combined weekly rates. Linens, cookware, and utilities are usually included. Sometimes a part-time cook, fishing or diving trips, and airport pickups are also part of the package.

The peak season is mid-December to mid-April. After that, room rates tend to drop by as much as a third. Price categories that follow apply to all of the Out Islands hotels. An 8% tax is added to your hotel bill, representing resort and government levies. Most hotels add a 10% gratuity for maid service, and a 3%–6% surcharge may be added to credit-card payments by some resorts. Be sure to ask about taxes, surcharges, and service charges when making your reservation—it can add over 20% to your bill.

For **private villa rentals** (starting at about $160 a night for two people) in Windermere Island in Eleuthera or Treasure Cay in the Abacos, call VHR Worldwide (☎ 800/633–3284 or 201/767–9393).

CATEGORY	COST*
$$$$	over $175
$$$	$125–$175
$$	$75–$125
$	under $75

All prices are for a double room in high season, excluding tax and service charges.

THE ABACOS

The Abacos, a boomerang-shape cluster of cays in the northeastern Bahamas, stretch from tiny Walker's Cay in the north to Hole-in-the-Wall, more than 130 mi to the southwest. Many of these cays are very small, providing exquisitely desolate settings for private picnics. The Abacos have their fair share of tranquil bays and inlets, lagoons, and pine forests where wild boar roam, but they also offer the commercial center of Marsh Harbour—the third-largest community in the Bahamas—with all the amenities of a small town, including a selection of shops, restaurants, and hotels. The two main islands, Great Abaco and Little Abaco, are fringed on their windward shore by an emerald necklace of cays that forms a barrier reef against the broad Atlantic.

The Abacos' calm, naturally protected waters, long admired for their beauty, have helped the area become the sailing capital of the Bahamas. The islands' excellent resorts are particularly popular with yachting and fishing enthusiasts because of the fine boating facilities available, among them the Treasure Cay Marina, the Boat Harbour Marina at Marsh Harbour, and Walker's Cay Club Marina. Man-O-War Cay remains the boatbuilding center for the Bahamas; its residents turn out traditionally crafted wood dinghies as well as high-tech crafts made of fiberglass. The Abacos play host annually to internationally famous regattas and to a half dozen game-fish tournaments. Outside of the resorts, the oceanside villages of Hope Town and New Plymouth also appeal to tourists for their charming New England–style ambience.

The Abacos' first settlers, New England Loyalists, arrived in 1783. Other families soon followed from Virginia and the Carolinas, bringing with them their plantation lifestyle and their slaves. These early arrivals tried to make a living from farming, but the Abacos' land was resistant to the growing of crops. Next, many settlers turned to the sea for sustenance; some of them started fishing, while others practiced wrecking.

By the end of the 18th century, charts of the Bahamian waters had not been drawn, and there were no lighthouses in the area until 1836. The wreckers of the Abacos worked at night, shining misleading lights to lure ships to destruction onto rocks and shoals—and then seizing the ships' cargo. Of course, not all these wrecks were caused by unscrupulous islanders; some ships were lost in storms and foundered on hidden reefs as they passed through the Bahamas. Nevertheless, by fair means or foul, wrecking remained a thriving industry in the Abacos until the mid-1800s.

The notorious deeds of the wreckers have long faded into history and legend. Today, about 10,000 residents live peacefully in the Abacos. Many of these enterprising, friendly people are seafarers, earning an honest living as boatbuilders, fishermen, and fishing guides. Because the Abacos are one of the most visited destinations in the Out Islands, an increasing number of residents work in the tourist industry.

Numbers in the text correspond to numbers in the margin and on the Abacos map.

Great Abaco Island

Most visitors to the Abacos make their first stop on the east coast of
① Great Abaco Island at **Marsh Harbour,** the third-largest city in the Bahamas and the commercial center of the Abacos. Besides having its own airport, Marsh Harbour is considered by boaters to be one of the easiest harbors to enter; and it offers several fine full-service marinas, such as the 150-slip Boat Harbour Marina and the 75-slip Conch Inn Marina.

This peaceful community is a good place to stock up on groceries and supplies on the way to other islands because its downtown area has several well-equipped supermarkets, department and hardware stores, banks, gas stations, and a few good, moderately priced restaurants. The main street, where most of the gift shops are located, has the island's only traffic light.

On a hilltop overlooking Marsh Harbour stands a **miniature castle** built by Dr. Evans Cottman, a high-school biology teacher from Madison, Indiana, who moved to the Bahamas and became an "unqualified practitioner" in the 1940s. Cottman wrote of his experiences in a fascinating book called *Out Island Doctor.* Visitors to Marsh Harbour in November may wish to participate in the **Abaco Week Festival,** which commemorates the arrival of the Loyalists after the Revolutionary War with fairs and parades, as well as golf, tennis, and fishing tournaments. For details, contact the Abaco Chamber of Commerce (☞ Abacos A to Z, *below*).

② About 20 mi south of Marsh Harbour is the little settlement of **Cherokee Sound** (population 165), whose inhabitants make their living by crawfishing and reside in wooden, shuttered houses with fruit trees in the yards. The beauty of this area is found in the deserted Atlantic beaches and the serene salt marshes.

③ **Sandy Point,** a rustic fishing village with a lovely beach that attracts shell collectors, lies just over 50 mi southwest of Marsh Harbour. Although there are no communities to visit south of Sandy Point, a major navigational lighthouse stands at **Hole-in-the-Wall,** on the southern tip of Great Abaco.

A rugged winding road leads off the Great Abaco Highway about 40 mi south of Marsh Harbour, passing through the dense pine wood-
④ lands of the **Bahamas National Trust Sanctuary,** a reserve for the endangered Bahamian parrot (your best chance of seeing the bird is at dawn). More than 100 other species have been sighted in this area by avid bird-watchers.

The Abacos

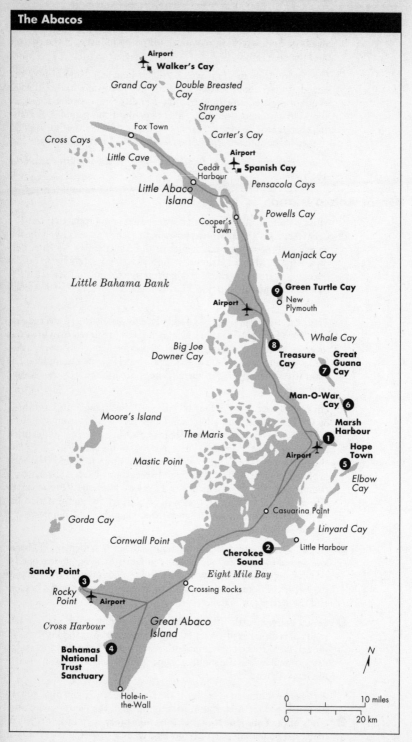

Dining and Lodging

$$$ ✕ **Conch Inn Café.** Near Mangoes on the docks, this dining room serves fresh seafood and Bahamian dishes such as minced lobster and coconut grouper, or lobster stuffed with mushrooms. There's a happy hour a couple of nights a week. If you dare, try a Conch Killer—a cocktail of four different rums with fruit juice. ⊠ *East Bay St., Marsh Harbour,* ☎ *242/367–2319. No dinner Tues.*

$$$ ✕ **Mangoes.** Located right on the active harbor, Mangoes is known for its spicy coconut shrimp, cracked conch, and pork tenderloin in mango sauce. ⊠ *East Bay St., Marsh Harbour,* ☎ *242/367–2366. Closed Sun.*

$$$ ✕ **Sapodilly's.** Head to the harbor when you have a taste for such Bahamian specialties as steamed conch and grilled fish, or if you just want a good sandwich. There is live music on Monday and Friday nights. ⊠ *Queen Elizabeth Dr., Marsh Harbour,* ☎ *242/367–3498. No lunch Mon.*

$$$ ✕ **Wally's.** In a two-story building that resembles a small mansion, across the road from the water, this is one of the Bahamas' most attractive restaurants. Inside, you'll find Haitian-style paintings and white wicker chairs on terra-cotta tiles. The gourmet local cuisine includes wild Abaco boar, turtle sautéed in onions and mushrooms, as well as grilled wahoo, tuna, or duck breast—and key lime pie. ⊠ *East Bay St., Marsh Harbour,* ☎ *242/367–2074. Closed Sun. and Mon.*

$$ ✕ **Different of Abaco.** In a cool, screened dining room, bells tinkle in the breeze while owner Nettie Symonette tells funny stories and mixes her famous bush tea. This tasty concoction is made from eleven local plants and coconut rum and is served in icy blue tin mugs. Nettie's tea—not to mention her Bahamian conch chowder, broiled lobster, wild boar, and peas 'n' rice—is worth the drive a few dusty miles beyond Cherokee Sound to Casuarina Point. A small museum displays the work of Nettie's daughter, Lorna Miller, a doll maker of worldwide acclaim. ⊠ *Casuarina Point, Great Abaco,* ☎ *242/366–2150.*

$$ ✕ **Jib Room.** This popular local spot has BBQ nights, serving New York strip steak Sundays and baby-back ribs Wednesdays. ⊠ *Pelican Shores, Marsh Harbour,* ☎ *242/367–2700. Closed Tues.*

$–$$ ✕ **Mother Merle's Fishnet.** Famous for Merle's special fried chicken and conch fritters, this unpretentious dining room is almost always busy. ⊠ *Dundas Town, Great Abaco,* ☎ *242/367–2770. Closed Wed. No lunch.*

$$$$ ✕🏨 **Abaco Beach Resort & Boat Harbour.** This sprawling hillside property on the Sea of Abaco is a hotel, conference center, marina, and planned residential community. Guests have a choice of a spacious room in the hotel or one of the fancier two-bedroom, two-bath villas, complete with kitchen, living room, and dining area; all accommodations have balconies with a grand view of the beach and sea. The hotel rooms in the newer wing are surprisingly attractive, decorated with tropical cherry furniture, tiled floors, granite vanity countertops, large baths with great water pressure (a rarity in the Out Islands), telephones, and TVs. The lanais even have Adirondack chairs. There are two pools, one with a swim-up bar. Angler's restaurant serves Bahamian cuisine while the Sand Bar whips up good bar food. The resort has a full-service dive shop and can arrange fishing charters, boat rentals, and sightseeing tours. A minimarket, liquor store, and boutique are on the grounds. ⊠ *Box AB 20511, Marsh Harbour, Abaco,* ☎ *242/367–2158 or 800/468–4799,* 𝔉𝔞𝔵 *242/367–2819. 52 rooms and 6 villas. Restaurant, 2 bars, lounge, 2 pools, 2 tennis courts, dive shop, dock, boating, fishing, bicycles, laundry service. AE, MC, V. EP.*

$$–$$$ ✕🏨 **Abaco Towns by the Sea.** This complex contains two-bedroom,
★ two-bath condominiums, each with a fully equipped kitchen, a dining
area, a master bedroom, a guest bedroom, and a private patio with a
small barbecue grill. All the villas can accommodate up to six people;
some are on the beach, some overlook the beach, and some face
nothing in particular. Choose the ones with at least a water view—the
"garden" units have all the ambience of a suburban condo complex.
The pool and two tennis courts overlook a decent beach and the Sea
of Abaco. The restaurant and bar, where there is live entertainment,
serves lunch and dinner. Fishing can be arranged, and there's a dive
shop across the street. ✉ *Box AB 20486, Marsh Harbour, Abaco,*
☎ *242/367–2227 or 800/322–7757,* ℻ *406/257–8575. 64 condos.*
Restaurant, bar, pool, 2 tennis courts, snorkeling, fishing. AE, MC, V.
EP.

$$ ✕🏨 **Conch Inn.** This casual, motelish hotel, situated between the ferry
dock and the town center, is one of the most popular gathering spots
on Great Abaco Island for yachters, private fliers, local residents, and
guests from other resorts. The inn, which is 2 mi from the airport, has
a swimming pool, and small beaches are within walking distance. Its
full-service 75-slip marina is one of the best and busiest in Marsh Har-
bour and is the Bahamas' headquarters for the Moorings yacht char-
ter service. The simple rooms have nautical-theme decor and small
patios overlooking the docks. The Conch Inn Café (☞ *above*) serves
great fare, including fried grits with salsa at breakfast. The ferry to Great
Guana Cay leaves from the inn. ✉ *Box AB 20469, Marsh Harbour,*
Abaco, ☎ *242/367–4000,* ℻ *242/367–4004. 9 rooms. Restaurant, bar,*
pool, dive shop, docks, baby-sitting, laundry service. AE, MC, V. EP.

$$ ✕🏨 **Different of Abaco.** This ecotourism resort at Casuarina Point is
the home of the Great Abaco Bonefishing Club (also known as Net-
tie's Heritage Club), but anyone seeking virgin beach and ocean reefs
will love it. There are blue holes for fishing or diving, and the snorkeling is excellent. If you find that you aren't busy snoozing in hammocks,
you can explore by bicycle, golf cart, or canoe. The rooms are right
on the water, each named for one of the local plants used in owner Nettie Symonette's bush tea (brewed herbs and rum), and they are spot-
less, airy, and comfortable. The screened dining room is decorated with
huge conch shells, blue Dutch platters, and tablecloths with brightly
painted fish. At night, this can be a lively scene, with fish tales flying.
Nettie serves very tasty, gourmet Bahamian fare (☞ *above*). From the
deck outside the dining room, one can feed ducks, geese, flamingos,
and schools of fish. Be sure to bring bug spray, however, as the sand
flies, or no-see-ums, are sometimes brutal at sunset. Next door is a replica
of an authentic thatched village, depicting the lifestyle of Lucayan Indians, the original Bahamians. ✉ *Box AB 20092, Marsh Harbour,*
Abaco, ☎ *242/366–2150 or 242/327–7921,* ℻ *242/327–8152. 28*
rooms. Bar, dining room, boating, fishing. No credit cards. FAP.

$$$ 🏨 **Pelican Beach Villas.** Five two-bedroom, two-bath villas with the
ambience of a lakefront cabin compound are tucked into the upscale
residential community of Pelican Shores at Marsh Harbour. The rooms,
all of which face the sea to catch the cooling trade winds, are light and
airy, with tropical furnishings, and fully equipped kitchens, including
microwave ovens. A resident caretaker is always available. Guests can
lunch at picnic tables out on the beach. There is a dock in back for
tying up boats—most guests rent their own. Children under 12 stay
for free. ✉ *Box AB 20304, Marsh Harbour, Abaco,* ☎ *242/367–3600*
or 800/642–7268, ℻ *242/367–3603. 5 villas. Beach, dive shop, dock,*
snorkeling, boating, laundry service. AE, MC, V. EP.

$$ ⊡ **Island Breezes.** With a few simple but attractive rooms, this orange-and-white, one-story hostelry provides every amenity at a bargain rate. Slatted wood ceilings, platform beds, ceiling fans, and satellite TV are in all rooms. ⊠ *Box AB 20453, Marsh Harbour, Abaco,* ☎ 242/367–3776, ℻ 242/367–4179. *8 rooms. MC, V. EP.*

$$ ⊡ **Lofty Fig Villas.** These six spacious villas are near the harbor and are adjacent to restaurants, marinas, bars, and a dive shop. The villa kitchens are fully equipped and the supermarket is about a 10-minute walk. For families or groups on a budget, this might be a good option. ⊠ *Box AB 20437, Marsh Harbour, Abaco,* ☎ ℻ 242/367–2681. *6 villas. Pool. MC, V. EP.*

Outdoor Activities and Sports

BOATING

Charters. Sailboats can be chartered by the week or longer, with or without crew. **The Moorings** (☎ 800/535–7289 or 242/367–4000) is located at the Conch Inn Resort & Marina in Marsh Harbour. This is the Bahamas' division of one of the foremost yacht-charter agencies in the world, which provides every service needed for yachters—from provisions to professional captains. **Swift Yacht Charters** (☎ 800/866–8340 or 508/647–1554, ℻ 508/647–1556) might be located in Massachusetts, but Hope Swift's personal knowledge of the Abacos' charter operations will put you in the right boat.

Marinas. The Abacos offer several fine full-service marina facilities, located at main points on the islands. In Marsh Harbour: **Boat Harbour Marina** (☎ 242/367–2736), **Conch Inn Marina** (☎ 242/367–4000), and **Marsh Harbour Marina** (☎ 242/367–2700).

Rentals. Renting a boat is a good idea if you're staying on the outer cays. Powerboats, from 15-ft Boston whalers to 26-ft Paramounts, can be rented on a daily, three-day, or weekly basis. Daily rates run from $65 to $135, three-day rates from $115 to $240, and weekly rates from $350 to $800. **Rich's Boat Rentals** (☎ 242/367–2742), **Sea Horse Boat Rentals** (☎ 242/367–2513), and **Laysue Rentals** (☎ 242/367–4414), offering catamarans only, are all in Marsh Harbour.

EVENTS

Several sporting events are held annually in the Abacos. The **Boat Harbour Billfish Championship** is held in June. July brings the weeklong **Regatta Time in Abaco,** a series of five races, accompanied by nightly parties and entertainment. To participate, write to Regatta Time in Abaco (⊠ Box 428, Marsh Harbour, Abaco), or contact David Ralph (☎ 242/367–2677, ℻ 242/367–3677). For information about any events on the Abacos, call the Bahamas Tourism office nearest you or the **Out Island Promotion Board** (☎ 954/359–8099 or 800/688–4752).

FISHING

You can find bonefish in the flats, yellowtail on the reefs, or marlin in the deep of the Abacos. **Great Abaco Bonefishing Club** (☎ 242/366–2150 in Marsh Harbour) lures the hook, line, and sinker crowd to Casuarina Point at Different of Abaco—an angler's paradise.

SCUBA DIVING

The clear waters of the Abacos, which teem with marine life, waving sea fans and coral, and multihued fish, are ideal for diving. You can arrange expeditions through your hotel. Some main dive sites include the wreck of the USS *Adirondack,* near Man-O-War Cay; Pelican Cays National Park at Marsh Harbour, with a full range of marine life; and ocean blue holes southwest of Hole-in-the-Wall. Most Abacos dive operators offer night dives and certification courses. **Dive Abaco** (☎ 242/367–2787) and **Great Abaco Beach** (☎ 242/367–2158), both in Marsh

Harbour, rent equipment and have daily reef and wreck dives. Also see
Scuba Diving *in* the other Abacos island sections, *below.*

TENNIS

Abaco Towns by the Sea (☎ 800/332–7757), and **Great Abaco Beach
Resort** (☎ 242/367–2158) both open their courts to visitors.

WINDSURFING

Windsurfing is offered at the **Great Abaco Beach Resort** (☎ 242/367–
2158) and **Different of Abaco**(☎ 242/366–2150).

Shopping

John Bull (✉ Marsh Harbour, ☎ 242/367–2473), situated near the
harbor, is a branch of a leading Nassau shop where you can purchase
watches and perfumes.

Johnston Studios Art Gallery (✉ Little Harbour, ☎ 242/367–3466)
displays original bronzes by the Johnstons.

Juliette Gallery (✉ Queen Elizabeth Dr., Marsh Harbour, ☎ 242/367–
4551) has Bahamian art, sculpture, stained glass, and handmade furniture.

Little Switzerland (✉ Queen Elizabeth Dr., Marsh Harbour, ☎ 242/367–
3191) sells watches and perfumes at the entrance to the Great Abaco
Beach Resort.

Loyalist Shoppe (✉ Don MacKay Blvd., Marsh Harbour, ☎ 242/367–
2701) specializes in pottery, china, and leather goods from England,
Italy, and Poland.

Elbow Cay

❺ The charming village of **Hope Town,** where most of the families among
its 300-odd residents have been here for generations, lies southeast of
Marsh Harbour, on Elbow Cay. You'll find few cars and other pesky
trappings of modern life here. In fact, most residents remember well
the day the island first got telephone service—since it wasn't until 1988!
Before that, everyone called each other the way many still do here and
in other Out Islands: by VHF, the party line for boaters.

In this peaceful, relaxed community, visitors are enthusiastically welcomed. Arrivals to Hope Town are greeted by the sight of a much-pho-
tographed Bahamas landmark, a 120-ft-tall, peppermint-stripe
lighthouse, built in 1838. The light's construction was delayed for several years by acts of vandalism because residents were afraid it would
put an end to their profitable wrecking practice. Today, the Hope
Town lighthouse is one of the last four hand-turned, kerosene-fueled
beacons in the Bahamas. If you're feeling energetic, the lighthouse
keeper will welcome you at the top (☉ Weekdays 10–4) for a superb
view of the sea and the nearby cays.

Ferry service within the harbor will take you to spots otherwise inac-
cessible on foot, for $1. For an interesting walking or bicycle tour of
Hope Town, whose saltbox cottages, white picket fences, and flowering gardens will remind you of a New England seaside community—
Bahamian style—follow the two narrow lanes that circle the village and
harbor. As in many small towns, a local beautification committee has
planted trees, palms, bushes, and flowers donated by the National Trust
in Nassau. The houses are painted in brilliant blues, purples, pinks,
and yellows, their porches and sills decorated with conch shells. You
may also want to stop at the **Wyannie Malone Historical Museum** (no
phone; ✉ Free, but donations welcome; ☉ Hrs vary) on Queen's
Highway, the main street. It contains memorabilia and photographs

of Hope Town. Many of the descendants of Mrs. Malone, who settled here with her children in 1875, still live on Elbow Cay.

Although the town is tiny, there are several churches. You can stand on a corner on a Sunday morning and hear two different sermons floating through open windows. Don't be surprised if while wandering the streets, you come across an alfresco Catholic service in the dockside park. Sometimes bikini-clad women and shirtless men can be seen climbing in and out of boats behind the priest! Residents joke that the priest has to stand in the hot sun while the congregation enjoys the shade of sprawling trees "so he won't talk so long."

Dining and Lodging

$$$ ✕ **Abaco Inn.** A few miles south of town, Abaco Inn serves American-Bahamian and vegetarian cuisine in a beautiful indoor and outdoor setting overlooking the ocean and White Sound. Call for free van service to pick you up. ⊠ *Hope Town, Elbow Cay,* ☎ *242/366–0133.*

$$$ ✕ **Club Soleil.** The menu in this wood-beamed dining room includes fresh seafood dishes, home-baked bread, and Bahamian peas 'n' rice. The spacious dining room is surrounded on three sides by water. Reservations are recommended for the famous champagne Sunday brunch. ⊠ *Club Soleil Resort, Hope Town, Elbow Cay,* ☎ *242/366–0003. Closed Mon. No dinner Sun.*

$$$ ✕ **Harbour's Edge.** This local Hope Town hangout serves excellent conch burgers, grilled grouper, or lobster salad for lunch and dinner and a Bahamian breakfast—usually chicken souse—on Sundays. You can also rent bikes here for $8 a day and cue up on the island's only pool table. Live bands occasionally play on weekends. ⊠ *Hope Town, Elbow Cay,* ☎ *242/366–0292. Closed Tues.*

$$$ ✕ **Hope Town Harbour Lodge.** Creamy lobster fettuccine is a favorite here, among other American-Bahamian–style dishes. The resort's restaurant is open for breakfast and dinner, and the beach-side Reef Bar serves lunch. The restaurant has a good wine list. ⊠ *Hope Town, Elbow Cay,* ☎ *242/366–0095. No dinner Sun. and Mon.*

$$ ✕ **Rudy's Place.** A favorite with locals for dinner—rave reviews go to the crawfish baked with Parmesan cheese—Rudy's is set in a renovated house. Complimentary pickup from your accommodation is available. ⊠ *Hope Town, Elbow Cay,* ☎ *242/366–0062. Closed Sun.*

$ ✕ **Captain Jack's.** This local hangout serves breakfast and pub-style lunches. ⊠ *Hope Town, Elbow Cay,* ☎ *242/366–0247.*

$ ✕ **Munchies.** This is the place for a late-night snack, as well as daily lunch and dinner specials, which include conch fritters, fish or turkey burgers, peas 'n' rice, and macaroni and cheese. Very casual, it offers outside seating at umbrella-shaded tables. ⊠ *Hope Town, Elbow Cay,* ☎ *242/366–0423. No dinner Sun.*

$$–$$$ ✕🏨 **Hope Town Harbour Lodge.** This amiable inn is perched on a hill
★ that faces both the gorgeous ocean beach and Hope Town harbor, with its distinctive red-and-white striped lighthouse. Six of the clean, unpretentious cottage rooms are clustered around the pool and two are on the ocean; the rest of the rooms in the main lodge overlook the harbor. All have air-conditioning, decks, and mini-refrigerators. Choose your ocean or harbor view carefully—there are no TVs or phones to distract you. There are two restaurants that serve Bahamian and Continental cuisine (☞ *above*), with vegetarian selections, as well as two bars. Diving, boating, or fishing can be arranged at the resort's dock; wonderful snorkeling opportunities are available only 15 yards off the beach. ⊠ *Hope Town, Abaco,* ☎ *242/366–0095 or 800/316–7844,* ℻ *242/366–0286. 20 rooms. 2 restaurants, 2 bars, lounge, pool, beach, dock. MC, V. EP.*

$$ ✕▥ **Abaco Inn.** This friendly beachfront resort overlooks the ocean
★ and bay in a setting of palms and sea-grape trees, about 2 mi south of
Hope Town. It offers six ocean- and six harbor-view villas; the sim-
ple, cheerful units have high ceilings with white beams and include com-
fortable furnishings. Each room has its own hammock outside for
dozing and a shelf full of books for reading. A weathered gazebo faces
the ocean, and a thatched solarium on the beach is available for nude
sunbathing. Excellent reefs for snorkeling and diving are nearby. There
are no phones or TVs in the rooms, but satellite TV is installed in the
bar, and the lounge has live music a couple of nights a week. After your
complimentary pickup in Hope Town, you'll probably want to rent your
own boat so you can zoom into town or to one of the smaller islets
around Elbow Cay; you can tie up at the resort. The restaurant (☞
above) serves creatively prepared seafood and vegetarian dishes. ⊠ *Hope
Town, Abaco,* ☎ *242/366–0133 or 800/468–8799,* ☏ *242/366–
0113. 12 rooms. Bar, dining room, lounge, pool, boating, fishing,
baby-sitting, coin laundry. MC, V. EP, MAP.*

$$ ✕▥ **Club Soleil Resort and Marina.** This Spanish-style resort, built in
1991, has an idyllic location in a grove of coconut palms, banana trees,
and hibiscus, just across the harbor from Hope Town and a short walk
from secluded beaches on the ocean side of Elbow Cay. The modern
rooms have cedar closets, tile floors, and private balconies. Rooms are
without phones, but do have TVs with VCRs; videos are available in
town. Using local driftwood and other beach finds, the Dutch owner
has created tasteful works of art for each room. The pool is a few steps
from the bar and popular restaurant (☞ *above*), where windows overlooking the water give the feeling of being on a ship. The hosts are happy
to help arrange boat rentals, diving, fishing, sailing, or touring. ⊠ *Hope
Town, Abaco,* ☎ *242/366–0003 or 800/626–5690,* ☏ *242/366–
0254. 6 rooms. Bar, dining room, in-room VCRs, pool, dock. MC, V.
EP, MAP.*

$$$–$$$$ ▥ **Sea Spray Resort and Villas.** The sea does indeed spray these one-
and two-bedroom villas nestled among 6 acres of nicely landscaped
grounds just 3½ mi from Hope Town. The immaculate villas—three
with an ocean view, three with a harbor view—have island-style fur-
nishings, full kitchens, and decks that overlook one of the best surf-
ing spots in the Bahamas. The clubhouse has satellite TV and Ping-Pong
and pool tables. Sailboats are available free of charge; boats, bikes, and
snorkeling gear are available to rent. Owners Monty and Ruth Albury
will deliver your Bahamian-style meal to your villa. ⊠ *White Sound,
Elbow Cay, Abaco,* ☎ *242/366–0065,* ☏ *242/366–0383. 6 villas. Pool,
Ping-Pong, diving, dock, snorkeling, boating, fishing, bicycles, bil-
liards. AE, MC, V. EP, MAP.*

$–$$$$ ▥ **Elbow Cay Properties.** Besides being the most cost-efficient way to
stay on Elbow Cay, renting a private house or villa for a week or more
is also one of the most comfortable. Many of the houses and villas for
rent are on the water, with a dock or a sandy beach right out front.
Owners Jane Patterson and Carrie Cash will find you a place to match
your wishes and budget. They can also arrange boat and bike rentals,
and set you up with a golf cart—perfect for negotiating Hope Town's
very narrow lanes. ⊠ *Hope Town, Abaco,* ☎ ☏ *242/366–0035. 26
houses and villas. No credit cards.*

$$$ ▥ **Hope Town Hideaways.** Across the harbor from Hope Town village
is this ideal vacation spot for those who really want to get away—vir-
tually the only way to get here is by boat. The owners, Abaco native
Chris Thompson and his wife, Peggy, who is American, create a warm,
relaxing atmosphere on this 11-acre spread and will make a variety of
arrangements, from boat rentals to picnic lunches. Peggy provides a charm-

ing list of things to do in Abaco, such as a treasure hunt in caves once frequented by pirates. The grounds are planted with peppers, bananas, avocados, and passion fruit, as well as wild orchids and other exotic flowers. The four villas have two bedrooms and are decorated with festive prints, light woods, ceiling fans and have telephones and televisions; as there is no channel reception here, the TVs come with a VCR and a selection of videotapes. A one-bedroom "honeymoon cottage" is also available. Kitchens come stocked with all necessities, as well as such extras as fresh fruit and guava jelly. There's no restaurant on site, but the patio area in front of the villas has a grill, and you're minutes away by boat from a choice of local restaurants. Peggy can also rent you a private villa or house just about anywhere else on Elbow Cay, as her company manages almost 20 houses and villas. ⊠ *Hope Town, Abaco,* ☎ *242/366–0224 or 800/688–4752,* FAX *242/366–0434. 4 villas, 1 one-bedroom cottage. In-room VCRs. AE, MC, V. EP.*

Outdoor Activities and Sports

BOATING
Marinas. Club Soleil (☎ 242/366–0003), **Sea Spray Resort** (☎ 242/366–0065), and **Hope Town Hideaways** (☎ 242/366–0224).

Rentals. In Hope Town, contact **Island Marine** (☎ 242/366–0282).

FISHING
Seagull Charters (☎ 242/366–0266) sets up guided deep-sea excursions with Captain Robert Lowe, who has over 30 years' experience in the local waters.

SCUBA DIVING
Dave's Dive Shop and Boat Rentals (☎ 242/366–0029).

WINDSURFING
Abaco Inn (☎ 242/366–0133) and **Sea Spray Resort** (☎ 242/366–0065).

Man-O-War Cay

6 Many of **Man-O-War Cay**'s residents are named Albury, descendants of early Loyalist settlers who started the tradition of handcrafting boats more than two centuries ago. They remain proud of their heritage and continue to build Fiberglas boats today. This shipwrighting center of the Abacos lies south of Green Turtle and Great Guana cays, an easy 45-minute ride from Marsh Harbour by water taxi or aboard a small rented outboard dinghy. Man-O-War Cay also has its own 60-slip marina.

A mile north of the island, you can dive to the wreck of the USS *Adirondack,* which sank after hitting a reef in 1862; it lies among a host of cannons in 20 ft of water. The cay is also a marvelous place to walk. Two main roads, Queen's Highway and Sea Road, are often shaded with arching sea-grape trees interspersed with palms and pines. The island is secluded, but it has kept up to date with satellite television and full phone service. There are a one-room schoolhouse and three churches, which most of the 300 residents faithfully attend. No liquor is sold here, but you're welcome to bring your own. Restaurants post their daily specials on "The Pole" in the center of town.

Dining and Lodging

$$ ✕ **Man-O-War Marina Pavillion.** Try the grouper fingers here or, if you stop in on a weekend, BBQ steak, chicken, or ribs. ⊠ *Waterfront, Man-O-War Cay,* ☎ *242/365–6185. Closed Sun.*

$–$$ ✕ **Ena's.** Consider this casual local spot when you want great conch burgers and coconut or pumpkin pie. ⊠ *Waterfront, Man-O-War Cay,* ☎ *242/365–6187. Closed Sun.*

$$$ ▣ **Schooner's Landing.** This small, Mediterranean-style resort with just four two-bedroom town-house condos is perched on a rocky promontory overlooking a long, isolated beach. It has the ultimate in secluded, romantic settings and modern amenities. Rooms are airy, with wicker furniture, ceramic tile floors, and TVs with VCRs. There's no restaurant, but within walking distance is almost everything on the cay, including a selection of restaurants. There's also a barbecue and wet bar in the gazebo, and nearby grocery stores deliver. Manager Brenda Sawyer knows the island well; dinner with her at Ena's or the Pavillion is a good way to learn the ropes. ✉ *Man-O-War Cay, Abaco,* ☎ *242/365–6072 or 800/626–5690,* FAX *242/365–6285. 4 condominiums. Bar, in-room VCRs, beach, boating, fishing, laundry service. AE, MC, V (5% surcharge). EP.*

Outdoor Activities and Sports
BOATING
Man-O-War Marina (☎ 242/365–6008).

SCUBA DIVING
Man-O-War Dive Shop (✉ At the Man-O-War Marina, ☎ 242/365–6013).

Shopping
Albury's Sail Shop (☎ 242/365–6014) is popular with boaters, who stock up on colorful canvas tote bags, briefcases, hats, and purses.

Caribbean Closet (☎ 242/365–6384) sells clothing and resortwear.

Island Treasure Gallery (☎ 242/365–6072) has a wide selection of T-shirts and souvenirs.

Great Guana Cay

❼ You'll be welcomed to **Great Guana Cay,** a narrow island off Marsh Harbour, by a hand-lettered sign that claims IT'S BETTER IN THE BAHAMAS, BUT . . . IT'S GOODER IN GUANA. If you love beautiful empty beaches and grassy dunes, you'll agree. The cries of roosters are about the loudest sound you'll hear in the drowsy village, and cars are absent from the narrow palm-lined roads that are bordered by clapboard cottages with picket fences.

Dining and Lodging

$$$–$$$$ ✕▣ **Guana Beach Resort and Marina.** This casual hotel, set against a background of thick tropical foliage, is the only hotel on one of the Abacos' prettiest islands, Great Guana Cay; the island, which is 7 mi long, has only 120 residents. The property will suit you whether you just want to relax or if you're keen on fishing, snorkeling, diving, kayaking, sailing, or cycling. Owners Gordon and Mary Sadler, formerly of New York, have a "no shoes" policy that sets the tone. They encourage the imbibing of rum-laden Guana Grabbers and the use of hammocks in the palm grove. The eight beachfront rooms and seven one- and two-bedroom villas with kitchens have no televisions or phones and could use a bit of a face-lift (renovations are being planned). The restaurant serves Bahamian and American dishes, with an emphasis on seafood. Although the resort has its own beach with thatched shelters, a 10-minute walk through town will lead you to a much more spectacular stretch of sand that runs the length of the island. And for boaters, there is a marina on-site as well. ✉ *Box AB 20474, Marsh Harbour, Abaco,* ☎ *242/365–5133 or 800/227–3366,* FAX *954/423–9733. 7 villas, 8 rooms. Bar, dining room, pool, beach, dock, babysitting. MC, V. EP, MAP.*

Treasure Cay

8 Running through large pine forests that are still home to wild horses and boars, the wide, paved Sherben A. Boothe Highway leads north from Marsh Harbour for 20 mi to **Treasure Cay,** which is technically not an island but a large peninsula connected to Great Abaco by a narrow spit of land. Here you'll find a few small communities and a 3,000-acre farm that grows winter vegetables and fruit for export. The main landmark of the area, however, is the sophisticated **Treasure Cay Resort and Marina,** with its championship golf course, 150-slip marina, and 3½-mi-long beach.

Dining and Lodging

$$–$$$ ✕▣ **Treasure Cay Resort and Marina.** The beach at Treasure Cay—a long strand of pearly white sand—is one of the best on Abaco. At the Treasure Cay Resort, individual guest rooms and suites overlook a 150-slip marina, and villas, scattered among gardens of palm trees and flowering shrubs, gaze out to the beach. The various rooms, decorated with handsome bamboo and rattan furniture, have TVs but no phones. A variety of water sports is available, including an underwater garden for divers and snorkelers. And you can rent boats to go to Elbow Cay, Man-O-War Cay, and Green Turtle Cay. The resort has the island's only 18-hole championship golf course, as well as eight tennis courts. In the evening, dine at the Spinnaker Restaurant or sip tropical drinks at the Tipsy Seagull bar at the marina. There are shops, a laundromat, bakery, doctor's office, bank, and post office nearby. ✉ *2301 S. Federal Hwy., Fort Lauderdale, FL 33316,* ☎ *954/525–7711, 242/365–8578, or 800/327–1584,* 𝖥𝖠𝖷 *954/525–1699. 95 rooms, 20 suites. 2 bars, dining room, lounge, pool, 18-hole golf course, 8 tennis courts, beach, diving, dock, snorkeling, windsurfing, boating, waterskiing, fishing, baby-sitting. AE, MC, V.*

Outdoor Activities and Sports

BOATING

Treasure Cay Resort and Marina (☎ 242/365–8250).

EVENTS

The **Treasure Cay Billfish Championship** is held in May. Call the **Out Island Promotion Board** (305/359–8099 or 800/688–4752) for information.

GOLF

The only golf course in the Abacos is located on Treasure Cay. The club, a half mile from the **Treasure Cay Resort and Marina,** (☎ 242/365–8535) has a par-72, 18-hole course designed by Dick Wilson. The resort has golf packages available for guests.

SCUBA DIVING

Treasure Cay Resort and Marina (☎ 242/365–8465).

TENNIS

Treasure Cay Resort and Marina (☎ 242/367–2570) has six of the best courses in the Abacos, and four are lighted for night play. Fees are $16 per hour for the hard courts, $18 per hour for the clay courts.

WATERSKIING AND WINDSURFING

Waterskiing and windsurfing are offered at the **Treasure Cay Resort and Marina** (☎ 242/365–8250).

Green Turtle Cay

9 **Green Turtle Cay** lies 2 mi off Treasure Cay. The tiny island is steeped in Loyalist history, and it is surrounded by several deep bays, sounds, and a nearly continuous strip of fine ocean beach. A 10-minute ferry ride from a dock on Treasure Cay will take you to the Green Turtle Club resort or to New Plymouth on the southern tip of Green Turtle Cay. An easy way to explore the entire island is by small outboard dinghy or Boston whaler, which can be rented by the hour or the day at most resorts and marinas.

New Plymouth, which was first settled in 1783, is the main community on Green Turtle. Most of its approximately 550 residents eke out a living by diving for conch or exporting lobster and fish through the Abaco Seafood Company. The village sits on a gentle hillside overlooking a harbor. Narrow streets flanked by wild-growing flora (such as amaryllis, hibiscus, and poinciana), wind between rows of quasi–New England–style white clapboard cottages with shutters trimmed in pink, brown, or green. During the Civil War, New Plymouth provided a port of safety for Confederate blockade runners. One Union ship, the USS *Adirondack,* was pursuing a gunrunner and wrecked on a reef in 1862 at nearby Man-O-War Cay. One of the ship's cannons now sits at the town harbor.

New Plymouth's most frequently visited attraction is the **Albert Lowe Museum** on the main thoroughfare, Parliament Street. It is dedicated to a model shipbuilder and direct descendant of the island's original European-American settlers. Housed in an 18th-century white-and-green clapboard building, it is fronted by a picket fence. Visitors learn island history through displays of local memorabilia from the 1700s, Lowe's model schooners, and old photographs, including one of the aftermath of the 1932 hurricane that almost flattened New Plymouth. The museum also features a selection of paintings by acclaimed artist Alton Lowe, son of the man for whom the museum is named. ✉ *Parliament St.,* ☎ *242/365–4094.* ✇ *$3.* ☉ *Mon.–Sat. 9–11:45 and 1–4.*

Just a few blocks from here, on Victoria Street, is **Miss Emily's Blue Bee Bar** (☎ 242/365–4181; ☉ Hrs vary), which stands next to a jail whose door is hanging on its hinges—it hasn't been used in recent history. The bar's owner, Mrs. Emily Cooper, is as well known for her stories as for making the best Goombay Smash in the islands. Although she is getting on in years, you can keep her daughter busy serving the concoction of rum, pineapple juice, and apricot brandy. Mementos of customers—dollar bills, expired credit cards, business cards—cover the bar walls. Lillian Carter, former President Jimmy Carter's mother, left her picture on the wall when she came here.

The past is also present in the **Memorial Sculpture Garden,** across the street from New Plymouth Inn—note that it is laid out in the pattern of the British flag. Immortalized in busts perched on pedestals are local residents who have made important contributions to the Bahamas. Plaques detail the accomplishments of American Loyalists, who came to the Abacos from New England and the Carolinas, their descendants, and the descendants of those brought as slaves, such as Jeanne I. Thompson, a contemporary playwright and the country's second woman to practice law.

Dining and Lodging

$$ ✕ **Laura's Kitchen.** This simple eatery on a narrow lane off Parliament Street, is a great place to pop into if your visit to New Plymouth keeps you through lunchtime. Choose from an inexpensive menu that features cracked conch, conch chowder, and fried hog snapper or grouper, as well as chicken. ✉ *Green Turtle Cay,* ☎ *242/365–4287.*

$$$$ ✕⛶ **Green Turtle Club.** A well-groomed yet informal haven for boaters,
★ this 80-acre resort is affiliated with the British Royal Yachting Association and the Palm Beach Yacht Club and organizes an annual billfish tournament in May. A large share of clientele, nonetheless, is
made up of nonyachting types who have an affinity for the water. The
buildings are on the water and nestled amid trees and shrubs on a hillside overlooking the harbor, and consist of villas as well as guest
rooms. The well-maintained one- or two-bedroom villas have kitchenettes, dining and living areas, private decks, and terraces, and most
have private docks. Decor varies considerably as villas are individually owned; opt for ones without wall-to-wall carpeting (not a good
idea in the humid tropics). The guest rooms are much more attractively
decorated in a mix of Queen Anne and plantation styles, with mahogany
headboards, a mix of rattan and mahogany furniture, hardwood floors,
Oriental rugs, and floral-print spreads. The resort has a small swimming beach—although the deserted 2-mi ocean beach, 12 minutes
away on foot, is far superior—and a 35-slip marina, the largest and
most complete yachting facility on the island. The dining room, which
serves tasty, elegantly presented meals with good wines, is also done
in Queen Anne style. The Tipsy Turtle Bar, wallpapered in $1 bills by
its guests, is an enjoyable place to have a cocktail. ✉ *Box AB 22792,
Green Turtle Cay, Abaco,* ☎ *242/365–4271 or 800/688–4752,* FAX *242/
365–4272. 34 rooms. Bar, dining room, lounge, pool, exercise room,
diving, dock, boating, fishing, laundry service. AE, MC, V. EP, MAP.*

$$–$$$ ✕⛶ **Bluff House.** The highest hill in the Abaco chain is home to this
romantic hideaway. Set among pine trees on 12 acres, it has panoramic
views of the sheltered harbor. Accommodations include split-level
town-house suites with ocean views, eight Colonial-style suites, and
rustic one-, two-, and three-bedroom beachside villas (with kitchens)
that can accommodate eight people. The comfortable, spacious rooms
were freshened up in 1995 and have wood paneling, tropical-style wicker
furniture, parquet floors, and ocean views, but are emphatically without television or telephone. A wooden walkway leads from the 30-slip
marina to the nautical-theme clubhouse, which has a lively bar and a
candlelit dining room that serves complimentary wine with excellent
Bahamian and American fare that incorporates local seafood. Guests
have access to 2 mi of almost deserted beach (about a 20-minute
walk); a beach bar serves drinks and lunch. There is one tennis court;
playing gear is provided. Charters are available for bonefishing and
deep-sea fishing, snorkeling, picnicking, and diving. Two evenings a
week, you can dance to live music. ✉ *Box AB 22886, Green Turtle
Cay, Abaco,* ☎ *242/365–4247,* FAX *242/365–4248. 6 rooms, 15 suites,
3 villas. Bar, dining room, lounge, pool, tennis court, dock. AE, MC,
V. EP, MAP.*

$$ ✕⛶ **New Plymouth Inn.** Built in 1830, this charming, two-story his-
toric hostelry with white balconies is in the center of New Plymouth.
It was a French mercantile exchange, a warehouse (in which shipwreckers
used to store their plunder), and a private residence before a Canadian
Air Force colonel opened it as a hotel in 1946. Owner Wally Davies
built a patio pool and expanded the tropical gardens. The cozy, care-
fully restored rooms have solid chests and chairs, old-fashioned hat racks,
quilts on the canopy beds, and private baths. The restaurant is popu-
lar with local residents and visitors alike, so you'll need to make a reser-
vation to enjoy such Bahamian dishes as conch and turtle steaks and
the selection of vintage wines. There is only one TV in the pleasantly
decorated dining room. ✉ *Green Turtle Cay, Abaco,* ☎ *242/365–4161
or 800/688–4752,* FAX *242/365–4138. 10 rooms. Bar, dining room,
lounge, pool. MC, V. MAP.*

$$$ ⬚ **Coco Bay Cottages.** Sandwiched between one beach on the Atlantic and another calmer sandy stretch on the bay, these four home-like cottages (three with two bedrooms and one with three) have water views. Attractively furnished, they come complete with modern kitchens and linens. Snorkeling and diving are excellent around the reef that protects the Atlantic beach. The bay, where sunset views are fabulous, is prime territory for shell-collecting and bonefishing. ⊠ *Green Turtle Cay, Abaco,* ☎ *242/365–5464 or 800/752–0166. 4 cottages. MC, V.*

$$$ ⬚ **Linton's Cottages.** Perched on a rise overlooking an isolated beach, these two cottages attract families, groups of friends, and couples looking for escape. Each has two comfortable bedrooms, a screened-in porch, a combination living-and-dining room, and a fully equipped kitchen. When you aren't fishing, snorkeling, scuba diving, waterskiing, sailing, windsurfing, shell-hunting, or using the barbecue, you can relax in hammocks. You can arrange to have someone shop and/or prepare meals. Boats are available for rent, and ask about fishing and diving guides. ⊠ *Box 158601, Nashville, TN 37215.* ☎ *615/269–5682. No credit cards.*

Nightlife

Nightlife on the Out Islands is virtually nonexistent, but the place to go in New Plymouth is the **Rooster's Rest** (☎ 242/365–4066), a pub and restaurant perched in a bright red building. On weekends, local bands shake the joint until the wee hours.

Outdoor Activities and Sports

BOATING

Marinas. Green Turtle Club (☎ 242/365–4271) and **Bluff House** (☎ 242/365–4247).

EVENTS

The **Green Turtle Yacht Club Fishing Tournament** is held in May. Call the **Out Island Promotion Board** (☎ 305/359–8099 or 800/688–4752) for information.

SCUBA DIVING

Brendal's Dive Shop (☎ 242/365–4411).

TENNIS

Bluff House (☎ 242/365–4247) and **Green Turtle Club** (☎ 800/688–4752).

WINDSURFING

Green Turtle Club (☎ 242/365–4271).

Spanish Cay

With several handsome beaches and only one small resort, this private island gives you the distinct impression that you have escaped the rest of the world. Artful landscaping includes palms, a variety of fruit trees, royal poincianas, and hibiscus.

Dining and Lodging

$$$$ ✕⬚ **Inn at Spanish Cay.** This 200-acre island has always been private. For 40 years, it was the preserve of a U.S. billionaire and his "rich and famous" friends. Now the beautifully landscaped house and grounds are open to well-heeled guests who reside in villa suites or one- or two-bedroom apartments. The suites have their own private gardens; the spacious apartments are by the marina. Each lodging comes with its own golf cart so that you can explore the island's five beaches and 7 mi of shoreline or just save your energy for the tennis court. There's fishing and diving on nearby reefs, and rental boats are available for exploring the uninhabited islands around Spanish Cay. Two restaurants

Pick up
the phone.

Pick up
the miles.

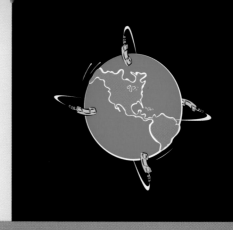

Use your MCI Card® to make an international call from virtually anywhere in the world and earn frequent flyer miles on one of seven major airlines.

Enroll in an MCI Airline Partner Program today. In the U.S., call **1-800-FLY-FREE.** Overseas, call MCI collect at **1-916-567-5151.**

1. To use your MCI Card, just dial the WorldPhone access number of the country you're calling from.
   (For a complete listing of codes, visit www.mci.com.)
2. Dial or give the operator your MCI Card number.
3. Dial or give the number you're calling.

# American Samoa	633-2MCI (633-2624)	# Guyana ÷	177
# Antigua	#2	# Haiti (CC) ÷	193
(Available from public card phones only)		Haiti IIIC Access in French/Creole	190
# Argentina (CC)	0800-5-1002	Honduras ÷	122
# Aruba ÷	800-888-8	# Jamaica ÷	1-800-888-8000
# Bahamas	1-800-888-8000	(From Special Hotels only)	873
# Barbados	1-800-888-8000	# Mexico	
# Belize	557 from hotels	Avantel (CC)	91-800-021-8000
	815 from pay phones	Telmex ▲	95-800-674-7000
# Bermuda ÷	1-800-888-8000	Mexico IIIC Access	91-800-021-1000
# Bolivia ♦	0-800-2222	# Netherlands Antilles (CC) ÷	001-800-888-8000
# Brazil (CC)	000-8012	Nicaragua (CC)	166
# British Virgin Islands ÷	1-800-888-8000	(Outside of Managua, dial 02 first)	
# Cayman Islands	1-800-888-8000	Nicaragua IIIC Access in Spanish	★2 from any public payphone
# Chile (CC)		# Panama	108
To call using CTC ■	800-207-300	Military Bases	2810-108
To call using ENTEL ■	800-360-180	# Paraguay ÷	008-112-800
# Colombia (CC) ♦	980-16-0001	# Peru	0-800-500-10
Columbia IIIC Access in Spanish	980-16-1000	# Puerto Rico (CC)	1-800-888-8000
# Costa Rica ♦	0800-012-2222	# St. Lucia ÷	1-800-888-8000
# Dominica	1-800-888-8000	# Trinidad & Tobago ÷	1-800-888-8000
# Dominican Republic (CC) ÷	1-800-888-8000	# Turks & Caicos ÷	1-800-888-8000
Dominican Republic IIIC Access in Spanish	1121	# Uruguay	000-412
# Ecuador (CC) ÷	999-170	# U.S. Virgin Islands (CC)	1-800-888-8000
El Salvador ♦	800-1767	# Venezuela (CC) ÷ ♦	800-1114-0
# Grenada ÷	1-800-888-8000		
Guatemala (CC) ♦	9999-189		

Is this a great time, or what? :-)

Urban planning.

CITYPACKS

The ultimate guide to the city—a complete pocket guide plus a full-size color map.

www.fodors.com

cater to guests' whims—in fact, the chef will fish with you, then prepare your catch. You can now fly directly into Spanish Cay's airstrip from Fort Lauderdale. ✉ *Box 882, Cooperstown, Abaco,* ☎ *242/365–0083, 800/688–4752, or 201/539–6450,* ℻ *242/365–0083. 5 villa suites, 7 apartments. 2 restaurants, 2 bars, in-room VCRs, 4 tennis courts, beaches, dive shop, dock, snorkeling, boating, fishing. MC, V. EP.*

Outdoor Activities and Sports

BOATING

Spanish Cay Marina (☎ 242/365–0083).

SCUBA DIVING

Spanish Cay Watersports (☎ 242/365–0083).

TENNIS

Spanish Cay Inn (☎ 242/365–0083).

WINDSURFING

Spanish Cay Inn (☎ 242/365–0083).

Walker's Cay

Fishing enthusiasts have been returning to this islet for years, and the lone hotel caters to anglers. With few of the wispy casuarina trees that abound on most Out Islands, Walker's Cay sprouts more of the gnarled, thick-trunked trees more common in cooler regions. Walker's Cay isn't known for its beaches—most visitors sail off to sandy shores on neighboring islands.

Dining and Lodging

$$–$$$ ✕🏠 **Walker's Cay Hotel and Marina.** A self-contained resort on the northernmost island of the Bahamas, this 100-acre island is served by its own airline out of Fort Lauderdale. The waters around here are renowned for their spectacular fishing opportunities, and the complex is a favorite with the yachters and fishermen who flock to the Annual Billfish Tournament, which is held here in April. Not surprisingly, the resort specializes in fishing and diving packages, and the full-service 75-slip marina offers some of the best yachting facilities in the Bahamas. Accommodations include elegant hotel suites and modern villas, nicely secluded in a wooded area. Rooms are cheerfully decorated with tropical-style rattan furniture and have private patios. The Lobster Trap restaurant and bar serves lunch and cocktails; sportsmen gather here to swap fish stories. The Conch Pearl dining room serves Bahamian and American specialties complemented by a superb wine list. ✉ *700 S.W. 34th St., Fort Lauderdale, FL 33315,* ☎ *954/359–1400 or 800/925–5377,* ℻ *954/359–1414. 62 rooms, 3 villas. 2 bars, dining room, lounge, 2 pools, 2 tennis courts, dive shop, dock, boating, fishing, laundry service. AE, DC, MC, V. EP, MAP.*

$ ✕🏠 **Tangelo Hotel.** Almost at the top of Abaco, a 25-mi ride from the Treasure Cay Airport, is this well-off-the-beaten-track motel-style property. Rooms, all in a single-story stone building, have wall-to-wall carpeting, matching bedspreads and drapes, and TVs. It's so remote that the taxi fare from the airport is a whopping $50 one way—the hotel can also arrange a $10 bus service if notified in advance. Restaurant prices are reasonable: The maximum you'll pay for dinner is $13. ✉ *Box 830, Wood Cay, Abaco,* ☎ *242/365–2222. 12 rooms. Restaurant, bar, boating, fishing. No credit cards. EP, MAP, FAP.*

Outdoor Activities and Sports

BOATING

Walker's Cay Hotel and Marina (☎ 242/352–5252).

May brings the **Bertram/Hatteras Shoot-out Tournament,** the Kentucky Derby for boats and the **Walker's Cay Billfish Tournament.** Call the **Out Island Promotion Board** (☎ 305/359–8099 or 800/688–4752) for information.

SCUBA DIVING
Sea Below Dive Center (⊠ At Walker's Cay Hotel and Marina, ☎ 242/352–5252) and **Neal Watson's Undersea Adventures** (☎ 800/327–8150).

TENNIS
Walker's Cay Hotel and Marina (☎ 800/432–2092).

Abacos A to Z

Arriving and Departing

BY MAIL BOAT
From Potter's Cay, Nassau, the M/V *Deborah K II* sails Wednesday to Cooper's Town, Green Turtle Cay, Hope Town, Marsh Harbour, and Turtle Cay; it arrives back in Nassau on Monday. The round-trip fare is $25, and the trip takes 12 hours. The M/V *Champion II* departs Nassau on Tuesday, calls on Wednesday at Sandy Point, Moore's Island, and Bullock's Harbour, returning to Nassau on Friday; the fare is $30. Schedules are subject to change due to weather conditions or occasional dry-docking. For details, call the **Dockmaster's office** (☎ 242/393–1064) at Potter's Cay.

BY PLANE
The Abacos have three airports: at Treasure Cay and Marsh Harbour on Great Abaco Island, and at Walker's Cay (private).

American Eagle (☎ 800/433–7300) flies to the Abacos daily from Miami.

Bahamasair (☎ 800/222–4262) flies daily from Miami and twice daily from Nassau to Treasure Cay and Marsh Harbour.

Gulfstream Airlines (☎ 305/871–1200 or 800/992–8532) flies daily into both public airports.

Island Express (☎ 954/359–0380) flies daily from Fort Lauderdale into both public airports.

Pan Am (☎ 800/359–7262) flies from Fort Lauderdale to Walker's Cay.

Twin Air (☎ 954/359–8266) has scheduled flights to Treasure Cay and flies to other parts of the Abacos by charter.

US Airways Express (☎ 800/622–1015) flies into both public airports from Orlando and Palm Beach.

Walker's International (☎ 954/359–1400 or 800/925–5377), serving the private airstrip at Walker's Cay, flies to the Abacos out of Fort Lauderdale.

Getting Around

BY BOAT
Because Abaco is made up of so many islands, many visitors find that a small boat offers both the easiest way to get around and the freedom to explore uninhabited areas and secluded beaches. **Rich's Boat Rentals** (☎ 242/367–2742), **Sea Horse Boat Rentals** (☎ 242/367–2513), and **Laysue Rentals** (☎ 242/367–4414) are all conveniently located in Marsh Harbour. **Island Marine** (☎ 242/366–0282) is in Hope Town on Elbow Cay. It's best to check with your hotel before renting; they

can either make arrangements for you or recommend the most convenient agent (☞ Outdoor Activities and Sports, *above*).

BY CAR

Although you can explore the main city of the Abacos, Marsh Harbour on Great Abaco Island, on foot, you will need a car to see the rest of Great Abaco and the other main island, Little Abaco. In Marsh Harbour, you can rent automobiles from **H & L Car Rentals** (✉ Shell Gas Station, ☎ 242/367–2854), **Reliable Car Rentals** (☎ 242/367–3015), and **A & P Rentals** (☎ 242/367–2655). Rentals are expensive at about $70 a day and up; weekly rentals are cheaper. It's easiest to have your hotel make your arrangements.

BY FERRY

Albury's Ferry Service (☎ 242/365–6010) leaves Marsh Harbour for the 20-minute ride to Hope Town daily at 10:30 AM and 4 PM and, additionally, at 12:15 PM on Monday, Thursday, and Saturday; ferries make the return trip at 8 AM, 1:30 PM, and 4 PM every day and also at 11:30 AM on Monday, Thursday, and Saturday. If you take the 4 PM ferry, you must stay overnight. A same-day round-trip costs $12; one-way costs $8. Albury's also provides service, though less frequently, between Marsh Harbour and Man-O-War Cay or Guana Cay.

Green Turtle Cay Ferry (☎ 242/365–4032) leaves the Treasure Cay airport dock at 10:30, 2:30, and 4:15, and returns from Green Turtle Cay at 8, 1:30, and 3; one-way fares are $8. **Guana Beach Resort Ferry** (☎ 242/367–3590) leaves the Conch Inn Marina in Marsh Harbour at 9:30 and returns from Guana Cay at 3:30. Fares are $12 one way, $18 round-trip on the same day.

BY TAXI

Taxi services meet arriving planes at the airports to take you to your hotel or to the dock, where you can take a water taxi to neighboring islands such as Green Turtle Cay or Elbow Cay. Hotels will arrange for taxis to take you on short trips and back to the airport. A combination taxi and water-taxi ride from Treasure Cay Airport to Green Turtle Cay costs $13. The ride from Marsh Harbour Airport to Hope Town on Elbow Cay costs $11. Fares are generally $1.50 per mile.

Opening and Closing Times

Banks are located at Marsh Harbour and Treasure Cay on Great Abaco Island, New Plymouth on Green Turtle Cay, Hope Town on Elbow Cay, and on Man-O-War Cay. These banks are generally open Monday–Thursday 9–1, Friday 9–5.

Contacts and Resources

EMERGENCIES

A few areas in the Abacos still do not have direct long-distance dialing, and emergencies have to be reported to the hotel management. BaTelCo (the Bahamas Telecommunications Corporation) has a system of microwave relay stations in the Abacos that provides direct-dial connections to the outside world without going through an operator.

Police or **fire** (☎ 919).

The **Marsh Harbour Clinic** (☎ 242/367–2510) has a resident doctor and a nurse.

GUIDED TOURS

Papa-Tango Tours (☎ 242/367–3753) depart daily from Marsh Harbour's Boat Harbour Marina for daylong trips that include touring the islands, shopping, fishing, shelling, and snorkeling.

VISITOR INFORMATION
Abaco Chamber of Commerce (✉ Box 20482, Marsh Harbour, Abaco,
☎ 242/367–2663).

ANDROS

Andros, the largest of the Bahamian islands (100 mi long and 40 mi
wide), is the least explored of them all, a place serrated by channels
and tiny inlets with such names as North Bight, Middle Bight, and South
Bight. Although not a frequently visited island, Andros is popular
with sports lovers for its excellent bonefishing and its diving opportunities. The Spaniards who came here in the 16th century called it *La
Isla del Espíritu Santo*—the Island of the Holy Spirit—and it has retained its eerie mystique to this day.

In fact, the descendants of a group of Seminole Indians and runaway
slaves who left the Florida Everglades in the mid-19th century settled
in Andros and remained hidden from the outside world until a few
decades ago. They continue to live as a tribal society with a leader they
acknowledge as their chief. Their village, near the northern tip of the
island, is called Red Bay, and they make a living by weaving straw goods.
The Seminoles are credited with originating the myth of the island's
legendary (and elusive) *chickcharnies*—red-eyed, bearded, green-feath-
ered creatures with three fingers and three toes that hang upside down
by their tails from pine trees. These mythical characters supposedly wait
deep in the forests to wish good luck to the friendly trespasser and vent
their mischief on the hostile.

Andros's western shore, which lies 170 mi southeast of Miami and 30
mi west of Nassau, is utterly barren and not recommended to yachters.
The island's lush green interior is covered with dense forests of pine
and mahogany, fringed on its western edge by miles of mangrove
swamp. The forests provide nesting grounds for parrots, partridges,
quail, white-crowned pigeons, and whistling ducks, and hunters come
to Andros from September to March in search of game. Only a dozen
settlements and a handful of hotels are located on the eastern shore.

The Andros Barrier Reef—the third-largest reef in the world—is within
a mile of this shore and runs for 140 mi. It has an enchanting variety
of marine life, and is easily accessible to divers. Sheltered waters within
the reef average 6 to 15 ft, but on the other side of the reef ("over the
wall") lie the depths (over 6,000 ft) of the Tongue of the Ocean, which
is used for testing submarines and underwater weapons by the U.S. and
British navies. They operate under the acronym AUTEC (Atlantic Underwater Test and Evaluation Center), and their base is located near
Andros Town.

*Numbers in the text correspond to numbers in the margin and on the
Andros map.*

Nicholl's Town

❿ **Nicholl's Town,** at the northeastern corner of Andros, is the largest village on the island, with a population of about 600. This friendly community has stores for your supplies and groceries, a few hotels, a
public medical clinic, a telephone station, and small restaurants that
serve Bahamian fare. A few miles north of Nicholl's Town is a crescent beach and a headland known as **Morgan's Bluff,** named after the
17th-century pirate Henry Morgan, who allegedly dropped off some
of his stolen loot in the area.

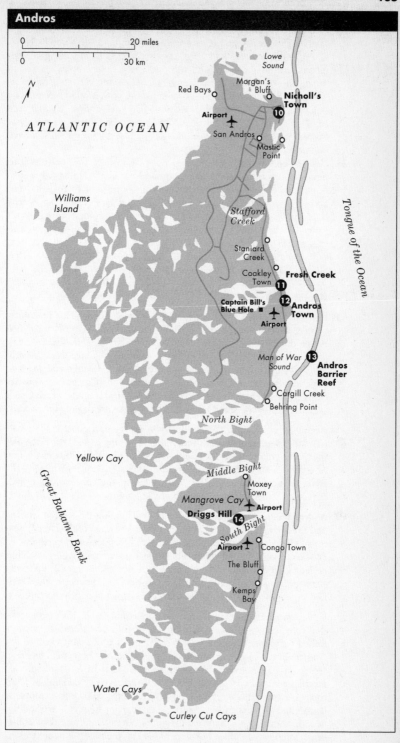

Andros

0 ——— 20 miles
0 ——— 30 km

N

ATLANTIC OCEAN

Red Bays

Morgan's Bluff

Lowe Sound

Nicholl's Town 10

Airport

San Andros

Mastic Point

Williams Island

Tongue of the Ocean

Stafford Creek

Staniard Creek

Coakley Town

Fresh Creek

11

Captain Bill's Blue Hole

Airport

12 **Andros Town**

Man of War Sound

13 **Andros Barrier Reef**

Cargill Creek

Behring Point

North Bight

Yellow Cay

Great Bahama Bank

Middle Bight

Moxey Town

Mangrove Cay

Airport

Driggs Hill 14

South Bight

Airport

Congo Town

The Bluff

Kemps Bay

Water Cays

Curley Cut Cays

Dining and Lodging

$$ ✕🏨 **Conch Sound Resort Inn.** Simple, clean, and spacious rooms with satellite TVs are situated among pine woods, just outside Nicholl's Town. Comfortable brown- and beige-carpeted rooms have mahogany furniture, handmade quilts, and soft cushioned chairs. Bonefishing and diving can be arranged; the beach is a 10-minute walk but the hotel will provide transportation. The restaurant, with a salad bar, offers a Bahamian menu featuring steamed conch, pork chops, grouper, and BBQ chicken. ✉ *Box 23029, Nicholl's Town, North Andros, Bahamas,* ☎ *242/329–2060 or 242/329–2341. 14 rooms. Restaurant, bar, pool, fishing. No credit cards. EP.*

$–$$ ✕🏨 **Green Windows Inn.** Formerly the Donna Lee Guest House, this inn offers rooms over the restaurant and bar in a building just a five-minute walk from the beach; two rooms have their own baths. The hotel is surrounded by neat landscaping and palm trees and has nearby flats for bonefishing aficionados (bonefishing guides are easily arranged). The restaurant serves seafood and Bahamian fare, such as steamed fish and peas 'n' rice. A package store is also available next door. ✉ *Box 23076, Nicholl's Town, Andros,* ☎ *242/329–2194,* FAX *242/329–2016. 12 rooms, 2 with bath. Restaurant, bar. AE. EP.*

Fresh Creek–Andros Town

⑪ Batik fabric called Androsia is made in **Fresh Creek.** This brilliantly colored fabric is designed and dyed by more than 75 people at the **Androsia Batik Works Factory** (☎ 242/368–2020; ⊘ Mon.–Fri. 8–4, Sat. 8–1, closed Sun.), a 3-mi drive from Andros Town airport. The batik fabric is turned into wall hangings and clothing for men and women, which are sold throughout the Bahamas and the Caribbean. Tourists can visit the factory to observe how the material is made. Fresh Creek is also home to the Small Hope Bay Lodge, the area's only dive resort.

⑫ About 30 mi south of Nicholl's Town on the east coast is the small hamlet of **Andros Town.** Although the only thing to see here is the airport, 5 mi inland from Andros Town is **Captain Bill's Blue Hole,** one of several on the island, a delightful freshwater spring with ropes for swinging across it. Also near Andros Town, you can commune with nature by strolling along forest paths and taking in the wild orchids.

⑬ **Andros Barrier Reef.** The fabulous bonefishing on the flats of Andros and the diving on the Andros Barrier Reef lure most of the island's visitors. Here is a world offering a variety of underwater experiences: Snorkelers can explore such reefs as the Three Sisters, where visibility is clear 15 ft to the sandy floor, and jungles of elkhorn snake up to the surface. Divers can delve into the 60-ft-deep coral caves of the Petrified Forest, beyond which the wall slopes down to depths of 9,000 ft.

Undersea adventurers also have the opportunity to investigate wrecks that have become home to multitudes of fish. The *Potomac,* a steel-hulled freighter that sank in 1952, lies in 40 ft of water close to the Andros Beach Hotel in Nicholl's Town. And off the waters of Fresh Creek, at 70 ft, lies the 56-ft-long World War II LCM (landing craft mechanized) known only as the Barge Wreck, which was sunk in 1963 to create an artificial reef. Divers also have the chance to explore an uncounted number of blue holes on the Barrier Reef and around the island. These huge submarine networks can extend more than 200 ft down into the coral. Blue holes are named for their inky-blue aura when viewed from above and for the light-blue filtered sunlight that is visible from many feet below. Some of the holes that have been explored include vast cathedral-like interior chambers with stalactites and stalagmites, offshoot tunnels, and seemingly endless corridors.

Dining and Lodging

$$$ ✕🏠 **Andros Lighthouse Yacht Club and Marina.** Andros Lighthouse has luxurious rooms and villas decorated in tropical fabrics, with ceiling fans, phones, televisions, refrigerators, and private patios. The dining room is elegant, with food to match. The resort is situated on a beautiful stretch of water, with a nice beach, a freshwater pool, and a modern 18-slip marina. Reef or bonefishing, diving, and boating are easily arranged. Due to the marina, the yachting crowd favors this spot, so you're sure to meet an ever-changing parade of people in the cocktail lounge and restaurant. ⊠ *Andros Town, Andros,* ☎ *242/368–2305,* FAX *242/368–2300. 20 rooms. Bar, dining room, refrigerators, pool, 2 tennis courts, beach, dock, bicycles. AE, D, MC, V. EP, MAP.*

$$$ ✕🏠 **Small Hope Bay Lodge.** Canadian Dick Birch, looking for the sim-
★ ple life, built this easygoing, well-known dive resort on Fresh Creek's Small Hope Bay in the early '60s. Today, sons Jeff and Peter manage the wonderfully casual all-inclusive property. It has long been popular with families and a favorite with divers because of the excellent undersea opportunities at the nearby Barrier Reef. Recently, fishermen, too, have been gathering here to experience some of the best bonefishing in the Bahamas. The resort consists of 20 rustic cottages made of coral rock and Andros pine, set on a beach amid tall coconut palms. All cottages have showers and ceiling fans and are decorated with local Androsia batik prints and straw work; none have phones or televisions. The central lodge houses a large fireplace for cool evenings (with throw pillows for sprawling), a game room and excellent library, a dining room, the glass room (a glass-walled room looking out to sea), and the *Panacea,* a fishing dory that serves as a bar. Meals served here tend to be hearty and excellent, with a choice of seafood or meat and an extensive salad bar at lunch and dinner. Out front, another bar serves as cocktail hour headquarters, where several hammocks allow you to soak up a drink and the trade winds at the same time. Off the jetty is a shielded solarium for nude sunbathing. Nearly everyone samples the snorkeling; novices are trained in a few minutes and don mask and gear to explore the shallow reefs. The resort has such specialty diving excursions as one-on-one guided explorations of blue holes and tunnels, and custom-diving packages for families, which include a private dive boat and dive master. As for bonefishing, the hotel has customized boats, experienced guides, and owns a villa in Fresh Creek that sleeps four to six and can be rented for self-catering or with full service. The hotel is 5 mi from the Andros Town airport and offers flight service from Fort Lauderdale, with a minimum of two guests. ⊠ *Box 21667, Fort Lauderdale, FL 33335,* ☎ *242/368–2014 or 800/223–6961,* FAX *242/ 368–2015. 20 rooms, 1 villa. 2 bars, dining room, lounge, hot tub, beach, snorkeling, windsurfing, boating, fishing, bicycles, recreation room, library, laundry service. AE, MC, V. FAP.*

$ ✕🏠 **Chickcharnie Hotel.** This whitewashed, two-story hotel at Fresh Creek has tiny rooms. Eleven of them have air-conditioning and a private bath; the five remaining rooms have ceiling fans and shared baths. Despite the brusque management, the inn is popular with anglers because of its cheap rates and the availability of fishing boats and guides. Guests can stock up on supplies at the mini-shopping center on the premises. The hotel is 3 mi from the Andros Town airport. The restaurant overlooks the water and is quite good, serving—although quite slowly—the best Bahamian fare around; consider trying the steamed conch, crawfish, or grouper fingers. ⊠ *Fresh Creek, Andros Town, Andros,* ☎ *242/368–2025. 16 rooms, 11 with private bath. Bar, dining room. No credit cards. EP.*

Outdoor Activities and Sports

BOATING AND FISHING

Chickcharnie Hotel (☎ 242/368–2025) at Fresh Creek has a dock, and boats to rent for fishing. Rates run about $250 a day for a bonefishing skiff and $400 a day for a 25-ft reef-fishing boat.

Small Hope Bay Lodge (☎ 242/368–2014 or 800/223–6961) offers bonefishing, deep-sea fishing (wahoo, kingfish tuna), fly-fishing, reef fishing, seasonal tarpon fishing, and a "west side overnight"—a two-night camping/bone- and tarpon-fishing trip into the uninhabited western end of the island. Rates run from $175 to $275 for a half day and $300 to $480 for a full day (full-day trips include all gear and lunch).

SCUBA DIVING

Andros probably has the largest number of dive sites in the country; they rank among the best in the Bahamas. Almost all the diving is connected with the Andros Barrier Reef; the island offers about 100 mi of drop-off diving into the Tongue of the Ocean. Two major dive sites are the Barge Wreck and Over-the-Wall near Fresh Creek. Divers can also explore the numerous blue holes along the barrier reef and around the island.

Small Hope Bay Lodge BDA (☎ 242/368–2014 or 800/223–6961) at Fresh Creek is the most venerable and possibly the best dive resort on Andros. It's a very informal place where the only thing taken seriously is diving; they have a fully equipped dive center for diving on the Andros Barrier Reef. If you join a dive at Small Hope Bay, expect to pay $55 for a two-tank dive.

Cargill Creek

Fishing—bonefishing in particular—is the principal appeal of this quiet area. Consider renting a car if you plan to spend time back in Andros Town and Fresh Creek.

Dining and Lodging

$$$–$$$$ ✕🏨 **Cargill Creek Fishing Lodge.** Fishermen who are looking for bonefish will find this a decent place to stay; local guides are available to take Hemingway types out in skiffs. All of the spacious rooms have views of the ocean, and two-bedroom, two-bath cottages are available. The dining room serves very good Bahamian and Continental fare, such as conch fritters, grouper fingers, locally grown fruit and vegetables, and freshly baked bread and desserts. ✉ *Cargill Creek G.P.O., Andros,* ☎ *242/368–5129,* 𝖥𝖠𝖷 *242/368–5046. 11 rooms, 3 cottages. Dining room, bar, pool, fishing. AE, MC, V. FAP.*

$$$ ✕🏨 **Andros Island Bonefishing Club.** Fishing is the name of the game here, and guests have access to 100 sq mi of lightly fished bonefish flats. Patterned after the Small Hope Bay Lodge (☞ *above*), accommodations are in comfortable cottages with two queen-size beds and ceiling fans; some have a refrigerator. The dining room/lounge has satellite television, a fly-tying table, and a well-stocked bar. It's a homey place, and the food is plentiful and good. The club has 12 boats for guests' use and provides fishing guides as part of its all-inclusive package. It is a half hour from Andros Town Airport at the mouth of Cargill Creek. ✉ *Box 959, Wexford, PA 15090,* ☎ *242/368–5167 or 800/245–1950. 13 rooms. Bar, dining room, lounge, fishing. MC, V (4% surcharge). FAP.*

Outdoor Activities and Sports

BOATING AND FISHING

Cargill Creek Fishing Lodge (☎ 242/368–5129) provides bonefishing packages that include lunch for $290 a day per boat.

Mangrove Cay

Another bonefishing mecca, this undeveloped cay is a good base for excursions to Bigwood Cay Flat, where the pale turquoise water seems to stretch forever. It's not uncommon to see manta rays gliding through the shallows, and from a boat you might spy mounds of sponges—sponge fishing is also big in these parts—drying on shores before being shipped to Nassau to be sold.

Dining and Lodging

$ ╳⌂ **Mangrove Beach Hotel.** This plain, orange-painted resort is especially appealing if you are looking for good reefs, bonefishing, or deep-sea fishing. Sand flats are open to guests who prefer to explore on foot. Standard rooms are right on the beach and include a single, queen-size, or double bed, dark-wood furniture, and floral-print wallpaper and bedspreads. The restaurant serves decent Bahamian fare, including crab and rice, crawfish, and fried or steamed turtle. ⌂ *Mangrove Cay, Andros,* ☎ *242/369–0004. 20 rooms. Restaurant, bar, grocery, fishing, car rental. AE. EP.*

South Andros-Driggs Hill

⑭ **Driggs Hill,** on South Andros, is a small settlement of pastel houses, a tiny church, a grocery store, and the Emerald Palms by the Sea Hotel. At the Bluff settlement, near Congo Town, which has the island's third airport, skeletons of Arawak natives were found huddled together. A local resident attests that another skeleton was found—this one of a 4-ft-tall, one-eyed owl, which may have given rise to the legend of the *chickcharnie,* a mythical elflike creature who, according to native legend, can cause great mischief if disturbed.

Dining and Lodging

$$–$$$$ ╳⌂ **Emerald Palms by the Sea.** This intimate property has tried to keep
★ pace with the luxury-resort trend, offering two oceanfront lanai suites and standard rooms with pool, ocean, or tennis-court view. The attractive furnishings in rooms—such as four-poster beds with mosquito netting and vanities—make this one of the more polished places to stay in the Out Islands. The dining room serves Bahamian and international cuisine. Most guests come for the fishing and opportunities for total relaxation. Chairs on private lanais and hammocks among the palms on the beach offer a pleasant alternative to water sports. ⌂ *General Post Office, Driggs Hill, Andros,* ☎ *242/369–2661,* ᴲᴬˣ *242/369–2667. 20 rooms. Dining room, pool, tennis court, snorkeling, boating, fishing, bicycles, car rental. AE, MC, V. EP, MAP.*

Andros A to Z

Arriving and Departing

BY MAIL BOAT

From Potter's Cay Dock in Nassau, the M/V *Lisa J II* sails to Lowe Sound, Mastic Point, and Nicholl's Town in the north of the island every Wednesday, returning to Nassau the following Tuesday. The trip takes three hours and costs $30. The M/V *Lady D* leaves Nassau on Tuesdays for Fresh Creek (with stops at Spaniard Creek, Blanket Sound, and Bowne Sound) and returns to Nassau on Sunday. The trip takes 3½ hours and the fare is $25. The M/V *Captain Moxey* leaves Nassau on Mondays and calls at Kemps Bay, Long Bay Cays, and the Bluff on South Andros. It returns to Nassau on Wednesday. The trip takes 7½ hours; the fare is $30. Schedules are subject to change due to weather conditions or occasional dry-docking. For more information, contact the **Dockmaster's office** (☎ 242/393–1064) at Potter's Cay.

Andros has three airports: at San Andros in the north, at Andros Town in Central Andros, and at Congo Town in South Andros. Check with a travel agent to find the airport closest to your hotel. The best-known resort is Small Hope Bay Lodge at Fresh Creek near Andros Town, which provides charter flights from Fort Lauderdale and Nassau.

Bahamasair (☎ 800/222–4262) has twice-daily flights (except Tues.) from Nassau to San Andros, Andros Town, and Congo Town.

Congo Air (☎ 242/377–8329) flies from Nassau to Mangrove Cay.

Island Express (☎ 954/359–0380) flies from Fort Lauderdale to Congo Town and Andros Town.

Getting Around

Andros has no tour operators, and cabdrivers will charge around $80 to $100 for a half-day tour of the island. Most visitors opt to get around by bicycle.

BY BICYCLE

Bicycles are available at **Andros Lighthouse Yacht Club and Marina** (✉ Andros Town, ☎ 242/368–2305), **Chickcharnie Hotel** (✉ Andros Town, ☎ 242/368–2025), **Small Hope Bay Lodge** (✉ Fresh Creek, ☎ 242/368–2014), **Whims Rentals** (✉ Spaniard Creek, ☎ 242/368–6456), and **Mangrove Cay Inn** (✉ Mangrove Cay, ☎ 242/369–0069).

BY CAR

If you need a rental car, your best bet is to have your hotel make arrangements.

BY TAXI

Taxis meet incoming planes at all airports, and they can also be arranged through the hotels. Rates are around $1.50 a mile. The average fare from Andros Town Airport to the Small Hope Bay Lodge is about $15.

Opening and Closing Times

The **Canadian Imperial Bank of Commerce** (☎ 242/329–2382), in San Andros, is open Wednesday from 10:30 to 2:30.

Contacts and Resources

EMERGENCIES

Telephone service is available only through the front desk at Andros hotels, so emergencies should be reported to the management. A doctor lives in San Andros. Medical clinics are located at Mastic Point, Nicholl's Town, and Lowe Sound, each with a resident nurse. A health center at Fresh Creek has both a doctor and a nurse. A clinic at Mangrove Cay has a nurse.

Police: North Andros (☎ 919); Central Andros (☎ 242/368–2626); South Andros (☎ 242/329–4733).

Medical Clinics: North Andros (☎ 242/329–2239); Central Andros (☎ 242/368–2038); South Andros (☎ 242/369–4620).

THE BERRY ISLANDS

The Berry Islands consist of two dozen–plus small cays stretching in a curve like a new moon north of Andros and New Providence Island. Although a few of the islands are privately owned, most of them are uninhabited—except by rare birds using the territory as their nesting grounds, or by visiting yachters dropping anchor in secluded havens. The Berry Islands start in the north at Great Stirrup Cay, where a lighthouse guides passing ships, and they end in the south at Chub Cay, whose club and marina attract anglers in search of bonefish in the nearby flats. Chub Cay lies only 35 mi north of Nassau.

Most of the islands' 700 residents live on Great Harbour Cay, which is 10 mi long and 1½ mi wide. Its main settlement, Bullock's Harbour, has a couple of small restaurants and a grocery store. The Great Harbour Cay resort, a few miles away from Bullock's Harbour, was developed in the early 1970s; it includes a golf course, a marina, and privately owned villas and town houses, which are now rented out. The resort is geared toward fishing enthusiasts. Both Chub and Great Harbour cays are located close to the Tongue of the Ocean, where big game fish roam.

The Berry Islands appear just north of Andros Island on the Bahamas map at the front of this guide.

Chub Cay

Dining and Lodging

$$$–$$$$ ✕🏨 **Chub Cay Club.** In 1994 this once-private resort opened its facilities to the public. The huge marina can handle more than 90 ocean-going craft, with big-game and flat fishing being the main pursuits here. The resort's 16 rooms, some with refrigerators and all with cable TV, are clustered next to an oversize freshwater pool or overlook the ocean. Nine one-, two-, and three-bedroom villas are on the horseshoe-shape beach, facing west. The villa porches are a great place to watch the sunset, and guests are occasionally treated to the "green flash" seen only in the tropics. An extensive landscaping face-lift has enhanced the grounds considerably. The Harbour House Restaurant serves a good variety of Caribbean and Continental dishes. With fresh fish, conch, and lobsters arriving daily, seafood is the obvious choice. The Hilltop bar has a pool table and large-screen TV for evening entertainment. Other diversions available are tennis, Ping-Pong, bird-watching, and bicycling around the tiny island. ✉ *Box 661067, Miami Springs, FL 33266,* ☎ *242/325–1490, 242/322–5590, 242/322–5599, or 800/662–8555,* 🆋 *242/322–5199. 16 rooms, 9 villas. Restaurant, 3 bars, dining room, grocery, refrigerators, 2 pools, tennis, Ping-Pong, beach, dive shop, dock, boating, fishing, bicycles. AE, MC, V. EP.*

Outdoor Activities and Sports

The **Chub Cay Club** (☎ 242/325–1490 or 800/662–8555) has charter boats with guides, diving facilities through Undersea Adventures, and two tennis courts.

Great Harbour Cay

Dining and Lodging

$$–$$$$ ✕🏨 **Great Harbour Cay.** The town houses and villas here are privately owned, and the resort rents them out on a daily or weekly basis. The furnishings, decor, and layouts differ, but all units have TVs, and sundecks; some have VCRs, attractive rattan furnishings, and a washer and dryer; none have phones. The number of bedrooms and the size of the kitchen facilities vary—studios, one-, two-, and four-bedroom units are available. About half overlook the marina, some are on the beach, some have only a view of the beach; the least expensive, as you might guess, have the poorest view. Management meets you at the airport and can help you find the services of fishing guides for bonefishing, bottom fishing, and deep-sea fishing. You can find a light lunch at the Beach Club, full meals at the Wharf on the marina, and a more expensive fish-and-seafood buffet a couple of nights a week at the yacht

club's private Tamboo Club, to which resort guests are admitted. ⊠ *3512 N. Ocean Dr., Hollywood, FL 33019,* ☎ *954/921–9084 or 800/343–7256,* FAX *954/921–1044. 15 villas, 6 town houses. 3 restaurants, bar, 9-hole golf course, beach, dock, snorkeling, boating, fishing, bicycles. AE, MC, V. EP.*

Outdoor Activities and Sports

The resort at **Great Harbour Cay** (☎ 242/367–8838, 954/921–9084, or 800/343–7256) has a nine-hole golf course and can arrange guides to take you bonefishing, sportfishing, and diving.

Berry Islands A to Z

Arriving and Departing

BY MAIL BOAT

M/V *Champion II* leaves Potter's Cay, Nassau, every Thursday for the Berry Islands. For schedules and specific destinations, call the **Dockmaster's office** (☎ 242/393–1064) at Potter's Cay.

BY PLANE

Both Great Harbour Cay and Chub Cay resorts provide transportation from the airport for their guests.

Island Express (☎ 954/359–0380) has charters from Fort Lauderdale to Chub Cay and Great Harbour Cay.

Tropical Diversions Air (☎ 954/921–9084 or 800/343–7256) flies to Great Harbour Cay from Fort Lauderdale.

Getting Around

Happy People's (☎ 242/367–8117) has rental bikes, Jeeps, and boats available for exploring the island.

Contacts and Resources

EMERGENCIES

Police (⊠ Bullock's Harbour, Great Harbour Cay, ☎ 242/367–8344).

Great Harbour Cay Medical Clinic (☎ 242/367–8400).

THE BIMINIS

The Biminis have long been known as the big-game-fishing capital of the Bahamas. The nearest Bahamian islands to the U.S. mainland, they consist of a handful of islands and cays just 50 mi east of Miami, across the Gulf Stream that sweeps the area's western shores. Most visitors spend their time on North Bimini. Throughout the year, more than a dozen billfish tournaments draw anglers to the Gulf Stream and the Great Bahama Bank from the United States, Canada, Britain, and the rest of Europe. Marinas such as Brown's, Weech's Bimini Dock, the Bimini Big Game Fishing Club, and Bimini's Blue Water, all on the eastern side of skinny North Bimini, provide more than 150 slips for oceangoing craft, many of them belonging to weekend visitors who make the short trip from Florida ports. The western side of North Bimini, along Queen's Highway, is one long stretch of beautiful beach.

All the hotels, restaurants, churches, and stores in the Biminis are located along North Bimini's King's and Queen's highways, which run parallel to each other. Everything on North Bimini, where most of the islands' 1,600 inhabitants reside, is so close together you do not need a car to get around. Sparsely populated South Bimini, separated from its big brother by a narrow ocean passage, is where Juan Ponce de León allegedly looked for the Fountain of Youth in 1513. Tourists are sometimes still approached by locals offering to show them the exact site

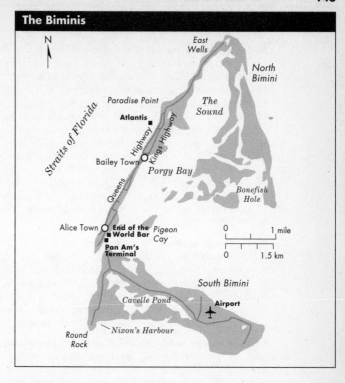

The Biminis

N

East
Wells

North
Bimini

The
Sound

Straits of Florida

Paradise Point

Atlantis ■

Kings Highway

Bailey Town ○

Porgy Bay

Queens Highway

Bonefish
Hole

0 ___ 1 mile

0 ___ 1.5 km

Alice Town ○ ■ **End of the**
World Bar

Pigeon
Cay

Pan Am's
Terminal ■

South Bimini

Cavelle Pond

Airport ✈

Round
Rock

Nixon's Harbour

---

of the Fountain of Youth, which is supposedly close to South Bimini's little airstrip.

Ernest Hemingway did battle with his share of game fish around North Bimini, which he visited for the first time in 1935 from his home in Key West. He made frequent visits here, where he wrote much of *To Have and Have Not* and *Islands in the Stream*. He is remembered in the area as a picaresque hero, not only for his graphic descriptions of his fishing exploits, but for his drinking and brawling, including a fist-fight he had with his brother Leicester on the Bimini dock. Other notables lured to the island have included Howard Hughes and Richard Nixon.

The Biminis also have a notorious history as a jumping-off place for illicit dealings; first during the Civil War, when it was a refuge for profiteers bringing in war supplies from Europe, and then during Prohibition, when it was a haven for rumrunners. Today, the Biminis attract fishermen and friendly tourists, especially Floridians, during the summer fishing season. Winters here are fairly quiet. Spring break brings lots of students, who rent sailboats and cruise over from Fort Lauderdale for wild nights at what was Papa Hemingway's favorite watering hole, the Compleat Angler.

Alice Town

The main community of the Biminis, Alice Town, is situated at the southern end of North Bimini; here, Pam Am Airbridge's seaplanes splash down in the harbor, lumber up a ramp, and park on the other side of King's Highway.

Bimini Bay Rod and Gun Club. Near the Pan Am seaplane landing area's customs and immigration office, along the narrow King's Highway, are

the Art Deco ruins of Bimini's first hotel, a resort and casino that was
built in the early 1920s and destroyed by a hurricane in 1926.

Bimini Blue Water Resort. This was one of Hemingway's Bimini hideaways, and its restaurant, the Anchorage, is believed to have been the
main setting for *Islands in the Stream*. You can still rent Marlin Cottage, where the author wrote much of the novel. The cottage, with its
matching cannons in front, remains the best place on the island for
watching the sunset and, on a clear evening, the reflection of Miami's
lights on the water. The Anchorage restaurant was also the former home
of Michael Lerner, who opened a laboratory on the island devoted to
dolphin and shark research in 1947; it was closed in 1974. The resort is just north of the Compleat Angler Hotel (☞ *below*). Although
the entrance to the hotel is on King's Highway, the building sits on
top of a 20-ft hill and faces Queen's Highway on the western side.
✉ *King's Hwy., Alice Town,* ☎ *242/347–3166 or 800/688–4752,*
FAX *242/347–3293.*

Bimini Historic Museum. Plans are under way in Alice Town for a new
museum showcasing Bimini's history. Exhibits will include Ernest
Hemingway's photographs of Bimini and his fishing log, as well as the
plaques of the Bimini Fishing Hall of Fame. The museum will be on
Kings Highway in a former government building (part of which was
the jail), one of the island's oldest structures. Work has been sporadic,
however, and the completion date is still unknown.

Compleat Angler Hotel. This was Ernest Hemingway's hideaway in the
'30s, and the Hemingway legend is perpetuated with a room full of
memorabilia related to the writer, including pictures of Hemingway
with gigantic fish and framed excerpts from his writings, most of them
concerning battles with sharks. A photo of Cuban fisherman Angelmo
Hernández, the supposed model for the hero of *The Old Man and the
Sea*, also hangs in the bar. The late Ossie Brown, who ran this hotel
until 1995, claimed a Cuban man named Bruce Garmendia walked into
the hotel some years ago, said he was Hernández's grandson, and
handed over the photograph. More recently the Angler was in the news
as the place where Gary Hart destroyed his hopes for the 1988 Demo-
cratic presidential nomination. He and Donna Rice were photographed
in full color whooping it up on the bandstand in the bar of the hotel;
the infamous picture now hangs in a place of honor. A short distance
from the Hotel, along King's Highway, is an **arch** on the roadside in-
scribed THE GATEWAY TO THE BAHAMAS. The arch was erected in com-
memoration of the 100th anniversary of the island's settlement in the
1840s. ✉ *Compleat Angler Hotel, King's Hwy., Alice Town,* ☎ *242/
347–3122.*

End of the World Bar. At this small, noisy tavern, which has a sandy
floor and visitors' graffiti, business cards, and even underwear plastered on every inch of wall, ceiling, and bar space, the back door is always open to the harbor. This place offers a good spot to meet some
local folk over a beer and a backgammon board. In the late '60s, the
bar became a hangout of the late New York congressman Adam Clay-
ton Powell who retreated to North Bimini while Congress investigated
his alleged misdemeanors; among other guests, Powell entertained
American reporters, who knew they could find him here, ready to dispense flowery quotes. A marble plaque in his honor is displayed in the
bar, and an annual Bimini fishing tournament is named in his memory. The bar is located a hundred yards away from the Bimini Bay Rod
and Gun Club ruins, on your right as you walk north on King's Highway (cars that meet head-on have to slow down so they can scrape past
each other). ✉ *King's Hwy., no phone.* ☉ *Daily 9 AM–3 AM.*

Dining and Lodging

$$$–$$$$ **✕▣ Bimini Big Game Fishing Club and Hotel.** This largest resting spot
★ on the island is a favorite not only of fishing and yachting types who
take advantage of the full-service 100-slip marina, but also of casual
visitors who receive a warm welcome from veteran manager Curtiss
Carroll. Owned by the Bacardi Corporation, the rum company, the hotel
has 35 large and comfortable guest rooms, as well as two elegant pent-
house apartments (often rented by VIPs) and 12 pleasant cottages, with
refrigerators, on the marina. If you're here to fish, you might prefer
one of the roomy cottages, where you can easily prepare a lucky catch
on an outdoor grill. The club has the only tennis court on North Bi-
mini. There are televisions in the rooms, a purely protective measure
to keep you from hanging around the tiny lobby and to give you an
added diversion on rainy days. The club's Gulfstream restaurant on
the harbor is the best on the island, specializing in fresh grouper, a Bi-
mini bouillabaisse, and cracked conch; steaks and lamb chops, which
are imported from Miami and are more expensive, are also served. The
Bimini Sports Bar serves seafood and sandwiches in an airy room that
overlooks the marina and has a large bar and four TVs. The pleasant
and swimmable Radio Beach is only a few minutes' walk away. If you
plan to stay here during one of the major fishing tournaments, reserve
well in advance. ⊠ *Box 699, Alice Town, Bimini,* ☏ *800/737–1007
or 242/347–3391,* ⤢ *242/347–3392. 49 rooms. Restaurant, 3 bars,
2 dining rooms, pool, tennis court, beach, snorkeling, boating, baby-
sitting, laundry service. AE, MC, V. EP.*

$$–$$$$ **✕▣ Bimini Blue Water Resort.** The main building of this resort is a blue-
shuttered white house on top of a hill. Its smallish rooms have blue-
and-white furniture, wood-paneled walls, private balconies, and TVs.
The resort's full-service marina, with 32 modern slips, is across the street,
and King's Highway's small shops are a short walk away. The grounds
extend to Queen's Highway and face a beautiful stretch of beach. On
the property stands Marlin Cottage, with three bedrooms, where Hemingway stayed in the '30s; ask the manager to lead you up the stairs
of the cottage to the little room where the writer worked. The wood-
paneled Anchorage dining room specializes in conch and lobster and
provides a gorgeous view of the Gulf Stream. The resort belongs to a
pioneer family in the islands, the Browns, who also own the Compleat
Angler (☞ *below*). ⊠ *Box 601, Alice Town, Bimini,* ☏ *800/688–4752
or 242/347–3166,* ⤢ *242/347–3293. 9 rooms, 1 3-bedroom cottage
(all have private bath). Bar, dining room, pool, beach. AE, MC, V. EP.*

$$–$$$$ **▣ Sea Crest Hotel and Marina.** This cheery, three-story, modern hotel
★ is, like everything else, located on King's Highway. The large rooms
have TVs and balconies, and are simply furnished with wood-veneer
furniture, tiled floors, and colorful spreads. Third-floor rooms have
elegant cathedral-beamed ceilings and gorgeous marina views from the
balcony. The beach is a two-minute walk. This motelish property is a
particularly excellent value to families, as children under age 12 stay
free. You can make arrangements at the full-service marina for fishing
or diving trips and boat rentals. ⊠ *Box 654, Alice Town, Bimini,*
☏ *242/347–3071,* ⤢ *242/347–3495. 11 rooms, 2 suites. MC, V
(5% surcharge). EP.*

$–$$ **▣ Compleat Angler Hotel.** This well-worn, informal, and friendly
wood-sided hotel dates back to the early '30s and will forever be as-
sociated with Hemingway, who often drank here after a day of stalk-
ing marlin. The cozy, unpretentious rooms are wood paneled and have
splashy green tropical-print spreads. Exterior rooms open onto the
wraparound porch, which overlooks the courtyard bar and the street.
The walls of the bar are plastered with fishing photographs and per-

sonalized auto-license plates. Hemingway memorabilia is kept in a separate room off the bar, hung on varnished, paneled walls. Drinks are served either inside or at an outdoor bar that encircles a huge almond tree. The bar remains the liveliest nightspot on the island, with live music on weekends, but this can be of questionable merit if you're trying to sleep upstairs. You can use the pool and marina facilities of the Blue Water Resort if you stay here—the two hotels are under the same management. ⊠ *Box 601, Alice Town, Bimini,* ☎ *242/347–3122,* 𝙵𝙰𝚇 *242/ 347–3293. 12 rooms. 3 bars, lounge. AE, MC, V. EP.*

$–$$ ☷ **Weech's Bimini Dock and Bay View Rooms.** This Alice Town marina (full-service, except fuel), has five clean, simply furnished rooms and one apartment available for rent. Two of the rooms and the apartment enjoy marina views. The pleasant but unadorned rooms have paneled walls, pastel spreads and drapes, and either two twins or a double and a twin bed; the apartment has a full kitchen and a seating area. Grills are available for guest use. The beach is a five-minute walk. ⊠ *Box 613, Alice Town, Bimini,* ☎ *242/347–3028,* 𝙵𝙰𝚇 *242/347–3508. 5 rooms, 1 apartment. Boating. No credit cards. EP.*

Outdoor Activities and Sports

BOATING AND FISHING

Events. The Biminis host the following fishing tournaments throughout the year: the **Hemingway Championship** (February), the **Annual Bacardi Rum Billfish Tournament** (March), the **Bimini Billfish Championship** (March), the **Big Game Club Bimini Festival** (May), the **Big Five Tournament** (June), the **Hatteras and Latin Builder's Tournaments** (July), the **Bimini Native Open Tournament** and **Bacardi Family Open Tournament** (August), **Small BOAT—Bimini Open Angling Tournament** (September), and the **Wahoo Tournament** (November). For information on dates and tournament regulations, call the **Bahamas News Bureau** (☎ 800/327– 7678).

Marinas. Bimini Big Game Fishing Club (☎ 800/737–1007 or 242/347– 3391), which has a first-class, full-service 100-slip marina serving as headquarters for many spring and summer fishing tournaments, charges $500 to $900 a day, and $400 a half day for deep-sea fishing. **Bimini Blue Water Marina** (☎ 242/347–3166) charges from $700 a day, and from $400 a half day, with captain, mate, and all gear included; this marina features 32 modern slips and usually hosts the annual Hemingway Billfish Tournament, among several other fishing events. **Brown's Marina** (☎ 242/347–3227) is a full-service 22-slip marina, and will take you reef, shark, or deep-sea fishing for $750 a day, and $450 a half day. **Weech's Bimini Dock** (☎ 242/347–3028), with 15 slips, has four Boston whalers, which it rents for $110 a day, and $60 a half day.

SCUBA DIVING

The Biminis offer some excellent diving opportunities, particularly for those who enjoy watching marine life. The **Bimini Barge** wreck rests in 100 ft of water; **Little Caverns** is a medium-depth dive with scattered coral heads, small tunnels, and swim-throughs; **Rainbow Reef** is a shallow dive popular for fish gazing. And, of course, there's **Atlantis** (☞ *below*).

Bimini Undersea Adventures (☎ 242/347–3089, 800/327–8150, or 800/348–4644) charges $39 for a one-tank dive, $69 for a two-tank, and $89 for three dives. Dive packages are also available. Guests taking advantage of the package stay at the Bimini Big Game Fishing Club, the Compleat Angler, or the Sea Crest Hotel.

SNORKELING

Bimini Undersea Adventures (☎ 242/347–3089, 800/327–8150, or 800/348–4644) rents and sells snorkel gear and arranges trips for $25 per person, including mask, snorkel, and fins. Excellent snorkeling is available mere steps from the beach.

TENNIS

The **Bimini Big Game Fishing Club** (☎ 242/347–3391) has one lighted court, which is available only to guests.

Elsewhere on North Bimini

Toward the north end of King's Highway, there are a couple of bars, grocery shops, clothing stores, a small straw market, and women sitting by the side of the road selling mouthwatering Bimini bread (it is sold warm, soft, and sweet). The northwestern part of the island bears the ruins of a planned luxury development that was begun only a few years ago, a $350 million resort community that was to include a marina, private homes, and a hotel. The developers ran out of money and abandoned the project, leaving the frames of a half dozen homes looking out on an untrampled, shell-strewn beach.

Atlantis. This odd-shaped 300-ft-long rectangular rock formation, some 20 ft under water, is not only a dive site. It is purported to be a lost city, and archaeologists estimate it to be between 5,000 and 10,000 years old. Carvings in the rock appear to some scientists to resemble a network of highways. Skeptics have pooh-poohed the theory, conjecturing that they are merely turtle pens built considerably more recently.

NEED A BREAK?

Whenever your stomach starts rumbling, you'll find a place to fill up while exploring Bimini. Go for breakfast at **Capt. Bob's** (✉ King's Hwy., ☎ 242/347–3260) for the terrific Bimini-bread French toast or fish and eggs. At lunch, hit **CJ's Deli** (✉ King's Hwy., ☎ 242/347–3295) for piles of the best cracked conch on the island—try it with either tartar sauce or ketchup.

Bailey Town. Most of the island's residents live here, in the island's second-largest settlement, in small, pastel-color concrete houses, a higgledy-piggledy combination of different shapes and sizes. Here you'll also find the attractive **Wesley Methodist Church**, built in 1858, with a bell tower on the roof. Bailey Town lies on Queen's Highway north of the Bimini Blue Water Resort.

OFF THE BEATEN PATH

Locals recommend the **Healing Hole** for curing what ails you—gout and rheumatism are among the supposedly treatable afflictions. Ask your hotel to arrange a trip out to this natural clearing in the mangrove flats of North Bimini; you can take a leap of faith into the water and have a refreshing dip, if nothing else.

Biminis A to Z

Arriving and Departing

BY MAIL BOAT

M/V *Bimini Mack* sails from Potter's Cay, Nassau, to Cat Cay and Bimini on a varying schedule. The trip takes 12 hours and costs $35. For information, call the **Dockmaster's office** (☎ 242/393–1064) at Potter's Cay.

BY PLANE

Pan Am Airbridge (☎ 800/359–7262) has several 25-minute flights daily into Alice Town, North Bimini, from Miami's terminal at Watson Island on the MacArthur Causeway, and from Fort Lauderdale (40 minutes). If you've just arrived at Miami International Airport, the taxi ride (about $10) to the Watson Island terminal across from the Port of Miami will take about the same time it takes to get to North Bimini. North Bimini is also served from Pan Am's base in Nassau/Paradise Island (☎ 242/363–1687). Pan Am uses amphibians, with takeoffs and landings on water. Baggage allowance is 30 pounds per passenger.

If you don't have heavy luggage, you might decide to walk to your hotel from the seaplane terminal in Alice Town, the main settlement on North Bimini. The Bimini Bus Company meets planes and takes incoming passengers to Alice Town in 12-passenger vans. The cost is $3. A $5 taxi-and-ferry ride takes visitors from the South Bimini airport to Alice Town.

Getting Around

BY BICYCLE

Undersea Adventures (☎ 242/347–3089) rents bikes for $5 per hour or $20 per day.

BY BUS

The **Bimini Bus Company** has minibuses available for a tour of the island. Arrangements can be made through your hotel.

BY CAR

Visitors do not need a car on North Bimini and usually walk wherever they go; there are no car-rental agencies.

BY GOLF CART

Rental golf carts are available at the Sea Crest Hotel Marina from **Capt. Pat's** (☎ 242/347–3477) for $75 a day or $20 for the first hour and $10 for each additional hour, or at the Compleat Angler from **Compleat Golf Cart Rentals** (☎ 242/347–3122) for $20 for the first hour and $10 for each additional hour.

Opening and Closing Times

The **Royal Bank of Canada** is open Monday and Friday from 9 to 3, and Tuesday through Thursday from 9 to 1. Note that most **stores** and **liquor stores** are closed on Sundays.

Contacts and Resources

EMERGENCIES

Police and **fire** (☎ 919).

North Bimini Medical Clinic (☎ 242/347–3210) has a resident doctor and a nurse.

TELEPHONES

Pay phones are scattered along King's Highway. If you have trouble placing your call, the office of the Blue Water Marina will place it for you for $1.50.

CAT ISLAND

At the summit of Cat Island's 206-ft Mt. Alvernia, the highest point in the Bahamas, you will find a tomb that is considered a shrine by the 1,698 inhabitants of this boot-shape land. Above the tomb's entrance, carved in stone, is the epitaph BLESSED ARE THE DEAD WHO DIE IN THE LORD and inside, past the wooden gate that hangs on its hinges, lies interred the body of an extraordinary man named Father Jerome; in 1956, at age 80, he was buried, supposedly with his arms outstretched, the pose resembling Christ's crucifixion. The mystique surrounding Father Jerome seems to envelop Cat Island, one of the Bahamas' farthest-flung destinations. It's 130 mi southeast of Nassau and is a close neighbor of San Salvador, the reputed landing place of Columbus. Little is known of Cat Island's history, perhaps because of its infrequent visitors. Nevertheless, the island's unofficial biographer, Frances Armbrister, a member of the pioneer family that runs Fernandez Bay, known simply throughout the island as Mrs. A, has many tales to tell about the place. Some of her stories involve the practice of Obeah, the Bahamian version of voodoo. Chatting with other residents, you might find some who knew or are related to native son Sidney Poitier, who left as a youth to become the famed movie actor and director.

The island may have been named after a frequent notorious visitor, Arthur Catt, a piratical contemporary of Edward "Blackbeard" Teach. Then again, Cat Island's name may derive from the fact that if you look at it from on high, you can see the shape of a cat sitting on its haunches. Slender Cat Island is 50 mi long, featuring high cliffs and dense forest. Its shores are ringed with mile upon mile of exquisite, untrampled beaches, edged with casuarina trees. Perhaps the tranquillity of the place is one of the reasons why some of the original inhabitants' descendants, who migrated long ago to New York, Detroit, and Miami, are slowly returning here; large, new homes have started to appear throughout the island.

Residents of the island fish, farm, and live a peaceful existence. The biggest event of the year remains the Annual Cat Island Regatta, which in summer brings the most fervent yachters to this faraway island. Otherwise, its resorts' guests are the professionals who are here to get away from it all.

Numbers in the text correspond to numbers in the margin and on the Cat Island map.

Arthur's Town and Bennett's Harbour

⓯ **Arthur's Town**'s claim to fame is that it was the boyhood home of actor Sidney Poitier, who has written about growing up here in his autobiography; his parents and other relatives were farmers. The village has little of interest, except for the telephone station and a few stores. If you drive south from Arthur's Town, which is located almost at the island's northernmost tip, the winding road passes through small villages and bays where fishing boats are tied up. At times, the road offers views of the sea and of beaches lined with coconut palms.

⓰ One of the island's oldest settlements of small, weather-beaten houses, **Bennett's Harbour,** is situated some 15 mi south of Arthur's Town; at the Bluff, you can see bread baked daily in whitewashed ovens beside many of the homes.

New Bight

⓱ The settlement of **New Bight,** where you'll find a small grocery store, a bakery, and the Bridge Inn, is near the New Bight (also called "The Bight") airport, and just south of **Fernandez Bay Village;** this resort, which sits on a long, curved bay, is the final destination for a large proportion of Cat Island's visitors. Between the airport and the town is the small, blue **First and Last Chance Bar,** run by Iva Thompson. This is a good place to have a beer with the locals and check out Miss Iva's straw work, which is some of the best in the Bahamas. New Bight is

Cat Island

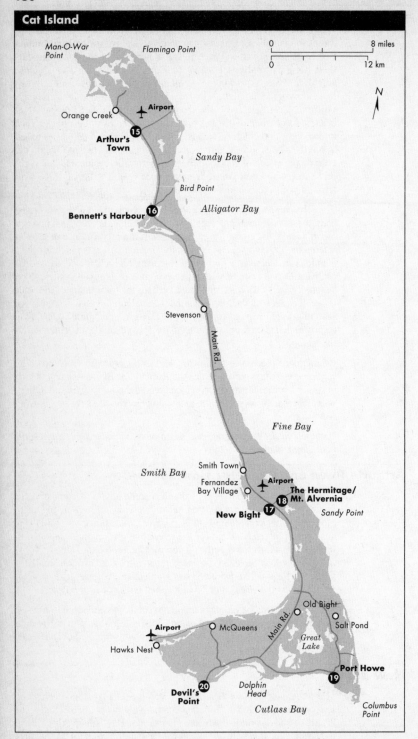

Man-O-War
Point

Flamingo Point

0   8 miles

0   12 km

N

Orange Creek

Airport

**Arthur's
Town** 15

Sandy Bay

Bird Point

Bennett's Harbour 16

Alligator Bay

Stevenson

Main Rd.

Fine Bay

Smith Bay

Smith Town

Fernandez
Bay Village

Airport

**The Hermitage/
Mt. Alvernia** 18

17

New Bight

Sandy Point

Old Bight

Main Rd.

Salt Pond

Airport

McQueens

*Great
Lake*

Hawks Nest

Port Howe 19

**Devil's
Point** 20

*Dolphin
Head*

*Columbus
Point*

Cutlass Bay

also the home of the **Sailing Club** (☎ 242/342–3054), a bar and restaurant specializing in fish, conch, and mutton; on Saturday nights, a local DJ keeps locals and a few tourists dancing until about 1 AM.

⑱ At the top of Mt. Alvernia, the **Hermitage** is Father Jerome's resting place. Early in this century, Father Jerome, born John Hawes, traveled the world and eventually settled in the Bahamas. An Anglican who converted to Roman Catholicism, he built two fine churches, St. Paul's and St. Peter's, on hills on Long Island (in the Bahamas, not New York), as well as the St. Augustine Monastery in Nassau, before he retired to Cat Island to live out the last dozen years of his life as a hermit. His final, supreme act of religious dedication was carried out here, where he carved steps up to the top of Mt. Alvernia. Along the way, he also carved the 14 Stations of the Cross, representing events from the Passion of Christ, and, at the summit, he built a child-size abbey with a small chapel, a conical bell tower, and three closet-size rooms that he used as living quarters.

The pilgrimage to the Hermitage begins next to the commissioner's office at New Bight, at a dirt path that leads to the foot of Mt. Alvernia. No one visiting the island should miss the experience of making the slightly laborious climb to the top. The Hermitage provides a perfect, inspired place to pause for quiet contemplation; it also has glorious views of the ocean on both sides of the island. The previously mentioned Frances Armbrister takes guests from the Fernandez Bay Village resort on pilgrimages to the Hermitage. A caretaker sees to it that someone clears the weeds around the tomb and lights a candle in Father Jerome's memory.

Dining and Lodging

$$$$ ✕⟦⟧ **Fernandez Bay Village.** Just north of New Bight, Tony and Pam
★ Armbrister run this resort built on land owned by Tony's parents. Five large brick-and-stonework villas are spread along a stunning white-sand beach; each accommodates four to six persons. There are also three single-story one-bedroom cottages. The villas have kitchens (there's a handy grocery store at the resort), terraces facing the sea, and individual gardens, where guests can shower; an outside wall ensures privacy. Only one telephone is available on the property, at the front desk. The dinner menu relies on freshly caught fish and locally grown vegetables; excellent, buffet-style meals are often served on the beach patio, though a comfortable, mahogany-beamed dining room is also used. Nightlife here usually involves conversation around a bonfire or stargazing from the moonlit beach. Guests can arrange with the resort for charter flights from Nassau. Donna, the ebullient manager, can be counted on to try to accommodate your every whim. There is a dive shop on the property, and fishing excursions can also be arranged. ⊠ *1507 S. University Dr., Suite A, Plantation, FL 33324,* ☎ *954/474–4821 or 800/940–1905,* ⨎⨉ *954/474–4864. 8 units. Bar, dining room, paddle tennis, beach, dive shop, snorkeling, boating, waterskiing, fishing, bicycles, laundry service. AE. EP, MAP.*

$$ ✕⟦⟧ **Bridge Inn.** This motel-like property, run by Cat Islanders Mr. and Mrs. Russell with the help of their large family, is about 300 yards from a beach where cottages have recently been built. About a mile down a back road is a more tranquil beach. The wood-paneled, high-ceilinged rooms (each can fit up to four people) have private baths, and cable TV. The hotel has a large, rustic dining room, and if you are on a special diet, you will find the managers very accommodating. Mr. Russell can arrange pickups in Nassau, landing you at the nearby New Bight airport. ⊠ *New Bight, Cat Island,* ☎ *242/342–3013 or 800/688–4752,*

FAX *242/342–3041. 12 rooms. Bar, dining room, beach, boating, billiards, baby-sitting. No credit cards. EP, CP, MAP, FAP.*

Port Howe

⑲ The road curves out toward **Port Howe,** named for an English admiral who fought in the American Revolution, at the bottom of the island. Nearby, you'll see the ruins of the **Deveaux Mansion,** a stark, two-story, whitewashed building overrun with wild vegetation. Once it was a grand house on a cotton plantation, home of Col. Andrew Deveaux of the U.S. Navy, who had been granted thousands of acres of Cat Island property as reward for his daring raid in 1783 that recaptured Nassau from the Spaniards. Just beyond the mansion ruin is the entrance road to the **Greenwood Beach Resort,** which sits on an 8-mi stretch of practically untouched velvet-sand beach.

Dining and Lodging

$$ ✕🏨 **Greenwood Beach Resort.** In 1992 this resort was bought by a
★ German family that has gradually upgraded the facilities. The smallish rooms have been remodeled, and received attractive spreads and drapes to complement the king-size beds. Half the rooms have ocean views; the four farthest from the beach are larger and have a twin in addition to the king bed. The clubhouse, with its cheery purple-and-white walls and colorful tropical paintings, is the center of activity here. There's also a small library, a lounge area, a bar, and the dining area. Outside is a large stone veranda which looks out at the ocean—a very pleasant place to have breakfast. A pool lies between the clubhouse and the rooms. The Cat Island Dive Center is steps off the beach and most of the guests join the twice-daily dive excursions. This isolated resort is about 45 minutes from the airport and lies on an 8-mi stretch of gorgeous Atlantic-side beach. ⊠ *Port Howe, Cat Island,* ☎ FAX *242/342–3053 or* ☎ *800/688–4752. 20 rooms. Bar, dining room, pool, beach, dive shop, snorkeling, boating, fishing, bicycles. MC, V (4% surcharge). EP, MAP, FAP.*

Devil's Point

⑳ The small village of **Devil's Point,** with its pastel-color, thatch-roof houses, lies about 10 mi west of Columbus Point. Here you'll also find the ruins of the **Richman Hill–Newfield plantation,** which once stretched from the lake to the ocean.

Dining and Lodging

$$–$$$ ✕🏨 **Hawk's Nest Resort & Marina.** At the southwestern tip of Cat Island, this small waterfront resort, just yards from a long sandy beach, has its own runway (for charter flights and private planes) and an eight-slip marina. The patios of the 10 guest rooms, as well as the dining room and lounge, overlook the ocean. With cheerful peach walls and bright bedspreads, all rooms have either one king-size or two queen-size beds. TV/VCRs are available when you aren't busy diving, snorkeling, shelling, sailing, biking, or simply relaxing on the lush grounds. For dinner, the Bahamian fried chicken is a crowd-pleaser—it's marinated in lime juice and red peppers, fried, then steamed with onions and more peppers. Families who like feeling at home while being away from home should consider renting the two-bedroom house next to a beach that is known for its multitude of shells. ⊠ *Devil's Point, Cat Island,* ☎ FAX *242/357–7257 or* ☎ *800/688–4752. 10 rooms, 2-bedroom house. Bar, dining room, beach, boating, fishing, bicycles. AE, MC, V. EP.*

Cat Island A to Z

Arriving and Departing

BY MAIL BOAT

The *North Cat Island Special* leaves Potter's Cay, Nassau, every Tuesday for Bennett's Town and Arthur's Town, returning on Thursday. The trip takes 14 hours and costs $35. M/V *Sea Hauler* leaves Potter's Cay on Tuesday for Bluff and Smith Bay, returning on Sunday. The trip is 10 hours long; the fare is $35. For information, call the **Dockmaster's office** (☎ 242/393–1064) at Potter's Cay.

BY PLANE

From Nassau, **Bahamasair** (☎ 800/222–4262) flies into Arthur's Town or New Bight Airport in the center of Cat Island twice weekly. The hotels we listed are closer to the New Bight airport—be sure to fly into that one. Several hotels also offer their own charter flights from Nassau: **Fernandez Bay Village** (☎ 800/940–1905), **Greenwood Beach Resort** (☎ 800/688–4752), and **Hawk's Nest Resort & Marina** (☎ 800/688–4752).

There are no taxis on Cat Island. Resort owners make arrangements beforehand with guests to pick them up at the airport. If you miss your ride, just ask around the parking lot for a lift; anyone going in your direction (there's only one road) will be happy to drop you.

Getting Around

BY CAR

The **New Bight Service Station** (☎ 242/342–3014; ask for Jason), rents cars for exploring.

Contacts and Resources

EMERGENCIES

Cat Island has three **medical clinics**—at Smith Bay, Old Bight, and Arthur's Town. There are few telephones on the island, but the front desk of your hotel will be able to contact the nearest clinic in case of an emergency.

CROOKED AND ACKLINS ISLANDS

Historians of the Bahamas tell us that as Columbus sailed down the lee of Crooked Island and its southern neighbor, Acklins Island (the islands are separated by a short water passage), he was riveted by the aroma of native herbs wafting out to his ship. Soon after, Crooked Island, which lies 225 mi southeast of Nassau, became known as one of the "fragrant islands." The first known settlers, however, didn't arrive in Crooked Island until the late 18th century, when Loyalists brought their slaves from the United States and established cotton plantations. It was a doomed venture because of the island's poor soil, and those who stayed made a living of sorts by farming and fishing. A salt and sponge industry flourished for a while on Fortune Island, south of Crooked Island, but the place is now a ghost town. Today the 400-plus inhabitants who live on Crooked and Acklins islands continue to eke out an existence by farming and fishing. The islands are best known to travelers for splendid tarpon and bonefishing, but not much else. They are about as remote as populated islands in the Bahamas get. Much of the islands still do not have power, and many residents rely on generators for electricity. Phone service, where available, often goes out for weeks at a time.

Although the plantations have long crumbled, two relics of those days are preserved by the Bahamas National Trust on the northern part of Crooked Island, which overlooks the Crooked Island Passage separating the cay from Long Island. One ruin, **Marine Farm,** may have been used as a fortification, for old Spanish guns have been discovered there. The other old structure, **Hope Great House,** has orchards and gardens that are still tended by the Trust.

Crooked Island is surrounded by 45 mi of barrier reefs that are great for diving. They slope from 4 to 50 ft, then plunge to 3,600 ft in the Crooked Island Passage, once one of the most important sea roads for ships following the southerly route from the West Indies to the Old World. From **Colonel Hill,** where the one-room airport is located, you get an uninterrupted view of the region all the way to the narrow passage between Crooked Island and Acklins Island. There are two lighthouses on these islands. The sparkling white **Bird Rock Lighthouse** (built in 1872) in the north once guarded the Crooked Island Passage. The rotating flash from its 115-ft tower still welcomes pilots and sailors to the **Pittstown Point Landings** resort, currently the only suitable accommodation on the islands. The **Castle Island** lighthouse (built in 1867), at the southern tip of Acklins Island, formerly served as a haven for pirates who used to retreat there after attacking ships.

Crooked and Acklins islands appear southeast of Andros Island on the Bahamas map at the front of this guide.

Dining and Lodging

$$ ✕🏠 **Pittstown Point Landings.** This all-inclusive property, which was briefly known as Caribe Bay but has restored its original name, attracts those interested in Crooked Island's excellent fishing and diving. This beachfront hideaway on the north end of the island has its own 2,300-ft landing strip for small private planes; the main Colonel Hill Airport is 15 mi away. The large, airy rooms are pleasantly furnished; seven of them are right on the beach, and the rest have a view of it. The dining room, overlooking both the ocean and the runway, serves Bahamian fare. It is situated in a mid-18th-century building that housed the first post office in the Bahamas. The completely isolated property has miles of open beach on its doorstep (the island's best), which should delight sun worshipers au naturel. As for diving, the resort can arrange your dives with a local outfitter. When making reservations, be sure to ask about what scuba gear to bring. ⊠ *Box 477, Mooresville, NC 28115,* ☎ *242/344–2507 or 800/752–2322,* 𝙵𝙰𝚇 *704/881–0771. 12 rooms. Bar, dining room, lounge, beach, snorkeling, boating. AE, MC, V. FAP.*

Crooked and Acklins Islands A to Z

Arriving and Departing

BY MAIL BOAT

M/V *Lady Mathilda* sails from Potter's Cay in Nassau to Acklins Island, Crooked Island, Inagua, and Mayaguana. The boat leaves Nassau on Wednesday and returns on Sunday; call the **Dockmaster's office** (☎ 242/393–1064) in Potter's Cay for fares and schedule information. A government ferry service between Crooked Island and Acklins Island operates daily 9–4.

BY PLANE

Bahamasair (☎ 800/222–4262) flies from Nassau to Crooked and Acklins islands twice a week. Airports are located in Colonel Hill, Crooked Island, and at Spring Point on Acklins Island.

Taxis wait at the airport. Pittstown Point Landings will also arrange transportation by prior arrangement.

Contacts and Resources

EMERGENCIES

Police (☎ 242/344–2599) and **Commissioner** (☎ 242/344–2197) on Crooked Island.

Government medical clinics are located on both islands. On Acklins Island they are at Spring Point and Chesters Bay. Crooked Island's clinic is found at Landrail Point. The resident doctor and nurse for the area live in Spring Point. Nurses are also available at Colonel Hill on Crooked Island, and Masons Bay on Acklins. You can contact any of these medical professionals through your hotel.

ELEUTHERA

Eleuthera is considered by many Out Islands aficionados to be one of the most enjoyable destinations in the Bahamas. Its appealing features include miles and miles of unspoiled beach, green forests, rolling hills, and rich, red soil in the north that produces pineapples and a variety of vegetables. Eleutheran residents, who live in boldly colored houses adorned with bougainvillea, welcome visitors warmly; most will be happy to let you know where to find bargains at a little tucked-away straw market or tell you the name of the best restaurant on the island for conch chowder.

Shaped like a praying mantis, Eleuthera, which is 110 mi long and mostly less than 2 mi wide, has 10,584 inhabitants (including those on Harbour Island and Spanish Wells), the second-largest population in the Out Islands. It lies 200 mi southeast of Florida and 60 mi east of Nassau. The island was named by a group from Britain who came here seeking religious freedom in 1648. Led by William Sayle, a former governor of Bermuda, the group took the name of the island from the Greek word for freedom. The Eleutheran Adventurers, as these Europeans called themselves, gave the Bahamas its first written constitution, which called for the establishment of a republic.

The Eleutheran Adventurers landed first on the middle of the island, close to what is now called Governor's Harbour. After quarreling among themselves, the group split up, and Sayle led one faction around the northern tip of the island by boat. This group was shipwrecked and took refuge at Preacher's Cave, where they held religious services. The cave, and the crude altar at which they worshiped, is still in existence, close to North Eleuthera.

Later in 1648, Sayle journeyed to the United States to seek help in settling his colony, but the people he left behind began to drift away from the island. By 1650, most of them had fled to New England, leaving only a few of the original Adventurers on Eleuthera to trade with passing ships in salt and brasiletto wood. Around 1666, Sayle returned to the Bahamas, this time to the island now called New Providence, which was ideally situated for shipping routes. Eleuthera was "revisited" at the end of the Revolutionary War by Loyalists who fled America with their slaves. The new settlers constructed colonial-style homes that still stand, and they started a shipbuilding industry. Today the population of Eleuthera—and of Harbour Island and Spanish Wells, which lie offshore in the north—consists of descendants of the original Adventurers, Loyalists, and the Loyalists' slaves.

Numbers in the text correspond to numbers in the margin and on the Eleuthera map.

Rock Sound

㉑ One of Eleuthera's largest settlements, the village of **Rock Sound** has a small airport serving the southern part of the island. **Front Street,** the main thoroughfare, runs along the seashore, where fishing boats are tied up. If you walk down the street, you'll eventually come to the pretty, whitewashed **St. Luke's Lutheran Church,** a contrast to the deep blue and green houses nearby, with their colorful gardens full of poinsettia, hibiscus, and marigolds. If you pass the church on a Sunday, you'll surely hear fervent hymn-singing, for the windows are always open to catch the breeze. A small supermarket shopping center, where locals come to stock up on groceries and supplies, is located on the west side of the street.

㉒ **Ocean Hole,** a large inland saltwater lake, is connected by tunnels to the sea. Steps have been cut into the coral on the shore so visitors can climb down to the lake's edge and feed the fish that find their way in from the sea and return to it at will. The hole is estimated to be more than 100 fathoms (600 ft) deep, but, in fact, its depths have never actually been measured. Ocean Hole is a mile east of Rock Sound.

㉓ The now defunct **Cotton Bay Club** is where you'll find the famed Robert Trent Jones golf course, studded with tree groves and nestled against the sea, that dominates the property. Cotton Bay was once an exclusive club, the domain of Pan Am's founder, Juan Trippe, who would fly his friends to the island on a 727 Yankee Clipper for a weekend of golf. The club is 12 mi from the Rock Sound Airport.

㉔ The tiny settlement of **Bannerman Town** (population 40) lies at the southern tip of the island along with its lighthouse, which was very important in navigating ships in the days before radar and satellite locating systems. The beach here is gorgeous and on a clear day you can see the highest point in the Bahamas, Mt. Alvernia (elevation 206 ft), on distant Cat Island. The town lies about 30 mi from the Cotton Bay Club (☞ *above*), past the quiet, little fishing villages of **Wemyss Bight** (named after Lord Gordon Wemyss, a 17th-century Scottish slave owner) and **John Millar's** (population 15), barely touched over the years.

Dining

$$–$$$ ✕ **Sammy's Place.** This reasonable (and spotless) stop for a taste of Bahamian food, owned by Sammy Culmer and managed mainly by his personable daughter Margarita, serves conch fritters, fried chicken and fish, and peas 'n' rice. ⊠ *Albury Lane, Rock Sound,* ☎ *242/334–2121.*

Outdoor Activities and Sports

GOLF

Robert Trent Jones Jr. course (⊠ Cotton Bay Club, Rock Sound, ☎ 242/334–6101), an 18-hole, 7,068-yard, par-72 course, is now open to the public. The once-luxurious hotel here, however, remains closed.

SCUBA DIVING

Dive Centers. South Eleuthera Divers–Tim Riley (⊠ Rock Sound, ☎ 242/334–2221) is the only dive operation in the southern part of the island. This full-service outfit offers diving to the seldom-visited reefs and wrecks off Rock Sound and Cape Eleuthera.

Shopping

Goombay Gifts (⊠ Fish St., ☎ 242/334–2191), owned by Janice and Michael Knowles, is the place to shop for shell necklaces, straw work, and souvenirs.

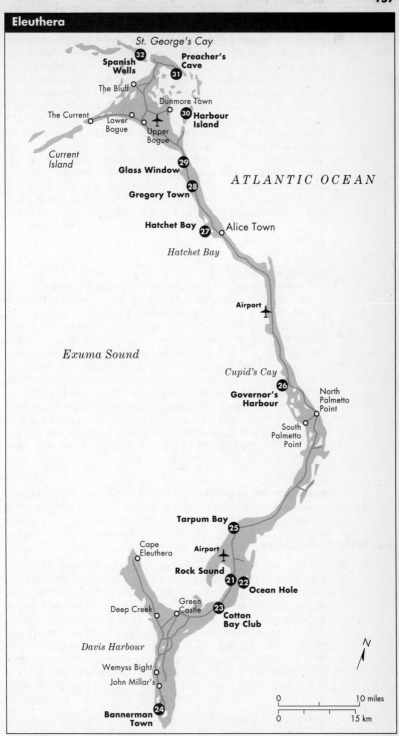

St. George's Cay

Spanish Wells 32

Preacher's Cave 31

The Bluff

Dunmore Town

The Current

Lower Bogue

Upper Bogue

30 **Harbour Island**

Current Island

29 **Glass Window**

28 **Gregory Town**

ATLANTIC OCEAN

Hatchet Bay 27 Alice Town

Hatchet Bay

Airport

Exuma Sound

Cupid's Cay

26 **Governor's Harbour**

North Palmetto Point

South Palmetto Point

Tarpum Bay 25

Cape Eleuthera

Airport

Rock Sound

21 22 **Ocean Hole**

Green Castle

23 **Cotton Bay Club**

Deep Creek

Davis Harbour

Wemyss Bight

John Millar's

24 **Bannerman Town**

0 ——— 10 miles

0 ——— 15 km

Tarpum Bay

㉕ Waterfront **Tarpum Bay** is one of Eleuthera's loveliest settlements, with hilly roads flanked by weather-beaten homes with colored shutters and goats roaming the streets. The town is the site of a small artists' colony. One of the island's more unusual characters—a self-proclaimed mystic and prodigious painter named G. MacMillan Hughes—lives here. A bearded, ponytailed Scots-Irish expatriate, he resides in a stone castle he built himself and from the top of which pennants fly. Behind a monumental, sculpted front gate, triangular steps lead to his **Castle Art Gallery** (✉ Lord St., ☎ 242/334–4091). Other forms—pyramidic, circular, arched—can be found around the gallery, and the artist is constantly adding mosaic touches to the decor. His striking paintings, which are modestly priced, depict themes of the sea; several canvases include mermaids. The gallery is open daily 9:30–5. Just south of the village of Tarpum Bay is **Flanders Art Studio** (☎ 242/334–4187), where Mal Flanders sells watercolors and canvases of local scenes, as well as driftwood paintings. The studio is open Monday through Saturday, 9–5.

Dining and Lodging

$ ✕🏨 **Hilton's Haven.** Not to be confused with the well-known U.S. hotel chain, this Hilton is an unassuming 12-room motel across the road from a beach and just around the corner from that unique attraction, the MacMillan Hughes Gallery and Castle. The place is run by a local nurse named Mary Hilton. Rooms have private baths and patios; downstairs they are fitted with air-conditioning, upstairs you'll find ceiling fans. Hilton serves good home cooking in her small restaurant. This is the kind of neat, unpretentious place you'll be happy to stay at overnight during a leisurely tour of the island. You can also ramble Tarpum Bay's narrow streets in the daytime to meet some of the residents and local artists. The hotel is a two-minute walk from the beach and about 6 mi from the Rock Sound Airport. ✉ *Tarpum Bay, Eleuthera,* ☎ *242/334–4231 or 800/688–4752,* ℻ *242/334–4020. 10 rooms, 1 apartment. Bar, dining room. No credit cards. EP, MAP.*

Shopping

Tarpum Bay Shopping Center (☎ 242/334–4022) is where you can stock up on groceries and snacks in town, and buy T-shirts and Bahamian souvenirs.

Governor's Harbour

㉖ Home to one of the ubiquitous Club Med resorts, **Governor's Harbour** nestles next to Cupid's Cay, the spot where the intrepid Eleuthera Adventurers landed. One feature of this attractive little town is the faded Victorian houses set in the half dozen blocks near the harbor. If you're here when the mail boats M/V *Bahama Daybreak III* and M/V *Eleuthera Express* chug in, you'll be treated to the sight of residents from around the island unloading mattresses, lumber, mail, stacks of vegetables, and other household necessities. You might also see the same Eleutherans loading their own vegetables and pineapples for export to Nassau. While they're here, they'll stop in at their mailboxes at the small post office in the town's pink government building.

Dining and Lodging

$$–$$$ ✕🏨 **Club Med Eleuthera.** This large, all-inclusive resort is oriented toward very young families and has a distinctive carefree Bahamian ambience. The 288 rooms are decorated in white and pastels, with twin or king-size beds, wood furniture, and marble fixtures in their private baths; none have TVs or phones. Rooms face either a long stretch of pinkish-sand beach or tropical gardens; a few have ocean views. Social life revolves around the main complex, which houses a dining room, an open-air cocktail lounge, a dance floor, a theater, a disco, and a boutique. You'll probably find that there's no other place on Eleuthera that has a circus workshop in which you can swing on a trapeze or bounce on a trampoline. The club also offers sailing, waterskiing, and snorkeling. Parents can leave babies (12–24 months) at the Baby Club, toddlers (ages 2–3) at the Petit Club, and older kids at the Mini Club, where they can learn to dive, sail, and play at the circus. The resort is 8 mi from Governor's Harbour Airport, and the Club Med Marina is a 10-minute shuttle ride away. Island-wide activities such as diving, boating and fishing can be arranged by the hotel. ⊠ *Box 80, Governor's Harbour, Eleuthera,* ☎ *242/332–2270, 800/258–2633,* ☒ *242/332– 2855. 288 rooms. 3 restaurants, 2 bars, pool, 8 tennis courts, aerobics, volleyball. AE, MC, V. FAP.*

$$–$$$ ✕⊡ **Unique Village.** Completed in 1992, this neat resort, just south of Governor's Harbour near North Palmetto Point, has 10 big, tile-floored rooms and two one-bedroom villas that face the Atlantic and a pink beach, as well as two villas with living-dining rooms and two bedrooms. The pleasant lounge has wicker furniture and twice-weekly entertainment. The excellent restaurant, with its pagoda-style natural wood ceiling and wonderful view of the beach, specializes in seafood, steaks, and Bahamian dishes. Rooms and villas have satellite TV. Snorkeling gear is provided free of charge; fishing trips can be arranged. ⊠ *Box EL 25187, Governor's Harbour, Eleuthera,* ☎ *242/332–1830 or 800/223–6510,* ☒ *242/332–1838. 10 rooms, 4 villas. Restaurant, bar, snorkeling, fishing. MC, V. EP, MAP, FAP.*

$$ ✕⊡ **Buccaneer Club.** On a hillside overlooking the town and the harbor, this former home has been transformed into a family-run inn. Bougainvillea, hibiscus, and coconut palms flourish on the beautifully landscaped grounds. The modern guest rooms, with two double beds and full baths, are attractively decorated with brightly painted furniture. On the top floor of this three-story building, you'll find the most spacious of the rooms, which also has a wonderful view of Governor's Harbour and the water. The beach is a leisurely 10-minute stroll away, and the harbor, where you can also swim, is within shouting distance. You can have drinks and lunch by the pool; the conch and grouper burgers are particularly good. ⊠ *Box 86, Governor's Harbour, Eleuthera,* ☎ *242/332–2000,* ☒ *242/332–2888. 5 rooms. Restaurant, bar, pool, shop. EP.*

$$–$$$ ⊡ **Palmetto Shores Vacation Villas.** Right on the bay, these spacious, south-facing villas are an attractive proposition for families, couples, or groups. They come with one, two, or three bedrooms—able to sleep up to six people—a large kitchen, lounges, and TVs. The villas have tile floors throughout and offer all the comforts of home, with easy strolls to beaches, a small restaurant, and shopping at a general store. ⊠ *Box 131, Governor's Harbour, Eleuthera,* ☎ ☒ *242/332– 1305. 15 villas. 2 tennis courts, dock, snorkeling, boating, fishing, bicycles, car and scooter rentals. AE, MC, V. EP.*

$$ ⊡ **Laughing Bird Apartments.** English architect Dan Davies and his wife Jean, a nurse, own four tidy apartments on a nicely landscaped acre of land at the water's edge. The roomy units—two with one bedroom and two studios—all have porches looking out to sea. The Davies furnish linens, crockery, and the first gallon of drinking water; you buy the rest. Four restaurants are within walking distance, or you can stock your kitchen from local stores. Laughing Bird is a quiet place, where relaxing and fishing are the easiest games in town. With a little effort, you can arrange for a variety of water sports or tour the island

by rental car. There's great fishing right off the beach, or the Davies can reserve boats. They have opened a boutique on-site. ⊠ *Box EL 25076, Governor's Harbour, Eleuthera,* ☎ *242/332–2012,* ℻ *242/332– 2358. 4 apartments. Beach, fishing. D, MC, V. EP.*

Outdoor Activities and Sports

TENNIS

Resort guests play free; visitors need to obtain permission to use courts, and fees will apply at **Club Med** (☎ 242/332–2270), which has the largest complex, with eight courts.

WATERSKIING/WINDSURFING

Club Med (☎ 242/332–2270) offers waterskiing and windsurfing.

Hatchet Bay

㉗ Side roads in **Hatchet Bay** are named even before houses are built on them, with such colorful designations as Lazy Road, Happy Hill Road, and Smile Lane. A sign will lead you to **The Cave,** a subterranean, bat-populated tunnel, complete with stalagmites and stalactites, that supposedly once was used by pirates to hide their loot. An underground path leads for over a mile to the sea, ending in a lofty, cathedral-like cavern; within its depths fish swim in total darkness. The adventurous may wish to explore this area with a flashlight, but it would be wise to inquire first at one of the local stores for a guide. Hatchet Bay also has mid-Eleuthera's only marina.

Dining and Lodging

$$–$$$ ╳ **Rainbow Inn.** One of the most popular restaurants on Eleuthera, Rainbow Inn is famed for its Bahamian steamed fish and minced lobster, as well as thick chowders, spicy boiled fish, fresh lobster, and tasty escargot adding a Continental touch to the menu. Owner "Krabby Kenny" hosts special rib nights (Wednesdays) and steak nights (Fridays). In his Nautical Bar, which is hung with authentic pilot wheels, salvaged from shipwrecks, try a Bahama Mama or a Goombay Smash, both made with rum and fruit juices. The inn sits on a bluff 2½ mi south of Hatchet Bay. ⊠ *2½ mi south of Hatchet Bay, Governor's Harbour,* ☎ *242/335–0294 or 800/688–0047. Closed Sun.*

$$ ╳▨ **Rainbow Inn.** The apartments that dot the inn's beachfront grounds have comfortable rooms with exposed wood, kitchenettes, and large private porches. The bar is a popular spot; you'll usually find a Bahamian folk singer strumming away on Friday evening. The inn's restaurant (☞ *above*), a cozy, nautical place with windows facing some of the best sunsets in the Bahamas, serves exceptional Bahamian fare. ⊠ *Box EL 25053, Governor's Harbour, Eleuthera,* ☎ ℻ *242/335– 0294 or* ☎ *800/688–0047. 6 apartments, 2 2-bedroom villas, 1 3-bedroom villa. Bar, dining room, kitchenettes, pool, tennis court. MC, V. EP, MAP.*

Gregory Town

㉘ **Gregory Town** sits on top of a cliff, though many of its charming pastel homes are actually located in a gully. If you'd like to see one of the hottest games of pool in town, pop into **Elvina's Restaurant and Bar** (⊠ On the main road, ☎ 242/335–5032). The menu might include Bahamian steamed or broiled fish with peas 'n' rice, Cajun jambalaya, Jamaican jerk pork, or West Indian curried chicken or mutton. This is the favorite hangout of the surfing crowd, who come to the island especially to ride the waves off Surfers' Beach, located at the end of rough-and-bumpy Ocean Boulevard at Eleuthera Island Shores just south of town.

At a very narrow point of the island a few miles north of Gregory Town, you'll find a place where a slender concrete bridge links two sea-battered bluffs that separate the Governor's Harbour and North Eleuthera districts. Sailors going south in the waters between New Providence and Eleuthera supposedly named this area the **Glass Window** because they could see through the narrow cavity to the Atlantic on the other side. The contrast in water color between the cobalt-blue Atlantic and the turquoise Gulf of Exuma is stunning.

Dining and Lodging

$$–$$$ ✕▥ **Cove-Eleuthera.** This seaside resort on 30 acres is secluded and peaceful. In front of the hotel, waves lap at the low, rocky promontories that jut into the ocean. A tiny, sandy cove offers superb snorkeling a few flipper beats from shore. Ask about the Cove's participation in the Jean Michael Cousteau Out Island Snorkeling Adventure Program. The comfortable rooms have been spruced up recently: New jewel-tone fabrics in tropical patterns complement the white rattan furniture and ceramic tiles. All have covered verandas and eight have ocean views. A large glass-walled restaurant—popular for sunset viewing—overlooks tropical gardens and the sea, as does the pleasant deck around the freshwater pool. The Pineapple Patio by the pool is a popular spot for alfresco luncheons and cocktails. Three moderately priced meals are served daily, with the dinner menu varying nightly. This hotel has the island's most extensive dessert menu, available throughout the day, featuring home-baked favorites such as coconut pie and pineapple crisp. ⌧ *Box 2007, Gregory Town, Eleuthera,* ☎ *242/335–5142, 954/974–3913, or 800/552–5960,* ℻ *242/335–5338. 26 rooms. Bar, dining room, lounge, pool, 2 tennis courts, snorkeling, boating, fishing, bicycles. AE, MC, V. EP, MAP.*

$ ✕▥ **Cambridge Villas.** This two-story motel with basic rooms and four two-bedroom apartments is a favorite with surfers on a budget because it's cheap and clean. The complex surrounds a terrace and a large saltwater pool. The cheerful bar is popular with locals and visitors. The dining room overlooks the pool and serves good Bahamian food, including conch chowder and broiled grouper. Diving and fishing can be arranged, and the hotel shuttles guests to either lovely swimming 1½ mi away or to the surfing beach. The resort is 20 mi from the North Eleuthera Airport and 22 mi from the Governor's Harbour Airport. ⌧ *Box 1548, Gregory Town, Eleuthera,* ☎ *242/335–5080 or 800/688–4752,* ℻ *242/335–5308. 25 rooms. Bar, dining room, refrigerators, pool, baby-sitting, car rental. AE, MC, V. EP, MAP.*

Outdoor Activities and Sports

TENNIS

Guests of the resorts play free; visitors need to obtain permission to use courts, and visitors' fees will apply at **Cambridge Villas** (☎ 242/335–5080) and the **Cove-Eleuthera** (☎ 242/335–5142).

Shopping

Island Made Shop (☎ 242/335–5369), run by Pam and Greg Thompson, is a good place to shop for Bahamian arts and crafts, including Androsia batik (made on Andros island), driftwood paintings, and prints.

Harbour Island

30 **Harbour Island** has often been called the prettiest of all the Out Islands because of its 3 mi of powdery pinkish sand beach (perhaps the most beautiful developed beach in the Bahamas) and its colorful colonial clapboard houses edged by picket fences and tropical flowers. The residents have long called it Briland, their faster way of pronouncing "Harbour Island." Although taxis, golf carts, and bikes are available, you can explore the island without too much exertion. Within its 2 sq mi, however, are tucked some of the Bahamas' most attractive small hotels, each strikingly distinct. At several that are perched on a bluff above the shore, you can fall asleep with the windows open and listen to the waves lapping the pink beach, which is tinted by powdered shells and coral. You reach Harbour Island by taking a five-minute ferry ride (✉ $4) from the North Eleuthera dock.

Old trees line the narrow streets of **Dunmore Town,** named after the 18th-century royal governor of the Bahamas, Lord Dunmore; it was once second only to Nassau in terms of its prosperity. Dunmore built a summer home here and laid out the town's plans. You can take in all of Dunmore Town's attractions during a 10-minute stroll. Stop off first at the yellow building opposite the ferry dock where the **Harbour Island Tourist Office** (☎ 242/333–2325) is located. This is where you can get a map and information on what to see and do on the island as well as on accommodations and restaurants. Across the street is a row of straw-work stands, including Dorothea's, Pal's, and Sarah's, where you'll find all kinds of straw bags, hats, accessories, T-shirts, and tourist tchotchkes. You may enjoy a visit to the oldest Anglican church in the Bahamas, **St. John's** (✉ Dunmore St.), built in 1768, and the distinguished 1848 **Wesley Methodist Church** (✉ Dunmore St.); services are still held here. **Loyalist Cottage,** one of the original settlers' homes built about 1792, has also survived. Many other old houses, with gingerbread trim and picket fences, have amusing names such as "Beside the Point," "The Grapevine," and "Up Yonder." Offshore lies a long coral reef, which protects the beach and offers excellent snorkeling; you can see multicolored fish and a few old wrecks.

Dining and Lodging

Note that most Harbour Island hotels are closed from September through late October or early November.

$$$$ ✗ **Pink Sands.** The chic cuisine coming out of the kitchen here is a fusion of Caribbean, Bahamian, and Asian styles and tastes. The prix-fixe dinner ($65) is served in a two-level patio, enclosed by lush vegetation. A lively Junkanoo BBQ buffet takes place Saturday nights at the Blue Bar on the beach ($45). ✉ *Chapel St., Harbour Island,* ☎ *242/333–2030.*

$$$$ ✗ **Runaway Hill Club.** To get a table for dinner you'll need to make reservations in the morning—if you can get them. Preparations are superb—such as carrot and orange bisque, shrimp scampi, and artfully seasoned fish—and the hosts of this small inn could hardly be more personable. ✉ *Harbour Island,* ☎ *242/333–2150. Closed Sun.*

$$–$$$ ✗ **Harbour Lounge.** Garlic-onion soup, jerk chicken, and grilled dolphinfish are among the dishes served here for lunch and dinner in an attractive setting. Arrive early if you want good seats for watching the sunset over cocktails on the front porch. ✉ *Harbour Island,* ☎ *242/333–2031.*

$$ ✗ **Miss Mae Tea Room & Fine Things.** If shopping for international imports at Fine Things works up your appetite, head into the Tea Room for breakfast—perhaps French toast or an omelet—or lunch—maybe spinach soup and quiche—in the sunny garden out back. ✉ *Harbour Island,* ☎ *242/333–2276 or 242/333–2002.*

$ ✗ **Angela's Starfish.** Set in a turquoise house on top of a hill off Dunmore Street, Angela's is the local favorite for cracked conch, grouper fingers, pork chops, and peas 'n' rice. ⊠ *Harbour Island,* ☎ *242/333–2253.*

$ ✕ **Dunmore Deli.** With tables on a pleasant veranda fringed with flourishing plants, the deli serves breakfast and lunch, including bagels, omelets, lobster salad, sandwiches, and a variety of cheeses. ⊠ *Harbour Island,*☎ *242/333–2644. Closed Sun.*

$ ✕ **Seaview Takeaway.** Right at the foot of the ferry dock, this spot is renowned for its cracked conch. ⊠ *Harbour Island,* ☎ *242/333–2542. Closed Sun.*

$$$$ ✕▥ **Dunmore Beach Club.** With a reputation for being formal and exclusionary, Dunmore Beach is trying to tone down its image with a more relaxed approach; yet men must wear a jacket (neckties are now optional) to dinner and women should dress accordingly. Of course, you will still find that the management prefers guests who either have already stayed at this club or are friends of those who have. Set just south of the Coral Sands Hotel, on Harbour Island's pink beach, this beach club offers comfortable rooms in six cottages. Furnishings include white and pastel accents, rattan, tile floors, handmade quilts, but no phones or TVs. The clubhouse, where you'll find the ocean-view honor bar, is decorated with rattan and chintz furniture, pale green and peach walls, jalousie windows, tan carpet, and various hanging plants and knickknacks. The Dunmore is proud of its guest/staff ratio (almost one-to-one) and the length of service of its employees (10 years is not considered a long time here). The restaurant serves a four-course international menu at 8 PM (virtually always for guests only). Island-wide activities such as diving and boating can be arranged by the hotel. ⊠ *Box EL 27122, Harbour Island, Eleuthera,* ☎ *242/333–2200,* ℻ *242/333–2429. 12 units in 6 cottages. Bar, dining room, tennis court. No credit cards. FAP.*

$$$$ ✕▥ **Ocean View.** Each of the nine guest rooms in this stunning home-
★ like hotel is individually decorated with antique armoires, side tables, and chests from southern France, old straw hats, original etchings and paintings, and intricate tile floors. The three largest rooms are upstairs, off the living/dining room, with a cozy sitting area by the fireplace and inlaid French provincial dining table. While guest rooms on the lower level are tiny, they are beautifully done in contrasting color schemes; all have cedar closets and a shared patio facing the ocean that licks the pink-sand beach below. On the sprawling upper patio, a giant chessboard with huge chess pieces overlooks the water. In the bar, walls are hung with weathered musical instruments (wind and string), as well as the colorful Haitian-inspired paintings of Amos Ferguson, probably the Bahamas' best-known artist. Canadian owner Pip Simmons promises that Ocean View will never have televisions or telephones in rooms. Trained in France and Switzerland, she is the head chef; she and her Bahamian staff whip up artful dishes such as puff pastry filled with spinach, cream of celery soup, beef tenderloin in béarnaise sauce, and chocolate pastries with homemade vanilla ice cream. If you are not staying here, you must make dinner reservations by 9 AM. Island-wide activities such as diving and boating can be arranged by the hotel. ⊠ *Box 134, Harbour Island, Eleuthera,* ☎ *242/333–2276. 9 rooms. Dining room, bar, beach. AE, MC, V. MAP.*

$$$$ ✕▥ **Pink Sands.** Chris Blackwell's latest and most luxurious hotel has
★ opened on one of the Bahamas' best beaches. If you can afford it, this is the trendiest place to stay in the Out Islands, if not the entire country—right down to the choice of ambient music—a joyful mix of Caribbean, West and southern African, and Brazilian sounds. The Island Records founder and hotel entrepreneur (he has opened hotels in Nassau, Jamaica, and Miami) has spared no expense since he bought

Pink Sands after Hurricane Andrew and transformed it into another gorgeous, small resort of handsome cottages with white stair-stepped roofs, spread out over 16 acres and 800 ft of beachfront. Some guests rent golf carts to get around the lush, expansive property, while others prefer using their feet. The cottages come in studio, one-, and two-bedroom configurations and are positioned for maximum privacy. Each has a kitchenette with a wet bar, stocked minibar, toaster, and coffeemaker, and a spacious bath with beautiful Italian tiles. Walls and tray ceilings are painted in pastels and highlight the rough, marble floors and Art Deco–style wooden furniture made by Miami craftsmen. Add to this the colorful African print bedspreads, pillows, chair cushions, and lamp shades, and you have a tasteful eyeful. All units come with a CD player and collection of Island Records CDs, a two-line phone with answering machine, and an in-room safe. The outside lanai has teak furniture. At the beach is the blue-on-blue Blue Bar, where lunch is served. Just below it is a thatched cabana where beachgoers relax in the shade. The grounds include three tennis courts (one lighted), a petite free-form pool, and an indoor-outdoor sound system with all-day music programmed by Mr. Blackwell himself. The main house has an entertainment center/library, a pool table, bar (with more than 30 types of Caribbean rum), fitness and exercise studio, an Island Outpost boutique, and a dining room (for inclement weather). The main dining area (☞ *above*) serves alfresco on terraced levels above the main house. Nonguests can use the pool, tennis courts, beach, and bars by applying for weekly, monthly, or annual memberships. Island-wide activities such as diving, fishing, and horseback riding can be arranged by the hotel. At press time, the resort is scheduled to break ground for a new cluster of cottages. ⊠ *Box 87, Harbour Island, Eleuthera,* ☏ *242/333–2030 or 800/688–7678,* ℻ *242/333–2060. 18 cottages with 29 rooms. Restaurant, 3 bars, dining room, room service. AE, DC, MC, V. MAP.*

$$$$ ✕▥ **Runaway Hill Club.** Perched on a bluff on Harbour Island's fa-
★ bled beach, this elegant yet intimate hotel on 8½ nicely landscaped acres connects to a flight of stairs that leads down to the beach. Once a private residence, the place maintains a homey ambience with tile floors and wicker furniture in spacious, individually decorated rooms upstairs and in an adjacent wing. Most rooms face the sea to catch the cool breezes (Room Two is especially nice); the rest overlook the gardens. Newer hilltop villas have larger, more uniform rooms with tray ceilings, tile floors, refrigerators, and front and rear decks. Rattan furnishings and pastel colors prevail throughout. All rooms have colorful patchwork quilts, bookshelves with an array of titles, and electronic safes. A small pool and deck hover over the beach. Locals know the main house as a great place to dine well on the chef's wonderful creations (☞ *above*); each morning you'll find the daily prix-fixe menu handwritten and displayed on an antique brass music stand in the front hall. Hosts Carol and Roger Becht and their staff quickly make vacationers feel like old friends. They are always happy to help arrange water sports and other activities and to fill visitors in on the island's (mainly weekend) nightlife scene. Among the inn's many repeat guests are groups of friends who return year after year; it's not unusual for people to book their stay for the following year as they check out. ⊠ *Box EL 27031, Harbour Island, Eleuthera,* ☏ *242/333–2150 or 800/728–9803,* ℻ *242/333–2420. 10 rooms. Bar, dining room, lounge, pool, beach. AE, MC, V. EP, MAP.*

$$$–$$$$ ✕▥ **Coral Sands Hotel.** Sharon King has run this easygoing, two-story
★ resort since 1968 with her former movie actor husband, Brett King (whom you may have caught in such films as *Flying Leathernecks* with John Wayne or *Payment on Demand* with Bette Davis). The hotel is

situated above Harbour Island's spectacular 3-mi-long pink beach, with 14 hilly acres descending to the heart of 300-year-old Dunmore Town. Congenial hosts, the Kings count well-heeled Europeans among their clientele. The number of repeat guests says something about their likable personalities and the charm of the place. The wicker furniture, colorful captain's chairs, and paintings done by the Kings' daughter Kimberly complement the palm trees right outside guest room windows. Upstairs rooms are reached by attractive, curving steps. Bahamian and American dinners are served in the romantic Mediterranean Cafe (which offers a light menu along with regular selections) and luncheon at the casual Beach Bar Lounge and Sundeck (high above the rosy sand); picnics to other islands can be arranged. The Yellowbird Bar offers guitar music; the game room has cable TV, a pool table, and card tables. Coral Sands has a tournament-quality lighted tennis court. ⊠ *Harbour Island, Eleuthera,* ☎ *242/333–2350, 242/333–2320, or 800/468–2799,* ⅏ *242/333–2368. 23 rooms, 8 suites, 2 villas. 3 bars, dining room, diving, snorkeling, boating, fishing. AE, DC, MC, V. EP, MAP.*

\$\$\$ ✕⊞ **Romora Bay Club.** Once a private club and now popular with young
★ couples and honeymooners, this Mediterranean-style resort faces the harbor. The island's famed pink beach is a brief stroll down a path and road. In 1996, the new owner gave Romora Bay a major face-lift. Outdoor sitting areas have been retiled in attractive designs. Guest rooms, located in separate cottages, have been completely redone, some with antique planter's chairs and imported lamps, mirrors, and area rugs from far-flung locales including Zaire, India, and France. All have balconies or patios that overlook the harbor or the pretty gardens with coconut palms and pine trees. In the evening, you can watch the sunset from the clubhouse perched on the water; the building houses a pleasant bar and lounge and a dining room that serves excellent Continental, American, and Bahamian dishes complemented by home-baked breads and pastries. After exploring Dunmore Town, you can take advantage of the resort's complete sailing, sportfishing, and diving programs. At press time, the owner has plans to add a harborside swimming pool. ⊠ *Box 146, Harbour Island, Eleuthera,* ☎ *242/333–2325 or 800/327–8286,* ⅏ *242/333–2500. 33 rooms. 2 bars, dining room, tennis court, dive shop, snorkeling, windsurfing, boating, fishing, bicycles, motorbikes, laundry service. AE, MC, V. EP, MAP.*

\$\$–\$\$\$ ✕⊞ **Valentine's Yacht Club and Inn.** Island-hopping yachters like to tie up at Valentine's modern 39-slip marina. The club hosts the North Eleuthera Regatta on Columbus Day, but it's a great place anytime to have a drink and a conch burger in the shaded dock restaurant. There's always a lot of activity, with anglers and divers coming and going. Valentine's has a complete dive shop, offering dives to the remnants of the Civil War Train Wreck; to Current Cut, where divers can coast through a bevy of sea life without moving a fin; and to Sink Hole and Bat Cavern, an introduction to the spooky pleasures of cave diving. Resort guests enjoy good Bahamian cooking and motel-style rooms. The lounge is a particular pleasure, with its wicker furniture, fluffy pillows, loaded bookshelves, and piano. ⊠ *Box 1, Harbour Island, Eleuthera,* ☎ *242/ 333–2142 or 800/323–5655,* ⅏ *242/333–2135. 21 rooms. 2 restaurants, 2 bars, pool, tennis court, diving, dive shop, fishing. AE, MC, V. EP, MAP.*

\$–\$\$ ✕⊞ **Tingum Village.** If you're on a budget, the clean and simple Tingum Village may be just your ticket. Located in town and a short walk from the famous pink-sand beach of Harbour Island, rooms here have white-tile floors, wood ceilings, ceiling fans, and comfortable, functional furnishings. Hammocks are strung between palms. Ma Ruby's Restaurant serves Bahamian food on a breezy covered patio three times a day. Popular menu items include steamed fish, conch burgers, and spareribs, along with home-baked coconut tarts and key lime pie. All kinds of activities can be arranged, such as diving, snorkeling, and fishing. ⊠ *Harbour Island, Eleuthera,* ☎ *242/333–2161,* FAX *242/333–2161. 12 rooms. Restaurant, bar. AE, MC, V. EP, MAP.*

Nightlife

Vic-Hum Club (⊠ Barrack St., ☎ 242/333–2161) occasionally hosts live Bahamian bands in a room decorated with classic record album covers; otherwise, you'll hear a variety of recorded music, from calypso to American pop and R&B.

Seagrapes (⊠ Colebrook St., ☎ 242/333–2439), featuring disco and live music on weekends, is usually packed.

Outdoor Activities and Sports

BOATING AND FISHING

Harbour Island is fish central around Eleuthera. There are abundant spots around the island to bonefish (at a cost of around $75 a half day), bottom fish ($75 a half day), reef fish ($20 an hour), and deep-sea fish ($250–$600 a full day). And there is great bonefishing right off Dunmore Town at Girl Bay. The Harbour Island Tourist Office (☞ Eleuthera A to Z, *below*) can arrange bone- and bottom-fishing trips and excursions, as can all the major hotels.

Romora Bay Club (☎ 242/333–2325) has Boston whaler and Sunfish boats for rent. **Valentine's Yacht Club** (☎ 242/333–2142) can arrange various types of fishing and has small boats for rent. **Big Red Rentals** (☎ 242/333–2045) offers Boston whalers (from 13 to 21 ft) and banana boat rides, along with snorkel gear.

SCUBA DIVING

Dive Centers. Romora Bay Club Dive Shop (☎ 242/333–2323) rents equipment and offers diving instruction, certification, dive packages, and daily dive trips. **Valentine's Dive Center** (☎ 242/333–2309) rents and sells equipment and provides all levels of instruction, certification, dive packages, and daily group and custom dives.

SITES

Current Cut, the narrow passage between North Eleuthera and Current Island, is loaded with marine life and provides a roller-coaster ride on the tides. **Devil's Backbone,** in North Eleuthera, offers a tricky reef area with a nearly infinite number of dive sites and a large number of wrecks. **Train Wreck,** parts of a Civil War–era railway train, lie in 20 ft of water near Harbour Island.

WATERSKIING/WINDSURFING

Valentine's Yacht Club (☎ 242/333–2142) has waterskiing and windsurfing, **Romora Bay Club** (☎ 242/333–2325) has windsurfing only.

Shopping

Briland's Ambrosia (☎ 242/333–2342) has a good selection of bathing suits, bags, and other items made from the bright batik fabric created on the island of Andros, as well as jewelry.

Miss Mae Tea Room & Fine Things (☎ 242/333-2276), stocks everything from leggings and T-shirts in an array of bold colors; jewelry, straw bags, and wood carvings from Kenya; and gourmet pasta and olive oil.

Sugar Mill (☎ 242/333–2173) sells prints by local artists, Bahamian coin jewelry, picture frames decorated with shells from Eleuthera, and wooden puzzles from the nearby island of Spanish Wells, along with multihued sarongs from Indonesia, ceramics from Italy, and Haitian steel drum cutout wall hangings.

North Eleuthera

Stratified and shaped over millions of years, **the Grotto** is part of an incredible formation of limestone cliffs, located on the eastern shore of North Eleuthera. You could fit a good-size restaurant in the yawning cave that is the centerpiece, although that would ruin its beauty. This part of the island is pineapple country; its rich, red soil fosters an abundance of the sweet-tasting fruit, which is made locally into a flavored rum.

㉛ **Preacher's Cave.** At the tip of the island, this cave is where the Eleutheran Adventurers took refuge and held services when their ship hit a reef more than three centuries ago. You can see inside the cave, with its original stone altar.

Spanish Wells

㉜ **Spanish Wells.** On the other side of northern Eleuthera from Harbour Island lies Spanish Wells on St. George's Cay. In the 17th century, the Spaniards, taking their riches from the New World to the Old, found this a safe harbor, and supposedly they dug wells from which they drew water on their frequent visits. Today, however, water comes from the mainland. Unfortunately, 1992's Hurricane Andrew devastated some of Spanish Wells's landmarks, but most now have been rebuilt. Residents live on the eastern end of the island in clapboard houses that look as if they've been transported from a New England fishing village. Tourists have little to do but hang out on the beach, dive, and dine on fresh seafood at the **Sea View** (☎ 242/333–4219). Descendants of the Eleutheran Adventurers continue to sail these waters and bring back to shore fish and lobster (most of the Bahamas' langoustes are caught in these waters), which are prepared and boxed for export in a factory at the dock. The 700 inhabitants may be the most prosperous Out-Islanders in the Bahamas, so lucrative is the trade in crawfish. Those who don't fish here grow tomatoes, onions, and the inevitable pineapples. You reach Spanish Wells by taking a five-minute ferry ride (🚢 $5–$9, depending on stop) from the North Eleuthera dock.

Eleuthera A to Z

Arriving and Departing

BY MAIL BOAT

The following mail boats leave from Nassau at Potter's Cay; for schedules, contact the **Dockmaster's office** (☎ 242/393–1064).

M/V *Current Pride* sails to The Current, Lower Bogue, and Upper Bogue on Thursday, returning Tuesday. M/V *Bahamas Daybreak III* leaves on Monday for South Eleuthera, stopping at Rock Sound, and returns on Tuesday; it then leaves Thursday from Nassau for The Bluff and Harbour Island, returning on Sunday. The fare is $20 for all Eleutheran destinations.

BY PLANE

Eleuthera has three airports: at North Eleuthera; at Governor's Harbour, near the center of the island; and at Rock Sound, in the southern part of the island. Because Eleuthera's resorts are scattered throughout the island, you'll need to find out in advance which airport is appropriate. If you're staying in Harbour Island or Spanish Wells, for example, your destination will be North Eleuthera Airport, and you'll take a taxi and ferry trip from there. If you are going to Windermere Isle, you will land at Rock Sound. For Club Med Eleuthera, you will fly to Governor's Harbour. Make sure you head for the airport closest to your hotel.

Taxis wait for incoming flights at all three airports and can also be found at most resorts. If you land at North Eleuthera and need to get to Harbour Island, off the north coast of Eleuthera, take a taxi ($4) to the ferry dock on Eleuthera, a water ferry ($4) to Harbour Island, and, on the other side, another taxi ($3 to Coral Sands, for example); some hotels are within walking distance from the Harbour Island dock. You follow a similar procedure to get to Spanish Wells, which is also off the north shore of Eleuthera. To get from Governor's Harbour Airport to the Rainbow Inn, Hatchet Bay (15 mi), it's $23.50 for two.

American Eagle (☎ 800/433–7300) offers daily flights to Governor's Harbour from Miami.

Bahamasair (☎ 800/222–4262) offers daily service from Nassau and Miami to all three airports.

Gulfstream Airlines (☎ 800/992–8532) has daily flights to North Eleuthera from Miami and Fort Lauderdale.

Twin Air (☎ 954/359–8266) flies three times a week to Governor's Harbour and Rock Sound and four times a week to North Eleuthera from Fort Lauderdale.

US Airways Express (☎ 800/622–1015) flies daily to Governor's Harbour and North Eleuthera from Fort Lauderdale.

Getting Around

BY BIKE, CAR, SCOOTER, AND GOLF CART

Big Red Rentals (⌧ Harbour Island, ☎ 242/333–2045) provides golf carts, scooters, and bicycles. **Baretta's** (⌧ Harbour Island, ☎ 242/333–2361) has minivans available for large groups or families. **Cecil Cooper** (⌧ Palmetto Point, ☎ 242/332–1575) has cars for rent. **Dingle Motor Service** (⌧ Rock Sound, ☎ 242/334–2031) has cars for rent. **Grant's** (⌧ Harbour Island, ☎ 242/333–2157) offers golf carts for hire. **Hilton's Car Rentals** (⌧ Palmetto Point, ☎ 242/335–6241) has cars for hire. **Johnson's Garage** (⌧ Harbour Island, ☎ 242/333–2376) rents golf carts. **Johnson's Rentals** (⌧ Governor's Harbour, ☎ 242/332–2226) has cars for rent. **Michael's Cycles** (⌧ Harbour Island, ☎ 242/333–2384) rents golf carts as well as bikes and mopeds. **Ross' Garage** (⌧ Harbour Island, ☎ 242/333–2122) rents golf carts.

BY TAXI

To explore the island, you would be well advised to rent a car, which is more economical than hiring a taxi, unless you don't mind paying the driver to be your tour guide. Taxis are available through your hotel, should you need one.

Opening and Closing Times

Barclays Bank has offices in Governor's Harbour and Rock Sound, and is open weekdays from 9:30 to 3, Mondays and Thursdays until 5.

Royal Bank of Canada in Harbour Island, Governor's Harbour, and Spanish Wells, is open weekdays from 9:30 to 3, Mondays and Thursdays until 5.

Scotia Bank is in North Eleuthera and is open weekdays from 9:30 to 3, Mondays and Thursdays until 5.

Contacts and Resources

EMERGENCIES

Police: Governor's Harbour (☎ 242/332–2111), Rock Sound (☎ 242/334–2244), Harbour Island (☎ 242/333–2111), and Spanish Wells (☎ 242/333–4030).

Medical Clinics: Harbour Island (☎ 242/333–2227), Governor's Harbour (☎ 242/332–2001 or 242/332–2774), Spanish Wells (☎ 242/333–4064), and Rock Sound (☎ 242/334–2226).

GUIDED TOURS

Arthur Nixon (☎ 242/332–2568 or 242/332–1006) is probably the most knowledgeable authority on Eleuthera. His presentation will make you want to stand up and applaud.

VISITOR INFORMATION

The **Eleuthera Tourist Office** (☎ 242/332–2142, FAX 242/332–2480) is the primary clearinghouse for information about all parts of Eleuthera.

Harbour Island Tourist Office (✉ Bay St., ☎ 242/333–2621, FAX 242/333–2622), on the second floor of the yellow building across from the Government Dock, has all kinds of information about what to see and do on the island and is also helpful in finding accommodations.

THE EXUMAS

On the Exumas, you'll still find wild cotton, which was first grown on plantations established by Loyalists after the Revolutionary War, and breadfruit trees, which a local preacher bought from Captain William Bligh in the late 18th century. The islands are now known as the onion capital of the Bahamas, although many of the 3,600-odd residents earn a living by fishing as well as farming. However, your first impression of the people of the Exumas may be that almost all of them have the surname Rolle. Lord John Rolle, who imported the first cotton seeds to these islands, had more than 300 slaves, to whom he bequeathed not only his name but also the 2,300 acres of land that were bestowed on him by the British government in the late 18th century. This land, in turn, has been passed on to each new generation and can never be sold to outsiders. Rolle's legacy was also perpetuated by the two settlements that bear his name, Rolleville and Rolle Town.

The Exumas begin less than 35 mi southeast of Nassau and stretch south for about 90 mi, flanked by the Great Bahama Bank and Exuma Sound. They are made up largely of some 365 fragmented little cays. The two main islands, Great Exuma and Little Exuma, lie in the south, connected by a bridge. The islands' capital, George Town, on Great Exuma, is the site of one of the Bahamas' most prestigious and popular sailing events, the Out Islands Regatta, when locally built wooden workboats compete with one another. During the winter, George Town's Elizabeth Harbour is a haven of yachts; the surrounding waters are legendary for their desolate islands, coves, bays, and harbors.

The Exumas certainly offer their share of impressive characters. One of them, Gloria Patience, who is in her seventies and lives south of George Town, is known as the Shark Lady because, until recently, she used to go out regularly in her 13-ft Boston whaler and catch sharks with a 150-ft-long hand line. Hundreds of makos, hammerheads, and lemon sharks have met their match with Ms. Patience, whose family came from Ireland and Scotland. Still making good use of various shark parts, she drills holes in their teeth and vertebrae to create pendants, necklaces, and earrings, and turns their jawbones into wall hangings, all of which she sells to visitors from **Patience House,** her home–museum–gift shop in The Ferry. You can find her through George Town's unofficial social center, the Club Peace & Plenty (☎ 242/336–2551) on Elizabeth Harbour.

Numbers in the text correspond to numbers in the margins and on the Exumas map.

Little Exuma and Great Exuma

③③ The old village of **Williams Town** lies at the southern tip of Little Exuma Island. Its main landmark is the **Hermitage,** a former plantation house; the ruins of slave cottages are situated nearby.

③④ **Rolle Town** is a typical Exuma village—without the tourist trappings. After The Ferry bridge, Queen's Highway runs in an almost straight line the length of Great Exuma, and about 5 mi south of George Town is the first of the Rolle settlements, called Rolle Town. Inhabitants grow onions, mangoes, bananas, and other crops.

③⑤ Not far from a settlement called The Ferry, at the bridge that links Little Exuma to Great Exuma Island, is **Pretty Molly Bay.** Molly is a mermaid, according to local legend, whom some residents have seen at night, possibly after a few of bartender "Doc" Rolle's special rum concoctions at the Club Peace & Plenty in George Town.

③⑥ Although **George Town** is the island's main settlement, it is hardly a hive of activity—the town does not even have a traffic light. The most imposing structure here is located in the town's center, the white-pillared, sandy pink, colonial-style **Government Administration Building,** modeled on Nassau's Government House and containing the commissioner's office, police headquarters, courts, and a jail. Atop a hill across from the government building is the whitewashed **St. Andrew's Anglican Church** (originally built around 1802, then rebuilt in 1991), whose blue doors welcome many of the locals every Sunday. Behind the church is the small Lake Victoria. A leisurely stroll around town will take you past a straw market and a few shops. You can buy fruit and vegetables and bargain with fishermen for some of the day's catch at the **Government Wharf,** where the mail boat comes in. The wharf is close to **Regatta Point** (☏ 242/336–2206), an attractive guest house named after the annual April sailing event, the Out Islands Regatta, which curls around Kidd Cove, where the 18th-century pirate Captain Kidd supposedly tied up.

Club Peace & Plenty. Overlooking Elizabeth Harbour stands one of the island's best-known landmarks, a historic inn that got its name from a slave ship that brought the Loyalists from Florida to Exuma in the late 18th century. Part of the hotel once served as slave quarters, and the lively bar was the slaves' kitchen. Because the hotel has no beach, owner Stanley Benjamin, a Cleveland industrialist, leases part of **Stocking Island** (with only six inhabitants) just over a mile away—you can take a free ferry there twice daily. The 7-mi-long island has a pier and a long stretch of white beach rich in seashells. Stocking Island also has the huge Mystery Cave, one of the blue holes, where divers can find a variety of marine life. Cousteau's team is said to have traveled a length of some 1,700 ft into this grotto beneath the island at a depth of 70 ft. Out on Stocking Island, a 10-room luxury hotel named Higgin's Landing has opened. ⊠ *Box 29055, George Town, Exuma,* ☏ *242/336–2551 or 800/525–2210.*

③⑦ From the top of **Mt. Thompson,** rising from the beach, there is a pleasing view of the **Three Sisters Rocks** jutting above the water just offshore. During your peregrinations, you may glimpse a flock of roaming peacocks on Great Exuma. Originally, a peacock and a peahen were brought to the island as pets by a man named Shorty Johnson, but when he left to work in Nassau, he abandoned the birds, who gradually proliferated into a colony. Some locals hunt these birds because they eat crops, but they are difficult to catch. Mt. Thompson is about 12 mi north of George Town, past Moss Town.

The Exumas

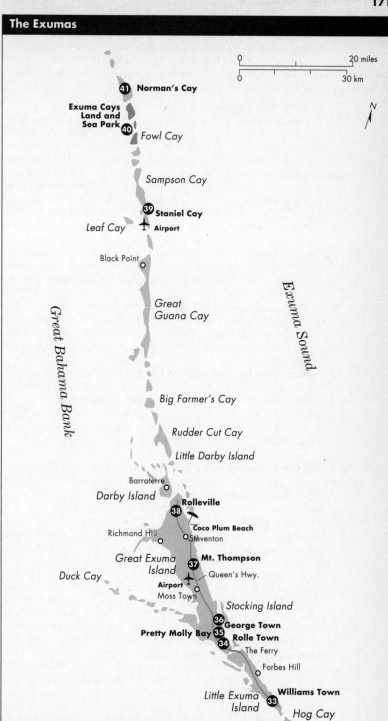

0   20 miles

0   30 km

N

41 Norman's Cay

Exuma Cays Land and Sea Park 40 *Fowl Cay*

Sampson Cay

39 Staniel Cay
✈ **Airport**

Leaf Cay

Black Point ○

Great Guana Cay

Exuma Sound

Great Bahama Bank

Big Farmer's Cay

Rudder Cut Cay

Little Darby Island

Barraterre ○

Darby Island

38 Rolleville

Coco Plum Beach
Richmond Hill ○   ○ Steventon

Great Exuma Island

37 Mt. Thompson
Queen's Hwy.

Duck Cay

✈ **Airport** ○
Moss Town

Stocking Island

36 George Town
Pretty Molly Bay 35 Rolle Town
34
The Ferry

Forbes Hill ○

Little Exuma Island

Williams Town
33

Hog Cay

㊳ The town of **Rolleville** sits on a hill above a harbor, 20 mi north of George Town. Old slave quarters stand here still, but they have been transformed into livable cottages. The town's most prominent citizen, Kermit Rolle, runs the **Hilltop Tavern** (☎ 242/336–6038), a seafood restaurant and bar guarded by an ancient cannon. The place is a popular meeting spot for locals.

Dining and Lodging

$$ ✕ **Eddie's Edgewater.** The specialty here is turtle steak (Madonna and PETA take note)—or you can leave the turtles alone and enjoy the "rake and scrape" band on Mondays—rakes and saws serve as instruments, hence the name. ⊠ *Charlotte St., George Town,* ☎ *242/336–2050.*

$–$$ ✕ **Iva Bowe's Central Highway Inn.** About 10 mi from George Town, close to Moss Town's airport, is a good place to stop for crawfish salad, cracked conch, or shrimp scampi when you're touring the island. ⊠ *Queen's Highway, Exhuma,* ☎ *242/345–7014. Closed Sun.*

$–$$ ✕ **Kermit's Hilltop Tavern.** If you're heading to the far northwest of Great Exuma and you have a taste for a local specialty such as panfried grouper or steamed conch, call in the afternoon for a reservation at this popular hangout in Rolleville, where Emancipation Day (in August) is celebrated with a vengeance. ⊠ *Clayton Rd., Rolleville,* ☎ *242/345–6006.*

$–$$ ✕ **Tino's.** The owner of this tiny local gathering spot (with pool table) doesn't close his doors until the last person leaves, which can be in the wee hours of the morning. The cracked conch, heaping portions of peas 'n' rice, and conch fritters are all good choices. ⊠ *George Town,* ☎ *242/336–2838.*

$ ✕ **Ruth's Deli.** The sandwiches and burgers here make this a good stop for a quick bite. ⊠ *Charlotte St., George Town,* ☎ *242/336–2596.*

$ ✕ **Town Café.** George Town's bakery serves breakfast—consider trying the stew fish or chicken souse—and lunch—seafood sandwiches with three sides or grilled fish. Town Café is open until 5:30. ⊠ *Marshall Complex, George Town,* ☎ *242/336–2194. Closed Sun.*

$$$–$$$$ ✕▨ **Hotel Higgins Landing.** The only hotel on luscious, undeveloped
★ Stocking Island, this solar-powered resort is truly a great escape. Antique chests, mirrors, and queen-size beds decorate the five cottages, each named for a tropical flower. Spacious decks afford wonderful views of the surrounding turquoise water. Cottages are sandwiched between Elizabeth Harbour and one of the island's talcum beaches on one side, and on the other, a lagoon that attracts many green sea turtles. The grounds are alive with colorful blossoms as well as egrets, hummingbirds, osprey, and herons. Reefs just offshore allow snorkelers to mingle with a variety of fish and other marine life. Borrow the hotel's pedal boat (with a canopy to block the sun) for a spin around these translucent waters. A Sunfish, Hobie Cat, rowing dinghy, and snorkel gear are also available. Rates include a full breakfast and a candlelit gourmet dinner (the prix fixe menu varies nightly). Lunch is also served, overlooking the water, and features lobster salad, grilled freshly caught fish, and conch burgers. No children under 18 are allowed during winter or spring season. ⊠ *Box EX 29146, George Town, Exuma,* ☎ *242/336–2460,* ℻ *242/357–0008 or* ☎ *800/688–4752. 5 cottages. Restaurant, bar, beach, boating, library. No credit cards. MAP. No smoking.*

$$$ ✕▨ **Coconut Cove Hotel.** This elegant resort has only 11 rooms, all of
★ which exude tropical warmth. The Paradise Suite has its own private hot tub on the terrace. All rooms except Paradise (which has a king-size bed) have queen-size beds with brightly colored quilts, tile floors, TVs, and views of the ocean, aquatic pond, and tropical gardens. You will find nice touches in your modern room, such as complimentary

bathrobes, minibars, and fresh-daily floral arrangements. The chef serves up such excellent gourmet fare as blackened grouper and seafood pasta, but you can also request low-calorie meals, as well as picnic baskets with a day's notice. ⊠ *Box EX 29299, George Town, Exuma,* ☎ *242/336–2659 or 800/688–4752,* ⅋ᴬˣ *242/336–2658. 11 rooms. Restaurant, bar, pool, diving, fishing, laundry service. MC, V. EP.*

$$ ✕🗊 **Club Peace & Plenty.** This two-story pink hotel is a perennial fa-
★ vorite with regular visitors who escape to this friendly, relaxing place. Holding court in the bar is Lermon "Doc" Rolle, who has been a hotel bartender since the '70s and has served his special drinks to such celebrities as Britain's Prince Philip and Greece's King Constantine. The indoor bar, which was once a slave kitchen, attracts locals and a yachting crowd, especially during the Out Islands Regatta; its walls are suitably decorated with ships' name boards, anchors, rudders, and assorted lights. In high season, the hotel is known for its festive Saturday night parties on the pool patio, where Bahamians and visitors let their hipbones slip to live bands. Most of the cheerful rooms, all with balconies, have water views. You can take a complimentary ferry twice a day to the beach just across the water on Stocking Island. At the beach club there are drinks and DoraLee's famous greasy burgers. The hotel's restaurant serves some of the best dishes in town. The resort has Windsurfers, Sunfish, paddleboats, and snorkeling gear for rent, and snorkeling trips to nearby reefs and islands can be arranged. Bonefishing aficionados are among the regular visitors to P & P, and fishing packages can be arranged. Many fishermen stay at the **P & P Bonefish Lodge** (☎ 242/345–5555), an eight-room hotel on Exuma's southern flats. Endless stretches of empty beach line this unprotected side of the island, perfect for exploring and shell gathering. ⊠ *Box 29055, George Town, Exuma,* ☎ *242/336–2551 or 800/525–2210,* ⅋ᴬˣ *242/336–2093. 36 rooms. 2 bars, dining room, pool, beach, diving, boating, fishing. AE, MC, V. EP, MAP.*

$$ ✕🗊 **Palms at Three Sisters Beach Resort.** This two-story hotel with 12 rooms and two cottages is located on a 1,000-ft stretch of white beach. All rooms in the motel-style resort have modern furnishings, wonderful views of the ocean, and TVs. Downstairs rooms have air-conditioning, while upstairs ceiling fans keep the air moving. The large restaurant has a high, exposed-beam ceiling with fans and serves good Bahamian and American fare. The resort lies only 2½ mi north of the airport but is quite isolated. Fishing trips are easily arranged, but no sporting gear is available, so bring your own. ⊠ *Box 29215, George Town, Exuma,* ☎ *242/358–4040,* ⅋ᴬˣ *242/358–4043. 12 rooms, 2 cottages. Restaurant, bar. MC, V. EP.*

$$ ✕🗊 **Peace & Plenty Beach Inn.** This 16-room resort, situated on 300 ft of beach, is located a mile west of its big brother, the Club Peace & Plenty, and a shuttle runs between the two four times daily. The bedroom and bathroom floors and walkways here are tiled in white, and rooms overlook the freshwater pool, Bonefish Bay, and Elizabeth Harbour. All rooms have TVs and mini-refrigerators. The dock bar juts out into the bay and lets you enjoy the hotel's lovely waterfront location throughout the evening, as boats pull up to join the festivities. Manager Charlie Pflueger is an affable presence and a wonderful source of island lore. ⊠ *Box 29055, George Town, Exuma,* ☎ *242/336–2250 or 800/525–2210,* ⅋ᴬˣ *242/336–2253. 16 rooms. Restaurant, bar, pool. AE, MC, V. EP, MAP.*

$$ ✕🗊 **Two Turtles Inn.** This two-story hotel with a small cannon guarding its entrance is made of local stone; overlooking Elizabeth Harbour, it is situated near the village green, where you'll find a straw market. Its plain, wood-paneled rooms have balconies and satellite TV, as well as ceiling fans and air-conditioning. A few efficiency units provide stove/sink/refrigerator combinations. On Tuesday and Friday nights locals flock to the inn for barbecues and happy hours at tables and benches on the patio. Diving, fishing, and boating can be arranged; the beach is 3 mi away. ⊠ *Box 29251, George Town, Exuma,* ☎ *242/336–2545,* FAX *242/336–2528. 12 rooms. Bar, dining room, fans, motorbikes, car rental. MC, V. EP.*

$$$ 🏨 **Flamingo Bay Club and Villas.** This complex boasts 1,300 acres of rolling hills and dense tropical vegetation that extend down to a long, secluded, golden beach on Flamingo Bay. The property is slowly undergoing a face-lift, and could use some attention to detail—such as landscaping. On the beach is a marker that notes that the Tropic of Cancer runs through the property. The hotel is a two-minute walk from the beach; the restaurant-bar is right on the water. There is one tennis court, a basketball court, and a volleyball net on the beach. ⊠ *Box 29090, George Town, Exuma,* ☎ *242/336–2661. 7 rooms, 1 villa. Tennis court, basketball, volleyball, baby-sitting, laundry service. No credit cards. EP.*

$$ 🏨 **Regatta Point.** This pleasant apartment complex overlooks Kidd Cove from its own small island, connected to George Town by a short causeway. The hotel has a delightful view of the yachts in Elizabeth Harbour. Large, high-ceilinged rooms have porches and are well designed to catch the cool, incoming trade winds. Sunfish and bicycles are available, and the resort has its own beach and dock; most guests choose to rent their own skiffs and tie them up here. Children may share their parents' room for a small charge. The resort has no restaurant, but the apartments have kitchens, so you'll have to eat in town or stock up on groceries. ⊠ *Box 29006, George Town, Exuma,* ☎ *242/336–2206 or 800/310–8125,* FAX *242/336–2046. 5 apartments. Beach, dock, boating, bicycles, laundry service. MC, V. EP.*

Nightlife

In season, most of George Town can be found at **Club Peace & Plenty** (☎ 242/336–2551) for the weekly poolside bashes, where a live band keeps Bahamians and vacationers on the dance floor.

Outdoor Activities and Sports

BOATING AND FISHING

The Exumas have some of the finest cruising areas in the Bahamas. The Upper Exumas are a nature wonderland, and yachters can observe a variety of wildlife, including birds and iguanas. Just north of **Staniel Cay**, the Exuma Cays Land and Sea Park, running from Wax Cay to Conch Cay, is a protected area also worth visiting. George Town on Great Exuma Island is generally the final destination of yachters visiting the area; it offers good anchorages and stores to stock up on supplies.

Deep-sea fishermen will find plenty of game-fish sport in Exuma Sound, off the Great Exuma's east coast, and good bonefishing off the west coast. In George Town, make arrangements for fuel and boating supplies at **Exuma Docking Services** (☎ 242/336–2578), **Exuma Fantasea** (☎ 242/336–3483), and—for bonefishing—at **P & P Bonefish Lodge** (☎ 242/345–5555). **Sampson Cay Colony Ltd.** (☎ 242/325–8864) has guides for hire.

EVENTS

Annual New Year's Day Cruising Regatta is held in January at the Staniel Cay Yacht Club, with international yachts taking part in a series of races. The **Out Islands Regatta** is the most important yachting event of the year in the Bahamas; it takes place in April. Starting from Elizabeth Harbour in George Town, island-made wooden sailing boats compete against one another for trophies; onshore, the town is a three-day riot of Junkanoo parades, Goombay music, arts and crafts fairs, and continuous partying in the hotels.

Centers. Divers should contact **Exuma Fantasea** (☎ 242/336–3483 or 800/760–0700) for trips to coral reefs, sea gardens, and the Mystery Cave at Stocking Island, off George Town. They also offer instruction and certification and specialize in eco-diving to protect and preserve the marine environment.

Sites. Stocking Island Mystery Cave, near George Town, which is full of schools of colorful fish.

Shopping

In the Exumas, George Town is the place to shop.

Exuma Market (⊠ Across from Scotia Bank, George Town, ☎ 242/336–2033) is the island's largest grocery. Air-conditioned and well-stocked, it is popular among boaters, who can use the skiff docks on Victoria Lake in the rear.

Helena's (⊠ Queen's Hwy., ☎ 242/336–2163) is George Town's version of a general store.

N & D Ice-Cream and Vegetable Stand (⊠ Queen's Hwy., ☎ 242/336–2236) allows you to savor an ice-cream cone while shopping for fresh produce. A few tables provide a good spot to cool your heels.

P&P Boutique (⊠ Opposite Club Peace & Plenty, ☎ 242/336–2551) has a good selection of Androsia shirts and dresses.

Sandpiper Boutique (⊠ Queen's Hwy., ☎ 242/336–2084) sells books and T-shirts.

Two Turtles Gift Shop (⊠ Queen's Hwy., ☎ 242/336–2545) is the place for a Two Turtles T-shirt.

Cays of the Exumas

A band of cays—with names such as Rudder Cut, Big Farmer's, Great Guana, and Leaf—stretches north from Great Exuma.

39 Staniel Cay is a favorite destination of yachters and makes the perfect home base for visiting the Exuma Cays Land and Sea Park. The island has an airstrip, two hotels, and one paved road. Virtually everything is within walking distance. Oddly enough, as you stroll past brightly painted houses and sandy shores, you are as likely to see a satellite dish as a woman pulling a bucket of water from a roadside well. At the two grocery stores (known as the pink one and the blue one), boat owners replenish their supplies. The friendly village also has a small red-roof church, a post office, and a straw market.

Just across the water from the Staniel Cay Yacht Club is one of the Bahamas' most breathtaking attractions: **Thunderball Grotto,** a beautiful marine cave that snorkelers (at low tide) and experienced scuba divers can explore. In the central cavern, shimmering shafts of sunlight pour through holes in the soaring ceiling and illuminate the glass-clear water. Scores of trumpetfish, yellowtail snapper, queen angels, and parrot fish all dash back and forth past submerged rocks decorated with bright orange, red, and green marine life. You'll see right away why this cave was chosen as an exotic setting for such movies as 007's *Thunderball* and *Never Say Never,* and the mermaid tale, *Splash.*

Above Staniel Cay, near the northern end of the Exumas, lies the 176-
40 sq-mi **Exuma Cays Land and Sea Park,** where the rare Bahamian

iguana is a protected species. Snorkelers, beachcombers, and bird-watchers must charter a small boat to reach the park, which has more than 20 mi of protected cays. Marked hiking trails are found on Hawksbill Cay and Warderick Wells (both with remains of 18th-century Loyalist settlements), as well as on Hall's Pond. At Shroud Cay, jump into "Camp Driftwood," where the strong current creates a natural whirlpool that whips you around a rocky outcropping to a powdery beach. Part of the Bahamas National Trust, the park appeals to divers who find a vast underworld of limestone, reefs, drop-offs, blue holes of freshwater springs, caves, and a multitude of exotic marine life, including one of the most impressive stands of rare pillar coral in the Bahamas. Strict laws prohibit fishing and taking coral, plants, or even shells away as souvenirs. A list of park rules is available at the headquarters on Warderick Wells.

41 At the northern end of the Exumas, **Norman's Cay** is a beautiful and now abandoned little island with 10 mi of rarely trodden white beaches that attract an occasional yachter. Norman's Cay was once the private domain of convicted Colombian drug smuggler Carlos Lehder, whose planes left from there for drop-offs in Florida. It's now owned by the Bahamian government.

Dining and Lodging

$$$ ✕🖼 **Staniel Cay Yacht Club.** Sunsets are particularly dramatic from this small group of cottages that are perched on stilts along a rocky bank just steps from a sandy beach. Once upon a time, this club drew luminaries such as Malcolm Forbes, before it fell into decline. It has now reemerged as a pleasant, rustic getaway for yachters. The cottages have been nicely redone, each in a different color scheme, inside and out. Balconies overlook the water. If you arrive at the island's airstrip you can rent boats at the club for trips to the scenic Exuma Cays Land and Sea Park, not far north, and other nearby locales. Snorkelers and scuba divers should not pass up a chance to visit gorgeous Thunderball Grotto, just across from the clubhouse (where meals are served). ✉ *2233 S. Andrews Ave., Fort Lauderdale, FL 33316,* ☎ *954/467–8920,* FAX *954/522–3248;* ☎ *242/355–2024,* FAX *242/355–2044 in Staniel Cay. 6 units. Restaurant, bar, boating, fishing. AE, MC, V. MAP.*

$ ✕🖼 **Happy People Marina.** You may find this casual hotel a bit isolated if you're not interested in yachting. The property is close to Staniel Cay, but it's a long way from the George Town social scene. A local band, however, plays at the Royal Entertainer Lounge, and a small but adequate restaurant is available for dining. The simple but comfortable motel-style rooms are situated along the beach; some have private baths. Children under 12 can stay at half price. ✉ *c/o Staniel Cay, Exuma,* ☎ *242/355–2008. 12 rooms. Bar, dining room, dock. No credit cards. EP.*

Nightlife

The island has two nightspots, the **Royal Entertainer Lounge** (✉ At the Happy People Marina, ☎ 242/355–2008), where live bands perform on special occasions, and the newer **Club Thunderball** (✉ East of Thunderball Grotto, ☎ 242/355–2012), a sports bar and dance club built on a bluff overlooking the water, serves lunch and has Friday evening barbecues and a mooring; it is run by a local pilot.

Outdoor Activities and Sports

BOATING AND FISHING

You can book fishing trips through your hotel or: **Happy People Marina** (☎ 242/355–2008) and the **Staniel Cay Yacht Club** (☎ 242/355–2024).

SCUBA DIVING

In order to take advantage of the area's outstanding dive sites, you will need to bring your own scuba and snorkeling gear.

Sites. Exuma Cays Land and Sea Park, just north of Staniel Cay, is a 176-sq-mi fish-and-bird sanctuary that runs from Wax Cay Cut to Conch Cut in the Upper Exumas.

Thunderball Grotto, facing the Staniel Cay Yacht Club, is an undersea cave with abundant fish. It is a fantastic place to snorkel at low tide or dive in any time (but never alone).

Exumas A to Z

Arriving and Departing

BY MAIL BOAT

M/V *Grand Master* travels from Nassau to George Town on Tuesday and returns to Nassau on Thursday. Travel time is 14 hours and fares range from $25 to $40 depending on your destination. M/V *Lady Francis* leaves Nassau on Tuesday for Staniel Cay, Farmers Cay, Black Point, and Baraterre, returning to Nassau on Saturday. The trip takes eight hours; fares are $25–$30. For more specific information contact the **Dockmaster's office** (☎ 242/393–1064) at Potter's Cay.

BY PLANE

Exuma International Airport, 9 mi from George Town, is the official airport for the Exumas, and the official port of entry. It's also one of the tidiest airports in the Bahamas. Taxis wait at the airport for incoming flights. The cost of a ride from the airport to George Town is about $22 for two. Little Staniel Cay, near the top of the chain, has a 3,000-ft airstrip that accepts private planes flying in U.S. citizens with homes there.

American Eagle (☎ 800/433–7300) has daily service from Miami.

Bahamasair (☎ 800/222–4262) has daily flights from Nassau and twice weekly flights from Miami to George Town.

Island Express (☎ 954/359–0380) flies from Fort Lauderdale to George Town and Staniel Cay.

Getting Around

BY CAR

In George Town, you can rent an automobile through **Exuma Transport** (☎ 242/336–2101) and the **Two Turtles Inn** (☎ 242/336–2545). Hotels also can arrange rentals of cars, scooters, and bicycles.

BY TAXI

Your hotel will arrange for a taxi if you wish to go exploring or need to return to the airport. You can also call **Kermit Rolle** (☎ 242/345–6038) for an enjoyable, informative island tour or a trip to or from the airport, or call the **Luther Rolle Taxi Service** (☎ 242/345–5003).

Opening and Closing Times

The **Bank of Nova Scotia** in George Town is open weekdays 9–1 and again on Friday 3–5.

Contacts and Resources

EMERGENCIES

George Town: **Police** (☎ 919 or 242/336–2666), **Medical Clinic** (☎ 242/336–2088).

VISITOR INFORMATION

The **Exuma Tourist Office** (☎ 242/336–2430, FAX 242/336–2167) is in George Town across the street from St. Andrew's Anglican Church.

INAGUA

Great Inagua, the third-largest island in the Bahamas, is 25 mi wide and 45 mi long. The terrain is mostly flat and covered with scrub. The island's unusual climate of little rainfall and continual trade winds created rich salt ponds, which brought prosperity to the island over the years. The Morton Salt Company harvests a million tons of salt annually at its Matthew Town factory. About 25% of Inaguans earn their living by working for the company. Inagua is best known not for its salt, however, but for the huge flocks of shy pink flamingos that reside in the island's vast national park and on the property belonging to the salt company. In addition to the famous flamingos, the island is also home to one of the largest populations of the rare Bahamian parrot, as well as to herons, egrets, owls, cormorants, and over a hundred other species of birds.

While the birds have moved in wholeheartedly, the island remains virtually undiscovered by outsiders. Avid bird-watchers make up the majority of the tourists who undertake the long trip to this most southerly of the Out Islands, about 300 mi southeast of Nassau and 50 mi off the coast of Cuba. Lack of exposure means, on the one hand, that people are still friendly and curious about each new face in town—you won't feel like just another tourist—and since crowds and traffic are nonexistent, there's nothing to bother you but the rather persistent mosquito population (be sure to bring strong insect repellent). On the other hand, tourist facilities are very few and far between. The only inhabited settlement on Inagua is Matthew Town, a small, dusty grid of workers' homes and essential services. The four "hotels" there are simply functional at best. There's no official visitor information office (although Great Inagua Tours is very helpful), and if you're a beach lover, Inagua is not for you. While there are a couple of small swimming areas near Matthew Town and a few longer stretches farther north, no perfect combination of hotel and beach has yet been built. However, the virgin reefs off the island have caused a stir among intrepid divers who bring in their own equipment. The buzz is that Inagua could become a hot dive destination. Great Inagua Tours may open a scuba operation, so divers, stay tuned.

Great Inagua Island appears in the southeast corner of the Bahamas map at the front of this guide.

Matthew Town

About 1,000 people live on Inagua, whose capital, **Matthew Town,** is on the west coast. The "town" is about a block long. There's the large pink, run-down government building (housing the commissioner's office, post office, and customs office), a power plant, a grocery and liquor store, Morton's Main House (a guest house), the After Work Bar, the bank, and the small Kiwanis park that comes complete with a bench for sunset-gazing. Most houses here have the ubiquitous, huge satellite dishes prominently displayed. It is rumored that a lot of the money for these, and the houses they are attached to, came from the heady drug-smuggling days of the 1980s. Today, a U.S. Coast Guard helicopter base at the airport has pretty much put an end to that gold rush.

The **Erickson Museum and Library** is a welcome part of the community, particularly the surprisingly well-stocked and equipped library. The Morton company built the complex in the former home of the Erickson family, who came to Inagua in 1934 to run the Morton company. The museum displays the history of the island, to which the company is inextricably tied. The house is at the northern edge of

Matthew Town across from the police station. ⊠ *Gregory St.,* ☎ *242/ 339–1863.* ◲ *Free.* ☉ *Weekdays 3–6:30, Sat. 9–6:30.*

The desire to marvel over the salt process entices few visitors to Inagua, but the **Morton Salt Company** is omnipresent on the island: It has over 2,000 acres of crystallizing ponds and over 34,000 acres of reservoirs. Over a million tons of salt are produced every year for such industrial uses as salting icy streets. (They produce more when the Northeast has a bad winter!) Even if you decide not to tour the facility, you'll be able to see the mountains of salt glistening in the sun from the plane. In an unusual case of industry assisting its environment, the crystallizers provide a feeding ground for the flamingos. As the water evaporates, the concentration of brine shrimp in the ponds increases, and the flamingos feed on these animals. Tours of the facility are available. ⊠ *Morton Salt Co., Inagua,* ☎ *242/339–1300.*

Dining and Lodging

$–$$ ✕ **Cozy Corner.** Cheerful and loud, Cozy Corner has a pool table and a large seating area with a bar—stop in for a chat with locals over a beer and cheeseburger. It's open daily for lunch and dinner. ⊠ *Matthew Town, Inagua,* ☎ *242/339–1440.*

$–$$ ✕ **Crystal Ruins.** Just north of town, this eatery serves breakfast, lunch, and dinner, and occasionally has live music. Bahamian cuisine is de rigueur. ⊠ *Crystal Beach View Hotel, Gregory St,* ☎ *242/339–1550.*

$$ ✕▧ **Crystal Beach View.** This one-story stone structure situated on a coral-stone stretch of coastline where the grounds are strewn with detritus, lies about half a mile from the airport and is the largest hotel in town. It is in need of some significant sprucing up, though the rooms are adequate. The island's sole pool (which is filled with salt water only when the hotel is fairly full—a major disappointment for off-peak guests and a hazard when empty) is found here. There's a beauty salon, and even a honeymoon suite with a tub in the middle of the room and a king-size bed on a raised platform (consider other honeymoon locales before this one!). A restaurant for guests called the Crystal Ruins (☞ *above*) serves three meals daily and has a bar. The lobby lounge is a friendly place to watch TV and chat with other guests. ⊠ *Matthew Town, Inagua,* ☎ *242/339–1550,* FAX *242/339–1670. 13 rooms. Restaurant, bar, lobby lounge, pool, beauty salon. MC, V. EP.*

$$$ ▧ **Sunset Apartments.** This is the name for apartments under eternal
★ construction right along the water on the southern side of Matthew Town. When completed, these four two-bedroom apartments will be the nicest accommodations on Inagua. At press time, only two units were open. Constructed from cement, the units have white walls and modern Caribbean-style, terra-cotta tile floors, and rattan furniture. Amenities include full kitchens, TVs, small terraces, and a picnic area with a gas grill. About a five-minute walk away is a small, secluded beach called the Swimming Hole. This is by far your best bet for accommodations on Inagua. ⊠ *c/o Ezzard Cartwight, Matthew Town, Inagua,* ☎ *242/339–1362. 2 apartments completed. Kitchenettes, boating. No credit cards.*

$ ▧ **Main House.** The Morton Salt Company operates this small, simple guest house. There are two floors; the air-conditioned rooms on the second floor share a sitting area with couches and a telephone. Rooms are spotless and spacious with dark-wood furnishings, Masonite paneled walls, and floral-print drapes and spreads. Room 6 is the largest. All rooms have TVs, which are all tuned to whatever station the master satellite tuner is on. (You have to find Edna, the Main House mistress, to change stations. The hospital next door is also on the same system, so there's competition for requests.) The green-and-white hotel is right in Matthew Town, behind the grocery store and directly across the street from the island's noisy power plant. But it's cheap and clean. ⊠ *Matthew Town, Inagua,* ☎ *242/339–1267. 5 rooms. No credit cards. EP.*

$ ⊡ **Walkine's Guest House.** Eleanor and Kirk Walkine operate this very basic, split-level stone guest house located just south of the center of Matthew Town. There are five rooms, three with private bath. There are no dining facilities, but Topps Restaurant is a half mile away. ⊠ *Matthew Town, Inagua,* ☎ *242/339–1612. 5 rooms. No credit cards.*

Elsewhere on the Island

In addition to the salt ponds on the island, birds and other wildlife also reside in the reserve set aside as the **Bahamas National Trust,** which spreads over 287 sq mi and occupies most of the western half of the island. Nature lovers, ornithologists, and photographers are drawn to the area and to Lake Windsor (a 12-mi-long brackish body of water in the center of the island) to view the spectacle of more than 60,000 flamingos feeding, mating, or flying (although you will rarely see all those birds together in the same place). When planning your trip, keep in mind that flamingo mating season is October–February, and the nesting season is March–April. Flamingos live on Inagua year-round, but the greatest concentrations come at these times. If you visit right after hatching, the scrambling flocks of fuzzy, gray baby flamingos are very entertaining—they can't fly until they're older. You don't have to tour the Trust property to see flamingos, but there are camping facilities on the grounds, and wardens will give guided tours. Arrangements can be made through your hotel or by calling Great Inagua Tours (☞ Contacts and Resources *in* Inagua A to Z, *below*).

From **Southwest Point,** a mile or so south of the capital, you can see the coast of Cuba on a clear day, just over 50 mi west, from atop the **lighthouse** (built in 1870 after a huge number of shipwrecks on offshore reefs). This is one of the last four hand-operated kerosene lighthouses in the Bahamas—be sure to sign the guest book after your climb.

Villa Rental

A four-bedroom cottage in a completely secluded area out toward the northwest point of the island rents for about $150 per day (negotiable depending on the length of stay). The cottage sits right on the beach and has a patio for sunset viewing. There's a fully equipped kitchen, dining area, an outdoor shower in addition to the indoor bath, and a private strip of beach with a section cleared of rocks for swimming. The cottage is not elegant, but it is completely private. Be warned however: If there has been a recent rain, mosquitoes will be fierce; be sure to ask about them when booking. Call Larry Ingraham at Great Inagua Tours (☎ 242/339–1862) with inquiries.

Inagua A to Z

Arriving and Departing

BY MAIL BOAT

M/V *Lady Mathilda* makes weekly trips from Nassau to Matthew Town, also stopping at Crooked Island, Acklins Island, and Mayaguana. The boat leaves Nassau on Wednesday and returns on Sunday. For information on specific schedules and fares, contact the **Dockmaster's office** (☎ 242/393–1064) at Potter's Cay.

Bahamasair (☎ 242/339–4415 or 800/222–4262) has flights on Monday, Wednesday, and Friday from Nassau to Matthew Town Airport.

Taxis sometimes meet incoming flights. It's best to make prior arrangements with your hotel to be picked up.

Getting Around
BY BICYCLE
The **Pour More Bar** (☎ 242/339–1232) and the **Crystal Beach View hotel** (☎ 242/339–1550) rent bikes for exploring.

BY CAR
Inagua Trading Ltd. (☎ 242/339–1330) has several cars for rent by the day.

BY TAXI
If you need a taxi for anything, ask your hotel to make arrangements, or call 242/339–1284 and ask for Rocky.

Opening and Closing Times
The **Bank of the Bahamas** in Matthew Town is open Monday–Thursday 9:30–2:30 and Friday 10–5:30.

Contacts and Resources
EMERGENCIES
Police (☎ 242/339–1263).

Hospital (☎ 242/339–1249).

VISITOR INFORMATION
Great Inagua Tours (☎ 242/339–1862, FAX 242/339–1204) is a full-service information and sightseeing operation run by Larry and Marianne Ingraham. The company specializes in ecotourism and organizes bird-watching and wildlife-viewing excursions, but Larry can arrange anything from a flamingo tour or a bonefishing trip to car rental and accommodations. He is an invaluable source of information and assistance for planning and executing your visit.

LONG ISLAND

Never more than 4 mi wide, Long Island, one of Columbus's stopping-off places, lives up to its name, for its Queen's Highway runs for close to 80 mi, through some 35 villages and farming towns where you'll always find a little straw market beckoning. One of the island's 4,500 residents once nicknamed the highway Rhythm Road, a reference perhaps to the many potholes that used to make driving it a syncopated ride. The government has finally completed construction, and Queen's Highway is now paved and smooth. The scenery on the way changes from shelving beaches and shallow bays on the west coast to rugged headlands that drop suddenly to the sea on the east coast. The southern end of the island has sea cliffs unique to the Bahamas.

Numbers in the text correspond to numbers in the margin and on the Long Island map.

Cape Santa Maria and Stella Maris

㊷ Columbus named the island's northern tip, **Cape Santa Maria,** in honor of one of his ships. The area has truly stunning beaches—among the best in the country—and is the home of the elegant **Cape Santa Maria Beach Resort.**

Long Island

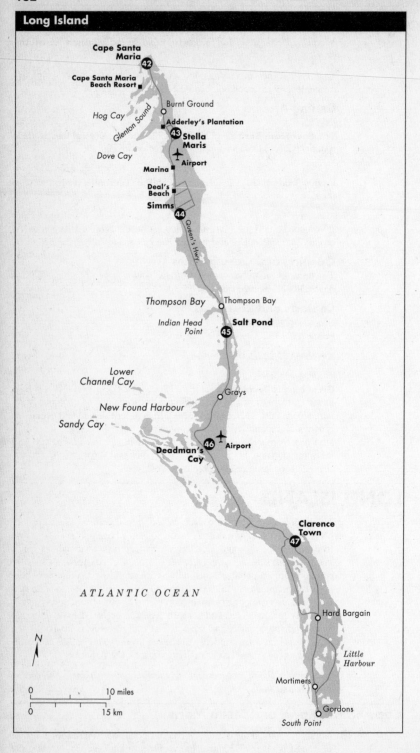

Cape Santa
Maria
42

Cape Santa Maria
Beach Resort

Burnt Ground

Hog Cay

Glenton Sound

Adderley's Plantation
43 Stella
Maris

Dove Cay

Airport

Marina

Deal's
Beach

Simms
44

Queen's Hwy.

Thompson Bay
Thompson Bay

*Indian Head
Point*
Salt Pond
45

*Lower
Channel Cay*

Grays

New Found Harbour

Sandy Cay

46 Airport

**Deadman's
Cay**

**Clarence
Town**

47

ATLANTIC OCEAN

Hard Bargain

*Little
Harbour*

Mortimers

Gordons

South Point

N

0   10 miles
0   15 km

Take a side trip on the unpaved road out to **Columbus Cove,** north of the Cape Santa Maria resort. Here are the monument and plaque that commemorate Columbus's landing, as well as tremendous views of the protected harbor he sailed into. Divers can explore the wreck of a ship, the M/S *Comberbach,* which lies just off the headland. The Stella Maris Resort sunk the leaky freighter in 1985 to create an artificial reef and an excellent dive site nearly 100 ft under. The road to the cove is too rough for most vehicles, but it happens to be a fine walk. An easier way to reach the Cove is by boat.

43 Translated, the name **Stella Maris** is the Star of the Sea, and it's home to the all-encompassing **Stella Maris Resort Club,** along with its airport. This is the only port of entry on Long Island. In a world of its own, the resort has a marina, yacht club, and tiny shopping complex, with a bank, a post office, and a general store.

At nearby **Shark Reef,** divers can safely watch groups of a dozen sharks at a time being fed fish by a scuba master. Stella Maris lies about 12 mi south of Cape Santa Maria, off Queen's Highway past the ruins of the 19th-century **Adderley's Plantation.** Long Island was another Bahamian island where fleeing Loyalists attempted, with little success, to grow cotton. You can still see parts of the plantation's three buildings up to roof level; the remains of two other plantations, **Dunmore's** and **Gray's,** are also on the island.

Dining and Lodging

$$$$ ✕⊞ **Cape Santa Maria Beach Resort.** This luxury resort consists of a
★ clubhouse and nine cottages (with two rooms each) spread along a gorgeous, 4-mi stretch of velvety white-sand beach. Catering to sportfishing enthusiasts but certainly welcoming anyone who is looking for peace and quiet in a stunning environment, the spacious, one- and two-bedroom units have marble or tile floors, elegant rattan furniture that includes a writing desk and dresser, cream-and-sea-foam walls and linens—but no televisions or phones. Dressing rooms have a well-lit mirror and plenty of counter space, plus a separate room for the tub and toilet. Each unit also has its own large, fully furnished screened porch for enjoying the outdoors without being bothered by mosquitoes. The friendly and efficient management team—Canadians Dan and Dorothy Baker—will endeavor to make your stay as relaxing as possible. The bar and dining room are in the beach house; the excellent cuisine usually features a catch of the day—opt for broiled lobster if it's on the menu. ⊠ *Oak Bay Marine Group, 1327 Beach Dr., Victoria, BC V8S 2N4,* ☎ 242/338–5273 or 800/663–7090, 𝖥𝖠𝖷 242/338–6013 or 604/598–1361. 18 rooms. Restaurant, bar, snorkeling, windsurfing, boating, fishing, bicycles. AE, D, MC, V. EP, FAP.

$$–$$$$ ✕⊞ **Stella Maris Resort Club.** Built on the grounds of the original Adderley plantation, this hotel, which sits atop a hill and overlooks the ocean, seems to attract many Germans and other Europeans. Standard rooms and one-bedroom cottages are closest to the clubhouse and have tropical decor, with rattan furniture and tile floors. All rooms have mini-refrigerators and ocean views; the one-bedroom apartments include kitchenettes. The resort also has two-, three-, and four-bedroom villas and bungalows, some with private pools. The clubhouse contains the dining room, bar, TV lounge, and gift shop. You can swim in three freshwater pools or explore east-coast beach coves with excellent snorkeling. Although diving and fishing are the most popular pursuits here, you can also take advantage of complimentary snorkeling trips, boat cruises, sunfish sailing, and bicycles. In addition, Stella Maris has its own cabana preserve on Cape Santa Maria with a stunning beach; a complimentary shuttle goes there daily. Guests can enjoy a weekly

"Out Island Cave Party" night of music and dancing on Monday, set in a huge cavern on the property, and a Wednesday rum punch party and BBQ. ⊠ *Box LI 30105, Stella Maris, Long Island; 1100 Lee Wagener Blvd., #319, Fort Lauderdale, FL 33315;* ☎ *954/359–8236, 242/336–2106, or 800/426–0466,* ℻ *954/359–8238. 50 rooms. Bar, dining room, lounge, 3 pools, 2 tennis courts, snorkeling, boating, waterskiing, fishing, bicycles. AE, MC, V. EP, MAP.*

Outdoor Activities and Sports

Cape Santa Maria Beach Resort (☎ 242/338–5273) offers sailing, windsurfing, snorkeling, and fishing: reef ($500 per day), deep sea ($600 per day), and bonefishing ($200 per day).

Stella Maris Resort Club (☎ 242/336–2106) takes divers to Shark Reef as well as a variety of wrecks and to Conception Island for world-class wall diving. The resort also offers snorkeling, bonefishing, and deep-sea fishing.

Simms and South

44 **Simms** is one of the oldest settlements on Long Island, 8 mi south of Stella Maris past little pastel-color houses. Some of these abodes display emblems to ward off evil spirits, an indication of the presence of Obeah, the superstitious voodoolike culture found in many of the Bahamian islands.

45 The annual Long Island Regatta is held in **Salt Pond** every May among competing Bahamian-made boats. The regatta is the island's biggest event, and attracts contestants from all over the islands. Salt Pond is 10 mi south of Simms.

46 The town of **Deadman's Cay** serves as home for most of the island's population. Here you'll find a few shops, churches, and schools. In Deadman's Cay is a cave that has stalactites and stalagmites and eventually leads to the sea. The cave has apparently never been completely explored, though Indian drawings were found on one wall. There are several other caves, supposedly pirate-haunted, around Millerton and Simms; knock on any door and the resident will point you in the right direction. The island's second airport is located here.

47 **Clarence Town** is the setting for Long Island's most celebrated landmarks, **St. Paul's Church** (Anglican) and **St. Peter's Church** (Catholic). They were both built by Father Jerome, a priest who is buried in a tomb in the Hermitage atop Mt. Alvernia on Cat Island. He constructed St. Paul's as he practiced the Anglican faith, while named John Hawes, and St. Peter's after his conversion to Catholicism. The architecture of the two churches is similar to that of the missions established by the Spaniards in California in the early 18th century. Clarence Town is the most picturesque settlement on Long Island, with a harbor and dock and the government headquarters in addition to the two churches.

Dining

$$ ✕ **Thompson Bay Inn.** Near Salt Pond, this is a popular local eatery that serves up Bahamian favorites such as boiled fish, cracked conch, and peas 'n' rice. Be sure to call ahead for reservations. ⊠ *Main Road, Thompson Bay,* ☎ *242/338–0052.*

$–$$ ✕ **Mario's.** Ward off a growling stomach with this haunt's local-style Bahamian food, such as "stew fish" or "boil fish" for breakfast or grouper fingers, cracked conch, and peas 'n' rice for lunch. ⊠ *Simms, no phone.*

Long Island A to Z

Arriving and Departing

BY MAIL BOAT

M/V *Abilin* makes a weekly trip from Nassau to Clarence Town on the south end of the island. The boat leaves Nassau on Tuesday; the trip takes 18 hours and the fare is $45. The M/V *Mia Dean* leaves Nassau on a varying schedule with stops in Salt Pond, Stella Maris, and Deadman's Cay. The travel time is 14 hours; fare is $45. For more information contact the **Dockmaster's office** (☎ 242/393–1064) at Potter's Cay.

BY PLANE

Virtually all guests will want to fly to the Stella Maris airport; flying into the Deadman's Cay airport if you're staying at Cape Santa Maria or Stella Maris will cost you a $100 taxi ride.

Bahamasair (☎ 800/222–4262) flies daily from Nassau to one of Long Island's two airports, Stella Maris and Deadman's Cay.

Island Express (☎ 954/359–0380) flies from Fort Lauderdale to the Stella Maris airport Thursday–Sunday.

Stella Maris Resort Club (☎ 954/359–8236, 242/336–2106, or 800/426–0466) has charter flights from Exuma and Nassau to Stella Maris. Taxis meet incoming flights. The fare to the resort from the airport is $3.

Getting Around

BY CAR

The **Stella Maris Resort Club** (☎ 242/336–2106) has automobiles for rent.

Opening and Closing Times

The **Bank of Nova Scotia** at the Stella Maris resort is open Tuesday and Thursday 10–2.

Contacts and Resources

EMERGENCIES

Police: Clarence Town (☎ 231); Deadman's Cay (☎ 242/337–0444); Simms (☎ 242/338–8555).

SAN SALVADOR

On October 12, 1492, Christopher Columbus disturbed the lives of the peaceful Lucayan Indians by landing on the island of Guanahani, which he named San Salvador. He knelt on the beach and claimed the land for Spain. (Never mind that doubting Thomases, spurred by the findings of a computerized study published in a 1986 *National Geographic* article, point to Samana Cay, 60 mi southeast, as the exact point of the weary explorer's landing.) Three monuments on the 7-by-12-mi island commemorate Columbus's arrival, and the 500th-anniversary celebration of the event was officially focused here in 1992.

A 17th-century pirate named George Watling, who frequently sought shelter on the island, changed San Salvador's name to Watling's Island. The Bahamas government switched the name back to San Salvador in 1926.

Numbers in the text correspond to numbers in the margin and on the San Salvador map.

Fernandez Bay to Riding Rock Point

In 1492, the inspiring sight that greeted Christopher Columbus by moonlight at 2 AM was a terrain of gleaming beaches and far-reaching forest. The peripatetic traveler and his crews—"men from Heaven," the locals called them—steered the *Niña, Pinta,* and *Santa María* warily among the coral reefs and anchored, so it is recorded, in **Fernandez Bay.** A cross erected in 1956 by Columbus scholar Ruth C. Durlacher Wolper Malvin stands at his approximate landing spot. Ms. Malvin's **New World Museum** (no phone), near North Victoria Hill on the east coast, contains artifacts from the era of the Lucayans. Admission to the museum is free; it's open by appointment (your hotel can make arrangements). An underwater monument marks the place where the *Santa María* anchored. Nearby, another monument commemorates the passage of the Olympic flame on its journey from Greece to Mexico City in 1968.

Fernandez Bay is close to what is now the main community of **Cockburn Town,** mid-island on the western shore. Queen's Highway encircles the island from Cockburn Town, where the weekly mail boat docks. This small village's narrow streets contain two churches, a commissioner's office, a police station, a courthouse, a library, a clinic, a drugstore, and a telephone station.

Columbus first spotted and recorded **Riding Rock Point.** The area now serves as the home for the **Riding Rock Inn,** a popular resort for divers. Just north of the point is the island's other resort, the **Club Med–Columbus Isle,** set at the foot of a 2-mi-long, gorgeous beach. Riding Rock Point is about a mile north of Cockburn Town.

Dining and Lodging

$$$$ ✕🖪 **Club Med–Columbus Isle.** This luxurious, 80-acre village opened in 1992 and is billed as the most luxurious of all the Club Med resorts, with superb, state-of-the-art dive facilities, elegant rooms, and a long stretch of private beach. German-born interior designer Gisela Trigano—effervescent wife of Club Med's vice chairman—has used as motifs the sun, moon, and stars, representing that which guided Columbus to the New World, throughout the resort. Most of the decorations were imported from Asia, Africa, and South America, including feathered Brazilian headdresses, Indian birdcages, 18th-century Pakistani pillars, Thai rice-paper flowers, Vietnamese jars, and carved doors from Mali. Hundreds of palm trees were brought from Miami to enhance the sparse landscape and protect the beach from erosion. The buildings are painted brilliant blues, greens, yellows, pinks, and purples. All rooms have patios or balconies, a walk-in closet, TV, telephone, and mini-refrigerator, and are brightly fitted with crisp turquoise spreads, white walls, tile floors, and handcrafted furniture and artwork. In baths there are plenty of mirrors and counter space and excellent water pressure in the tiled shower. A gym with cardiovascular machines, free weights, weight machines, and aerobics classes will help keep you buff. Guided bike tours introduce vacationers to island life beyond the resort. Unlike some Club Meds, this one caters primarily to upscale couples, and the atmosphere is more low-key than at most. More than 40 pristine dive sites are a half hour from shore. The dive facilities include three custom-made 45-ft catamarans and a decompression chamber. ✉ *40 W. 57th St., New York, NY 10019,* ☎ *800/258–2633 or 242/331–2000,* 🖷 *242/331–2222. 260 rooms. 3 restaurants, lounge, pool, beauty salon, massage, 9 tennis courts, exercise room, bicycles, nightclub, theater, laundry service, car rental. AE, MC, V.*

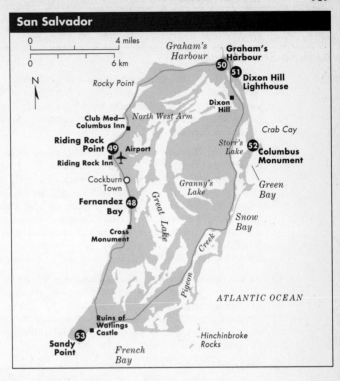

San Salvador

0 — 4 miles
0 — 6 km

N

Graham's Harbour

Graham's Harbour **50** **51** Dixon Hill Lighthouse

Rocky Point

Dixon Hill

Club Med—Columbus Inn

North West Arm

Crab Cay

Riding Rock Point **49** Airport

Storr's Lake **52** Columbus Monument

Riding Rock Inn

Cockburn Town

Granny's Lake

Green Bay

Fernandez Bay **48**

Great Lake

Snow Bay

Cross Monument

Pigeon Creek

ATLANTIC OCEAN

Ruins of Watlings Castle

Sandy Point **53**

Hinchinbroke Rocks

French Bay

$$ ✕🏠 **Riding Rock Inn.** This white, motel-style resort attracts divers because of the excellent reefs offshore and its variety of dive packages. It's also the only place to stay on San Salvador where you can avoid the relentless enthusiasm of the Club Med staff. The inn's three buildings house rooms facing either the ocean or the freshwater pool. Standard rooms are painted off-white, with wooden furniture and redwood patios. Deluxe modern oceanfront rooms (recommended) have tile floors, wicker furniture, telephones, cable TV, and refrigerators. The restaurant, which can seat 60 people, serves Bahamian dishes, such as fried grouper, conch, and peas 'n' rice, as well as such American favorites as hearty pancake breakfasts. The comfortable and friendly Driftwood Bar has a TV, VCR, and a stack of paperbacks for rainy days. Pieces of driftwood and oars signed by diving groups decorate the walls. The inn also has two one- or two-bedroom villas with kitchens; the two-bedroom units will sleep up to six. ✉ *1170 Lee Wagener Blvd., Suite 103, Fort Lauderdale, FL 33315,* ☎ *954/359–8353 or 800/272–1492,* 𝖥𝖠𝖷 *954/359–8254. 24 standard, 18 deluxe rooms. Restaurant, bar, pool, tennis court, dive center, fishing, bicycles. MC, V (5% surcharge). EP, FAP.*

Outdoor Activities and Sports

Club Med (☎ 242/331–2000) has state-of-the-art dive boats and a decompression chamber. In addition, there are nine tennis courts, sailing, and windsurfing, among other sports.

Riding Rock Inn (☎ 800/272–1492) is affiliated with Guanahani Dive Ltd., which has year-round dive packages. It also offers resort and certification courses, and a modern underwater photographic facility. They rent all kinds of camera gear and do slide shows of divers' work. The dive outfit also uses mostly buoyed sites to avoid any damage to the marine environment by dropping anchor. Riding Rock rents bicycles and snorkel gear as well, and will arrange fishing trips ($180–$400 for a half day and $300–$600 for a full day).

Around San Salvador

50 Columbus describes **Graham's Harbour** in his diaries as large enough "to hold all the ships of Christendom." A complex of buildings near the harbor houses the **Bahamian Field Station,** a biological and geological research institution that attracts scientists and students from all over the world.

51 A couple of miles south of Graham's Harbour stands **Dixon Hill Lighthouse.** Built around 1856, it is still hand-operated, and the light from its small kerosene lamp beams out to sea every 15 seconds to a maximum distance of 19 mi, depending on visibility. The lighthouse keeper must continually wind the apparatus that projects the light. A climb to the top of the 160-ft landmark offers a fabulous view of the island, which includes a series of inland lakes. The keeper is present 24 hours a day. Knock on his door and he'll take you up to the top and explain the machinery. Drop $1 in the box when you sign the guest book on the way out.

52 No road leads to the **Columbus Monument** on Crab Cay. You have to make your way along a bushy path. This initial tribute to the explorer was erected by the *Chicago Herald* newspaper in 1892, far from the presumed site of Columbus's landing. A series of little villages winds south of here for several miles, such as **Holiday Track** and **Polly Hill,** that once contained plantations.

53 **Sandy Point** anchors the southwestern end of the island, overlooking French Bay. Here, on a hill, you'll find the **ruins of Watling's Castle,** named after the 17th-century pirate. The ruins are more likely the remains of a Loyalist plantation house than a castle from buccaneering days. You can walk from Queen's Highway up the hill to see what is left of the ruins, which are now engulfed in vegetation.

San Salvador A to Z

Arriving and Departing

BY MAIL BOAT

M/V *Maxine,* out of Nassau, leaves Tuesday for San Salvador and Rum Cay. The long trip takes 18 hours, for a fare of $40. For information on specific schedules and fares, contact the **Dockmaster's office** (☎ 242/393–1064) at Potter's Cay.

BY PLANE

Taxis meet arriving planes at Cockburn Town Airport. Club Med meets all guests at the airport (your account is charged $10 for the three-minute transfer). Riding Rock provides complimentary transportation for guests.

Bahamasair (800/222–4262) flies Monday, Wednesday, Thursday, Friday, and Sunday from Nassau to Cockburn Town Airport.

Riding Rock Inn (☎ 954/359–8353 or 800/272–1492) has charter flights every Saturday from Fort Lauderdale.

Getting Around

Riding Rock Inn (☎ 954/359–8353 or 800/272–1492) rents cars for $85 a day and bicycles for $8 a day.

Contacts and Resources

Police (☎ 218).

Medical Clinic (☎ 207).

OUT ISLANDS A TO Z

Contacts and Resources

Emergencies
There are health centers and clinics scattered throughout the islands, but in the event of emergency illnesses or accidents requiring fast transportation to the United States, **Air Medical Services** (☎ 800/443–0013) provides aero-medical services out of Fort Lauderdale International Airport. Its 14 aircraft are equipped with sophisticated medical equipment and a trained staff of doctors, nurses, and paramedics.

Guided Tours
The following companies can arrange Out Islands tours:

FROM THE UNITED STATES
Adventure Vacations (✉ 10612 Beaver Dam Rd., Hunt Valley, MD 21030, ☎ 800/638–9040), **Bahamas Travel Network** (✉ 1047 S.E. 17th St., Fort Lauderdale, FL 33316, ☎ 954/467–1133 or 800/513–5535), **Caribbean Trends** (110 E. Broward Blvd., Box 1525, Fort Lauderdale, FL 33301, ☎ 954/522–1440 or 800/221–6666, FAX 954/357–4687), **Changes in L'Attitudes** (✉ 4986 113th Ave. N, Clearwater, FL 34620, ☎ 813/573–3536 or 800/282–8272), **Ibis Tours** (✉ 5798 Sunpoint Circle, Boynton Beach, FL 33437, ☎ 800/525–9411 for kayak tours), **Swift Yacht Charters** (✉ 209 S. Main St., Sherborn, MA 01770, ☎ 800/866–8340 for yacht charters).

FROM CANADA
Americanada (✉ 139 Sauve O, Montreal, Quebec H3L LY4, ☎ 514/384–6431) and **Holiday House** (✉ 110 Richmond St. E, Suite 304, Toronto, Ontario M5C 1P1, ☎ 416/364–2433).

Visitor Information
The **Bahama Out Islands Promotion Board** (✉ 1100 Lee Wagener Blvd., No. 204, Fort Lauderdale, FL 33315, ☎ 954/359–8099 or 800/688–4752) has a helpful staff that provides information about lodging, travel, and activities in the islands and can book reservations at many of the hotels. On request, the board will send color brochures about island resorts.

6 The Turks and Caicos Islands

From above, it looks as if someone poured pancake batter on the sea, that is how flat these islands are. Though there may not be pretty hills and valleys to view, the islands are ringed by sugary sand beaches and offer plenty of places to stroll along the clear blue sea. For the more adventurous, there's excellent scuba diving and sportfishing.

THE TURKS AND CAICOS ISLANDS are relatively unknown except to scuba divers and aficionados of beautiful beaches, who religiously return to these waters year after year. Miles-long, soft, sparkling white-sand beaches ring the flat islands, and offshore, pristine reefs overflow with a variety of fish, crustaceans, and coral, making for excellent snorkeling and scuba diving. The islands' slogan, "Beautiful by Nature," reflects its tranquillity and natural wonders.

Updated by
JoAnn
Milivojevic

It is claimed that Columbus's first landfall was on Grand Turk. First settled by the English more than 200 years ago, the British Crown Colony of Turks and Caicos is renowned in two respects: Its booming banking and insurance institutions lure investors from the United States and elsewhere, and its offshore reef formations entice divers to the world of colorful marine life surrounding its more than 40 islands and small cays, only eight of which are inhabited. The total landmass is 193 sq mi; the population of the eight inhabited islands and cays is some 12,350.

The Turks and Caicos are two groups of islands in an archipelago lying 575 mi southeast of Miami and about 90 mi north of Haiti. The Turks Islands include Grand Turk, which is the capital and seat of government, and Salt Cay, with a population of about 200. According to local legend, these islands were named by early settlers who thought the scarlet blossoms on the local cactus resembled the Turkish fez.

Approximately 22 mi west of Grand Turk, across the 7,000-ft-deep Christopher Columbus Passage, is the Caicos group, which includes South, East, West, Middle, and North Caicos and Providenciales. South Caicos, Middle Caicos, North Caicos, and Providenciales (nicknamed Provo) are the only inhabited islands in this group; Pine Cay and Parrot Cay are the only inhabited cays. "Caicos" is derived from *cayos,* the Spanish word for cay, and is believed to mean "string of islands."

Around 1678, Bermudians, lured by the wealth of salt in these islands, began raking salt from the flats and returning to Bermuda to sell their crop. Despite French and Spanish attacks and pirate raids, the Bermudians persisted and established a trade that became the bedrock of the Bermudian economy. In 1766 Andrew Symmers settled here to hold the islands for England. Later, Loyalists from Georgia obtained land grants in the Caicos Islands, imported slaves, and continued the lifestyle of the pre–Civil War American South.

Today, the government has devised a long-term development plan to improve the visibility of the Turks and Caicos in the Caribbean tourism market. Providenciales, in particular, is well under way as a tourist destination and also as an offshore financial center and company registrant. Mass tourism on the scale of that of some other island destinations, however, is not in the cards; government guidelines promote a "quality, not quantity," policy toward tourism, including conservation awareness and firm restrictions on building heights and casino construction. Without a port for cruise ships, the islands remain uncrowded and peaceful.

GRAND TURK

Bermudian colonial architecture abounds on this string bean of an island that is just 6 mi long and 1 mi wide. Buildings have walled-in courtyards to keep wandering donkeys from nibbling on the foliage.

Exploring Grand Turk

Pristine beaches with vistas of turquoise waters, small local settlements, historic ruins, and native flora and fauna are among the sights to see on these islands. Keep an eye out for fruit-bearing trees like lime, papaya, and custard apple. Birds to look for include the great blue heron, the woodstar hummingbird, and the squawking Cuban crow. It's hard to get lost on any of the islands, as there aren't many roads; given the low amount of traffic, motor scooters can be a fun way to explore.

Numbers in the text correspond to numbers in the margin and on the Turks and Caicos Islands map.

Fewer than 4,000 people live on Grand Turk, a 7½-sq-mi island. Diving is definitely the big deal here. Grand Turk's Wall, with a sheer drop to 7,000 ft, is well known to divers.

❶ The buildings in **Cockburn Town,** the colony's capital and seat of government, reflect the 19th-century Bermudian style of architecture. The narrow streets are lined with low stone walls and old street lamps, now powered by electricity. Horses and cattle wander around as if they own the place, and the occasional donkey cart clatters by, carrying a load of water or freight. In one of the oldest native stone buildings in the islands, the **Turks & Caicos National Museum** houses the Molasses Reef wreck of 1513, the earliest shipwreck discovered in the Americas. The natural-history exhibits include artifacts left by African, North American, Bermudian, French, Hispanic, and Taino settlers. An impressive addition to the museum is the coral reef and sea-life exhibit, faithfully modeled on a popular dive site just off the island. ☎ 649/94–62160. ☒ $5. ⊙ Mon.–Tues. and Thurs.–Fri. 9–4, Wed. 9–6, Sat. 10–1.

| NEED A BREAK? | The **Pepper Pot** (no phone) is a little blue shack at the end of Front Street where Peanuts Butterfield makes her famous conch fritters. |

Beaches

There are more than 230 mi of beaches in the Turks and Caicos Islands, ranging from secluded coves to miles-long stretches. Most beaches are soft coralline sand. Tiny uninhabited cays offer complete isolation for nude sunbathing and skinny-dipping. Many are accessible only by boat.

Governor's Beach, a long white strip on the west coast of Grand Turk, is one of the nicest beaches on this island.

Dining

Like everything else on these islands, dining out is a very laid-back affair, which is not to say that it is cheap. Because of the high cost of importing all edibles, the cost of a meal is usually higher than that of a comparable meal in the United States. A 7% government tax and a 10% service charge are added to your check. Reservations are not required. Dress is casual throughout the island.

CATEGORY	COST*
$$$	over $25
$$	$15–$25
$	under $15

per person for a three-course meal, excluding drinks, service, and 7% sales tax

$$ ✕ **Sandpiper.** Candles flicker on the Sandpiper's terrace, set beside a flower-filled courtyard. The leisurely pace here creates a relaxing setting to experience such blackboard specialties as lobster, filet mignon, seafood platter, or pork chops with applesauce. ⊠ *Sitting Pretty Hotel, Duke St.,* ☎ *649/94–62232. AE, D, MC, V.*

$$ ✕ **Secret Garden.** Menu highlights include a seafood platter, grilled lobster tail, pork chops, and roast leg of lamb. For dessert, try the tasty apple pie. The Sunday dinner and sing-along are popular. The outdoor garden is beautifully landscaped with hibiscus, bougainvillea, palms, and other tropical plants; sea nets, glass balls and local paintings round out the decor. Like most places on the island, casual dress like shorts and T-shirts are fine, however, locals are apt to dress-up more for an evening out. ⊠ *Salt Raker Inn, Duke St.,* ☎ *649/94–62260. AE, D, MC, V.*

$–$$ ✕ **Turk's Head Inn.** The menu changes daily at this lively restaurant, touted by many residents as the best on the island. Some staples include escargots, pâté, and a handful of other delectables, including local grouper fingers perfectly fried for fish-and-chips. Look for lobster, quiche, steaks, and homemade soups on the blackboard menu. You may not want to leave after your meal—come nightfall, the inn's bar is abuzz with local gossip and mirthful chatter. ⊠ *Turk's Head Inn, Duke St.,* ☎ *649/94–62466. AE, MC, V.*

$ ✕ **Regal Begal.** Drop by this popular local eatery for native specialties such as cracked conch, minced lobster, and fish-and-chips. The atmosphere is casual and the decor unmemorable, but the portions are large and the prices easy on your wallet. ⊠ *Hospital Rd.,* ☎ *649/94–62274. No credit cards.*

$ ✕ **Water's Edge.** Relaxed waterfront dining awaits you at this pleasantly rustic eatery. The limited menu covers the basics with a twist—from barbecued grouper to a fresh seafood crepe. A kids' menu is also available. The food is authentic and filling, and the view at sunset breathtaking, but the irresistible homemade pies are enough to justify a visit. ⊠ *Duke St.,* ☎ *649/94–61680. MC, V. Closed Mon.*

Lodging

CATEGORY	COST*
$$$$	over $250
$$$	$170–$250
$$	$110–$170
$	under $110

All prices are for a standard double room in winter, excluding 7% tax and 10%–15% service charge. Please note that some hotels are now charging 8% tax.

$$–$$$ 🏨 **Guanahani Beach Hotel.** One of the finest stretches of beach on the island belongs to this hotel; the palm-tree-lined property is popular with honeymooners. Fully renovated by new owners in 1994, the rooms have pale ceramic tile floors and bright, primary-color Caribbean-print bedspreads and curtains. Every room has an ocean view, two double beds, and a full bathroom. A crewed 35-ft yacht is available to rent for day trips or romantic moonlight rides. Dive packages are available. ⊠ *Box 178,* ☎ *649/94–62135,* ℻ *649/94–61460. 16 rooms. Restaurant, 2 bars, pool, shop. MC, V.*

$$ 🏨 **Sitting Pretty Hotel.** Formerly known as Kittina and under new own-
★ ership, the hotel is split in two by the town's main drag. On one side, comfortable, lodge-style rooms and sleek balconied suites with kitchens sit on a gleaming white-sand beach. In 1996 beachfront rooms were completely refurbished with new furniture and updated baths. Across the street, the older main house holds a lively dining room and rooms that ooze island atmosphere. Behind the house are the pool and garden. All rooms and suites are air-conditioned and have tile floors. ⊠ *Duke St., Box 42,* ☎ *649/94–62232,* ℻ *649/94–62877. 40 rooms, 2*

Turks and Caicos Islands

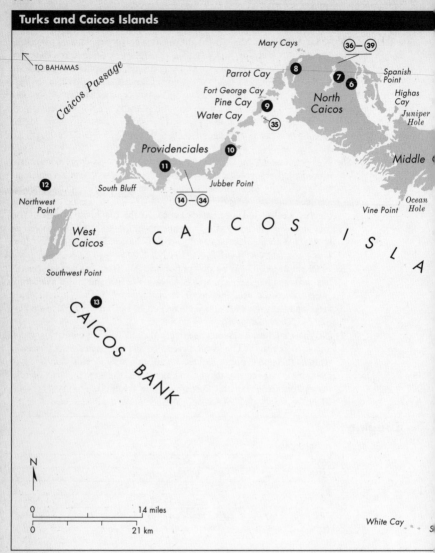

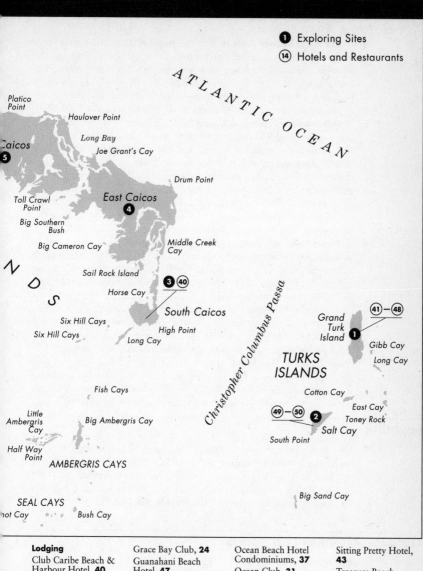

- ① Exploring Sites
- ⑭ Hotels and Restaurants

ATLANTIC OCEAN

Platico Point

Haulover Point

Long Bay

Joe Grant's Cay

Caicos ❺

Drum Point

Toll Crawl Point

East Caicos ❹

Big Southern Bush

Big Cameron Cay

Middle Creek Cay

Sail Rock Island

❸ ㊵

Horse Cay

South Caicos

Grand Turk Island ①

㊶ — ㊽

Gibb Cay

Long Cay

Six Hill Cays

Six Hill Cays

High Point

Long Cay

TURKS ISLANDS

N D S

Christopher Columbus Passa

Fish Cays

Cotton Cay

Little Ambergris Cay

Big Ambergris Cay

East Cay

Toney Rock

㊾ — ㊿ ②

Salt Cay

Half Way Point

AMBERGRIS CAYS

South Point

SEAL CAYS

...ot Cay · · · · Bush Cay

Big Sand Cay

Lodging

Club Caribe Beach & Harbour Hotel, **40**

Club Med Turkoise, **23**

Club Vacanze Prospect of Whitby Hotel, **36**

Coral Reef Beach Club, **41**

Erebus Inn Resort, **27**

Grace Bay Club, **24**

Guanahani Beach Hotel, **47**

Island Princess, **20**

JoAnne's B&B, **38**

Le Deck Hotel & Beach Club, **21**

Meridian Club, **35**

Mount Pleasant Guest House, **50**

Ocean Beach Hotel Condominiums, **37**

Ocean Club, **31**

Ocean View Hotel, **48**

Pelican Beach Hotel, **39**

Salt Raker Inn, **42**

Sandals, Turks and Caicos, **34**

Sitting Pretty Hotel, **43**

Treasure Beach Villas, **25**

Turk's Head Inn, **45**

Turquoise Reef Resort & Casino, **22**

Turtle Cove Inn, **26**

Windmills Plantation, **49**

suites. 2 restaurants, 2 bars, air-conditioning, room service, pool, dive shop, windsurfing, boating, bicycles, shop, baby-sitting, travel services. AE, MC, V. EP, MAP.

$ 🏨 **Coral Reef Beach Club.** One- and two-bedroom units here have complete kitchens, air-conditioning, and contemporary furnishings. The resort is a short drive from town, and the beach is a few steps from your door. ⊠ *Box 10,* ☎ *649/94–62055,* FAX *649/94–62911. 18 units. Restaurant, bar, air-conditioning, pool, tennis court, health club, water sports arranged with dive operations, shop. AE, MC, V. EP, MAP.*

$ 🏨 **Salt Raker Inn.** Across the street from the beach, this galleried house was the home of a Bermudian shipwright 180 years ago. The rooms and suites are not elegant but are individually decorated and have a homey atmosphere, and each has air-conditioning and a mini-refrigerator. The three garden rooms are desirable for their screened porches and ocean views. Dive packages are available. ⊠ *Duke St., Box 1,* ☎ *649/94–62260,* FAX *649/94–62817. U.K. reservations:* ⊠ *44 Birchington Rd., London NW6 4LJ,* ☎ *0171/328–6474. 10 rooms, 2 suites. Restaurant, bar, air-conditioning, bicycles. AE, D, MC, V. EP.*

$ 🏨 **Turk's Head Inn.** Built in 1850 by a prosperous salt miner, this classic Bermudian building has had incarnations as the American Consulate and as the governor's guest house (the queen reportedly took a room here on her last visit to the island). Now run by a Frenchman known as Mr. X, the inn has acquired a strong European flavor. A plethora of Brits and other expat Europeans make it their stomping ground. The seven distinctive rooms have the owner's own drawings, and detailed maps adorn many of the walls. In the front courtyard, an oversize hammock provides the perfect vantage point from which to admire the well-tended garden. The beach is only a few strides away. The bar and restaurant area bustle at night. Dive packages are available. ⊠ *Duke St., Box 58,* ☎ *649/94–62466,* FAX *649/94–62825. 7 rooms, 1 apartment. Showers only. Restaurant, bar, air-conditioning. AE, MC, V.*

Nightlife

On Grand Turk, Xavier Tonneau (a.k.a. Mr. X) leads sing-alongs in his bar at the **Turk's Head Inn** (⊠ Duke St., ☎ 649/94–62466) almost every night. There's folk and pop music at the **Salt Raker Inn** (⊠ Duke St., ☎ 649/94–62260) on Wednesday and Sunday nights. Weekends and on holidays, head over to the **Nookie Hill Club** (⊠ Nookie Hill, no phone) for dancing.

Outdoor Activities and Sports

Bicycling
In Grand Turk on Duke Street, both the **Salt Raker Inn** (☎ 649/94–62260) and the **Sitting Pretty Hotel** (☎ 649/94–62232) rent bikes for $10 per day, $40 per week.

Horseback Riding
Horses roam lazily around the main roads on Grand Turk. While there is no organized riding program, most hotels will make arrangements for their guests, and rates can be negotiated with individual owners.

Scuba Diving
Diving is the top attraction here. (All divers must carry and present a valid certificate card before they'll be allowed to dive.) These islands are surrounded by a reef system of more than 200 sq mi—much of it unexplored. Grand Turk's famed wall drops more than 7,000 ft and is one side of a 22-mi-wide channel called the Christopher Columbus Passage. From January through March, an estimated 6,000 eastern Atlantic humpback whales swim through this passage en route to their

winter breeding grounds. There are undersea cathedrals, coral gardens, and countless tunnels. Among the operations that provide instruction, equipment rentals, underwater video equipment, and trips are **Sea Eye Divers** (⊠ Duke St., Grand Turk, ☎ 649/94–61407), **Blue Water Divers** (⊠ Front St., Salt Raker Inn, Grand Turk, ☎ 649/94–62432), and **Off the Wall Divers** (⊠ Pond St., Grand Turk, ☎ 649/94–62159).

Note: Divers in need of a hyperbaric/recompression chamber are airlifted to the one on Provo—a 30-minute flight.

Snorkeling

Blue Water Divers (⊠ Front St., Salt Raker Inn, Grand Turk, ☎ 649/94–62432) and **Sea Eye Divers** (⊠ Duke St., Grand Turk, ☎ 649/94–61407) both offer equipment and trips, as well as diving packages and instruction.

Tennis

The **Coral Reef Resort** (⊠ The Ridge, ☎ 649/94–62055) has one lighted court.

PROVIDENCIALES

About 6,000 people live on Provo (as everybody calls it), a considerable number of whom are expatriate U.S. and Canadian businesspeople and retirees. Provo's 44 sq mi are by far the most developed in the Turks and Caicos.

Exploring Providenciales

In the mid-18th century, so the story goes, a French ship was wrecked near here and the survivors were washed ashore on an island they gratefully christened La Providentielle. Under the Spanish, the name was changed to Providenciales.

With its rolling ridges and 12-mi beach, the island is a prime target for developers. More than two decades ago a group of U.S. investors, including the DuPonts, Ludingtons, and Roosevelts, opened up this island for visitors and those seeking homesites in the Caribbean. In 1990 the island's first luxury resort, the Turquoise Reef Resort & Casino, opened, and with it, the island's first gourmet Italian restaurant. The luxurious Ocean Club, a condominium resort at Grace Bay, was also completed in 1990 and was followed by the upscale Grace Bay Club resort in 1992. The newest luxury resort is the Royal Bay, which opened in 1995. Competition created by the new resorts spurred many of the older hotels to undertake much-needed renovations.

⓫ Near Providenciales International Airport, **Downtown Provo** is really a strip mall that houses car-rental agencies, law offices, boutiques, banks, and other businesses.

NEED A BREAK? Stop in at **Fast Eddie's** (⊠ Airport Rd., ☎ 649/94-64075), a casual eatery, for a drink and a platter of seafood.

⓾ **Island Sea Center.** On the northeast coast, this is the place to learn about the sea and its inhabitants. Here you'll find the **Caicos Conch Farm,** a major mariculture operation where the mollusks are farmed commercially. The farm's tourist facilities include a video show, boutique, and a hands-on tank with conches in various stages of growth. There are more than 2.5 million conch in their inventory. Established by the PRIDE Foundation (Protection of Reefs and Islands from Degradation and Exploitation), the **JoJo Dolphin Project,** named after a 7-ft-long male bottlenose dolphin who cruises these waters and enjoys playing with local divers, is also here. You can watch a video on JoJo and learn how to interact with him safely if you see him on one of your dives. ⊠ *Island Sea Center,* ☎ 649/94–65330; ⊠ *Caicos Conch Farm,* ☎ *649/94–65849.* ☞ *$6.* ☉ *Mon.–Sat. 9–5.*

Beaches

A fine white-sand beach stretches 12 mi along the northeast coast of **Providenciales.** There are good beaches at **Sapodilla Bay**; for excellent close-to-shore snorkeling there's a reef near the White House off Penn's Road.

Dining and Lodging

$$$ ✕ **Gecko Grille.** Gourmet dining can be enjoyed either indoors amid tropical hand-painted murals or out on the garden patio. The menu features creative dishes such as almond-cracked conch with a lime *rémoulade* (a cold, mayonnaise-based sauce), and grilled pork chops marinated in papaya juice. Portions are quite large, so either share or bring a hearty appetite. ⊠ *Ocean Club Resort, Grace Bay,* ☎ 649/94–65880. AE, MC, V.

$$$ ✕ **The Terrace.** The cuisine here has a Euro-Caribbean flair, and the menu changes according to the freshest ingredients available. You can make a meal from such delicious starters as freshly baked tomato-and-goat-cheese tarts, lobster bisque, and simmered mussels. Main courses include roast rack of lamb, and fresh conch encrusted with pecans. Top it all off with a classic crème brûlée. ⊠ *Turtle Cove,* ☎ 649/94–64763. AE, MC, V. Closed Sun.

$$–$$$ ✕ **Alfred's Place.** Austrian owner Alfred Holzfeind caters to an Amer-
★ ican palate with an extensive menu featuring everything from prime rib to chicken salad. The alfresco lounge is a popular watering hole for locals and tourists alike ⊠ *Turtle Cove,* ☎ 649/94–64679. AE, D, MC, V. Closed Mon. July–Oct. No lunch weekends.

$$–$$$ ✕ **Anacaona.** At the impressive Grace Bay Club, this exquisitely de-
★ signed restaurant offers a true gourmet dining experience minus the tie, the air-conditioning, and the attitude. Start with a bottle of fine wine from the extensive cellar, and then enjoy a three- or four-course meal of the chef's light but flavorful cooking, which combines traditional French recipes with fresh seafood and Caribbean fruits, vegetables, and spices. Oil lamps on the tables, gently circulating ceiling fans, and the natural sounds of the breeze, ocean, birds, and tree frogs all add to the Eden-like environment. ⊠ *Grace Bay Club, Providenciales,* ☎ *649/94–65050. AE, MC, V.*

$–$$ ✕ **Dora's.** This popular local eatery serves up island fare—turtle, shredded lobster, spicy conch chowder—seven days a week, from 7 AM until the last person leaves the bar. Plastic print and lace tablecloths, hanging plants, and Haitian art add to the island ambience. Soups ($4) come with homemade bread, and entrées such as fish-and-chips, conch Creole, and grilled pork chops come with a choice of vegetable. Be sure to come early for the packed Monday- and Thursday-night all-you-can-eat $20 seafood buffet. The price includes round-trip transportation to your hotel. ⊠ *Leeward Hwy.,* ☎ 649/94–64558. No credit cards.

$–$$ ✕ **Fast Eddie's.** Plants festoon this cheerful restaurant, which is across from the airport. Broiled turtle steak, fried grouper fingers, and other island specialties are joined on the menu by old American standbys such as cheeseburgers and cherry pie. Wednesday evening there's a $20 ($10 for children) all-you-can-eat seafood buffet. Friday is prime rib and live music night. Free transportation to and from your hotel is provided. ⊠ *Airport Rd.,* ☎ 649/94–13175. MC, V.

$–$$ ✕ **Hong Kong Restaurant.** A no-frills place with plain wood tables and chairs, the Hong Kong offers dine-in, delivery, and take-out. The menu includes lobster with ginger and green onions, chicken with black-bean sauce, sliced duck with salted mustard greens, and sweet-and-sour chicken. ✉ *Leeward Hwy.,* ☎ 649/94–65678. V. *No lunch Sun.*

$ ✕ **Banana Boat.** Buoys and other sea relics deck the walls of this brightly painted casual restaurant on the wharf. Grilled grouper, lobster-salad sandwiches, conch fritters, and a refreshing conch salad are among the menu options. Excellent tropical drinks include the house specialty, the rum-filled Banana Breeze. ✉ *Turtle Cove,* ☎ 649/94–15706. AE, MC, V.

$ ✕ **Caicos Cafe.** There's a pervasive air of celebration in the uncovered outdoor dining area of this popular eatery. Choose from a selection of local and American cuisine, including lobster sandwiches, hamburgers, and a variety of excellent salads. ✉ *Across from Turquoise Reef,* ☎ 649/94–65278. AE. *No lunch Sun.*

$ ✕ **Hey, José.** Frequented by locals, this restaurant claims to serve the ★ island's best margaritas. Customers also return for the tasty Tex-Mex treats: tacos, tostados, nachos, burritos, fajitas, and José's special-recipe hot chicken wings. Creative types can build their own pizzas. ✉ *Central Square,* ☎ 649/94–64812. AE, MC, V. *Closed Sun.*

$ ✕ **Pub on the Bay.** If beachfront dining is what you're after, it doesn't get much better than this. Located in the Blue Hill residential district, a five-minute drive from downtown Provo, this restaurant serves fried or steamed fish, oxtail stew, barbecue ribs, chicken, various sandwiches, and even turtle steak. There is no air-conditioning inside the restaurant, so you may as well cross the street to one of three thatched roof "huts," which stand on the beach. ✉ *Blue Hill Rd.,* ☎ 649/94–15309. AE, MC, V.

$ ✕ **Top O' the Cove Gourmet Delicatessen.** You can easily walk to this tiny café on Leeward Highway from the Turtle Cove and Erebus Inns. Don't be put off by the location in the Napa Auto Parts plaza. Order breakfast, deli subs, sandwiches, salads, and cool soft-swirl frozen yogurt. It's open every day but Christmas and New Year's from 7 to 3:30. ✉ *Leeward Hwy.,* ☎ 649/94–64694. *No credit cards.*

$$$ ▥ **Club Med Turkoise.** This lavish $23 million resort is one of the most sumptuous of all Club Med's villages. One-, two-, and three-story bungalows line a mile-long beach, and all the usual sybaritic pleasures are here. This club is especially geared toward couples, singles aged 28 and over, and divers. The one-price-covers-all-except-drinks package includes all the diving, water sports, and daytime activities you can handle, plus nightly entertainment. ✉ *Providenciales,* ☎ 649/94–65500 or 800/258–2633; 212/750–1684 or 212/750–1687 in NY; FAX 649/94–65501. *298 rooms. 3 restaurants, bar, snack bar, pool, 8 tennis courts, exercise room, beach, dive shop, water sports, fishing, bicycles, shop, dance club, video games, library. AE, MC, V. All-inclusive (except for drinks).*

$$$ ▥ **Grace Bay Club.** Staying at this Swiss-owned, Mediterranean-style ★ resort is a little like being the guest of honor of a very gracious host with unbeatable taste. The suites, which all feature a breathtaking view of Grace Bay's stunning turquoise waters, are furnished with rattan and pickled wood. Mexican-tile floors are elegantly appointed with throw rugs from Turkey and India. If you choose to take advantage of the myriad activities (from diving to golf to individually planned and catered picnics on surrounding islands), you will be expertly provided for; but the main attraction here is natural beauty. Relax and enjoy a getaway that is peaceful, invigorating, and wonderfully pampering. ✉ *Box 128, Providenciales,* ☎ 649/94–65757 or 800/946–5757, FAX 649/94–

65758. 22 suites. Restaurant, bar, pool, hot tub, 2 tennis courts, beach, water sports, video games, library. AE, MC, V. EP, MAP.

$$$ ⊞ **Sandals, Turks and Caicos.** A row of giant palm trees lines the approach to this new, elegant pink-and-white resort, a couples-only, all-inclusive retreat. Stroll among the lush tropical landscaping, take a dip in the free-form lap pool, and dine in one of the delicious restaurants—there are plenty of sports and activities to work off the extra calories. You'll be sufficiently pampered with bar service that extends to the beach. Luxurious accommodations combined with white-glove service make this all-inclusive resort a truly relaxing experience. ⊠ *Grace Bay,* ☎ *649/94–68000 or 800/726–3257,* FAX *649/94-68001. 200 rooms. 3 restaurants, pool, hot tub, 2 tennis courts, exercise room, water sports, dive shop. AE, MC, V.*

$$$ ⊞ **Turquoise Reef Resort & Casino.** Oversize oceanfront rooms have
★ rattan furniture and a rich Caribbean color scheme. Furnished with a king or two double beds, all rooms are air-conditioned and have a color TV and ceiling fan, and either a terrace or a patio. The island's only casino is here, and there's live nightly entertainment. Guests enjoy a free daily activities program that includes pool volleyball and children's treasure hunts. ⊠ *Box 205, Provo,* ☎ *649/94–65555,* FAX *649/94–65522. 228 rooms. 3 restaurants, 3 bars, air-conditioning, fans, room service, pool, hot tub, 2 tennis courts, exercise room, beach, dive shop, water sports, shops, casino, dance club, baby-sitting, travel services. AE, MC, V. EP, MAP.*

$$ ⊞ **Island Princess.** Wood walkways at this hotel lead up to and around the rooms, which are in two wings. All rooms have cable TV and a private balcony. This is a suitable little hotel for families. It's on the beach, the restaurant serves excellent Italian and Caribbean food, and there's nightly entertainment. ⊠ *The Bight,* ☎ *649/94–64260,* FAX *649/94–64666. 80 rooms. Restaurant, bar, 2 pools, water sports, boating, recreation room, playground. AE, D, MC, V. MAP.*

$$ ⊞ **Le Deck Hotel & Beach Club.** This 27-room pink hostelry was built
★ in classic Bermudian style around a tropical courtyard. It offers clean rooms with a tile floor, color TV, phone, and air-conditioning. Le Deck is especially popular with divers, and its atmosphere is informal and lively with a mostly thirty-something-and-over crowd. ⊠ *Box 144, Grace Bay, Provo,* ☎ *649/94–65547,* FAX *649/94–65770. 27 rooms, including 2 suites. Restaurant, bar, air-conditioning, pool, beach, water sports, shop. AE, D, MC, V. EP, CP, AP, MAP.*

$$ ⊞ **Ocean Club.** "Escape the Stress of Success" is the slogan for this luxury beachfront suite resort. It's on Grace Bay's 12-mi stretch of pristine beach, a short walk away from Provo's only golf course. The all-suite accommodations range from efficiency studios to deluxe versions with ocean view, full screened balcony, kitchen, dining room, and living room. Third-floor rooms have striking slanted ceilings, and all but efficiency accommodations include washer and dryer. Efficiency suites fall into our $ category. ⊠ *Box 240, Providenciales,* ☎ *649/94–65880 or 800/457–8787,* FAX *649/94–65845. 2 restaurants, bar, pool, 18-hole golf course, tennis court, exercise room, dive shop. AE, MC, V. EP.*

$$ ⊞ **Treasure Beach Villas.** These one- and two-bedroom modern, self-catering apartments have fully equipped kitchens and ceiling fans. You may want a car or bike (Treasure Beach has rentals) to reach the grocery store or restaurants; bus service is limited. Provo's 12 mi of white sandy beach is just outside your door, and the hotel can organize fishing, snorkeling, and scuba expeditions. ⊠ *The Bight,* ☎ *649/94–64325,* FAX *649/94–64108; or* ⊠ *Box 8409, Hialeah, FL 33012. 8 single, 10 double rooms. Pool, tennis court. AE, D, MC, V. EP.*

$$ ⊞ **Turtle Cove Inn.** A marina, a free-form pool, a dive shop with equipment rentals and instruction, and lighted tennis courts attract the sporting crowd to Turtle Cove. There's a free boat shuttle to the nearby beach and snorkeling reef. All rooms have a TV, phone, and air-conditioning, and eight also have mini-refrigerators. A handful of good restaurants are within walking distance. ⊠ *Providenciales,* ☎ 649/94–64203 or 800/887–0477, ℻ 649/94–64141. *30 rooms, 1 suite. 2 restaurants, 2 bars, air-conditioning, 2 tennis courts, pool, dive shop, bicycles. AE, MC, V. EP.*

$–$$ ⊞ **Erebus Inn Resort.** This environmentally sensitive resort sits on a cliff
★   overlooking Turtle Cove and has wonderful panoramic views. All units have two double beds, modern wicker furnishings, and original island artwork, including some lovely and unique Haitian wall hangings. Rooms in the older chalet cost under $110 a night (double occupancy) in winter. For those preferring creature comforts, we recommend the units in the newer section ($$); each has air-conditioning, cable TV, and phone. Frequent bus shuttles take guests to a nearby beach. The restaurant and bar, always one of Provo's liveliest spots, has a menu of French and Caribbean cuisine. Five affordable restaurants are within walking distance, as are snorkeling sites, a shopping center, and several dive operations. ⊠ *Turtle Cove, Box 238, Providenciales,* ☎ 649/ 94–64240, ℻ 649/94–64704. *30 rooms. Restaurant, bar, air-conditioning, 2 pools (1 saltwater), 2 tennis courts, aerobics, exercise room, baby-sitting. AE, MC, V. EP, MAP.*

Nightlife

On Provo, the newest hot spot is **Casablanca** (⊠ Next to Club Med, ☎ 649/94–65449), a Monte Carlo–style nightclub complete with mirrors and a decked-out crowd. **Disco Elite** (⊠ Airport Rd., ☎ 649/ 94–64592) has strobe lights and an elevated dance floor. A full band plays native, reggae, and contemporary music on Thursday night at the **Erebus Inn** (⊠ Turtle Cove, ☎ 649/94–64240). **Le Deck** (⊠ Grace Bay, ☎ 649/94–65547) offers one-armed bandits every night. Locals frequent **Smokey's on da Beach** (⊠ Near Le Deck hotel, ☎ 649/94– 13466), a lively restaurant-bar that, as the name suggests, is right on the beach, and a great place to watch the sunset. A lively lounge can be found at the **Turquoise Reef Resort** (⊠ Grace Bay, ☎ 649/94– 65555), where a musician plays to the mostly tourist crowd. **Port Royale** (⊠ Turquoise Reef Resort, ☎ 649/94–65508) is the island's only gambling casino.

Outdoor Activities and Sports

Bicycling

Provo has a few steep grades to conquer, but they're short, and there's little traffic. Bikes can be rented at the **Island Princess** hotel (☎ 649/ 94–64260) at the Bight for $10 a day, through **Turtle Inn Divers** (⊠ Turtle Cove Inn, ☎ 649/94–15389) for $12 a day and $60 a week, or at the **Turquoise Reef Resort & Casino** (⊠ Grace Bay, ☎ 649/94– 65555) for $14 a day.

Boat Rentals

You can rent a boat with a private captain for a half or full day of sportfishing through **J&B Tours** (⊠ Leward Marina, Provo, ☎ 649/94–65047) for about $300 a day. **Dive Provo** (⊠ Turquoise Reef Resort, Grace Bay, Provo, ☎ 649/94–65040) rents small sailboats for $20 per hour and provides beginning instruction for $40 for up to two hours. Sailing not your bent? Try open-cockpit ocean kayaking, available at Dive Provo for $10 per hour for one and $15 per hour for two.

Fishing

Silver Deep (⊠ Turtle Cove Marina, Provo, ☎ 649/94–15595) will take you out for half- or full-day bonefishing or bottom-fishing expeditions, bait and tackle included. The same outfit will arrange half- or full-day deep-sea fishing trips in search of shark, marlin, kingfish, sawfish, wahoo, and tuna, with all equipment furnished. Deep-sea, bone-, and bottom-fishing are also available aboard the **Sakitumi** (☎ 649/94–64065).

Golf

A 6,529-yard golf course opened on Providenciales in late 1991. **Provo Golf Club** (☎ 649/94–65991) has a par-72, 18-hole championship course, designed by Karl Litten, that is sustained by a desalination plant producing 250,000 gallons of water a day. The turf is sprinkled in green islands over 12 acres of natural limestone outcroppings, creating a desert-style design of narrow "target areas" and sandy waste areas—a formidable challenge to anyone playing from the championship tees. Fees are $90, which includes a shared electric cart. A pro shop, driving ranges, and a restaurant and bar round out the club's facilities.

Parasailing

A 15-minute flight is available for $45 at either **Dive Provo** (⊠ Turquoise Reef Resort, Provo, ☎ 649/94–65040 or 800/234–7768) or **J&B Tours** (⊠ Leward Marina, ☎ 649/94–65047).

Scuba Diving

As diving is the number one tourist activity on the island, there are lots of dive operators to choose from. **Art Pickering's Provo Turtle Divers** (⊠ Turtle Cove Marina, Provo, ☎ 649/94–64232), **Aquanaut** (⊠ Turtle Cove, Provo, ☎ 649/94–64048), **Caicos Adventures** (⊠ Turtle Cove Marina, Provo, ☎ 649/94–63346), **Dive Provo** (⊠ Turquoise Reef Resort, Provo, ☎ 649/94–65040 or 800/234–7768), **Flamingo Divers** (⊠ Turtle Cove, Provo, ☎ 649/94–64193), **J&B Tours** (⊠ Leward Marina, ☎ 649/94–65047).

Note: A modern hyperbaric/recompression chamber is located on Provo in the **Menzies Medical Centre** (☎ 649/94–64242) on Leeward Highway.

Sea Excursions

The **Ocean Outback** (☎ 649/94–64080), a 70-ft motor cruiser, has barbecue-and-snorkel cruises to uninhabited islands. Both the 37-ft catamaran **Beluga** (☎ 649/94–15196, $39 per half day) and the 56-ft trimaran **Tao** (☎ 649/94–65040) run sunset cruises, as well as sailing and snorkeling outings. A full-day outing on the *Tao* is $59 per person, including snorkel rental and lunch. For $20 per person, **Dive Provo** (⊠ Ramada Turquoise Reef Resort, ☎ 649/94–65040 or 800/234–7768) gives two-hour glass-bottom-boat tours of the spectacular reefs. **Turtle Inn Divers** (⊠ Turtle Cove Inn, ☎ 649/94–15389) offers full-day Sunday excursions for divers for $64.50 per person ($25 per person for nondivers and snorkelers). The **Turks and Caicos Aggressor** (⊠ Turtle Cove Marina, ☎ 504/385–2416, FAX 504/384–0817) offers luxury six-day dive cruises with full accommodations.

Snorkeling

Dive Provo (⊠ Turtle Cove Marina, Provo, ☎ 649/94–65040 or 800/234–7768) and **Provo Turtle Divers** (⊠ Turtle Cove Marina, Provo, ☎ 649/94–64232) provide rentals for about $10 and trips for $20.

Spectator Sports

Cricket is the most popular game in town. The season runs from July through August. Tennis, basketball, softball, and darts are other local favorites. You're welcome to join in. Inquire at the tourist board (☎ 800/241–0824) for a list of events.

Tennis

There are two lighted courts at **Turtle Cove Inn** (☎ 649/94–64203), eight courts (four lighted) at **Club Med Turkoise** (☎ 649/94–65500), two lighted courts at the **Turquoise Reef Resort** (☎ 649/94–65555), two lighted courts at the **Erebus Inn** (☎ 649/94–64240), one unlighted court at **Treasure Beach Villas** (☎ 649/94–64211), and two lighted courts at **Grace Bay Club** (☎ 649/94–65050).

Waterskiing

Waterskiers will find the calm turquoise water ideal for long-distance runs. **Dive Provo** (✉ Turquoise Reef Resort, Provo, ☎ 649/94–65040) charges $35 for a 15-minute run.

Windsurfing

Rental and instruction are available at **Dive Provo** (✉ Turquoise Reef Resort, Provo, ☎ 649/94–65040).

Shopping

Shopping is limited to hotel gift shops, airports, and occasional street vendors, except on Provo, where new shops and franchises open every month. Most of these stores can be found in five main shopping complexes: Market Place, Central Square, Caribbean Place, all on Leeward Highway; Turtle Cove Landing, in Turtle Cove; and the newest complex, Ports of Call, in Grace Bay. Delicate baskets woven from the local top grasses and small metalworks are the only crafts native to the Turks and Caicos, and they are sold in many shops.

The **Bamboo Gallery** (✉ Market Place, Provo, ☎ 649/94–064748) sells all types of Caribbean art, from vivid Haitian paintings to wood carvings and local metal sculptures. **Greensleeves** (✉ Central Square, Provo, ☎ 649/94–64147) is the place to go for paintings by local artists, island-made rag rugs, baskets, jewelry, and sisal mats and bags. **Mama's Gifts** (✉ Ports of Call, Provo, ☎ 649/94–13338) sells hand-woven and embroidered straw baskets, handbags, hats, and shell and wood jewelry. **Maison Creole** (✉ Grace Bay, Provo, no phone) sells unique Caribbean arts and crafts, including painted metal sculptures, furniture, carved wood masks, canes, and bowls. **Pelican's Pouch/Designer I** (✉ Turtle Cove Landing, Provo, ☎ 649/94–64343) displays resort wear, sandals, Provo T-shirts, perfumes, and gold jewelry on the ground floor; head upstairs for basketry, sculpture, and watercolors. **Paradise Gifts/Arts** (✉ Central Square, Provo, ☎ 649/94–64637) has a ceramics studio on the premises; in addition to ceramics, jewelry, T-shirts, and paintings by local artists are sold here. **Royal Jewels** (✉ Leeward Hwy., Provo, ☎ 649/94–64885; ✉ Turquoise Reef Resort, Provo, ☎ 649/94–65311; ✉ Airport, Provo, ☎ 649/94–65311) sells gold and jewelry, designer watches, and perfumes—all duty-free.

OTHER ISLANDS

Middle Caicos

This is the largest (48 sq mi) and least developed of the inhabited Turks and Caicos Islands. Since telephones are a rare commodity, the boats that dock here and the planes that land on the little airstrip provide the island's 275 residents with their main connection to the outside world. **J&B Tours** offers boat tours from Provo to the mysterious Conch Bar Caves.

❺ The limestone **Conch Bar Caves** have eerie underground lakes and milky-white stalactites and stalagmites. Archaeologists have discovered Arawak and Lucayan Indian artifacts in the caves and the surrounding area.

North Caicos

Thanks to abundant rainfall, this island is the garden center of the Turks and Caicos Islands. Bird lovers will see a large flock of flamingos here, and fisherman will find the creeks full of schooling bonefish and tarpon. Bring all your own gear, as this quiet island has no water-sports shops.

❻ The ruins of old plantations in the settlement of **Kew**, which includes a small post office, school, and church, are set among lush tropical trees bearing limes, papayas, and custard apples. To visit Kew is to gain a better understanding of what life is like for many native islanders.

❼ **Flamingo Pond** is a regular nesting place for the beautiful pink birds. They tend to wander out in the middle of the pond, so bring binoculars to see them better.

❽ Getting to the town of **Sandy Point** is half the fun, as you rattle along dirt and stone-filled roads. You'll pass salt flats where you'll very likely see flamingos standing around in the shallow waters. They're shy birds, so bring binoculars to see them better. A secluded cove here provides excellent snorkeling.

Beaches

The beaches of North Caicos, a 41-sq-mi island, are superb for shelling and lolling, and the waters offshore offer excellent snorkeling, bonefishing, and scuba diving (there are no scuba outfitters on the island, so divers will have to make arrangements with dive shops on Provo). **Three Mary's Cays** has excellent snorkeling with a friendly ancient barracuda named Old Man.

Lodging

$$$ 🏨 **Club Vacanze Prospect of Whitby Hotel.** An Italian resort chain, Club
★   Vacanze, took over this secluded retreat in 1994. Miles of beach are yours for sunbathing, windsurfing, or snorkeling. Spacious guest rooms are simple; in true getaway fashion, they lack TVs and radios. The restaurant here is quite good. ✉ *Kew Post Office, North Caicos*, ☎ 649/94–67119, FAX 649/94–67114. 28 rooms, 4 suites. Restaurant, bar, pool, tennis court, dive shop, windsurfing, baby-sitting, travel services. AE, MC, V. EP, MAP.

$$ 🏨 **Ocean Beach Hotel Condominiums.** This unpretentious place provides family-style accommodations on a 10-mi stretch of sheltered beach. The spacious units, each with kitchenette, all face the ocean. Cool and constant trade winds, invited in through large sliding glass doors, replace the need for air-conditioning. The hotel offers an intimate lifestyle away from the fray. ✉ *Whitby, North Caicos*, ☎ 649/94–67113 or 800/710–5204; 905/336–2876 in Canada; FAX 649/94–67386. 10 units. Restaurant, bar, fishing, bicycles, car rental. MC, V. MAP.

$$ 🏨 **Pelican Beach Hotel.** This hotel has large rooms done in pastels and dark wood trim. Ask to stay on the second floor, where rooms have high wood ceilings and fabulous ocean views. Ceiling fans and constant sea breezes keep you cool. ✉ *Whitby, North Caicos*, ☎ 649/94–67112, FAX 649/94–67139. 14 rooms, 2 suites. Restaurant, bar, fishing. MC, V.

$ 🏨 **JoAnne's B&B.** This no-frills, charming bed-and-breakfast on the beach is the perfect spot for those seeking peace and quiet. Rooms are light and airy with cool, white tile floors. Two friendly dogs escort you to the sea and trot along with you as you shell and sun on a very private stretch of beach. The owner, a former Peace Corps worker, also runs

Papa Grunts, an excellent restaurant nearby. Her island stories entertain and delight. Faxing is the best way to make reservations. ✉ *Whitby, North Caicos,* ☎ FAX *649/94–67301. 3 rooms. MC, V.*

Pine Cay

One of a chain of small cays connecting North Caicos and Provo, 800-acre Pine Cay is privately owned and under development as a planned **9** community. The island is home to the exclusive **Meridian Club** resort, playground of jet-setters, and its 2½-mi beach is the most beautiful in the archipelago. The island has a 3,800-ft airstrip and electric carts for getting around.

Lodging

$$$$ 🏨 **Meridian Club.** High rollers vacation in high style on this privately
★ owned 800-acre island. Club guests enjoy an unspoiled cay with 2½ mi of soft white sand and a 500-acre nature reserve with tropical landscaping, freshwater ponds, and nature trails that lure bird-watchers and botanists. A stay here is truly getting away from it all, as there are no air conditioners, telephones, or TVs. The accommodations range from spacious rooms with king-size beds (or twin beds on request) and patios to one- to four-bedroom cottage homes that range in decor and amenities from rustic to well appointed. There's also a "round room" cottage and two ocean-view atrium units that are separated by a lovely interior garden. Rooms in the main complex run over $485 a night for two in winter and include all meals. Cottage homes start at $3,000 a week EP. ✉ *Pine Cay,* ☎ *800/331–9154,* FAX *649/94–65128. 12 rooms, 13 cottage homes. Restaurant, bar, pool, tennis court, windsurfing, boating, bicycles. No credit cards. EP, AP.*

Salt Cay

Only 200 people live on this tiny 2½-sq-mi dot of land. There's not much in the way of development, but there are splendid beaches on the north coast. Salt sheds and salt ponds are silent reminders of the days when the island was a leading producer of salt. February through March, whales pass by on the way to their winter breeding grounds. Scuba divers can dive the *Endymion,* a recently discovered 140-ft wooden-hull British warship that sank in 1790.

2 What little development there is on Salt Cay is found in **Balfour Town.** It's home to the Windmills Plantation hotel, the Mount Pleasant Guest House, and a few stores.

Beaches

There are superb beaches on the north coast of **Salt Cay. Big Sand Cay,** 7 mi to the south of Salt Cay, is also known for its excellent beaches.

Lodging

$$$$ 🏨 **Windmills Plantation.** The attraction here is the lack of distrac-
★ tion: no nightlife, no cruise ships, no crowds, and no shopping. Owner-manager-architect Guy Lovelace and his interior designer wife, Patricia, built the hotel as their version of a colonial-era plantation. The great house has four suites, each with a sitting area, four-poster bed, ceiling fans, and a veranda or balcony with a view of the sea. All are furnished in a mix of antique English and wicker furniture. Four other rooms are housed in two adjacent buildings. Room rates, which during the height of winter run from $415 a night and up for two people, include snorkeling equipment, three meals, and unlimited bar drinks, wine, and beer. ✉ *Salt Cay,* ☎ *649/94–66962 or 800/822–7715,* FAX *649/94–66930. 4 rooms, 4 suites. Restaurant, bar, pool, hiking, horseback riding, beach, snorkeling, fishing, library. AE, MC, V. AP.*

$-$$ 🏠 **Mount Pleasant Guest House.** This simple, somewhat rustic hotel offers guests inexpensive lodging at a remote location. Not all rooms have private baths. ⊠ *Salt Cay,* ☎ *649/94–66927 or 800/821-6670. 7 rooms, 1 with bath. Restaurant, bar, horseback riding, scuba diving, bicycles, library. MC, V.*

Outdoor Activities and Sports

SCUBA DIVING

Porpoise Divers (⊠ Salt Cay, ☎ 649/94–66927) rents all the necessary equipment.

South Caicos

This 8½-sq-mi island was once an important salt producer; today it's the heart of the fishing industry. The beaches here are small and unremarkable, but the vibrant reef makes it a popular destination for divers. Spiny lobster and queen conch are found in the shallow Caicos bank to the west and are harvested for export by local processing plants. The bonefishing here is some of the best in the West Indies. At the northern end of the island are fine, white-sand beaches; the south coast is great for scuba diving along the drop-off; and there's excellent snorkeling off the windward (east) coast, where large stands of elkhorn and staghorn coral shelter a variety of small tropical fish.

❸ **Cockburn Harbour.** The best natural harbor in the Caicos chain is home to the South Caicos Regatta, held each year in May.

Beaches

Due south is **Big Ambergris Cay,** an uninhabited cay about 14 mi beyond the Fish Cays, with a magnificent beach at Long Bay. To the north is **East Caicos,** an uninhabited island has a beautiful 17-mi-long beach along its north coast. The island was once a cattle range and the site of a major sisal-growing industry. Both these cays are accessible only by boat.

Lodging

$-$$ 🏠 **Club Caribe Beach & Harbour Hotel.** Cockburn Harbour, the only natural harbor in the Turks and Caicos Islands, is the perfect setting for this hotel. The 16 beachfront villas, which can be rented as studios or as one-, two-, or three-bedroom apartments, have cool tile floors and kitchenettes equipped with mini refrigerator and microwave. Half of the rooms don't have air-conditioning, but they get a nice breeze around the clock. The 22 harbor rooms are smaller than the others but have air-conditioning. There's a dive shop with a full-time instructor. ⊠ *Box 1, South Caicos,* ☎ *649/94–63444 or 800/722-2582,* 📠 *649/94–63446. 38 rooms. Restaurant, bar, dive shop, windsurfing, bicycles. AE, D, MC, V. EP, MAP.*

West Caicos

Accessible only by boat, this island is uninhabited and untamed, and there are no facilities whatsoever. A glorious white beach stretches for a mile along the northwest point, and offshore diving is among the most exotic in the islands. A wall inhabited by countless species of large marine life begins ¼ mi offshore. If you do tour West Caicos, take along several vats of insect repellent. It won't help much with the sharks, but it should fend off the mosquitoes and sand flies. Be advised, too, that the interior is overgrown with dense shrubs, including manchineel.

⓭ **Molasses Reef** is rumored to be the final resting place of the *Pinta,* which is thought to have been wrecked here in the early 1500s. Over the past few centuries numerous wrecks have occurred in the area between West Caicos and Provo, and author Peter Benchley is among the treasure seekers who have been lured to this island.

⑫ Dive off **Northwest Reef** to see great stands of elkhorn coral and acres of staghorn brambles. But this area is only for experienced divers. The wall starts deep, the currents are strong—and there are sharks in the waters.

TURKS AND CAICOS ISLANDS A TO Z

Arriving and Departing

By Boat

Because of the superb diving, three live-aboard dive boats call regularly. Contact the **Aquanaut** (⊠ c/o See & Sea, ☎ 800/348–9778), the **Sea Dancer** (⊠ c/o Peter Hughes Diving, ☎ 800/932–6237), or the **Turks and Caicos Aggressor** (⊠ c/o Aggressor Fleet, ☎ 504/385–2628 or 800/348–2628, FAX 504/384–0817).

By Plane

American Airlines (☎ 800/433–7300) flies daily between Miami and Provo. **Turks & Caicos Islands Airlines** (☎ 649/94–64255) is the only regularly scheduled carrier that flies between Provo, Grand Turk, and other outer Turks and Caicos islands. Many air charter services also connect the islands (☞ Guided Tours, *below*).

From the Airport

Taxis are available at the airports; expect to share a ride. Rates are fixed. A trip between Provo's airport and most major hotels runs about $15. On Grand Turk, a trip from the airport to town is about $5; from the airport to hotels outside town, $6–$11.

Getting Around

Buses

On Provo, shuttle buses operated by **Executive Tours** (☎ 649/94–64524) run from the hotels into town every hour, Monday through Saturday 9–6. Fares are $2 each way. A new public bus system on Grand Turk charges 50¢ one-way to any scheduled stop.

Car Rentals

Local rental agencies on Provo are **Turks & Caicos National** (☎ 649/94–64701), **Provo Rent-a-Car** (☎ 649/94–64404), **Rent a Buggy** (☎ 649/94–64158), and **Turquoise Jeep Rentals** (☎ 649/94–64910); on Grand Turk, try **Dutchie's Car Rental** (☎ 649/94–62244). Rates average $40 to $65 per day, plus a $10-per-rental-agreement government tax. To rent cars on South Caicos, check with your hotel manager for rates and information.

Ferries

Ferries are available between some islands; check with local marinas. The only government ferry (no phone) runs between Grand Turk and Salt Cay.

Scooters

You can scoot around Provo by contacting **Scooter Bob's** (☎ 649/94–64684) or the **Honda Shop** (☎ 649/94–64397). On North Caicos, contact **North Caicos Scooter Rentals** (☎ 649/94–67301). Rates generally start at $25 per day for a one-seater and $40 a day for a two-seater, plus a onetime $5 government tax and gas.

Taxis

Taxis are unmetered, and rates, posted in the taxis, are regulated by the government. In Provo, call the Provo taxi association (☎ 649/94–65481).

Contacts and Resources

Currency

The unit of currency is U.S. dollars.

Emergencies

Police: Grand Turk, ☎ 649/94–62299; Providenciales, ☎ 649/94–64259; North Caicos, ☎ 649/94–67116; South Caicos, ☎ 649/94–63299. **Hospitals:** There is a 24-hour emergency room at **Grand Turk Hospital** (⊠ Hospital Rd., ☎ 649/94–62333) and at **Providenciales Health-Medical Center** (⊠ Leeward Hwy., ☎ 649/94–64201). **Pharmacies:** Prescriptions can be filled at the **Government Clinic** (⊠ Grand Turk Hospital, ☎ 649/94–62040) and at the **Providenciales Health-Medical Center** in Provo (⊠ Leeward Hwy., ☎ 649/94–64201).

Guided Tours

A **taxi** tour of the islands costs between $25 and $30 for the first hour and $25 for each additional hour. On Provo, contact **Paradise Taxi Company** (☎ 649/94–13555). **Turtle Tours** (☎ 649/94–65585) offers a variety of bus and small-plane tours. You can also fly to Middle Caicos, the largest of the islands, for a visit to its mysterious caves or to North Caicos to see the ruins of a former slave plantation. If you want to island-hop on your own schedule, air charters are available through **Blue Hills Aviation** (☎ 649/94–15290), **Flamingo Air Services** (☎ 649/94–62109 or 649/94–64933), and **SkyKing** (☎ 649/94–15464).

Language

The official language of the Turks and Caicos is English.

Lodging

Hotel accommodations are available on Grand Turk, North Caicos, South Caicos, Pine Cay, and Provo. There are also some small, non-air-conditioned guest houses on Salt Cay and Middle Caicos. Accommodations range from small island inns to the splashy Club Med Turkoise to the luxury Grace Bay Club in Providenciales. Because of the popularity of scuba diving here, virtually all the hotels have dive shops and offer dive packages. Dive packagers offering air-hotel-dive packages include **Dive Provo** (☎ 800/234–7768) and **Undersea Adventures** (☎ 800/234–7768). Most of the medium and large hotels offer a choice of EP and MAP. People who don't rent a car or scooter tend to eat at their hotels, so MAP may be the better option. Another option favored by many visitors, particularly families, is renting a self-contained villa or private home; contact the **Ministry of Tourism** (☎ 649/94–62321) three to six months in advance for more information. Please note that the government hotel tax does not apply to guest houses with fewer than four rooms.

Opening and Closing Times

Most offices are open weekdays from 8 or 8:30 till 4 or 4:30. Banks are open Monday–Thursday 8:30–2:30, Friday 8:30–12:30 and 2:30–4:30.

Passports and Visas

U.S. citizens need some proof of citizenship, such as a birth certificate (original or certified copy), plus a photo ID or a current passport. British subjects must have a current passport. All visitors must have an on-going or return ticket.

Precautions

Petty crime does occur here, and you're advised to leave your valuables in the hotel safe-deposit box. Bring along a can of insect repellent: The mosquitoes and no-see-ums can be vicious.

If you plan to explore the uninhabited island of West Caicos, be advised that the interior is overgrown with dense shrubs that include manchineel, which has a milky, poisonous sap that can cause painful, scarring blisters.

In some hotels on Grand Turk, Salt Cay, and South Caicos, there are signs that read PLEASE HELP US CONSERVE OUR PRECIOUS WATER. These islands have no freshwater supply other than rainwater collected in cisterns, and rainfall is scant. Drink only from the decanter of fresh water your hotel provides; tap water is safe for brushing your teeth or other hygiene uses.

Taxes and Service Charges

Most hotels collect a 7%–8% government tax; all add a 10%–15% service charge to your bill. Restaurants collect a 7% government tax and add a 10% service charge to your bill. Taxi drivers expect a token tip. The departure tax is $15.

Telephones and Mail

You can call the islands direct from the United States by dialing 809 and the number. To call home from Turks and Caicos, dial direct from most hotels, from some pay phones, and from **Cable and Wireless,** which has offices in Provo (☎ 649/94–64499) and Grand Turk (☎ 649/94–62200), open Monday–Thursday 8–4:30 and Friday 8–4. You must dial 0, followed by the country code (1 for U.S. and Canada; 44 for U.K.), area code, and local number.

Postal rates for letters to the United States, Bahamas, and Caribbean are 50¢ per half ounce; postcards, 35¢. Letters to the United Kingdom and Europe, run 65¢ per half ounce; postcards, 45¢. Letters to Canada, Puerto Rico, and South America cost 65¢; postcards, 45¢.

Visitor Information

For tourist information contact the **Turks and Caicos Islands Tourist Board** (☎ 800/241–0824). The **Caribbean Tourism Organization** (✉ 20 E. 46th St., New York, NY 10017, ☎ 212/682–0435) is another source of information. In the United Kingdom, contact **Morris-Kevan International Ltd.** (✉ International House, 47 Chase Side, Enfield Middlesex EN2 6NB, ☎ 0181/367–5175).

On Grand Turk, the **Government Tourist Office** (✉ Front St., Cockburn Town, Grand Turk, ☎ 649/94–62321; ✉ Turtle Cove Landing, Provo, ☎ 649/94–64970) is open Monday–Thursday 8–4:30 and Friday 8–5.

7 Portrait of the Bahamas

In Search of Columbus

IN SEARCH OF COLUMBUS

I **FIRST HEARD** the singing toward the middle of the night, as the mail boat M.V. *Maxine* plowed southward between Eleuthera and the Exumas. The sound drifted faintly to where I lay doubled up on a bench in the main cabin with my head on a cardboard crate of pears and a copy of the *Bahama Journal* shielding my eyes from a yellow bug light.

It was a two-part chant, almost African in its rhythm. I looked down the dim corridor to the bridge, where the crewman at the wheel was singing softly in harmony with his companion on the midnight-to-four watch. The second man was shuffling back and forth, keeping time. It was a scene out of Conrad, and a reminder that this is still what transportation is like in much of the world: pitching through the waters of a dark archipelago, sleeping with your head on a box of fruit, while guys sing and dance on the bridge.

The *Maxine* was 14 hours out of Potter's Cay, Nassau, the Bahamas, on the 22-hour run to the island of San Salvador. I had long since abandoned my claustrophobic upper bunk in the boat's only passenger compartment and had stayed out on deck until dark, sprawling over a tarp that covered bags of cement, taking shallow breaths to ration the stench of diesel fuel. Finally, half soaked from the waves constantly breaching the port rail, I had retreated to the last remotely habitable place on board—the big common room with its table and benches and its clutter of cargo for the islands. Four dozen eggs, the cartons taped together. An oscillating fan. Gallon jars of mayonnaise, their future owners' names written on the labels. Two galvanized tubs. Homemade sound equipment for the band that plays in the bar on San Salvador. My pillow of pears, consigned to Francita Gardiner of Rum Cay. Bags, boxes, crates—and, secured somehow on the opposite bench, with ears alert and bright, eager eyes, a life-size ceramic German shepherd, soon to be a boon companion to someone in a place where a real German shepherd probably would die of heat prostration. Every time

I woke to shift positions during that endless night, I would glance across the cabin, and there would be the good dog, looking as if he were waiting for a biscuit.

It is altogether possible to fly from Nassau to San Salvador in an hour and a half, but I had cast my lot with the mayonnaise and the galvanized tubs because I wanted to reach the island by water. San Salvador is arguably the most famous landfall in history: In 1992 the New World and the Old celebrated (or lamented, depending on one's politics) the 500th anniversary of the arrival of the *Niña, Pinta,* and *Santa María* at this coral-gilt outcrop. Anticipation of the tourism the quincentennial would inspire is no doubt the reason why the creaking and malodorous *Maxine* was eventually replaced by a new 110-ft mail boat with air-conditioned cabins. Fruit-box pillows are finally going out of style in the Bahamas.

My plan was to retrace, by whatever transportation was available, the route Christopher Columbus followed through Bahamian waters after his landing at San Salvador on October 12, 1492. On the face of it, this seems a simple enough task: The log of the first voyage, lost in the original but substantially transcribed by the near-contemporary chronicler Bartolome de Las Casas, describes the fleet's circuitous route through the archipelago and the series of island landfalls it made. The problem is, the island names given are those that Columbus coined with each new discovery. From San Salvador he sailed to what he called "Santa María de la Concepción," then to "Fernandina," then to "Isabela," then to the southwest and out of the Bahamian archipelago on his way to Cuba. With the exception of San Salvador, which was called Watling Island until 1926, none of these islands bears its Columbus name today. And the distances, directions, and descriptions of terrain given in the surviving version of the log are just ambiguous enough, at crucial junctures, to have inspired nine major theories as to exactly which sequence of island landfalls was followed. Some of the theories are more than a bit tenuous, depending heavily on a blithe disregard of their own weak points and an amplification of everyone else's departures from the log or from common sense. You begin to wonder, after a while, if someone couldn't take the Las Casas translation and use it to prove that Columbus landed on Chincoteague and sailed into the Tidal Basin by way of Annapolis.

But two plausible theories stand out. One, championed by the late historian and Columbus biographer Admiral Samuel Eliot Morison, is based on a first landing at today's San Salvador. The other says the first landing was at Samana Cay, a smaller, uninhabited island on the eastern fringes of the chain. Samana Cay's most recent proponent has been Joseph Judge of the National Geographic Society; in 1986 he published an exhaustive defense of his position, based in part on a computer's estimation of where Columbus should have ended up after the Atlantic crossing. The jury is still out on both major theories, as it is on the less commonly held ones. It probably always will be. For the purposes of my trip, though, I had to choose one version and stick with it. On the basis of my layman's reading of the log, I decided to go with Morison.

In this version, San Salvador is San Salvador, Santa María de la Concepción is today's Rum Cay, Fernandina is Long Island, and Isabela is Crooked Island. This was the sequence I planned to follow as the *Maxine* approached San Salvador's Fernandez Bay at 9 o'clock in the morning.

This island is fairly large and very flat. It is green, with many trees and several bodies of water. There is a very large lagoon in the middle of the island and there are no mountains. It is a pleasure to gaze upon this place because it is all so green, and the weather is delightful.

— Christopher Columbus's log, October 13, 1492

We docked at Cockburn Town, the only settlement of any size on San Salvador. Cockburn Town, population several hundred souls, was the type and model of the Bahamian Out Island communities I would see along the Columbus track over the next few days: three or four streets of cinder-block-and-stucco houses, some brightly painted; a grocery store and a bar—the Harlem Square Club, site of a big domi-

noes tournament that week; a post office/radiophone station; and a couple of churches. On the facade of the Catholic church, Holy Savior, there was a peeling relief portrait of Christopher Columbus.

In the late morning heat I walked the half mile of blacktop—scrub brush on one side and ocean views on the other—that separates Cockburn Town from the Riding Rock Inn.

The latter is a handful of cottages, a short block of plain but cheerful motel units, and a restaurant/bar, all right on the water; up at the bar most of the talk you hear has to do with skin diving. Divers are the principal clientele here. When I arrived, the place was securely in the hands of a California club called the Flipperdippers. At the poolside cookout just after I pulled in, the first snippet of conversation I caught was a tyro Flipperdipper asking an old hand if a basket starfish would eat until it exploded. The answer was no, and without waiting around to find out why the questioner suspected such a thing I got up for more rice and crabs. That's when the *maîtresse de barbecue* hove into my path and told me about the dance that night: "If you don't dance, you don't get breakfast."

With the assistance of a Flipperdipper or two, I earned my breakfast. The band was a Cockburn Town outfit of indeterminate numerical strength. Guitarists and conga drummers came and went, and everyone kept commenting that things were really supposed to start jumping when the Kiwanis meeting at the Harlem Square Club let out. Shortly after 10, the band did get a transfusion of new talent, all wearing white cabana shirts patterned with yellow-and-black Kiwanis emblems. They played a couple of good sets, but they did an even better job of exemplifying the phenomenon scholars call the "Columbian Exchange," that cross-pollination of peoples, cultures, flora and fauna, foodstuffs, and microorganisms that followed in the wake of the admiral's fleet and has been transmogrifying the Eastern and Western hemispheres ever since. Here were six descendants of African slaves, wearing the insignia of an American fraternal organization, playing music written by a Jamaican who thought Haile Selassie was God, for a merry throng

Excerpted from The Log of Christopher Columbus, *by Robert H. Fuson, courtesy of International Marine Publishing,* © 1987.

of skin-diving orthodontists from California on an island discovered by an Italian working for Spain but settled along with the rest of the archipelago by British and American planters who imported the slaves to begin with.

About all that was missing were the Lucayans, the native Bahamians extirpated by the Spaniards—who worked them to death in the mines of Hispaniola—within a generation after Columbus's arrival. It was the Lucayans' island I set off to see the following morning, by motor scooter and on foot.

The people here call this island Guanahani in their language, and their speech is very fluent, although I do not understand any of it. They are friendly and well-dispositioned people who bear no arms except for small spears, and they have no iron. I showed one my sword, and through ignorance he grabbed it by the blade and cut himself.

— October 12

The San Salvador of the Lucayans is but a memory, as they are. When Columbus arrived, there were tall trees on the island, but the planters of the late 18th and early 19th centuries deforested the place so that now virtually the only vegetation is the dense, stickery brush called "haulback." The island's interior, though, still conveys the same sense of impenetrability and desolation that it must have to the first Europeans who came here, and no doubt to the Lucayans themselves. Fishermen as well as cultivators must have stayed close to shore, except to travel from one end of San Salvador to the other by dugout canoe across a system of brackish lakes that covers nearly half of the interior. From a crude concrete-and-wood observation platform on a rise near the airport, you can take in the sprawl of these lakes and the lonely, thicketed hills (the terrain isn't all as flat as Columbus described it) that break them into crazy patterns. No one lives there; it's hard to imagine that anyone ever goes there.

I drove the scooter the length of the island's circuit road, past crescent beaches with white sand so fine it coats your feet like flour, past ruined plantation buildings, past "Ed's First and Last Bar," a homey little joint out in the sticks that would be beerless until the cases made it up from the mail

boat dock, past four monuments to Columbus's landing at four different places (a fifth marker is underwater, where somebody decided his anchor hit bottom), and past the Dixon Hill Lighthouse ("Imperial Lighthouse Service"), billed as one of 10 left in the world that run on kerosene. Past, and then back again—I bullied the scooter up Dixon Hill, because you don't get to climb to the top of a lighthouse every day.

I went looking for the light keeper, but instead I found my ride to Rum Cay, according to Morison the second of Columbus's landfalls on his first voyage. It was a family of blue-water sailors—an American named Kent, his German wife, Britta, and their two-month-old baby, Luke, who had cruised to San Salvador from St. Thomas in their 32-foot sailboat. Having hitchhiked up from Cockburn Town, the baby in a shaded basket, they too were waiting for the light keeper to show up; after she did, and took us to the top, the sailing couple offered to let me hitch with them the next day on the 30-mile run to Rum Cay. I soon learned I would be in good hands: Later that day, Kent asked a local if he knew anything about Rum Cay.

"What do you want to know?" the man responded.

"What's the anchorage like in a southeast wind?"

I'd have asked where to eat, or if the Kiwanis had a band.

I made sail and saw so many islands that I could not decide where to go first . . . Finally, I looked for the largest island and decided to go there.

— October 14

Christopher Columbus left San Salvador on October 11, 1492, and later that day arrived at the island he named Santa María de la Concepción. My adopted family and I weighed anchor at Cockburn Town and sailed out of Fernandez Bay early in the morning of a bright June day, flying fish scudding around our bows and cottony trade clouds riding briskly above. Luke, already a veteran mariner, slept in his basket below. We sighted Rum Cay when we were 10 miles out from San Salvador— Columbus had a much higher mast to climb—but the distant shoreline was to loom for a long time before we could draw very close to it. The east shore and much of the south shore of Rum Cay are girded with lethal reefs, and both the charts and the *Yachtsman's Guide to the Bahamas* go to great pains to point out so precise a route to the anchorage that it might as well have been the directions to a parking space in George Town. Six other boats had negotiated the coral gauntlet that day, including one whose captain gave us half of a blackfin tuna he'd just caught. How Columbus safely pulled it off (his anchorage was at a point west of ours) is beyond imagining.

Rum Cay, which once made a living selling sea salt to Nova Scotia's cod packers, has shriveled in population until barely 60 people today inhabit its sole settlement of Port Nelson. An American, David Melville, opened a small skin-diving resort called the Rum Cay Club a mile from town a few years back: When I arrived, the place was closed for renovations. There were no Flipperdippers here—just Melville, a couple of handymen, and the locals down the road. Rum Cay was, for the moment, almost out of things to do and people to do them.

Almost, but not quite. There's always Kay's Bar, where proprietor Dolores Wilson turns out lovely baked chicken and coconut bread to wash down with the Out Islands' requisite gallons of beer and rum in an atmosphere dominated by a satellite TV, an antique space-age jukebox, turtle shells with colored lightbulbs in them, and a giant poster of Bob Marley wearing a beatific grin and knitted hat that looks like a Rasta halo. People who sailed to the Bahamas years ago have told me that Dolores was once something of a hellraiser, but she seems to have settled into sweet grandmotherliness by now. For ethyl-powered amusement, I had to rely on an expatriate Oklahoman named Billy. Billy, whose personal style ran to the pirate-biker look, was Melville's mechanical factotum at the Rum Cay Club. His avocation, as I discovered when I took a Jeep ride with him to the other side of the island, is nonstop talking. In the space of an hour, Billy went chapter and verse on everything from his archery prowess in Oklahoma, to how he could build an ammonia-powered icehouse like the one in *The Mosquito Coast,* to his deepest feelings about the universe: "You know, I like everything and I hate everything."

"That's called having a lover's quarrel with the world," I told him, remembering Frost.

"Oh, they have a name for it now?"

I decided not to linger very long at Santa María de la Concepción, for I saw that there was no gold there and the wind freshened to a SE crosswind. I departed the island for the ship after a two hours' stay.

— October 16

It was Billy who drove me to catch a plane to Long Island—Columbus's Fernandina, his third landfall—on the following afternoon. Back on San Salvador, I'd been told that the ticket to getting off Rum Cay without waiting for the next mail boat was to "ask for Bobby with the plane." But there was no plane on the island's crushed-coral landing strip. Bobby had flown somewhere, so rather than spend another night I asked Melville to radio the Stella Maris Inn on Long Island for a plane. They sent a Cessna four-seater, which landed just as Billy was pouring me a rum-and-powdered-lemonade at his house—he insisted on this hospitable stopover, since it was a whole mile between Kay's Bar and the airstrip. Besides, his own much-loved blue plastic cup was empty.

Long Island: a day's sail from Rum Cay for the *Niña, Pinta,* and *Santa María* on October 17, 1492; 15 minutes in the Cessna. As we approached the landing strip, I looked down to see territory that looked almost like a manicured suburb compared with the trackless scrub forests of Rum Cay and San Salvador. Here were roads, trees, villas, broad beaches, swimming pools . . . in short, a modest but complete resort, and run by Germans to boot. This last fact is worthy of remark because of the concept known as "Bahamian time," best defined as a devil-may-care approach to the minute hand. Somehow, the Germans and Bahamians had arrived at a compromise: The shuttle to the beach leaves more or less on time, but you don't have to eat breakfast at 7:23 AM.

I wanted to follow Columbus up and down this island. Near its northern tip is a shallow cove outside of which he anchored while several of his men went ashore for water. If local legend can be trusted, they filled their casks at a deep natural well in the coral rock, which a Stella

Maris driver showed me. He had drawn water there as a small boy, just 450 years after the Spanish expedition.

A couple of miles from the well was the cove, a harbor with "two entrances," according to the 1492 log, which the admiral sounded in his ships' boats. At least it seemed to me to be the place, and "Where Was Columbus?" is a game that anyone with a copy of the log can play. I explored the cove and, while snorkeling, was reminded of the entry for October 17: "Here the fishes are so unlike ours that it is amazing."

To reach Columbus's final Long Island anchorage, at a place called Little Harbour in a village with the pretty name of Roses, was not such an easy job. I rented a VW bug and drove south for nearly 80 miles to the tip of this 2-mile-wide island. The road passed through one little town after another, each with its neat cinder-block school and tiny Protestant church. At Roses I found a storekeeper who knew the road to Little Harbour. It ended at a dump a mile into the bush. I walked nearly another mile—had I been heading due east I would have been in the water. I wasn't going to find Little Harbour, not in this pounding sun on a trail narrowing to the width of an iguana, any more than Columbus was going to find Japan.

Columbus got farther than I did, though. He wandered southeast from Long Island to Crooked Island, then southwest to the southernmost of the Ragged Islands, where the tiny outpost called Duncan Town now stands. This was his last Bahamas anchorage before he sailed off to Cuba, Hispaniola, and immortality.

The odd thing is, Columbus had an easier time pressing ahead than I would have had. Although it's true that he was not only lost in the Caribbean but stuck in the 15th century, at least his fleet was self-contained, and one island was as good as another. For me, the Cessnas were too expensive, the mail boats too infrequent, the lodgings from Long Island south, on Crooked Island and at Duncan Town, nonexistent. These places are as far away as they ever were. They are, in fact, parts of the New World that haven't really been discovered yet.

— William G. Scheller

A resident of Newbury, Massachusetts, William G. Scheller contributes travel pieces regularly to *National Geographic*, *Condé Nast Traveler*, and the *Washington Post Magazine*.

INDEX

X = *restaurant*, ⊞ = *hotel*

Fodor's Travel Publications

Available at bookstores everywhere, or call 1–800–533–6478, 24 hours a day.

Gold Guides

U.S.

Alaska

Arizona

Boston

California

Cape Cod, Martha's Vineyard, Nantucket

The Carolinas & Georgia

Chicago

Colorado

Florida

Hawai'i

Las Vegas, Reno, Tahoe

Los Angeles

Maine, Vermont, New Hampshire

Maui & Lāna'i

Miami & the Keys

New England

New Orleans

New York City

Pacific North Coast

Philadelphia & the Pennsylvania Dutch Country

The Rockies

San Diego

San Francisco

Santa Fe, Taos, Albuquerque

Seattle & Vancouver

The South

U.S. & British Virgin Islands

USA

Virginia & Maryland

Walt Disney World, Universal Studios and Orlando

Washington, D.C.

Foreign

Australia

Austria

The Bahamas

Belize & Guatemala

Bermuda

Canada

Cancún, Cozumel, Yucatán Peninsula

Caribbean

China

Costa Rica

Cuba

The Czech Republic & Slovakia

Eastern & Central Europe

Europe

Florence, Tuscany & Umbria

France

Germany

Great Britain

Greece

Hong Kong

India

Ireland

Israel

Italy

Japan

London

Madrid & Barcelona

Mexico

Montréal & Québec City

Moscow, St. Petersburg, Kiev

The Netherlands, Belgium & Luxembourg

New Zealand

Norway

Nova Scotia, New Brunswick, Prince Edward Island

Paris

Portugal

Provence & the Riviera

Scandinavia

Scotland

Singapore

South Africa

South America

Southeast Asia

Spain

Sweden

Switzerland

Thailand

Toronto

Turkey

Vienna & the Danube

Special-Interest Guides

Adventures to Imagine

Alaska Ports of Call

Ballpark Vacations

Caribbean Ports of Call

The Official Guide to America's National Parks

Disney Like a Pro

Europe Ports of Call

Family Adventures

Fodor's Gay Guide to the USA

Fodor's How to Pack

Great American Learning Vacations

Great American Sports & Adventure Vacations

Great American Vacations

Great American Vacations for Travelers with Disabilities

Halliday's New Orleans Food Explorer

Healthy Escapes

Kodak Guide to Shooting Great Travel Pictures

National Parks and Seashores of the East

National Parks of the West

Nights to Imagine

Rock & Roll Traveler Great Britain and Ireland

Rock & Roll Traveler USA

Sunday in San Francisco

Walt Disney World for Adults

Weekends in New York

Wendy Perrin's Secrets Every Smart Traveler Should Know

CNN✈
Airport Network

Your
Window
To The
World
While You're
On The
Road

Keep in touch when you're traveling. Before you take off, tune in to CNN Airport Network. Now available in major airports across America, CNN Airport Network provides nonstop news, sports, business, weather and lifestyle programming. Both domestic and international. All piloted by the top-flight global resources of CNN. All up-to-the-minute reporting. And just for travelers, CNN Airport Network features intriguing segments such as "Travel Facts." With an information source like Fodor's this series of fascinating travel trivia will definitely make time fly while you're waiting to board. SO KEEP YOUR WINDOW TO THE WORLD WIDE OPEN. ESPECIALLY WHEN YOU'RE ON THE ROAD. TUNE IN TO CNN AIRPORT NETWORK TODAY.

WHEREVER YOU TRAVEL, *H*ELP IS NEVER FAR AWAY.

From planning your trip to providing travel assistance along the way, American Express® Travel Service Offices are always there to help.

Bahamas

Mundy Tours (R)
Suite 20, Regent Center 4
Freeport
809/352-4444

Playtours (R)
303 Shirley Street
Nassau
809/322-2931

Travel

http://www.americanexpress.com/travel